W9-DFD-536

"All We Are Saying..."

THE PHILOSOPHY OF THE NEW LEFT

"All We Are Saying..."

Edited by

The Philosophy of the New Left

Arthur Lothstein

G. P. Putnam's Sons   New York

TO CHRISSIE AND TEDDY:

the two most beautiful people I know

Acknowledgments

I am happy to acknowledge the help given to me by many colleagues in preparing this book for publication. Special thanks must be given to Professor Peter T. Manicas of the Department of Philosophy at Queens College, who encouraged the project from beginning to end and who read and criticized much of the material assembled in the book. Bruce Brown gave me very valuable bibliographic advice, as did Stanley Aronowitz, Paul Piccone, and Paul Buhle, and many of their suggestions, especially Bruce Brown's, have been incorporated in the book. I must also acknowledge the help given to me by many friends, especially Frank King, Tom Whitehill, Tom Pomposello, Louis Markowitz, Michael Elsas, Rick Salutin, Michael Goldman, Michael Brown, and Ken Smith, with whom I have talked about most of the problems raised in the book and who have helped clarify my own thinking in several important respects on these problems. I was aided also by the Center for Movement Research, affiliated with the Department of Sociology at Queens College, whose extensive Movement library was made available to me by its director, Professor Michael Brown. Finally, I must thank my wife, Chrissie, my brother, Les, and my father, who participated actively in the project at every stage, who read all the material, and who, as always, proved to be my best critics.

Contents

10   CONTENTS

PART III. *The Revolution of the Future: Tactics
and Goals*

Introduction

We are forces of chaos and anarchy
Everything they say we are we are
And we are very
Proud of ourselves.

JEFFERSON AIRPLANE

What is new about the New Left? How is it distinguished from older types of leftist thought and practice? What were the historical circumstances under which it arose? What is its analysis of contemporary social experience? What strategies for change has it articulated? What is its vision of the future?

These are some of the questions that the readings assembled in this book try to answer. No attempt will be made here to summarize what those answers are or to evaluate the conclusions of the articles that make up the anthology. For brief summaries of the arguments of each of the various essays the reader should consult the prefatory notes which accompany each essay in the book.

The purpose of this book, as the subtitle suggests, is to define the philosophical context of contemporary New Left politics. We argue below that there is no one philosophy of the New Left, in the sense of a single philosophical angle of vision shared by all New Leftists. This is not to say, however, that all New Leftists do not share certain basic philosophical attitudes and beliefs, or that the philosophical differences that exist between them are more important than the philosophical attitudes and beliefs they hold in common. Neither do we mean to imply that their philosophical differences are of minor importance. On the contrary, we argue that these differences are both important and salutary. They are important, because they reflect the loose agglomeration of interests and the wide variety of experiences that characterize the New Left; and they are salutary, because they suggest the multifariousness of all human experience and therefore the pedagogical value of diversity.

11

The common theme of all the essays in the book is the irrationality and barbarity of the advanced capitalist societies and the need to forge radical alternatives to bourgeois culture and institutions. All of the essays are written by radicals—many of whom are leading protagonists in the Movement—and all are very powerful—and we think seminal—statements of contemporary radical politics. As much as space has permitted, we have tried to include representative work of the European New Left, because we believe that the most incisive theoretical work now being done in the Movement is being done in Europe, and because most of that work is either unknown or unavailable to the average English-speaking reader. While the articles in the book do not represent any single philosophical point of view or encompass the whole spectrum of New Left philosophical opinion, they nevertheless deal with most of the important theoretical and practical questions the New Left now faces.

Despite the fact that there is no one common body of political and philosophical assumptions which all people who consider themselves New Leftists share with equal weight, there are nonetheless significant family resemblances among New Leftists and New Left organizations or groups to justify referring to them by a single name. The following is a brief list of characteristics which are generally descriptive of contemporary New Left attitudes and beliefs and which help to define the new radical politics. The reader should bear in mind that the list is unavoidably superficial, as all such lists are. Each of the problems discussed is extremely complex and merits close and separate study.

A. *The great majority of New Leftists are students* (mainly white middle-class students). The New Left originated as a student movement in the United States in the early 1960's, with the formation of the Student Nonviolent Coordinating Committee (SNCC) in 1960 (the word "nonviolent" has since been dropped and been replaced by the word "national") and the Students for a Democratic Society (SDS) in 1962 (we date the birth of SDS from the founding convention at Port Huron). That SNCC has virtually collapsed and that ideological bickering has fractionalized the SDS (the SDS is now composed of the Weatherman faction or RYM-I and the Revolutionary Youth Movement or RYM-II faction), following the expulsion of the Progressive Labor Party from SDS in the summer of 1969, do not vitiate the fact that the American New Left is still primarily a student movement. (See Roland Aronson and John C. Cowley's essay in Part I.) This is equally true of the New Left movements outside the United States.

B. *The New Left is a radical political movement.* It is not content to be a parliamentary opposition or a countervailing political power as, for example, the Old Left was. It challenges the vested interests, entrenched institutions, and dominant life-styles endemic to the advanced capitalist societies and to a lesser extent the totalitarian socialist societies. It is a *movement,* in the sense of being an ongoing, developmental, mass public phenomenon. (See Carlo Donolo's essay in Part I.)

C. *The New Left is not a national political phenomenon, nor is it yet a totally global political phenomenon.* Its scope includes all the advanced capitalist societies (France, West Germany) and to a lesser extent those countries under the dominion of U.S. capital in which there is an incipient anti-imperialist and anti-authoritarian struggle (Brazil). It is also a viable phenomenon in those few countries (Yugoslavia) in which the institutional trappings of socialism exist, but where sclerotic vestiges of bourgeois culture—hierarchical decision-making, authoritarian knowledge—proscribe the building of a fully libertarian socialist community.

D. *The New Left is an anti-authoritarian movement.* This may come as a surprise to the reader in the light of current liberal criticism of the New Left as authoritarian. But the liberal attack is at best fatuous. It confuses moral outrage with political hooliganism and the repudiation of repressive tolerance with the perpetration of a tyranny of the minority. If there is authoritarianism on the New Left, its sources are *not* those cited by liberals. More likely it is to be found in the "knee-jerk" Marxism of the left sect groups that push an inflexible Marxist-Leninist or Maoist line.

By anti-authoritarianism we mean the New Left's struggle against the institutional authoritarianism of the neo-capitalist societies. Since the New Left argues that institutional authoritarianism—i.e., top-down control, manipulative bureaucracy, hierarchical decision-making—is endemic to neo-capitalism—and is therefore irremediable within the sociocultural framework of neo-capitalism—its anti-authoritarianism necessarily implies an anti-institutional strategy—that is, a strategy for the radical reconstitution of bourgeois culture and institutions, what the German student revolutionary, Rudy Dutschke, has described as a "long march through the institutions." (See Carlo Donolo's essay in Part I.)

The New Left argues that the institutional authoritarianism of the neo-capitalist societies is a necessary concomitant of the capitalistic system in its later stages. Given (a) the private ownership of property and the private accumulation of wealth, and (b) the ownership and control of the means of production by a few—the ruling class—and (c) the class basis of social relationships produced by the economic hegemony of the ruling class, the neo-capitalist social system is, it is argued, ineluctably authoritarian. For social relations under neo-capitalism are determined by the fact that the labor power of the overwhelming majority of people is appropriated by a small minority simply for the purpose of realizing profits for that small minority. Thus the status of the largest sector of the population is one of economic vassalage; and because social behavior is parasitic upon economic status, it is one of social and political vassalage too. (See Fredy Perlman's essay in Part I.)

In contrast to the institutional authoritarianism of the neo-capitalist societies, the New Left argues for the creation of decentralized, anarchistically self-regulating communities, controlled from below and free of class relationships. Accordingly, it seeks to abolish those economic institutions—private property, wage-labor, hierarchical work relations—which cater for possessive individualism, alienated labor, and social anomie and which therefore render obsolete the possibility of humanizing communal experience. More generally, the New Left argues for the radical reconstruction of human experience around "de-alienated" social principles, such as personal openness, mutual aid, and face-to-face encounter, and for the experimentation with new social life forms—extended family structures—to replace those social institutions—the nuclear family—which are integral to the reproduction of daily life in the neo-capitalist societies. (See Murray Bookchin's essay in Part III.)

A good example of the New Left's anti-authoritarianism is its concept of participatory democracy. While only nebulously defined, participatory democracy is nevertheless a patent repudiation of the elitist and exclusionary nature of bourgeois democracy and of the equation of technical expertise with moral competence. Both a utopian social goal and a concrete political strategy for the radical restructuring of existing lines of power, the central idea of participatory democracy is that people should exercise *complete* control over their own lives, that they should participate *meaningfully* at *all* levels of social, political, and economic decision-making. Accordingly, participatory democracy is a strategy for radically overhauling established forms of representative and parliamentary democracy, which owing to the class basis of distribution of power in the neo-capitalist societies serve only to legitimize the economic hegemony of the ruling class, and to perpetuate class politics. In sum, participatory democracy is a strategy for returning to the people the power to determine their collective social destiny—power which has been usurped by the ruling class by virtue of its economic suzerainty and which is wielded by the latter for the twin purposes of economic self-aggrandizement and political domination.

On a different level, participatory democracy is a negation of formalistic or legalistic definitions of democracy—that is, of the identification of democracy with the mere institutional trappings of representative government. For the New Left, democracy is not only a system of political decision-making, but also a means of codifying interpersonal experience and shared moral perceptions. The attempt on the part of New Left organizations to structure decision-making apparatuses that are participatorily democratic and to replace political anonymity and charismatic leadership with face-to-face encounter and collective responsibility is a revealing example of participatory democracy and of how social institutions may be refashioned along participatory democratic lines. (See Ronald Aronson and John C. Cowley's essay in Part I.)

Another example of the New Left's anti-authoritarianism is its rejection (with few exceptions) of doctrinaire social theory and its celebration of the pedagogical value of spontaneity and personal experience. In part this is a reaction to endemic institutional authoritarianism and to the claustrophobic political atmosphere engendered by the disappearance of meaningful life options. It is also, however, a profound philosophical recognition of the centrality of lived experience in the working out of a humanizing radical social perspective. (See Ronald Aronson and John C. Cowley's essay in Part I, and Murray Bookchin's essay in Part III.)

Committed to the world of process, the politics of the New Left is perforce experimental and open-ended. It is continually subject to radical redefinition in the light of developing social realities and immediately perceived needs. Thus the new politics is as radically contingent as life itself. The role of the political actor is circumscribed only by the limits placed on political action by what are generally perceived to be the possibilities for meaningful self-expression. Jerry Rubin speaks for the New Left when he says: "Politics is how you lead your life, not whom you vote for."

Moreover, political behavior is not restricted to special areas of daily life; it suffuses the total endeavor. Thus no area of daily life is immune to politicization or repoliticization, as the case may be. In fact, "the long march through the institutions" entails the thorough-going politicization of *all* areas of daily life, from the seemingly most peripheral—neighborhood clubs—to those generally perceived to be crucial—the unions, the universities, the army. From the point of view of an anti-institutional struggle there are no areas of daily life which are irrelevant to the radicalization process. (See Carlo Donolo's essay in Part I.) This is not to say, however, that every area of daily life is as crucial to the radicalization process as every other area. While none is irrelevant, there are areas which are more crucial than others. Accordingly, the radicalization process must be tempered by a basic theoretical understanding of the total social situation. If it involves more than simply raising the level of consciousness, if it involves also the incarnation of radical consciousness in pivotal institutions—which it must if it is to be self-sustaining—the radicalization process must be tethered to a well-defined—but nonetheless freewheeling—theoretical perspective. If it is not, if it makes no attempt to analyze, for example, the mutability of institutional structures, the viability of alternate institutions, the possibility of repression or co-optation, etc., radical politics is thereupon reduced to a ritualistic existentialism, to a headless confrontation politics. Alternatively, whatever theoretical understanding of the total social situation is articulated, thought must forever remain married to experience, and the commitment to the world of process must forever be sustained. Otherwise what is now most humanizing about the New Left's politics—namely, its processual, open-ended structure—will be destroyed by vicious intellectualism.

We noted above that for the New Left spontaneity and personal experience are pedagogical. That the roots of the new politics are located in the instinctual life, in lived immediacy, in gut moral feelings does not imply, however, that the new politics is a new irrationalism. One must not confuse its repudiation of the chlorophorming, administrative rationality of Establishment politics with a blanket condemnation of reason. The New Left does not place the emotions before reason, but rather seeks to reconstitute reason so that it is libidinal and affective—that is, energized by ongoing life experience. Similarly, its emphasis on existential commitment or the will to act is not a clarion call for headless action, but rather an attempt to rupture the repressive continuum of Establishment politics and to carve out counter-images of liberating political experience.

The New Left struggle against the *cultural* hegemony of the bourgeoisie is part and parcel of its anti-authoritarian strategy. For the New Left is as much concerned with the questions of psychic liberation and a revolutionary counter-culture as it is with those of economic and political well-being. As the radical economist James O'Connor has recently argued, the political battlelines are more and more being drawn in terms of those who are radicalizing their life-style, reconstituting their repressive needs, and "proletarianizing" their consciousness, and those who are not. It is in this light that the question of a counter-culture or of parallel or alternate institutional growth must be understood and evaluated. While it is true that the so-called counter-culture lacks refined socialist consciousness, it is also true that the demand by radicals for a high-energy, erotic, freewheeling culture is the keystone in the arch of the anti-institutional struggle. For the integrity of neo-capitalism demands socialization to a repressive social system—that is, to life-negating values and to stereotypic, middle-class life-styles—which is in its form, as well as content, antipathetic to the goals of the counter-culture. To the extent that the counter-culture embodies a total transvaluation of values—that is, a nonrepressive reality principle—it telescopes the essential outlines of a libertarian radical culture. (See Carlo Donolo's essay and *Ten Days That Shook the University* in Part I; and Murray Bookchin's essay in Part III.)

E. *The New Left is anti-racist and anti-imperialist.* While the New Left argues that all the advanced capitalist societies are racist and imperialist to varying degrees, its principal target is the United States. The justification for focusing on the United States is simply its historically entrenched institutional racism and its genocidal foreign policy.

Vis-à-vis prevailing liberal ideology, the New Left argues that racism is not an aberration of an otherwise benevolent social system, but rather a root institutional phenomenon of the advanced capitalist societies. Consequently, it denies that racism in those countries—especially in the United States where it is so widespread—has been significantly ameliorated by token compliance with black, brown, and red demands or by enlightened social legislation or even that racism can be abolished within the institutional framework of monopoly capitalism. The New Left argues that racism will be destroyed only when the class basis of social relationships under neo-capitalism is destroyed—that is, when humane interpersonal living becomes functional to the ongoing social system. At present the opposite is the case; racism is perhaps morally and socially abhorrent to many people —many more are unconscious of it, and still others defend it—but it is not economically and politically deleterious. For example, it sustains the necessary unemployment rate—between 4 percent and 6 percent—and through polarization of the working class population militates against the formation of a unified workers' front against the despotism of capital.

Racism is crucial to an analysis of the economic imperialism and foreign policy of the advanced capitalist countries. For example, the economic exploitation of the Third World is demonstrably racist. The economic disenfranchisement of the native masses of the Third World, produced by the incursion and entrenchment of foreign capital and by the pillaging of natural resources by the Western robber barons, begets a master-slave culture, in which, as Frantz Fanon and others have argued, white Western interests reign supreme and ride herd on indigenous cultural institutions and value structures.

In essence, neo-capitalist foreign policy—*vis-à-vis* the Third World—is governed by the twofold aim of creating an international political status quo for the realization and absorption of the economic surplus and of stymieing and, where possible, of destroying anti-capitalist national liberation struggles. (See James O'Connor's essay in Part II.) The rationale for opposing national liberation struggles (whether in the form of clandestine CIA counter-insurgency operations, as in Laos, or of overt genocidal warfare against a whole people, as in Vietnam) is not the proclaimed moral and political desire to make the world safe for democracy, but the more sundry economic desire to make the world safe for foreign investments and for the proliferation of new markets. (See David Horowitz's essay in Part II.) As such, every victorious national liberation struggle strikes a death blow to the neo-capitalist imperialist Leviathan, because each victory emboldens Third World opposition to Western economic imperialism and exposes the venality of capitalism. (See Göran Therborn's essay in Part II; and Herbert Marcuse's essay in Part III.)

More generally, the liberal thesis that Western foreign policy is arrived at democratically and in the interests of the common good is patently absurd. As the revisionist historians and others have shown, the foreign policy of the Western imperialist nations is determined by a corporate elite in the private interests of international capital, not by the people of those countries in their enlightened self-interest. Consequently, liberal rhetoric about "the national interest" as the criterion of foreign policy decision-making is but a verbal imprimatur for the imperialist schemes of the white corporate ruling class. Cold-war mythmaking about Communist imperialism obfuscates this fact and is used to justify the existence of an economically parasitarian military-industrial-governmental complex, which in the name of freedom produces genocide for profit. In sum, the neo-capitalist state is a warfare state—not a welfare state—which is bent upon global hegemony, and which produces both untold suffering and misery at home and genocidal warfare abroad. (See David Horowitz's essay in Part II.)

The university plays a key role in the racism and imperialism of the advanced capitalist societies. The New Left argues that the university is not politically neutral—as the liberals claim—but is a vital armature of the corporate liberal Establishment. As evidence of the apologetical function of the university, the New Left cites its systematic "laying on of culture," its class structure, its propagation of authoritarian knowledge, and its complicity with the war-machine (through government-sponsored and government-supervised war research, job recruitment by war profiteers, ROTC, etc.).

The New Left argues that the university is neither an ivory tower nor a community of scholars, but a knowledge factory where the socially necessary labor force is reproduced and where the socialization of the future bourgeoisie is ensured by educational tracking and the "embourgeoisement" of consciousness. (See André Gorz's essay in Part II.) It cites the collapse of critical reason and the general "moronization" of learning as further evidence of the ideological function of the university. In addition, it argues that the emphasis on atomistic *vis-à-vis* cross-disciplinary learning, and the separation of thought and practice render the learning experience self-alienating, and produce atomistic individuals, and socialize people to "affirmative culture"—that is, culture which is synonymous with the leisured activities of elites. More generally, the New Left argues that the bastardizing of critical reason in the name of "value free inquiry" and "scientific objectivity" obscures the irrationality of the social system and the logic of political domination, insofar as the ideological basis of Establishment social science and unitary scientific method remains inscrutable.

Accordingly, liberal rhetoric about the "integrity of higher learning" is a verbal ruse to hide the fact of compulsory miseducation and is but a transparent rationalization of the cultural hegemony of the white, Waspish ruling class.

F. *The New Left is utopian,* in the sense that it is a living negation of existing social reality. Its social ideals are not, however, pollyannaish, nor does its visionary sociology imply a paradisiacal future or a social messianism. (See Murray Bookchin's essay in Part III.)

Given the irrationality of the neo-capitalist social system, the function of utopian thinking is to keep alive counter-images of rational social existence. Those who would decry the utopianism of the New Left should ask themselves who the true custodians of reason are in an irrational society: the utopians who refuse to be supine and who attempt to construct humanizing social alternatives to the status quo or the "realists" who sheepishly capitulate to the status quo? This is not to say that radicalism is synonymous with building castles in the air, but that where reason is systematically violated the most reasonable course is *not* to be "realistic," in the sense in which this implies accommodation to a maleficent and irrational social system.

New Left utopianism is not incompatible, however, with a strategy of anti-capitalist structural reforms. Fighting for anti-capitalist reforms should not be confused with fighting for reforms per se. The first is genuinely revolutionary and should play a central role in any revolutionary socialist struggle. The second, on the other hand, is supportive of the status quo, and should be eschewed as counter-revolutionary. (See Ernest Mandel's and André Gorz's essays in Part III.)

To be utopian, then, is not something the New Left can or cannot choose. By virtue of being "left"—that is, a negation of the status quo—the New Left is perforce utopian. What is an object of choice are the strategies for change which the New Left ought to adopt, and here it ought to adopt any strategy for change which facilitates the overthrow of corporate capitalism and which enhances the prospects of libertarian socialist revolution.

Among the leading utopian social goals of the New Left are: (1) the elimination of toil and alienated labor—that is, labor which is enforced and determined by the private needs of monopoly capital, instead of by rational social needs; and ultimately the creation of a truly post-scarcity society in which work would be converted into play and the market abolished by complete automation of the labor process (see Murray Bookchin's essay in Part III); (2) the creation of a non-repressive culture, governed by the conversion of need into desire, by the transformation of sexuality into Eros— that is, the passage from genital sexuality to an eroticizing of the whole human personality and the total social milieu—and by the freeing of the human body from repressive de-sublimated sex; (3) the creation of decentralized and fully libertarian communities of authentic selves—shored on a liberating technological and ecological base—where the fulfillment of the common good would be a necessary condition for the personal self-realization of all (see Murray Bookchin's essay in Part III); (4) the abolition of cultural ethnocentrism and the creation of a world-cultural community, free of economic avarice and political domination, and nourished by love and mutual self-understanding; (5) the abolition of private property, the collective ownership of the means of production, and the utilization of economic resources for the pacification and harmonization of all the peoples of the earth; and (6) the structuring of new, experimental social life paradigms—extended family structures, communes, etc. (See Margaret Benston's essay in Part II.)

G. *The New Left is anti-male chauvinist.* The rise of a politically sophisticated women's liberation movement in the United States has refocused attention on the institutional basis of women's oppression —sex-typed jobs—and has called into question the legitimacy of the very institutions which oppress women under monopoly capitalism— the nuclear family. In addition, the raising of "the women's question" has had a democratizing influence on the Movement itself, insofar as it has revealed widespread sexist attitudes among male radicals and has sensitized the latter to the incompatibility of male supremacy with libertarian communal life. Moreover, the new and more important political roles played by radical women within Movement organizations and the deepening awareness by radical women of the political power of the idea of sisterhood have brought to bear a great deal of pressure on male radicals to redefine their roles as political actors and have contributed significantly to the diminution of overt male chauvinism within the Movement.

This notwithstanding, the ethic of sexual exclusivity articulated by many of the radical feminist groups—the man haters—is a fact to be mourned. Only when the radical feminists see themselves as proletarians first and as a sexual class second will they escape their parochial preoccupation with sexual exploitation (parochial from the viewpoint of an anti-institutional strategy) and pose a more truly revolutionary threat to the status quo. Nevertheless, the question of women's oppression should be raised as a special question, if only as an interim strategy, because male supremacy—like white-skin privilege—is so deep-rooted and so inscrutable. The fact that socialist revolutions in Cuba, China, etc. have not completely eliminated the oppression of women is further evidence of how really deep-rooted the problem of male supremacy is. Moreover, it will be necessary to internationalize the women's struggle—at present it is mainly confined to the United States—for the oppression of women is global and is probably worse in Europe and in other areas of the world. (See Margaret Benston's essay in Part II.)

We have tried to define—however superficially—the experimental temper of New Left politics. A major implication of our analysis is that the various forms this politics will assume in the future cannot be circumscribed in advance. For these will in large part depend on the possibilities for meaningful political self-expression, crystallized by developing social realities, whose own forms also remain radically contingent and therefore unpredictable. The ideals discussed in Part III deal with the general long-range strategy of the contemporary New Left, but they leave open the question of what new social, political and economic configurations will come into play in the near future.

For many the open-endedness of the new radical politics will be disappointing, but for those of us committed to the world of process this is a challenge we fully embrace. The revolution will be made by men and women who, rejecting certitude, opt for a life of excess and creative adventure, who are experimentalist in spirit and visionary in philosophical outlook. It will be made by men and women who *live* the revolution in their daily life, who are continually redefining their roles as political actors in the context of ongoing social experience, and whose controlling passion is the building of a living socialist community. It will not be made by men and women who either because of ideological intransigency or bourgeois life-style hang-ups are cut off from the world of process and novelty.

The battle lines are now being drawn, reader. Are you going to be part of the problem or part of the solution? You are not being asked to make a political decision, but to stake. your being! Perhaps we shall meet in the streets!!

All power to the people!

Part I

Concepts of Ideology

Ronald Aronson
and John C. Cowley

Ronald Aronson is a former editor of *Studies on the Left* and is the author of several influential articles on New Left politics. John Cowley is a former associate editor of *Studies on the Left* who teaches political sociology at the City University, London, England. He has recently written "The Strange Death of the Liberal University" for *The Socialist Register, 1969*.

The following essay originally appeared in *The Socialist Register, 1967*. The footnotes are omitted here.

Aronson and Cowley briefly analyze the new contradictions which have given birth to a revivified leftist movement in the United States. While the character of the American New Left has changed considerably since 1967 when this essay was first published, Aronson and Cowley's analysis is for that a very seminal and perceptive statement of the new radical politics ushered in by the American New Left.

THE NEW LEFT IN
THE UNITED STATES

The New Left: An agglomeration of thousands of young Americans self-righteous but courageous, radical but not specifically socialist, democratic but not anit-communist, far-out but reformist, liberated yet enormously confused. A journalistic literature has sprung up in the past year which describes this strange phenomenon but unfortunately most of the discussion remains on the level of description. Certain vital questions remain unanswered: Why the New Left? Why now? Is it merely the reassertion—after the McCarthy hiatus—of a tradition of student rebellion? Do the traits of the New Left represent a new trend of radical politics? Or rather, are they the necessary result of its peculiar process of self-birth? Does the New Left reflect any fundamental contradictions of American society, contradictions which can be expected to become aggravated? Does it have any chance of developing a coherent ideology and mushrooming into a full-scale radical movement?

If these are some of the most pressing questions, one thing should be clear: to raise fundamental questions about the New Left is to raise fundamental questions about the nature and direction of contemporary American society. The present analysis is tentative and exploratory. The traits of the New Left are well known. The purpose here is to explain the most salient of these traits in terms of the society in which the New Left arose. Our underlying premise is that specific traits of American society made possible a movement such as the New Left, and that the nature and course of development of the New Left follows, to some degree at least, lines made possible by the nature of American society. Through analyzing one in terms of the other, then, it is hoped to arive at a better understanding of both.

Twentieth century American capitalism is a system atop a system. Protecting and preserving the capitalist structure of the American economy is a system of controls, mechanisms, and devices, which extends from Madison Avenue to seventeen hundred overseas military bases, from Vietnam to price-fixing, from Guatemala and Iran to automobile junkyards, from welfare payments to the moon: everywhere and in every way one confronts American capitalism's means of ever-more-profitable survival. These mechanisms and devices which absorb opposition while exploiting and squandering resources are *required* for American capitalism's continued survival—and they seem to have indeed succeeded. A high standard of living prevails; the major labor unions are solidly in the system and actively supporting it. In the 1950's and early 1960's American capitalism appeared to have resolved what Marxists had insisted were its fundamental underlying contradictions. So much so that its ideologues called for "the end of ideology" and its opponents with bitterness and despair called it "the Great American Celebration" and the "One Dimensional Society."

A brief description is necessary of these mechanisms which have made the "Great Society" out of the underemployed, underproducing capitalist system of the 1930's, a system which had seemed to fulfill classical Marxism's anticipations.

The Great Depression disappeared with the war-time mobilization of the 1940's. It is now evident that the New Deal provided a number of the necessary conditions but not the sufficient cause for the post-thirties recovery and rehabilitation of the American economy. In short, it was the permanent war-economy ushered in during the forties which led to the revolutionizing of productive capacity and the subsequent remarkable rise in living standards of the 1950's.

Within this general movement of recovery the tendency noted by Berle and Means in 1932, for the economy to come under the dominance and control of a few hundred large corporations, continued to assert itself. As a result, a few hundred supercorporations have come to control the strategic areas, "the commanding heights," of the economy. As one economist has concluded: "The removal of 150 super-corporations would effectively destroy the American economy. . . ." These supercorporations control a productive capacity that not only makes America the richest nation in the world, but also provides the foundations upon which the allocation of resources, jobs, wealth and income are based. All aspects of this society, from occupation to housing, education to health, scientific research to television entertainment, are dependent on the corporate-controlled area of the economy.

The rise of the supercorporation has taken place within the context of a still war-mobilized economy. A central feature of this warfare economy has been the rapid growth of a "military-industrial complex" absorbing millions of men and billions of dollars of investment. The defense and defense-connected industries are proving to be an indispensable prop to the post-war economy. This enormous military-industrial complex not only helps stabilize the domestic economy but is also proving to be an essential adjunct to the world-wide practice of American capitalism. Since the 1930's, the United States has emerged as the undisputed leader and protector of the "Free World," and the demands made by this role in turn necessitate the preservation of the war-mobilized economy. America's military machine is vital for the maintenance of the world market economy. A "nuclear umbrella" has been created by the United States under which it participates in the training of numerous foreign armies and police forces and conducts counter-insurgency operations from Thailand to Peru, while at the same time maintaining a network of 275 major base complexes and 1,400 other bases around the world.

Since the 1940's, American corporations have extended their world-wide activities. Today the foreign market for domestic and overseas United States owned firms is roughly equivalent to two-fifths the domestic market. In terms of the Third World, this extension of American interests has included not only the attempt to gain control over scarce resources such as oil, but also the attempt to establish captive markets. The growing importance of, and the growing need for, such assured markets on the part of many large corporations strengthens America's overall commitment to maintaining the authority of market relations on a world scale. It must preserve a structure of superordinate and subordinate market relations that are founded upon an historically transient international division of labor. It is not surprising that the United States, with only 6 per cent of the world's population and yet producing and consuming over 35 per cent of the world's manufactured goods, enjoys a virtually unassailable hegemony over world markets.

This extension of the market in *breadth* (overseas), although of fundamental importance for American capitalism, is but one dimension of its post-thirties expansion. Attention must also be paid to its expansion in *time* (planned obsolescence), and in *depth* (creation of artificial wants, selling through advertising and consumer credit). There is no doubt that the extension of the domestic market in these other directions has proved crucial for the post-war American economy. The corporations have succeeded in establishing administered markets domestically: markets compartmentalized, controlled through mechanisms of managed prices, the brand image and "quality control," and buoyed-up by enormous injections of credit. What competition does take place today, takes place between corporation and consumer via the media of mass communications which are themselves a vital and integral part of the world of the large corporation.

It appears that American capitalism only survives in so far as it can produce and sell enormous quantities of waste-articles satisfying no vital human need. One need only reflect here on the acknowledged tie between the fate of Detroit's automobiles—produced far beyond any rational need, and becoming obsolete in outrageously brief periods —and the economy as a whole. The waste economy, in order to expand and perpetuate itself, extends and intensifies exploitation backwards to the worker in the corporation and forwards to the consumer, and in the process it increasingly invades every area and moment of the individual's life—through advertising, pressures to buy and consumer credit. There has been created, over and above basic individual needs, a structure of *induced* needs. The individual becomes enmeshed in this structure of artificial wants. More and more, the individual, in obediently supporting his economy, surrenders areas of autonomy. The system's demands on him, the stereotyped and standardized forms of amusement, leisure activity and pleasure, block out any possibility for the development of individual interests, needs and desires. In short, the economy has had to extend itself deeply into the individual.

In order to survive, American capitalism has had to expand relentlessly, developing a productive capacity serving no vital needs, but which requires the manufacture and manipulation of induced needs. But while the individual has no choice but to satisfy his vital life needs the artificial needs must be sold to him. And the individual can hardly accept these waste needs as his own without accepting the entire style of life and society they represent. In buying that way of life, the individual identifies with and becomes enmeshed in this society. Much more of him—his hopes, needs and fears—is bound-up with the economy than ever before. Structurally unable to meet the basic needs of everybody, American capitalism moves deeper and deeper into the lives of its affluent members.

Parallel to this extension of market practice has been the ever growing concentration of control into fewer and fewer hands. A few hundred supercorporations, world-wide in their activities, are increasingly controlled by fewer and fewer people, and in the process are acquiring ever greater efficiency and consequently an ever more tightly structured chain of command, controlling at a moment's notice vast areas of resources, and establishing captive markets at home and abroad and setting prices with little fear of open price competition. The concentration and consolidation of the supercorporation has resulted in a rapid extension of top-down controls which destroy the possibility for exercising individual initiative and responsibility.

The growth of bureaucracy is a function of this centralization in the economic sphere. Bureaucratization is an integral element to the post-thirties phenomenon of organized capitalism: a capitalism in which the state has become the agency of mediation for the complex of interlocking bureaucracies. The state is now the focus of the protective apparatus.

Today the American ruling class mediates, justifies and shields its corporation-based dominance and privileges through an institutional and bureaucratic structure which is both private and public in extent. The executive and middle-managers in the large corporations, federal and state employees and administrators in politics, education and health, all have a material and ideological commitment to the existing structure of American society. They are the functionaries of organized capitalism, the links in the chain of top-down command, and they owe their position, status and comforts to the existing institutional structure of American society. These social strata have grown in number as the public and private bureaucracies and regulatory agencies of organized capitalism have grown.

The increasing centralization of control, the elaboration of higher and middle strata of functionaries, and the tendency to eliminate at all levels and in all dimensions of social life individual initiative and responsibility, has culminated in a voluntary form of totalitarianism. But this self-imposed totalitarianism, the elimination of significant choice at every level, and the consequent identification with a pre-defined whole way of life, is ultimately predicated upon the anti-communist ideology produced by capitalism's epochal conflict with communism. Unquestioned identification with *the American* way of life is the other aspect of anti-communist prejudice.

The Cold War has made it possible to reject all other forms of society. Perhaps indeed the expression of and hostility to any alternative is a necessary psychological precondition for the production and consumption of useless goods, for it creates the required identification with *this* way of life. Thus more than just a simple ideological unity is being generated by the Cold War. The Cold War has helped to eliminate any alternative to the status quo, and by so doing it has disguised the fact that capitalism's transiency has been demonstrated. American society, as Marcuse argues in *One Dimensional Man,* is mobilized politically and intellectually to disguise this fact. Communism thus becomes its sustaining menace, its required enemy.

The Cold War's elimination of any alternative to the *status quo,* the enormous expansion of production and the consequent expansion of wages, and, finally, the development of such welfare-state measures as medicare for the aged, social security, limited public housing, welfare payments, workman's compensation, and minimum wage scales, have been the devices that help cement the "Great Society" consensus. It has also been aided in the political sphere by a political, governmental, law-enforcing structure of checks and balances which operate on the principle of integrational politics. The political parties have proved to be the necessary additional apparatus for closing the arena of divisive politics. Today the narrow sphere of electoral politics is managed. It has become the exclusive preserve of highly organized political parties steered and run by professional politicians and political bureaucrats: functionaries directing a politics in which representatives choose their electors. Electoral politics has become the mechanism through which the American ruling class builds up and maintains an alliance of classes and social strata. In the 1964 elections, the Democratic Party succeeded to a greater extent than ever before in joining businessmen, farmers, professionals, white-collar workers, organized labor, and the Negro community in an electoral alliance, united by a program which incorporated the various minimum demands of the different groups into a hierarchy of aims which promised a lessening of tensions and problems within American society. The program of promises to meet this aggregate of minimum demands was labeled the "Great Society."

Organized capitalism is, fundamentally, a society without opposition on the political level, and without alternatives on the individual level. It is a system which increasingly penetrates and shapes every area and phase of social and individual life. It needs, demands, and attains the individual's identification and subordination to a system which is increasingly hostile and external to him. It is, in the profoundest sense of the word, a *system:* a centralized, a hierarchical structure in which all elements and phases are interlocking and interdependent, and, in the final analysis, interpenetrative and inseparable. The autonomy of the whole is supreme. In its epochal conflict with communism, all become subservient to the movement and structural requirements of the whole. The system demands, whether in its waste production or its anti-communism, identification with, and acceptance of the whole. In order to survive, American capitalism has developed a protective apparatus dependent not on vital needs but on the manufacture and manipulation of induced needs—ultimately it sells the individual a whole way of life. The dismal picture, conveyed starkly in Herbert

Marcuse's *One Dimensional Man,* of a closed and controlled universe, a sleek and clean society, is also a picture of the success of American capitalism. The consensus, mobilization against the enemy, the welfare-warfare society, the endless proliferation of useless gadgets—here one is confronting American capitalism's means of overcoming the contradictions made so evident during the Great Depression.

This, then, is the American "solution." Yet in spite of it, in the past few years we have witnessed Vietnam and Watts, Berkeley and Selma. We have witnessed the rise of a student movement and a Negro movement, often side by side. Why these explosions? Why this New Left, if American capitalism has been so successful?

In point of fact, the "solution" has merely temporized and repressed the basic difficulties. Indeed, they continue to recur, often in their traditional form: unemployment and poverty. Often, in fact, the various forms of the solution contain their own problems—as Vietnam indicates. The point is, of course, that whatever forms they may take, the basic problems of American capitalism have not vanished. The protective apparatus eliminates choice, contracts the space for individual initiative, while at the same time the system in its continuing need and search for profits excludes whole strata from the comforts of affluence. Profitable affluence has produced the ghetto and the depressed rural areas, the unemployed and the unemployable, the high school drop-out and the Bowery derelict.

We have suggested that the most basic facts in the "solution" of the system's difficulties are the extension of its demands into all areas of social and individual life, its growth into gigantic institutions, and the concentration of more and more vital decision-making powers in the hands of fewer and fewer men. The elite control bound-up with capitalism becomes more and more pronounced as capitalism makes greater and greater demands on the individual, as the institutions become larger, as they merge and entrench themselves and as they become more manipulative in their search for profits. Choice, whether in the market or politics, is eliminated.

Yet American democratic values—which have proved so vital a weapon in the war against communism—foster expectations which these structures invariably frustrate. These values, rooted as they are in a possessive individualism surviving from an historical period when there was some social space for individual and group movement, still hold sway and dominate in a society which now denies any such space. The notion on which these values are premised W. E. B. Dubois called "the American Assumption": the assumption, that is, that in America there had been created a unique arrangement of societal relations that provided a framework for individual opportunity and self-fulfillment. Today this assumption stands in sharp contradiction to the system's actual practice, yet continues to be intellectually affirmed.

This contradiction between ideology and reality has been felt most strongly by those who take the ideology most seriously—students. It was among the students that the New Left originated: individuals choked-off from the system at one of its most vulnerable points—the very institutions in which America's ideas are most strenuously propagated. A refusal has been made to go on meeting the all-embracing demands of organized capitalism. A generation of students has rejected the specialization of interest, the narrowness of pursuit, the stereotyping of mind, the standardizing of personality demanded of them. It has been a total reaction; a single and decisive act of disinvolvement from the ongoing—a point blank refusal to continue accepting the pre-packaged way. This dramatic act of disentanglement has been the first step in the emergence of a New Left.

The student left that has emerged was not mechanically determined but rather it created itself, and it has done so under conditions imposed by the very society in which it arises. The distinctive features and the character of this new movement represent its response to the very specific situation in which it has created itself.

The first element to note in the specific situation is the absence of an opposition labor movement. The American trade union movement (AFL-CIO) is not only integrated into the system, but is solidly behind it. Its commitment strengthens the peculiar ideological unity of American politics. In terms of the tone this integration imparts to American politics, it would be academic to ask whether the AFL-CIO represents a majority of the workers. The workers it represents are the decisive ones: the privileged workers of the corporate sector, operating the key areas of the economy. The important point here is not the question of labor's future potential, nor what might happen to those liberal elements existing within the AFL-CIO (elements stifled by the firmly entrenched conservative leadership), but rather the character of the trade union movement: its hierarchical and bureaucratic structure and its over-riding aim of maintaining the privileged position of its membership. The AFL-CIO now constitutes a major obstacle to any radical activity and politics in America. This does not, of course, preclude either the possibility or the need for attempting organizing efforts among the workers outside the AFL-CIO, whether they be unskilled, white collar or those of seemingly middle class and semi-professional standing. No act of will, however, is going to overcome this immediate obstacle of the AFL-CIO.

If there is no workers' opposition, neither is there a radical party within which the New Left could have developed. Besides having been isolated and discredited by the Cold War, the traditional Left parties have been polarized around the issues arising from the Russian and Chinese revolutions, having little or nothing to say about the key issue for the New Left—the quality of life in American society. Their insights into poverty and the Vietnam war are appealing, but their fixation on a frozen Marxism, Leninism, or Trotskyism blinds them to the most current developments of advanced capitalism. Moreover, their organizational structure tends to reduplicate that of the existing order, making them unappealing as an alternative.

If the New Left has grown up in relation to neither party nor workers' movement, then it has not been able to shape itself in terms of a coherent theory and organizing strategy, and it has not been able to shape itself in terms of an ongoing movement whose experience permitted insight into the underlying socio-economic structure. Neither theory nor first-hand insight into the system's underlying contradictions have been available to it.

But, in fact, the New Left *has* grown up in relation to a movement —the Civil Rights movement. The complexion and situation of the Civil Rights movement has been decisive in shaping the character of the New Left; for many it was the formative experience of their lives. Here is where we must look for a more positive understanding of the characteristics of the New Left.

Until very recently the unifying goal of the Civil Rights movement was integration and the full enfranchisement of American Negroes. The failure to implement full adult suffrage and formal equality has stood in stark contradiction to the society's cherished democratic ideals. The immediate visibility of Southern racism profoundly affected thousands of students. Intimate contact with a people *outside of* the totally absorbing system, a people not yet standardized, proved to be a critical experience: it sharpened the contradiction between ideology and reality.

More than the student left, the Negroes are suffering because of the traditional problems of American capitalism: under-employment, low wages, inadequate and over-crowded housing and extremely poor educational facilities and opportunities. They exist on the margin of American society, having made their most important gains only during the two periods of World War. Their position represents America's inability to come to terms with its own slave-owning past. A failure which has resulted in such a deepening of race prejudice that racism is imminent throughout the institutions and practices of American society. American Negroes represent a peculiar colonial problem: historically they were integral to the white colonization of the Americas, but their drive for full emancipation has awaited the political emancipation of Africa. Their peculiar colonial status has not only awakened an interest in Africa, but has also encouraged among some Negroes their self-identification as Afro-Americans. With the use of a "black mercenary army" in Vietnam two phases of past and present American practice are coming together.

But the Negroes are not placed in a strategic position vis-à-vis the economy and they do not have an immediate awareness of its basic structure. This absence of a direct tie to the central processes of American capitalism, this marginality, makes it difficult for student organizers, whether black or white, to see how the Negroes' problems will be solved, or how the society itself can be transformed. The Negroes do not readily identify with working class exploitation, nor are they in a position themselves to project a structural alternative. Thus the development of a socialist consciousness is impeded. The student left has not been able to conceive of any alternative, because no existing social forces, by their activity or relationship to the system, project any such alternative.

The Negro community's extreme dislocation, and internal lack of cohesion and malaise, produced by more than three hundred years of slavery, capitalist exploitation and race prejudice, does not extend but simply reinforces the student left's perception of what the system denies—control over one's life. Involvement with a people largely outside of the totally absorbing system makes for a moral urgency and an immediacy of demands. Although there is a radical rejection of the system, the absence of any socialist politics within the labor movement and the absence of any vital current of socialist theory within American thought leads to radical energies being transmuted into reformist politics. Radical energies are directed, for the lack of any other direction, at effects of the system rather than the system itself. Naturally bound-up with this tendency is a further one of an alternating despair and utopianism. Both of these tendencies are at present embodied in SNCC.

For the majority of the student left, as typified by SDS, involvement with the Negro movement has not encouraged this new radical consciousness to overcome and destroy its natural impulse towards reformism. The concern with local and direct control and the quality of life remains at the level of simple spontaneity, rather than a clearly defined alternative to the established society. This fact helps account for a whole range of New Left characteristics, which are related to the kind of system advanced capitalism has become in its efforts to preserve itself.

The American New Left has arisen in response to the peculiar characteristics of contemporary capitalism—its need for a foreign empire, and for wars to defend that empire; its exclusion of Negroes; its enormous and expanding depersonalized institutions; its tendency to bring more and more areas of individual lives under the control of ever more remote bureaucracies; its economic need that individuals not merely produce and consume its goods, but further adopt a whole way of life based on its profit requirements; and, finally, the growing contradiction between a democratic ideology and a capitalism that is demanding and totalitarian in its pressures. Even so, the peculiar traits of the New Left—its emphasis on feelings and people, its vitality, its bohemianism and anti-intellectualism, its reformist politics—are not merely a mechanical reflex to the overall social conditions.

The pre-history of the New Left is to be found in the beat movement of the 1950's—an unorganized and non-political form of social protest. The beatnik was a disillusioned individual who resigned from middle class society and searched for his identity in a community of exiles —voluntary outcasts from middle class comforts and conformity. Traits from this primitive protest survive in the New Left of today.

The intention here, however, is to outline some of the more important of the New Left's characteristics that have developed in the process of its birth within this society. Right at the heart of the student protest is an over-riding sense of moral urgency and need for personal witness: a sense of individual responsibility born out of frustration with the impersonalness of the system. Intensely personal modes of behaving and relating have developed in opposition to the general destruction of individual characteristics that has accompanied the growth of organized capitalism: there is a rejection of its coldness. The rejection manifests itself, in part, in distinctive but carefree modes of dress, personalized styles that bear witness to the conventionalization that has accompanied the organization of American capitalism. There is much experimentation with sex, pot and drugs in opposition to the standardized and totally constricted behavior required for employment in any of the major corporations and in opposition to the customary notions of what constitutes "success."

The anti-intellectualism that characterizes large sections of the student left is a two-fold response: first, it is a rejection of an intellectual and educational system which trains for jobs, makes specialists, imparts experience not knowledge, an educational system which undercuts the possibility of individual recognition and criticism; and secondly, it is a rejection of an intellectualism which has retreated into a search for exactitude in the name of science, protecting itself in the process from open and direct criticism—an intellectualism, that is, that has cut the heart out of intellectual activity, no longer concerning itself with human values and human aspirations. In short, what is rejected is an intellectualism which itself is anti-intellectual and anti-theory. The New Left has rejected an intellectualism which has itself negated the intellectual's critical function.

Another of the New Left's peculiar characteristics is its demand for an unstructured movement. It stands in opposition to structures because they don't conform to human needs, and it emphasizes people's needs as the central dimension of any new radical politics. The New Left searches for, and hopes to re-establish, the human dimension in American life. It demands that structures should be based upon human needs.

These are the salient characteristics of the student left, and they have both angered the Old Left and frustrated those Marxist intellectuals who wish to make their commitment to socialism something more than a personal preference. But no admonishing will alter the root cause of the problem: namely, the lack of a movement, outside of the ghetto, to which the student left can relate. It is this void that puts the New Left in perpetual danger. The break with the system may be sharp and genuine, but the absence of any visible alternative tendency can lead to despair, to the demand for immediate solutions, and to reformism. The absence of visible alternative tendencies, coupled with the enormous strength of the system and the great weakness of the New Left itself leads to the constant threat of disillusionment with politics.

The analysis of contemporary capitalism has suggested the raison d'être for the New Left. In order to perpetuate itself, the system has had to extend itself in every direction: the individual must lose control of his life in ever-increasing ways. Although it is certainly true that every oppressive system has denied the individual's emotional and physiological needs, contemporary capitalism is decisively different: no system proclaiming itself the fulfillment of man's hopes has ever demanded so much from its members. As was pointed out, the basic tendency is to require more and more that the individual meet a structure of induced needs superimposed on his individual needs. Indeed, emotions and instincts are increasingly denied, the space for individuality shrinks as leisure becomes increasingly a social task. No realm of life is left for self-determination because no realm of life is free from the need for profit. Every area of life that "pays"—which means virtually every area—is being tapped. The key to this extension of capitalism in space, time, and depth, we have suggested, is its inability to survive by merely producing the necessary goods. New necessities must be created, for production must expand.

If there is no longer any room for individual emotions and instincts at home, after work, with one's family, or in one's section of town— if the whole is a standardized apparatus imposed on the individual; further, if for these classes scarcity is no longer a problem; then traditional notions of what is truly "political" and what is merely "psychological" can no longer be applied. That is, the chief accusation against capitalism is no longer that it cannot produce the goods necessary for a decent standard of living; but that it fails to create the fundamental conditions for human freedom and self-expression. It does not permit, at any level, individual self-determination. It does not permit the members of the society to decide about themselves or the society. It denies individuality by denying men's intellectual, sexual and emotional needs.

Thus the bohemianism of the New Left—in which all of these denied dimensions are asserted and demanded—is not simply a protest against an accidental byproduct of the system. It rather attacks the necessary requirements for the perpetuation of capitalism: the total absorption of the needs of man by the needs of the system. This is not to say that this concern with life styles, individual feelings, the quality of life, spontaneity, is *per se* political. But it is to insist that these issues are not at all irrelevant to politics and that a mass radical movement in the affluent society will put such questions at its very center.

In discussing the origin and nature of the New Left we have mentioned the spontaneous development of a new critical consciousness. This new radical consciousness, in its demand for participatory democracy, suggests the "determinant negation" of this society.

In other words, the historical alternative to a given social form is not an arbitrary matter, to be discovered by chance, but rather—if it is to have historical meaning—it must arise directly from the structural malfunctioning of the prevailing society. It must represent the needs that are denied by the present society and which may be realized in the specific social forms made possible by and growing out of the present society. In classical capitalism the most telling structural problems resulted in low wages, underemployment and unemployment for the mass of the workers. State control and rationalization of industry was seen as necessary for eliminating these structural defects of capitalism. Today the underlying system cannot be meaningfully separated from its vast protective apparatus when structural malfunctioning no longer affects the proletariat so keenly and directly. State control and nationalization hardly express the historical alternative of organized capitalism. Perhaps the decentralization and direct individual involvement on every level which are implied in participatory democracy foreshadow the still-to-be-elaborated alternative to organized capitalism: black power, student power, faculty power, workers power, and above all community power.

A founding member of SDS, Tom Hayden, has explained the term participatory democracy in the following way:

> "The emphasis in the movement on 'letting the people decide,' on decentralized decision-making, on refusing alliances with top leaders, stems from the need to create a personal and a group identity that can survive both the temptations and the crippling effects of this society. Power in America is abdicated by individuals to top-down organizational units, and it is in the recovery of

this power that the movement becomes distinctive from the rest
of the country and a new kind of man emerges."

Participatory democracy represents an attack on the realities of organized capitalism: its production of profitable affluence, and its concentration of control into fewer and fewer hands while at the same
time eliminating choice and closing out individual initiative and responsibility. The student left has correctly perceived that the issue of control is central to organized capitalism. Perhaps it is the area of the
system's greatest vulnerability, for to survive the system must take
control from the individual over ever greater areas of his life. Basically
capitalism must deny meaningful popular control because control over
the means of production by a small class in the interests of that class
is its very essence. Its struggle for survival is a struggle to retain power
in those few hands. But those who remain without power, those who
are to serve the need for profit, must by that very token *be* managed.
In the factory, if the worker is not to control the work process, is not
to participate in planning and management, then there needs to be a
hierarchical structure of functionaries—planners, experts, and personnel officers to manage people. To the extent that all institutions of organized capitalism become patterned after and intertwined with the
corporation this becomes so throughout the society. If teachers (with
or without the participation of their students) are not to control their
own work, the shaping of the physical facilities as well as the cur-
riculum, then again there needs to be a strata of functionaries, a bureaucracy to perform these functions. To the extent that popular participation and control is eliminated from government and public administration, an extensive bureaucracy is needed. As administrative
institutions develop and grow so the top-down chains of command
invade every area. If, for example, the administration of the current
poverty program is not to be in the hands of the poor themselves,
then a new extension to the bureaucratic structure must be created.
Poverty, embracing as it does over forty million people existing in the
midst of a prosperous society, requires an extensive bureaucracy of
administrators, welfare workers and police. Participatory democracy
represents an attack on these realities. Implicit also in the formulation, but as yet unarticulated, is the understanding that bureaucracy
and control from above is necessary for a certain mode of production,
but not modern industrial production *per se*. Also implicit is the under-

standing that this over-extended bureaucracy, with its layers of functionaries and attached experts, performs—under the guise of impar-
tiality—the function of legitimizing the dominant values and theoretically justifying the structure of organized capitalism. These bureaucratic structures required to perpetuate capitalism, structures which
reduce individual control over individual lives to mere assent to one of
two pre-packaged alternatives, are relatively new to American society.

The New Left has spontaneously developed this radical critique of
American capitalism. At the center of the student left's thinking is the
idea that "men must share in the decisions which affect their lives."
This idea has led the New Left to focus its energies on organizing and
mobilizing the poor and the powerless of the depressed rural areas of
the South, such as Lowndes County (Alabama), and the decayed urban ghettoes of the North, such as "Uptown" Chicago. The organizers
of these projects stress the need for individual and local community
control; they seek to build a new form of movement. Participatory
democracy also provides an instrumental theory, a guide to tactics
however limited it may be, for the fight against paternalistic bureaucratic control whether it is the university administration at Berkeley
or the city administration in Newark, New Jersey. In the anti-war and
anti-draft movements it finds an echo in the argument that stresses the
individual's ultimate responsibility for his actions, an argument that
utilizes the case put forward by the Allied prosecution at the Nuremberg Trials.

By raising the issue of control, the New Left suggest the basis for a
conception of human freedom which demonstrates the need for a new
arrangement of social relations. Implicit within this spontaneously developed consciousness is an alternative vision of what society could
be: a free and equal association of men controlling the decisions that
affect their lives—in short, a socialist society. This new radical consciousness is, to paraphrase Lenin, a socialist consciousness in its embryonic form. It is the beginnings of a self-awareness of capitalism in
its organized, totalitarian phase.

But so long as it remains at this level of simple spontaneity, the
natural tendency of this new radicalism is towards reformist politics.
The tendency is for New Left consciousness to remain confined to intuitively perceived insights concerning the structure of organized capitalism, and, as a result, to tend towards a subordinate reformism, a
tendency which is already clearly discernible in the New Left: in its

failure to break with and clearly confront the dominant liberal-demo-
cratic ideology, in its attraction to the "new politics" of liberalism
and its failure so far to develop the notion of participatory democracy
into a conception of a qualitatively new form and structure of society.
In addition, as presently defined by its advocates, participatory democracy does not include within it the basis for an adequate socio-economic critique of organized capitalism, so that it speaks of elite rule
and subordination only, failing to grasp the significance of class rule
and exploitation.

If the New Left is to continue the process of its self-creation it must
develop a socialist consciousness capable of directly challenging the
existing intellectual and moral supremacy of liberalism; it must break
the present ideological unanimity. This needs to be done if it is to develop a movement which aims not only at organizing those already
excluded by the system, and providing a haven for those who reject it,
but also those who at present identify, not with the system as such, but
with the dominant ideology. The existing gap between ideology and
reality needs to be expressed in an alternate theory and a vision, which
rejects the attempt simply to rehabilitate existing social conditions. In
other words, not only a practical basis but also an intellectual basis for
a socialist movement has to be created in the United States. The central concept of any contemporary socialism will be popular control—
participatory democracy.

At the present time the development of a socialist movement appears to be dependent upon circumstances, such as the world-wide
practice of American capitalism, and the rise of the Negro revolt,
which lie outside the immediate purview of the new radicals. But work
aimed at creating the basis of a socialist movement is both necessary
and possible, although it will be prolonged and protracted. The basis
for such activity exists in American society. The tendency for the system to choke off individuals is built in. The New Left is an organic,
not an accidental, movement, the product of a system which continues
to create the demand for its overthrow.

Carlo Donolo

Carlo Donolo is a young Italian sociologist and activist who has written widely on New Left politics for European radical journals. He lived for quite a while in Germany, and his analysis of the Movement owes much to the German SDS experience and to the writings of Rudy Dutschke. He was active in organizing the free university in Turin.

The present essay originally appeared in the Italian radical journal *Quaderni Piacentini,* June, 1968, and was reprinted in *Leviathan,* June, 1969. The translation is by Angela Terzani.

Donolo analyzes the process by which students are politicized, arguing that the class composition of the Movement—which is petit bourgeois—is less important than its "strategy and objective function." He examines the anti-authoritarianism and anti-Jacobinism of the Movement, defining its "objective function" as the "re-opening [of] the political system" through the reconstitution of "the conditions for the formation of a non-institutionalized opposition to the system." Owing to "the de-politicization of reality" in the advanced capitalist societies, Donolo argues for a redefinition of politics, the central aim of which would be the "political resocialization of individuals" and which would perforce entail the politicization of "traditionally non-political fields." More generally, Donolo argues for an anti-institutional strategy—that is, a cultural revolution—by means of which "the Movement can repoliticize the social universe." After discussing the ramifications of this anti-institutional strategy, he rejects the view that to be successful such a strategy must transcend the level of "a coalition of relatively autonomous and heterogeneous groups" and embody a "monolithic structure." According to Donolo, the masses—the socially heterogeneous masses—not a small vanguard, will play the "pilot role" in the articulation of this anti-institutional strategy.

POLITICS REDEFINED

Students and Politics

To understand the politicization of students we must consider some
of their sociological characteristics:

a) The student has a specific role in a specialized institution. While
this role covers only a segment of his social status, it has at least two
dimensions that connect it with, and found it in, systems of more
general roles: first, the role of "age" which is characterized by submission to socializing authorities (family, school) and by limited responsibility; and second, a cognitive role wherein the student's specific
task is to acquire a more or less specialized technical-scientific knowledge. The progressive homogenization of these socio-cultural characteristics tends to make of the social category "students" a subcultural
group in the scholastic institution.

It is however only a tendency, for there continue to be differences
in the material conditions of life. The most relevant factor here is
probably the status of the student's family which reproduces social
stratification within the subcultural group. Not only does this status
determine the student's material conditions of life, but it also structures
his motivation to study, the type of subjects he chooses, his linguistic
and cultural patrimony, the level of his aspirations, and the material
possibilities of achieving them. As a matter of fact, the level of aspirations (the image of one's own professional future) is precisely the
factor which determines the propensity of the student to accept his
role as part of the ruling class in formation, or, for the majority of
the students, to accept a subordinate position within the ruling class.
The level of aspirations is symptomatic of the degree of identification
with the socio-cultural values of the system, and the various degrees of
identification have an eminently political meaning. However, while
these differences are relevant for the internal social relations of the
group, they do not altogether overcome the relatively unitarian consciousness and homogeneous self-interpretation of social function.
Students generally tend to project themselves as a "symbolic" class, a
class that is paradoxically more "for itself" than "in itself"—to use

the Marxian terminology. In other words, while the material elimination of original class differences is still a long way off, the development of a uniform culture and politics anticipates it.

b) The complexity of the student's role suggested above produces a strong ambiguity in the definition of the role itself. This ambiguity emerges first from the very real inconsistency of the student's status (high outside the university, low inside); second, from his role ambivalence (between that of the youth and that of the adult); and third, from the uncertainty of his position (whether or not he will achieve established professional goals). These conflicts accumulate into an identity crisis which is correspondingly related to the student's past (the social status of his family, position of youth within the family), to his present (his role within the institution and among his peers) and to his future (his professional perspectives). In this context it is important to note that the interpretation of these contradictions arises for the most part out of both the political and pre-political subculture of the group. In fact, it is within the group that needs which can be satisfied neither by family, school nor professional perspective, develop and acquire legitimacy. Family and school contribute because they tend to prolong minority and an emotional, economic and disciplinary dependency without at the same time providing compensation on an emotional and intellectual level. Professional prospects contribute for they anticipate the constrictions of the future professional life during the years of study, when immediate satisfactions must be sacrificed for the ethic of postponement.

Such contradictions become stronger with the passage from the elite university to the mass university, with the prolonging of the student's training period, and with the growing pressure that the social system exercises on the scholastic institutions. Not only does the number of students, and hence the variety of their social origins, increase, but the very social meaning of the student role is modified. Whereas in the past the student (member of the ruling class) became socialized in the values of his own class in order to inherit vested positions, today socialization in the dominant values of the system is achieved in the mass universities independent of one's social origins. Two ideologies tend to establish themselves as a result: the meritocratic one, which mediates between school and profession on a motivational level, centering

on individual performance as a factor of social mobility; and the technocratic one, which guarantees the cultural isolation of the students
from traditions of critical thought.

The system thus provides a motivation adequate to the contemporary struggle for existence—the career. At the same time, it guarantees
a depoliticization which complements that motivation. That is why the
student is no longer an "intellectual" temporarily detached from social
obligations. On the contrary, as a member of the new labor force in
training, the student belongs to a category which already holds social
responsibilities. It is not an accident that one of the preferred arguments of the official ideologists is that because society invests such a
great amount of money in the schools, students have the social duty
to study quickly and well and to do nothing else. Society thus demands
from students a sense of responsibility in their studies, and at the
same time a socio-political irresponsibility.

There is, in fact, an increasing tendency for the institutional definition of the student role to be socially oriented. In many of the capitalist countries the universities and the entire school system are about
to undergo a rationalization in that sense. But it is precisely in this
phase of transition that the ambivalence between the above definition
of the student role and this new attempt to define it in an authoritarian
sense becomes acute. The very "rationalizing" provisions taken by the
authorities make the student role an even more problematic one by demanding that the individual student identify with society's rules. It is
in this very delicate transitional phase that the system is incapable of
guaranteeing consensus. Masses of students become more and more
aware of the gap between themselves and the role foreseen and expected from them by the educational system.

In a certain way, it is this gap which is the material basis for the
student revolt. At first it is experienced individually as a vague uneasiness—as a personal problem. To become a motivation for political
action other conditions, specific to the student role, are necessary. In
particular, the relatively advantageous situation of the students, their
access to information, and the availability of critical interpretations of
society (developed mostly by small sect groups of the New Left), all
play an important part. At the same time, the collapse of such institutions as fatherland, nation or even family as sources of practical and
political orientation is also relevant. Finally, nearly every institution of
the existing society has only a precarious legitimacy in the eyes of the

students; the subcultural group to which he belongs and the meaning of revolutionary experience on a world scale take on a definite legitimacy in their own right as a source of meaning for the individual life.

The scheme for the politicization of the students can therefore be described as follows: the motivational energy derives from the first obscure individual resistance to the immediate experience of social repression. The political interpretation of the uneasiness and the sense of need are derived from that which is most remote and apparently abstract with respect to the individual experience: the contradictions of imperialism on a world level and the examples of struggle against it. The individual resistance to repression, usually manifested in a refusal to satisfy society's demands (perhaps by the choice of a non-professional major, by postponing graduation, by renouncing a career, etc.) becomes political dissent the very moment it is interpreted within the broader context.

Nature of the Movement

The student movement arises out of the supra-structural nature of the contradictions lived by the students, and while it possesses a definite subculture its basis is still socially heterogeneous. At first sight, these characteristics seem to suggest an analogy with preceding student and youth movements, the best examples of which may be found in German history, for example, the *Wandervogelbewegung*. The political ambiguity and the irrationality of the motivations of students have indeed induced some more advanced groups of the New Left to consider the movement as ephemeral, merely protestative, and useful simply as a source for cadres, or, alternatively, as an unmanageable mass which is only able to create tensions. However, analysis of the movement within the international framework seems to deny both these interpretations (as well as the opposite one which looks on the student movement as an elite or vanguard or even as a new revolutionary subject).

Particularly inadequate and ill-founded is that interpretation which speaks of the petit-bourgeois nature of the student movement. It is inadequate because it fails to recognize that the class composition of the movement is an element of secondary importance compared with its strategy and objective function. This statement, which in other cases could be extremely dubious, is justified here by the nature of the contradictions in advanced capitalism and by the "closure" of the political system. The strategy and objective function of the student movement derive their importance from the fact that the political system is blocked both on a governmental and on an oppositional level. Every really radical movement therefore projects itself from the very beginning as an extra-parliamentary opposition. As the only potential mass movement capable of political initiatives that are relevant on a national level, the student movement has the objective function of "reopening" the political system by reconstituting the conditions for the formation of a non-institutionalized opposition to the system. As we shall see, this will be essentially an anti-authoritarian and anti-institutional opposition. In the long run, these structural characteristics will be much more relevant than the fact that the students are middle class or lower middle class. Finally, other characteristics of the movement, such as its quick transition from the simple raising of demands and issues to the overt struggle against the system, the anti-authoritarianism by which it is inspired, and its anti-jacobinism, seem to deny its petit-bourgeois nature.

Even more unfounded is another interpretation of the movement which sees it as a manifestation of left-wing fascism. It establishes a false historical analogy with experiences such as those prefigured by Julien Sorel. Today the movement is not confronted by weak bourgeois democracies, but rather by stabilized socio-political systems, even if they are inefficient and irrational. There is no situation of chaos or political disorientation, but a programmed development of society which one wants to impede. It is precisely the objectively authoritarian tendency of neo-capitalism in its phase of rationalization that provokes the revolt. The opponent, indeed, is not a liberal system in crisis, but a system that has reached a high level of political integration. Moreover, the revolutionary tradition which inspires the student movement does not contain those irrational, aggressive elements of which even socialism at the beginning of the century may not have been devoid. There is undoubtedly an anarcho-actionist element in the movement, but this cannot be identified with fascism of the left. At best this part of the movement would like to realize a sort of cultural revolution (*"L'imagination a pris le pouvoir"*—Imagination has seized power—Ed.); at worst it expresses the negative dialectic of immediate satisfaction.

Apart from these ultra-leftist and moderate interpretations, there remains the legitimate interpretation. The nature of the movement is not totally defined and depends just as much on its potentialities as on its past. If it is true, as we have said, that the class nature of the movement, *i.e.,* its revolutionary nature, depends on its objective role and on its strategy primarily, then it is also true that the determination of the strategy and of the historical meaning of the movement depends on its capacity to adequately comprehend itself. What this implies is that to develop such self-comprehension, many remnants of the traditional notions of revolutionary politics (still held by most of the left sect groups) will have to be destroyed.

Politics Redefined

The student movement has developed (albeit unevenly and on different levels) some characteristics which are now part of its definition. On the whole they typify a new way of making politics, and also, a new way of defining what politics is. One such characteristic is the struggle against authoritarianism. The notion of authoritarianism contains several sociological and political ideas. It refers in the first place to the power structures within the institutions and social organizations of the society which are not functionally legitimized, and which can be justified only by private material interests. Secondly, it refers to both passive and more or less directed violence exercised against subordinated individuals in their different social roles, especially including repression within the family. Finally, it refers to the political-social climate of a society undergoing rationalization, when it is not prepared to tolerate the satisfaction of wants other than those which it imposes.

Authoritarianism is a new word for an old fact: exploitation. It can, however, be generalized into forms of underprivilege and oppression which are not included in the old notion. Thus it is possible to include in a radical program relatively privileged, yet still subordinate social groups, which the system deprives not so much of surplus value as of the power of self-determination and the possibility of emancipation. This idea reflects the increasing importance of institutional manipulation that serves to depoliticize and to integrate people into the system. It also reflects the fact that the direct exploitation of the worker is possible not only because of the discipline imposed on him in his working place, but also because of the "global" effect of the social controls exerted on him outside the factory, whose net effect is to convince him of the obviousness of the present division between social and political work.

Authoritarianism is the term that describes the logic of a society completely mediated by the dominant interests and which utilizes for its own survival the repressive functions of pre-capitalist, bourgeois and technocratic institutions. It also allows for a political interpretation of internal repression, of subliminal institutionalized violence, as well as of explicit and material violence. Authoritarianism is, finally, the system of preferences imposed on society in order to make liberation from repressive wants impossible.

The movement does not appear to have appreciated the relevance of the individual experience of repression in the politicization of its members, nor of its effects on the dynamics of the movement itself. A source of resistance to the development of this awareness is the survival of traditional conceptions of politicization taken over from the workers' movement and from the praxis of the left sect groups. There is, as well, an underestimation of the importance of developing "non-repressive needs," or "radical needs" (Marcuse, Dutschke) which would avoid reproducing within the movement the same processes of repression by which the system nourishes itself. This has become concretely evident in the underestimation of the relevance of the element of "participatory democracy" as against an emphasis on direct decision making, i.e., in the incapacity to acknowledge in political decisions the results of collective discussions or opinions, in the resumption of charismatic relationships, and in the beginning of divisions of labor in political work. All these are directly proportionate to the lack of self-comprehension within the movement.

The anti-authoritarian consciousness as an essential part of the political consciousness characterizes the new type of *militant* which the movement has up until now more projected than produced. This new figure is defined mainly by his relative political autonomy, by his ability both to evaluate and to make decisions. He must be capable of autonomously evaluating the situation in which he is operating and of formulating a political line of thought that is adequate for the concrete case. His role is thus defined in relation to the decentralized structure of the movement. He must be neither a transition line between the top and the base, nor an official who sells the ideology of a party. Rather, he must be a political "pedagog" who, from an examination of the specific contradictions within a given "working site," is capable of drawing general political implications that can be utilized as arguments for the politicization of the individuals involved.

The new militant distinguishes himself from the professional revolutionary inasmuch as the plausibility of his reasoning depends on his being "within the system," *i.e.,* from his holding a specific role (student, teacher, professional, etc.), and from his being a "rooted revolutionary intelligence." The abstract projection of the role of the revolutionary (which produces a new division of political work) must indeed be avoided. With the extension of the movement, the number of people dedicating themselves primarily to political activity will of course increase; what is important is that the mass of activists consists of persons holding roles within the social organizations and institutions, both for methodological reasons, and because it is important to have political access to the relevant social structures without being limited to attacking them from without.

Summing up the characteristics of the student movement, we may say that its unique characteristic lies precisely in its being a movement: a public and mass phenomenon. To be a movement, a mass acting publicly, means to represent oneself politically as on the one hand rooted in the contradictions of the social structure, and on the other hand, capable of constituting a practical political alternative to the existent. The movement distinguishes itself from the left sect groups and the establishment parties in the way that it conceives of and makes politics. Thus it is *within* the system as far as it is carried on by one or two social groups and initiated by specific contradictions concerning the social situation of those groups. In other words, it is connected with the system through a "radical chain" which gives it an objective sense of necessity and of relevance despite either fluctuations or stagnation. The movement is *outside* the system, nevertheless, because it is an unforeseen element in the system's plans, and even more important, because it cannot be controlled by the simple traditional methods of police, the courts, isolation and co-optation—although the latter is still problematic.

Social Co-optation

Like every process of innovation, a movement is also a mechanism for modernizing the social system, at least in the long run. It helps to eliminate norms and institutions which have become inadequate for the most advanced exigencies of rationalization. The history of most Western workers' movements teaches us to be basically pessimistic about the possibility of escaping this assimilation.

However, there are some positive signs indicating that the contrary may hold true today. One is the movement's refusal to interest itself in any participation in administering the spoils of the system (which in Italy is manifested by the refusal to co-administer the university). Another such sign is the movement's rejection of "democratic" reforms which are basically equivalent to the triumph of a more technocratic reason over an archaic one. In practice, the movement's proposals for radical reform of particular institutions are mainly intended to develop the critical, non-specialized capacities of the individual professional, and to effectively reduce regimentation and repression. (This applies mainly to the university, the only institution which the movement has as yet radically attacked.) Yet another positive sign is the tendency to establish wherever possible situations of "parallel power." Here the politically significant effects are, first, the introduction of conflict and dissent into institutions which are otherwise coercively integrated; second, the development of spheres that escape institutional control within the institutions themselves; and third, the creation, at least in the bud, of alternative structures to the existing ones.

In spite of these promising tendencies the revolutionary potential of the movement is not at all self-evident. Nor is it guaranteed by anti-authoritarian and "incorruptible" actions alone.

In the present conditions of capitalist society, a radical protest movement needs more, not less, reflection and theory. It is necessary for the movement to be able to dominate, both theoretically and practically, the dialectic between repression and integration which is the intrinsic logic of the system. This will be possible only if while the movement applies itself to the principle of anti-institutional struggle, it is able to distinguish its own policy from that of the official institutions *and* from the left sect groups.

Very synthetically, we may say that politics in the official sense (both for the government and the opposition) is both participation in the division of spoils (socio-economic values such as wealth, power, influence, privileges, etc.) and self-preservation. The first corresponds to the rules of the game within a "pluralistic society." According to those rules, politics is reduced to compromises on the distribution of national income as well as of other goods and values. This is true on the level of the visible political system and on the level of the sub-government. The second aspect corresponds to the logic of bureaucratic organisms which leads to defending their own field of influence and their own slice of the political and social market.

The necessity for the movement to distinguish itself from the politics of the left sect groups may be somewhat less obvious, inasmuch as many who participate in the movement have been formed in these sects. The irrelevance of the sects for anti-institutional struggle, however, is clear. For them political activity basically means political *training*—sometimes terroristic, almost always clandestine. The more negative aspects of their activity are the relentlessness with which they must defend their individuality against competing strategic and theoretic concepts, and the restriction of "creative" work to a few people whose positions remain unaccountable to criticism from outside the sect. Characteristically, these grouplets are prone to mystify the working class; and while they justify any work directed toward the working class as implicitly revolutionary, their own activity is generally restricted to the formation of cadres and the diffusion of traditionally "revolutionary" ideas.

Neither the organizational style of a minority sect, nor an exclusive fixation on the working class is suitable for the student movement which has other quantitative and qualitative dimensions, and which moves simultaneously through different social strata and institutional fields. The movement's comprehension of itself must be broader: it culminates in the redefinition of politics. While the politics of the official institutions is reabsorbed by the system, and thus transformed into a stabilizing or modernizing element, the politics of the sect groups (thanks to their objective characteristics, not to incapacity or error) remains completely outside the system, unable to influence political history. In each case politics remains *specialized*—both in the sense that the political role of the individual has little to do with his social role, and in the sense that politics is assumed to belong to the competence of certain qualified people.

In its entirety the social system itself constantly strives to define what is to be considered political, by guaranteeing the political neutrality or irrelevance of questions which in reality are substantially political. This depoliticization of reality not only points to the political apathy of the citizens, but it also refers to something important to the system: the image of the normal society. There is nothing natural, and therefore nothing non-political, in phenomena such as mental illness, criminality, unemployment, national and international migrations, the persistency of underdevelopment, and in the historical problems of the Italian social system. Yet almost without exception these questions are being handled by administrative bodies without even being discussed by those directly concerned, *i.e.,* all the citizens.

One might say that subjective political apathy is a consequence of the depoliticization of reality. The first priority of radical action then is to reconquer for politics all those aspects of the social system which the system makes appear as non-contradictory or non-political. This repoliticization must take place on three levels: in the private sphere (family, consumption), in the professional roles, or working hours, and in the awareness of the pervasiveness of social repression. It is not a matter of counterposing to society a more or less concrete utopia, but of realizing the specific forms of repression in a given society, even if they manifest themselves only as individual idiosyncrasies. They must then be turned into motivations for individuals and groups to act in a revolutionary sense and into themes for a political struggle.

The necessity of redefining politics derives in part from the realization that without some emancipating dynamic within the movement, which includes a political resocialization of individuals, it will not be possible to adequately fight the system. Further, it derives from an historical analysis of the workers' movement and its failures. The new definition must acknowledge the fact that politicization in advanced capitalism has to include what are traditionally non-political fields, and that it must be of deep consequence to the individuals involved. Finally, without a more global concept of politics it will not be possible to reconquer for revolutionary praxis a series of protest experiences which are in fact taking place at all different points of the social structure, but which are generally left to appear non-political, as the "moral witness" of a few isolated individuals, or as sectional reformism.

Anti-Institutional Struggle and
Cultural Revolution

The strategy of the movement is the anti-institutional struggle; its political working method and its organizational model are precisely those of a cultural revolution. In general terms, the cultural revolution is the provoking of a crisis by practical criticism of the institutional processes on an individual, collective and structural level. It is also the struggle against the social institutions insofar as they are examples of control and repression by a no longer legitimized power structure. Finally, it is the struggle for the liberation of the individual and collective consciousness from the image of the "normal" society. It demands tying the emancipation of consciousness to the liberation of the institutions, in order to avoid having institutional reforms which are passed "over the heads" of the individuals. Thus the idea of politicization changes: it is no longer the adhesion to and identification with canned ideology and with the organization that diffuses it. Nor is it the irrational gesture of immediate revolution. Both of these examples are basically indifferent to the relationship between the social and political role of the individual and between his political action and his capacity for critical self-reflection.

Within the conditions of the advanced capitalist countries, the cultural revolution is the means by which the movement can repoliticize the social universe. To be a cultural revolution it must be put forth by a movement, that is, by a publicly organized mass during periods of discussion and elaboration and periods of practical intervention. As a method it consists of the collective reflection of a group on its position within the social structure, and on the conditions of its own structure and of the total meaning of the functions it holds. As a way of organizing it is a coalition, built around a largely homogeneous political line, while reflecting a variety of classes, strata of society, etc.

The unity of the movement is not guaranteed by its class nature in the traditional sense. Rather it derives from its strategy, *i.e.,* from the idea of anti-institutional struggle. It is a strategy which transforms the publics of classical bourgeois society into *critical publics,* publics which have joined the full exercise of traditional political rights with certain forms of extra-parliamentary action necessary to combat the misinformation, practical disorientation and ideological blindness of consensus politics. As a strategy it originates with a refusal to accept the rules of the game and with a conscious violation of those rules in politically meaningful situations for precise ends. It leads to the paralysis of the institutions (by occupations, strikes, other forms of non-collaboration) to the creation of embryonic alternative structures, and to the formation of "oppositions" within the institutions which attenuate the conflict between the logic of the institutions and the logic of the people's needs.

The meaning of the anti-institutional struggle lies in the fact that these institutions are the columns of society, that they are instances of repression and control, and that within a more advanced society they are all functionally interconnected. The institutions are attacked from without and/or within depending on whether it is possible to win the interest of at least part of their subjects for a revolutionary praxis. The fact that the initiative is to be taken by a group working inside the institutions, rather than by a group working from without, is of great relevance. This does not mean waiting for some spontaneous occurrence, but rather it involves an awareness of the value that lies in the initiatives being taken by those most interested in reconstituting their own autonomy.

The movement thus reproduces itself by a continuous branching out. Obviously, the more areas and institutions that are involved, the more the movement becomes differentiated. The unifying factor is given by the political line and by the methods used for politicization, as well as by the organizational model. The "long march through the institutions" of which Dutschke speaks is a fine metaphor for this process of broadening which corresponds to an attack from within on the capitalist social system.

The idea of the anti-institutional struggle as a strategy for the movement rests on the notion that the revolution does not happen right away, that it is a long historical process. In other words, the anti-institutional struggle takes into account the fact that in complex societies the revolution must not be conceived as a unique historical act, but rather as a series of more and more serious *political crises*. Previously the revolution was connected with the necessary, inevitable disposition to economic crisis of the capitalist system. Today it is the political crises (which are obviously connected with structural contradictions) that seem to be the most probable form of a revolutionary overthrow. Even if the economic crises do not add up to a crash, the fact remains that capitalism is not capable of eliminating its own contradictions. Thus, renouncing the idea of an economic crash as *the* revolutionary opportunity does not imply either renouncing revolution as a means of qualitatively modifying the system, or postponing preparation for the revolution—in terms of mass politicization and organization—to some remote horizon when the system will be completely incapable of maintaining itself. The contradictions of the system exist today and provoke crisis after crisis, even if each of them is not decisive or the "real" occasion for revolution. They become revolutionary events as soon as protest struggles have been initiated on many levels of the social structure, struggles which may be relatively independent from the oscillations of the economic system. These struggles may sharpen the political consequences of these crises by diminishing the consensus to the system and by broadening the gap between citizen-subjects and the institutions and their values.

While the economic crises are connected with the objective laws of capitalist development, the political crises may be systematically induced by activating processes of politicization within subordinated social groups, even if they are relatively privileged. These processes should start with the immediate discomfort these groups suffer daily. Just as this strategy does not rely on the possibility of a crash or crisis to be carried out, it also can be started without the immediate involvement of the working class. Of course, the abandoning of the notion "crash and revolution," the legitimacy and relative autonomy of action within specific superstructural spheres, the renunciation of the immediate involvement of the working class—all are partly rationalizations *a posteriori,* subsequent to the events of the last few years. But they are also the political lessons that should be drawn from those events.

Expansion and Structure of the Movement

Once the movement has eliminated reformism and consciously established revolutionary goals, the central problem becomes that of the criteria for its own expansion and of the characteristics of the organizational structure it should assume. The movement has to determine which institutional spheres it wants to attack, and therefore must define some general criteria of priority. Here the relevant factors are: the strategic importance of the institutions or social group; the political resistance that could be brought to bear; the characteristics of the movement itself; finally, the opportunity that could arise outside the framework of priorities that have been established on the grounds of the first three factors.

During the "long march through the institutions" one does in fact proceed by working in those institutions that can be attacked from the point of view of their inherent nature, the methods that can be utilized for politicization of individuals, the organizational patterns, etc. This suggests the *school* as the first area for protest action. This should be followed up by attacks on the institutions of *control and repression* (mass communication, mass media, social welfare, the judiciary, etc.), on those which produce *culture,* on *professionals* and *technicians* whose fields are relevant to the development of society (engineers, doctors, etc.); and finally on *public opinion* (which refers here not to the institutions which manipulate it, but to the manipulated individuals, *i.e.,* to the general public). According to the specific case, and therefore to the nature of the objective, one will aim at paralyzing the institution itself, at mobilizing and organizing groups, at the development of alternative institutions, or simply at demonstrations aimed at breaking down the false consciousness of particular groups or of the public in general. It is not a matter of alternative goals but a matter of emphasis. Each anti-institutional praxis aims, of course, at broadening the social base of the movement, or at politicizing and organizing groups that are as yet non-political and apathetic.

As it grows, the movement sharpens the latent contradictions and induces the system to reveal its most violent and repressive aspects. It therefore becomes inevitable for the movement to soon find itself face-to-face with those institutions it would rather have avoided; to be forced to confront social powers of which it may have not yet developed an analysis or which it does not have the strength to fight. In general, it will be impossible to avoid this clash. The movement, however, if it is to avoid playing the game according to the system's rules, has to be aware of the first two criteria of its strategy. This will be the only way that the movement can avoid falling into the trap of consuming itself against an obstacle which is as yet too great. Clearly, this is especially true of the clash with the police and the courts. These battles can be occasions for the movement to grow, both in terms of awareness and in the development of solidarity among oppressed groups. This, however, should not produce the illusion that the movement can establish itself through such clashes. The NLF in Vietnam and the Black Power movement in the United States should teach the movement how to develop strategies and tactics which are more subtle —less exposed to the direct repression of the system. Concluding, it is important not to lose "opportunities" whenever they are favorable to the movement, but it is equally important that these opportunities not dictate strategy.

The search for a more organic connection between the student movement and other social groups leads to the problem of the possible politicization of the modern intelligentsia. An important aspect of the student movement is the idea of politicization through reflection on the role the individual plays in a particular institution: in this case roles associated with the production, reproduction and utilization of technical and scientific knowledge. Such roles are characterized essentially by: (a) the identification of the individual with the role; (b) the availability of technical and social power.

Recognizing science and technology as elements of the social praxis creates problems for those individuals holding cognitive roles—problems of identification with the content of the performance of their roles and even more of identification with the social rules and the power structure. It puts the professional ideology in a crisis. The movement can appeal to this crisis of identity by providing a political interpretation of the role, by freeing it from its institutional definition, and finally, by turning it against the system itself. The power delegated from above would then no longer be turned against the base, against employees, customers, pupils, etc., but against the top of the hierarchy. This would be a typical anti-institutional praxis, beginning with an exposure of professional ideology through inner-organizational disruption, proceeding to paralysis of social function and to the embryonic development of alternative models for intellectual and technical work.

From what has been said above it should be clear that a "new working class" does not need to be theorized into existence to receive the charisma of historical subject as the classical proletariat did before it. The problem rather is to distinguish within the groups holding cognitive roles those which may be involved in the struggle, *i.e.,* those for whom the legitimacy of the system is uncertain and precarious. The decisive element is the amount of identification with the values and the social rules of the profession: he who identifies profoundly will obviously not be interested in struggling. Even in these cases the relevance of false consciousness must not be underestimated. It can be broken down in the course of struggle. The other element to evaluate therefore is the distribution of social compensation: money, power, influence, etc. Such compensation is asymmetrical within the system even for basically similar roles. Whenever the relative privileges over other social groups does not balance inferior conditions, impoverishment and cultural isolation, politicizing those performing the role should be possible. It entails decreasing their identification with "superiors," and increasing identification with the recipients of their different services.

What has been said up until now holds true for the cognitive role in general, and therefore goes beyond the traditional liberal professions. It involves the numerous specialized cultural, scientific, and technical roles that are characteristic of a capitalist society. Although it is difficult to draw a precise border line, there is certainly a limit beyond which this method of politicization does not seem to be applicable. The series of roles below that border include the mainly executional or manual roles. In these roles, we do not find identification with the content of the performance or the availability of technical power. Correspondingly, there is also no professional ideology and thus no false consciousness of one's own social role.

The difference can be exemplified by a border case. The highly skilled workers insofar as they have a "craft," tend to differentiate themselves from the common workers. When the rationalization of production (*e.g.,* with the introduction of computers) sharpens the contradictions of their role, they are faced with a dilemma: either to become technicians, thus holding a cognitive if subordinate role, or to become workers, thus abandoning any "cultural" identification with one's own role. It is not ruled out that this dilemma may individually give rise to an identity crisis.

In those cases where the job is primarily manual labor, and where it cannot be mediated through a craft, the relationship between the individual and the role is externalized: he considers it only as a means of reproducing his own life, without identifying it with any inherent aspirations or expectations. This is all the more true the more the compartmentalization of tasks is advanced. Then the politicization of the people holding such jobs is not likely to result from criticism of a role from within. Rather it is much more likely to result from political action which underscores the cultural impoverishment which that sort of work entails in the work place and in social life. In order to escape the ghetto of isolation and impotence in which the system holds him, it is particularly important for the worker to understand the organization of exploitation in which he is kept in civil society, that is to say his class condition. This political work would entail cultural revolution, too, so as to contend with the dominant praxis of the institutional representatives of the working class, such as trade union or party, which always tend to define the social contradictions in trade-unionist and reformist terms. The big themes of any revolutionary policy must therefore involve the repoliticization of the working class, by emphasizing the contradiction between productive forces and the relations of production, the problem of the national and international division of labor, and the relation between the development of social consciousness and the increase of productive forces. This is the way in which the working class could become the bearer of a new politics—this is its contribution to the redefinition of politics.

As the movement broadens in the direction of the working class and of other social groups, it loses its student character and becomes clearly political. The anchorage in the schools will then be of secondary importance, that is, it will be equivalent to any other anchorage in institutions and systems of roles. In the initial phase (in which we still find ourselves) the connection with the schools is, however, very important. Actually, there has been no movement, but a series of contemporary movements: each university has produced a movement with particular characteristics. Thus, already implicit in the structure of the movement is the autonomy of its various sections. With the extension of the struggle, it is no longer a natural quality, but rather the fruit of a political conception, an organizing principle. A movement is such in that it develops as a coalition of relatively autonomous and heterogeneous groups, not as a monolithic structure. This certainly complicates the problem of communication, and even more, the problems of coordination within the movement. Therefore, the development of an adequate political consciousness by members of the movement, reducing sectarianism as much as possible, becomes extremely pressing. It becomes all the more necessary to have a clear consensus on the strategic line on which all must converge. Therefore one has to invent forms of collaboration between different groups that will lead to the growth of relatively political perspectives. Examples of this might include the exchange of activists (as has already been done in Italy), or the establishment of action and discussion centers as forums of the new opposition and as meeting points for all the elements of the coalition (as has mainly been done in Germany).

The relative autonomy of the different parts of the movement must, however, not be considered as an element typical of the initial phase of a still immature protest movement, even if today this may at times be correct. It should instead be seen as characteristic of a new way to make politics. Very briefly we may say that within the political and institutional conditions of the advanced capitalist countries the system can be overthrown only by a great mass movement, and not by a classical revolutionary (minority) party. The reasons for this are manifold, but can be summed up by the advanced institutionalization of the conflicts and by the, at least formal, integration of all citizens into the political system. In all societies in which the state, governmental, and political apparatus are no longer on the outside of civil society, the system and its equilibrium are defended by an institutional barrier which cannot be surmounted by a competing minority organization. Such an organization indeed remains fundamentally outside and indifferent to the extremely complex mechanisms by which the ruling class ensures consensus. What is required instead is an anti-institutional praxis and a cultural revolution that destroys the consensus, not for a small vanguard, but for the masses.

On that level, revolutionary action can be produced only by a mass movement that is not a class movement in the strict sense, but rather socially heterogeneous. The movement should simultaneously upset different institutional spheres, starting perhaps with those which the system relied on most because they were considered non-political. However, when we say that it is possible to overthrow the system and to take power only through a mass movement, and not through a classical revolutionary party, we do not mean to say that the second alternative is practically impossible. Rather, it could not solve any of the problems which justify a revolution in advanced capitalist countries. It would in fact give no guarantee of reducing the additional repression, of substantially modifying the power structure, or of increasing the general social consciousness. These are all goals that only an anti-institutional praxis and a cultural revolution can help to reach. While in underdeveloped countries the pilot role of a centralized party may still be transitionally necessary, in the advanced countries the conditions entrust such a role to a vast and heterogeneous movement which fore-shadows in itself an alternative political society.

No movement will be able for long to renounce political leadership. But this problem must be distinguished from that of the vanguard party. Once the movement has been accepted as the structure for revolutionary praxis, its political direction will have to be constantly justified, in the course of the struggle, before its various components. It is no longer possible to think of a bureaucratic-authoritarian solution to the problems of strategy and leadership; the problems must be determined by the conditions of the political struggle. If in the course of such actions the movement should make use of historically surpassed formulae, the entire innovating nature of its policies would be compromised.

Struggle and revolution are forms of praxis that require more, not less, historical reflection and political awareness. A revolutionary movement is the practical criticism of the existent. Today more than ever it is necessary that this criticism be referred also to the movement itself; today less than ever can the movement afford to shorten the path that connects theory with praxis.

Tom Nairn

Tom Nairn is a member of the editorial committee of *New Left Review*. He lectured on the history of art at Hornsey College in England until his expulsion in 1968. He is the author of numerous articles on New Left politics and on the work of Marshall McLuhan, and is also the coauthor, with Angelo Quattrocchi, of *The Beginning of the End* (1968), a historical and analytical account of the May, 1968, events in France.

The following essay is the last chapter of that book. The whole second section of the book was written by Nairn.

Nairn argues that the "new conflict" in the advanced capitalist societies is rooted in the creation of a "mental surplus." The new conflict is also the "ultimate" conflict of the bourgeois social order, because it is "last in time" and "can never be resolved inside the system." His argument is as follows: The ultimate phase of capitalist productivity is "the mass production of consciousness as a commodity" through education and "the exploding communication and information systems." However, consciousness opposes its conversion into a commodity by "its very dialectical and social character." As such, the formation of a "mental surplus" becomes the "revolutionary agent" which makes possible the transition from civilization to communism, as the formation and use of a "material surplus" made possible the transition from primitive society to civilization. Ironically, the very agent which capitalism has produced to accelerate its material growth—namely, the mass production of consciousness—is now undermining the capitalist system of accumulation. The "mental surplus" is inherently social and thus cannot be appropriated (as the material surplus was) by the ruling class for the purpose of self-aggrandizement. It is therefore "a prefiguration of the future in its *form*," the adumbration of a classless society, the "transcendence of the split between manual and mental labor."

Reprinted by permission of Tom Nairn.

NEW CONTRADICTIONS

All these other questions return one insistently to the central one: what had changed in the heart of social reality, to make what was inconceivable yesterday into a matter of fact? The unpredictability of the phenomenon, the dramatic opening of what Sartre called the "horizons of the possible" in May, the profound novelties thrown up almost casually by the movement on every hand—everything suggests that if society has secretly transformed itself to make such originality possible, then this transformation must be of the utmost importance, must represent a turning-point second to none in the development of human history.

The proximate, visible cause of the upheaval lay in the student revolt, in the universities. That is, in society's "higher nervous system," in a rebellion of the higher "nerve-centers." Pursuing the metaphor then, one must ask what the nature of this system is, why it is capable of generating rebellion on such a scale. We say already that it can scarcely be coincidence that the first "perfect" generation produced by capitalism is like this—but what is the machinery of the comedy? And—still more important—what is the new relationship between the "nervous system" and the whole social body, which allows the former to be the initiator of revolution?

These "nerve-centers" of western society, the institutions of higher education and particularly the universities, have obviously changed very greatly in the last half-century, in a way that constantly crops up in every diagnosis of student revolt. They are enormously larger, and have a different and larger significance for society. They are now the products of an "academic revolution" which has transformed them from their old function, the formation of a narrow and privileged elite of social administrators, to a new one. Today, they train a far larger number of intellectual specialists of all sorts, more widely diffused throughout the social body. The old university produced what Gramsci called "traditional intellectuals" (writers, men of letters, teachers, clergy, professional men and social administrators who belonged to the same culture-world). The new university, as well as a much greater number of these, and their modern successors (e.g., journalists, media-men), also produces a great number of what he called "organic intellectuals" more closely and necessarily related to the economic structure (e.g., technicians, managers, ad-men, and so on).

This "academic revolution" is in turn the product of something else. That is, of the immense growth in the productive forces of western society during the same period. The creation of "intellectuals" on a scale so much greater than in the past is the sign that this growth is not simply a growth in quantity, but contains a qualitative change within itself. The crisis among these "intellectuals," then, differs in essential nature from previous intellectual disturbances to the extent to which it embodies this change. It is the sign that the change is not a linear progress, but a dialectical development containing contradictions of its own, not reducible to the older social categories, and only now beginning to display their real character. As a commentator on the American academic revolution (in many ways more advanced than the European) puts it:

> It may be true that the more advanced social systems of our own era may well be caught up in unprecedented dialectical conflicts of their own that threaten their internal stability. Societies consist not of classes and institutions only, but of the human beings who give them substance; if institutions systematically frustrate the needs and aspirations of considerable numbers of their ablest and most valuable functionaries, then a quasi-Marxian analysis may still be appropriate. To my knowledge no one has disproved such a possibility in the circumstances that concern us here.*

The "unprecedented dialectical conflict" exposed in May in the form of revolution can only be understood in terms of this underlying change of equilibrium. That is, in terms of a mutation which gives us the proper criterion of what constitutes the maturity of capitalist-industrial society. Revolution could not come before maturity, and maturity is the phase in which the forces of material production—the mainspring of all historical change so far—have brought about a decisive development in the *forces of mental production*.

The development of these forces assumes two closely-related

* H. D. Aiken, "The Revolting Academy," in the *New York Review*, 11th July, 1968.

forms, corresponding to the "traditional" and "organic" categories mentioned above. One is associated with the major growth in the old elite of ideologists and administrators deriving from the swelling complexity of contemporary society and its prodigious and ever-increasing apparatus of *communication:* the mass media, popular culture, and the transformation of the conscious environment these have brought about. The other is rooted more directly in the development of industrial and administrative technology, and consists of the specialized intellectual skills the process requires. Its great symbol is the computer, the highest form of technical intelligence, and its tendency is to transform an ever-larger sector of the economy—along with the cities which house economic organization, and the State which services it—into the processing of *information* (the "information revolution").

Thus, an ever-greater part of the modern economy and of social life generally is given over to the production of *consciousness.* But this entire development sprang necessarily from within the forces of material production, from the industrial production and the commercial distribution of *things,* "commodities." It is the ultimate triumph of the latter in post-war American and European capitalism which has precipitated the former forward at such a rate. "Advanced" capitalism, or "consumer capitalism," the definitive victory of materialism in a universal worship of the commodity-fetish, is impossible without the mass media, advertising, and automation, without a parallel expansion of the social "brain" and the nerves of communication. Naturally, in western society such evolution is harnessed to commodity-production—the increasing powers of "mental production" are subordinated to the dominating powers of material production and circumscribed within its categories. But it does not follow that this subordination is the whole truth of the historical situation, as so many have assumed.

It has always been recognized that humanity will become "free" and adult to the extent to which it transcends the necessities of material production. That is, when it leaves behind the millennial effort of laboriously transforming the environment and can finally stand upright on this secure material basis and cultivate its own intrinsic, human potential. Such cultivation must evidently take the form of "culture," the enormous development of social consciousness, and consequent enrichment of everyone's individual experience.

According to Marx's conception of man's advance towards this condition, capitalism will necessarily be the ultimate stage of the development of the forces of material production. The prodigious magic of Capital will unfold, carrying men farther in a few years than in all the past millennia to the edge of freedom. Only when this edge is reached, when the colossal apparatus of commodity-production has unfolded "fully," will it permit liberation from its own alienation. It will then be transcended by a revolutionary process. There is a graphic account of this "mature" state in the *Grundrisse:*

> The great historic role of Capital is the creation of surplus labor, labor which is superfluous from the standpoint of mere use value, mere subsistence. This historical function is fulfilled when, on the one hand, needs have been developed to the point where such surplus labor . . . has itself become a general need which is expressed in the needs of individual people, and—on the other hand—when the strict discipline of Capital has schooled successive generations in industriousness, and this quality has become a common inheritance, and when (finally) the productive powers of labor, constantly spurred on by Capital in its limitless drive towards accumulation, have ripened to the point where the maintenance of social wealth requires no more than a very limited amount of labor-time, and where scientific processes regulate the reproduction and growth of this wealth towards ever greater abundance. In other words, where a reified, machine-like human labor has ceased altogether.*

However, "reification" (the form in which capitalism persists, even in maturity) will only vanish on the other side of the revolutionary transition. Later on, Marx points out that such a capitalist "affluent society" where automation plays an increasing part in production itself negates many conventional capitalist categories. It renders absurd the estimation of value in terms of old-fashioned individual "labor-time," since the power of labor is so many times magnified by automation, and what is really being harnessed is the *"collective* productive power" of society, its *intelligence* of nature and consequently ability to dominate it. The social nature of production be-

* *Grundrisse der Kritik der politischen Ökonomie* (Rohentwurf), *Berlin* 1953, p. 231; French translation, *Fondements de la Critique de l'Economie Politique* (Editions Anthropos, Paris 1967), Vol. I, p. 273. Author's translation.

comes more important, and more evident. Things begin to appear as they really are, through the fragmentation and mystification of the system—

> Nature does not build machines . . . these are the products of human industry, of natural materials turned into instruments of human will and activity. . . . They are *instruments of the human brain,* created by the hand of man, the materialized organs of his knowledge.*

The conflict between the social nature of production and the endless series of alienating splits which bourgeois society inflicts upon it (between the worker and his tools, between the worker and the product of his work, between one unit of production and another, etc., etc.) therefore comes to a head in capitalism's maturity. The "social" becomes embodied in the "brain," in the social intelligence, the knowledge that increasingly "regulates the reproduction and growth of wealth."

The last phase of Capital's progress, hence, does more than simply establish the "material conditions" for liberation (in the sense of relief from primary poverty, the development of productive forces to the stage where some kind of socialism is "materially possible"). It also *anticipates* the future state of society, beyond the revolution, in its *form*- in the *real* organization of production within the persisting (or even intensified) alienation of the system (its chronic "misorganization"). Evidently, there must be an essential contradiction operative here, peculiar to the later stages of the system. And it would be surprising indeed if it could be reduced to the terms of those older contradictions previously generated within capitalism (the contradictions of "immature," evolving bourgeois society, still preserved in the unfolded system).

It would be no less surprising if Marx had been able to foresee the nature of this contradiction fully. In fact, the new conflict— which is also the ultimate conflict of the bourgeois social order, in the double sense of being last in time, and such that it can never be resolved inside the system—is rooted in the great development of the forces of mental production, in a multitude of forms whose character and effect were only dimly visible until much more recently. One way

* *Grundrisse,* pp. 593–4; *Fondements,* Vol. 2, pp. 221–3.

of indicating the nature, and novelty, of the change is perhaps to say that the central contradictions of later capitalism are focused in what would traditionally have been called the social "superstructure" (because they involve social consciousness and ideology, and the quintessentially "superstructural" institution of the university), but they cannot really be opposed to the contradictions or problems of the socio-economic "structure" (i.e. the apparatus of material production, and the form it takes in existing society) because they evidently derive from it. The material forces of production in western capitalism would not sustain themselves or advance one half-centimeter farther without the continued operation and expansion of this "superstructure" —without the *real* activity of the "intellectuals," both organic and traditional, and the constantly growing importance of their function. Late capitalist society is infinitely more *united* than the conventional categories allow for, and this unity (because the system remains divisive at the same time) is itself an omnipresent contradiction.

Perhaps the sense of the contradiction may be clear if one recalls the past history of society's powers of mental production. These powers are in essence identical with the distinctively human or "social" structure. This social structure (which distinguishes human from all animal "societies") is a dialectical and inherently contradictory one between the individual and social group he belongs to materially. This relationship of individual and group is the extremely developed communicative one of *language*. Through this communication-network of various linguistic codes, the collective consciousness of the "social" group is created, and continuously reproduced within the individual skull, internalized through language. In one sense, therefore, the linguistic relationship characterizing "society" looks like a complicated form of subordination of the individual awareness to society, a form of social control.

But the inner contradiction of the relationship—which explains both the immense superiority of human society to any other gregarious form imaginable, and the instability that is inseparable from it—lies in the necessary development of individual potential which its working entails. For a communication-system to work as the armature of a group, individual communicative power must be developed, as individual consciousness potentially distinct from that expressed in the codes. To "understand" *is* to speak; in linguistic terms, to speak is to internalize the code as an individual reality: to "speak to oneself" or think. Hence, society in constantly re-creating itself within the individual also constantly *loses itself* in the individual. The "subordination" of the individual, mediated in this fashion, is also potentially at every instant the loss of society within the indivdual, the subordination of society to an individual consciousness (and therefore to more than one such consciousness, since the code is precisely a social phenomenon of diffusion). The "individual" awareness, in "personal" speech or thought, is nothing without the social communication-code; but the code or language is itself nothing but so many individual "expressions," so many acts of speech. This is the sense in which man is a "species-being," according to Marx's definition in the 1844 *Manuscripts:* "he" (the individual) *is* the network of socio-linguistic relationships around him, and it *is* him and the other individuals who embody it.

Human "history" is founded upon this dynamic of interaction, the living dialectic which haunts every moment of human consciousness. This, rather than the tool, is the lever which tears men out of nature (for material instruments can only be developed and transmitted in a context of language). But the history that is the development of this potential—the "powers of mental production" which are the essence of society—is also, necessarily, the negation of it, the repression and distortion of its true meaning.

In primitive society, first of all, it is trapped within the dense conservatism marking the group's struggle against the overwhelming pressure of the natural environment. Then in the history of "civilization" that follows, it is harnessed to the secular task of transforming this environment—to the slow development of the material forces of production. Because history is material, in this sense, consciousness is subordinated to its needs in the form of the classical division between "mental" and "manual" labor. The consciousness of the social body is canalized into a small governing elite that presides over the slavery of the majority, forced into the apparatus of material production. Because the latter is more important historically, the mental domination of the former takes the form of "ideology," a *false* consciousness of control and coercion unconsciously rooted in material production.

The successful "conquest of the environment," the development of material production to the point where scarcity is eliminated, obviously means the release of the social "essence"—of the intrinsic "idealism" of human existence from the half-human compulsions of matter. Western capitalism is now on the threshold of this condition; it is possible at least to foresee it. But hitherto, this has been seen as the final material state of civilization: the last plateau of material abundance (which must be transcended, still, out of material causes —because of the contradictions built into alienated material production). In fact, though (as we saw), this phase of history is also a prefiguration of the future in its *form*—because of the ripening development of the "social" inside it, in the shape of collective intelligence and consciousness.

The transition from primitive society to civilization was made possible by the slow creation and use of a *material surplus*—the amount over and above what was necessary for social survival. The transition from civilization to communism, in turn, is made possible by the creation of a "mental surplus"—that is, by the development of mental production to the point where it exceeds the demands of the material matrix. This, rather than the tensions inherent in the matrix of material production, becomes the directly "revolutionary" agent which will finally compel the transformation. Capitalism generated this revolutionary agent to serve itself, it produced education and the exploding communication and information systems in order to intensify its own material growth, as capital-accumulation. Now, however, these forces are turning into apprentice-sorcerers, undermining the whole reified structure of accumulation. The ultimate phase of capitalist productivity, in other words, is the mass-production of consciousness as a commodity. But consciousness resists the form of commodity-production by its very dialectical and social character.

This contradiction is clearly manifested in the two principal positions taken up by theorists who have considered the problem. One arm of it is represented, for instance, by T. W. Adorno, who sees the influence of "mass culture: as—

> Regimentation, the result of the progressive societalization of all human relations . . . (which) . . . imposes itself as relentlessly on the autonomous mind as heteronomous orders were formerly imposed on the mind which was bound. Not only does the mind mold itself for the sake of its marketability, and thus reproduce the socially prevalent categories. Rather, it grows to resemble ever more closely the *status quo* even where it subjectively refrains from making a commodity of itself. The net-

work of the whole is drawn ever tighter, modeled after the act of exchange. It leaves the individual consciousness less and less room for evasion, preforms it more and more thoroughly [hence] the regression of spirit and intellect. In accordance with the predominant social tendency, the integrity of the mind becomes a fiction.*

Hence, the system is being *entirely successful* in tying the development of culture down to the old, alienated basis. The mass consciousness generated by the new means of production is even more the slave of the "socially prevalent categories" than before—it is either crystallized directly within these categories, or else indirectly, as a "drug" or an escape-route to a "leisure" whose whole purpose is the recreation of labor energy.

On the other hand, there is the strikingly contrasted thesis associated with, for instance, Marshall McLuhan and his school. They see the growth of modern communications as in itself a revolutionary liberation of—and a qualitative change in—social consciousness. The new powers of mental production contained in our "electric technology" release us from the "mechanical patterns" of the past, so that—

The aspiration of our time for wholeness, empathy and depth of awareness is a natural adjunct of electric technology. The age of mechanical industry that preceded us found vehement assertion of private outlook the natural mode of expression. Every culture and every age has its favorite model of perception and knowledge that it is inclined to prescribe for everybody and everything. The mark of our time is its revulsion against imposed patterns. We are suddenly eager to have things and people declare their beings totally. . . .**

Far from imprisoning us still more completely and subtly, therefore, this culture is the implicit negation of the imprisoning categories. As a consequence of automation, claims McLuhan,

Wealth and work become information factors, and totally new structures are needed. . . . With electric technology, the new

* T. W. Adorno, *Prisms* (trans. S. W. Weber, 1967), p. 21. See also *L'Industrie culturelle,* by the same author, in No. 3 of the review *Communications* (Ecole Pratique des Hautes Etudes, Paris).
** H. M. McLuhan, *Understanding Media* (McGraw-Hill, 1964), p. 5.

kinds of instant interdependence and interprocess that take over production also enter the market and social organizations. For this reason markets and education designed to cope with the products of servile toil and mechanical production are no longer adequate. Our education long ago acquired the fragmentary and piece-meal character of mechanism. It is now under increasing pressure to acquire the depth and inter-relation that are indispensable in the all-at-once world of electric organization.*

He indicates elsewhere how the most marked expression of this pressure within the educational system is the revolutionary "teach-in" (which reached its apotheosis in the Sorbonne debates in May).**

The confusion and mythological nature of McLuhanism and its deeply reactionary background meaning ought not to obscure the imaginative sensibility of many of McLuhan's insights. On the other hand, even though Adorno and his school are working within the major European tradition of social analysis deriving from Hegel and Marx, they are often astonishingly insensible to the subject-matter. In fact, both propositions are right and wrong, because neither comes to terms with the central contradiction at work in the development of such forces.

This contradiction is the reproduction on a revolutionary, world scale of the root contradiction of human society which can emerge only now from the chrysalis of material production. While society lay within this chrysalis, "matter" dominated "mind" and society dominated the individual. The resolution of these conflicts is only possible though the creation of the "social individual," at the point where men begin to become capable of "making their own history" (capable of freedom). Then the other face of the basic sociological contradiction—the domination of society by its individual members—is released for the first time. This occurs through the development of the forces of mental production and the formation of a "mental surplus" whose social fate is the inverse of the material surplus hitherto decisive. Whereas the material surplus was (necessarily) appropriated by a minority, the ruling class, to free itself from drudgery and develop civilization, the mental surplus is inherently social—the most social of phenomena—and cannot be "appropriated" in this way. It arises

* *Understanding Media,* p. 357.
** H. M. McLuhan, *The Medium Is the Message* (McGraw-Hill, 1967), pp. 100–101.

as the potential unity of society, the prefiguration of the classless social body, the transcendence of the split between manual and mental labor (which could only occur under the emergent dominance of the latter). However, because this occurs within the historical alienation associated with the material surplus, it must struggle to exist—in the last major contradiction of history; it must assume a political form, a revolutionary form, and destroy its own source.

The clearest intellectual sign of the emergence of the contradiction —before May—was surely the growing contemporary obsession with the whole subject matter of communication and language. While in traditional social theory this hardly counted as a problem, and there was no distinct area of study focused on it, it has now very quickly come to the forefront of sociological concern. This concern extends from the spectacular manifestation of McLuhanism, on the one hand (a general theory of history as determined by modes of communication), and the Situationist theme of "la societé du spectacle" (modern society seen as already mainly devoted to the production of "scenes," appearances rather than things), to the abstruse theories of French structuralism, on the other. A large sector of American sociological theory is also oriented in this direction. Marxism, naturally, has remained aloof from the intellectual harbingers of the real revolution, in comfortable contemplation of the past (identifying the mythical aspects of such novelties—signs of their deep social significance—with sad deviations from the truths of historical materialism).

It is not possible here to consider in greater detail the functioning of the contradiction. But plainly, its operation is concentrated—and felt most urgently—in the expanding workshops of mental production. Although it is a general social contradiction certain ultimately to embrace the whole social body, it is natural that it should be focused in "higher education" and (initially) spread in shock-waves from this center, awakening every latent contradiction of society.

There have been attempts to give some formulation to the problem already. Thus, the Professor of Sociology at Nanterre University asked (two months before the May uprising):

> Today, is it possible to avoid any longer posing this question: are these student movements, from Berlin to Nanterre, from Prague to Trento, the avant-garde signs of a new contestation of society in both theory and practice, revealing new forms of domination and new social conflicts? If it is true that knowledge and tech-

nological progress are the motors of the new society, as capital
accumulation was of the old, then does not the university now
occupy the same place in society as the great capitalist business
once did, and does not the student movement have the same significance as the workers' movements of the previous epoch? *

This parallelism between student movements and working-class
movements has also been developed more thoroughly by two American
writers in a study called "Youth as a Class." They argue that—

. . . the new proletariat is (1) the masses of the backward countries; and (2) the young of the United States.

This new "internal proletariat" has grown up because—

The American economy is increasingly dominated by two industries that are large, public, and rapidly growing—defense and
education [hence] the essential exploited class for the perpetuation of the existing economic system is now the young. The
youth occupy the critical workplaces; they man the war-machine
and the idea-factories.**

Previously, "youth" was the biological period for the formation of
the bourgeois-individualistic personality. The name of the prolonged
repressive limbo which did the molding was "adolescence." But the
whole evolution of capitalism has made this process otiose: society
no longer requires entrepreneurial personalities, however it may cling
to the folklore of the heroic age of the bourgeoisie. The increasingly
social character of production demands, instead, "organization men."
At this point the gap between generations endemic to bourgeois society becomes catastrophic, for the new generation is much more
instinctively social than its predecessors (following the erosion of the
traditional repressive mechanisms), and this sociality encounters both
the fossils of the bourgeois *ancien régime* (parents and teachers) and
the new forms of alienation (harsher, rhythms of work in higher education, a machine-like preparation for a circumscribed role in a big

* A. Touraine, "Naissance d'un Mouvement Etudiant," in *Le Monde* (7th
13th March, 1968).
** J. and M. Rowntree, in the *International Socialist Journal,* No. 25 (February, 1968).

organization, etc.). Caught between two forms of authoritarianism, this "cool" (social) generation is also the focus of the most sensible and dramatic developments of the forces of mental production:

> Youth culture can be seen as becoming increasingly collective and activist in the last decade . . . forms of collective activity are more frequent and more comprehensive, and, most importantly, modes of communication have become much more intensive and sophisticated. . . . Viewed in one way, "youth culture" is an invention of merchandisers and a vehicle of false consciousness. However, it can *also* be the crucial support for alienated youth, making it possible to translate disaffection into open revolt.*

These are the social conditions under which "youth" can for the first time assume an other than biological meaning, a positive social meaning as the bearer of those pressures in the social body which prefigure a new society instead of the reproduction of the old one. When de Gaulle spoke with condescension of "the new blood of France," to be "given a voice" after May, he revealed only his own ignorance of a generation which spewed out *that* "France" along with the priests, professors, and policemen, and adopted "Nous sommes tous des Juifs-Allemands" ["We are all German Jews"—Ed.] as its motto, doing more for the cause of internationalism and European unity in one day of May than the governments and labor bureaucracies of western Europe had achieved in twenty years.

The analogy suggested by Touraine and the Rowntrees between the factory yesterday and the university today is interesting, as an approach to the problem. However, it is really only a metaphor, which may tend to hide the essential novelties in the present situation. The contradictions at work in it are qualitatively different from the old ones, and it is ultimately much more important to see why the university is *not* what the factory once was, why students are *not* a later generation of alienated workers (but precisely the antithesis of this, revolutionary because they negate alienation), and why youth is *not* another "class" fitting into a conventional analysis of the social structure.

* J. and M. Rowntree, *op. cit.*

Where such radical novelties have already come into existence, and a new world has uttered its first cries, theory has to be very audacious merely to catch up with practice.

> July 1968, Hornsey
> College of Art, London,
>   in the sixth week
> of the student occupation,
> in a classroom where I was
> once paid to explain this
> century to those too young
> to understand it.

Situationist International

The following is the final chapter of *Ten Days That Shook the University,* the "infamous pamphlet" written in 1966 by situationist students at the University of Strasbourg. The *Situationist International,* which published the pamphlet, introduced it with these words:

In November 1966, Strasbourg University was the scene of a preliminary skirmish between modern capitalism and the new revolutionary forces which it is beginning to engender. For the first time, a few students abandoned pseudo-revolt and found their way to a coherent radical activity of a kind which has everywhere been repressed by reformism. This small group got itself elected, amidst the apathy of Strasbourg's 16,000 students, to the committee of the left-wing students' union. Once in this position of power, they began to put union funds to good use. They founded a Society for the Rehabilitation of Karl Marx and Ravachol. They plastered the walls of the city with a Marxist comic-strip, 'The Return of the Durutti Column.' They proclaimed their intention to dissolve the union once and for all. Worst of all, they enlisted the aid of the notorious Situationist International and ran off ten thousand copies of a lengthy pamphlet which poured shit on student life and loves (and a few other things). When this was handed out at the official ceremony marking the beginning of the academic year, only de Gaulle was unaffected. The press—local, national and international—had a field-day. It took three weeks for the local Party of Order—from right-wing students to the official left, via Alsatian mill-owners—to eject these fanatics. The union was closed by a court order on the 14th of December.

The situationist students argue for the radical reconstruction of the revolutionary project, "starting with a clear grasp of the failure of those who first began it." They denounce Stalinism "in all its forms," as well as the co-optation of "present revolutionary action" by "the modernism of the system." The students contend that the separation of theory and practice was the chief cause of the failure of "the old revolutionary movement" and that the success of "a new revolutionary movement" will depend on whether or not organizations are fashioned which embody "a *total* critique of the world" and which facilitate the development of a revolutionary praxis in keeping with "the final criterion" of the "coherence" of "a new revolutionary movement" —namely, *"the international and absolute power of Workers' Councils."* Consequently, the students reject the Leninist theory of organization. Central to their defense of complete workers' autogestion or self-management is the students' denunciation of "the alienation produced by the commodity system," whose abolition, they maintain, is a necessary condition for "the free construction of social life." Toward this end the students argue for "the suppression of work and its replacement by a new type of free activity" and for the destruction of "the spectacle" of false needs engendered by the commodity system, in favor of "the infinite multiplication of real desires and their gratification."

TEN DAYS THAT SHOOK THE UNIVERSITY: To Create at Long Last a Situation Which Goes Beyond the Point of No Return

"To be avant-garde means to keep abreast of reality" (*Internationale Situationniste 8*). A radical critique of the modern world must have the totality as its object and objective. Its searchlight must reveal the world's real past, its present existence and the prospects for its transformation *as an indivisible whole*. If we are to reach the whole truth about the modern world—and *a fortiori* if we are to formulate the project of its total subversion—we must be able to expose its *hidden history;* in concrete terms this means subjecting the history of the international revolutionary movement, as set in motion over a century ago by the Western proletariat, to a demystified and critical scrutiny.

"This movement against the total organization of the old world came to a stop long ago" (*Internationale Situationniste 7*). *It failed.* Its last historical appearance was in the Spanish social revolution, crushed in the Barcelona "May Days" of 1937. Yet its so-called "victories" and "defeats," if judged in the light of their historical consequences, tend to confirm Liebknecht's remark, the day before his assassination, that "some defeats are really victories, while some victories are more shameful than any defeat." Thus the first great "failure" of workers' power, the Paris Commune, is in fact its first great *success,* whereby the primitive proletariat proclaimed its historical capacity to organize all aspects of social life *freely.* And the Bolshevik revolution, hailed as the proletariat's first great triumph, turns out in the last analysis to be its most disastrous defeat.

The installation of the Bolshevik order coincides with the crushing of the Spartacists by the German "Social-Democrats." The joint victory of Bolshevism and reformism constitutes a unity masked by an apparent incompatibility, for the Bolshevik order too, as it transpired, was to be a variation on the old theme. The effects of the Russian counter-revolution were, internally, the institution and development of a new mode of exploitation, bureaucratic state capitalism, and externally, the growth of the "Communist" International, whose spreading branches served the unique purpose of defending and reproducing the rotten trunk. Capitalism, under its bourgeois and bureaucratic guises, won a new lease on life—over the dead bodies of the sailors of Kronstadt, the Ukrainian peasants, and the workers of Berlin, Kiel, Turin, Shanghai, and Barcelona.

The third International, apparently created by the Bolsheviks to combat the degenerate reformism of its predecessor, and to unite the avant-garde of the proletariat in "revolutionary communist parties," was too closely linked to the interests of its founders ever to serve an authentic socialist revolution. Despite all its polemics, the third International was a chip off the old block. The Russian model was rapidly imposed on the Western workers' organizations, and the evolution of both was thenceforward one and the same thing. The totalitarian dictatorship of the bureaucratic class over the Russian proletariat found its echo in the subjection of the great mass of workers in other countries to castes of trade union and political functionaries, with their own private interests in repression. While the Stalinist monster haunted the working-class consciousness, old-fashioned capitalism was becoming bureaucratized and overdeveloped, resolving its famous internal contradictions and proudly claiming this victory to be decisive. Today, though the unity is obscured by apparent variations and oppositions, a *single social form* is coming to dominate the world—this modern world which it proposes to govern with the principles of a world long dead and gone. The tradition of the dead generations still weighs like a nightmare on the minds of the living.

Opposition to the world offered from within—and in its own terms —by supposedly revolutionary organizations, can only be spurious. Such opposition, depending on the worst mystifications and calling on more or less reified ideologies, helps consolidate the social order. Trade unions and political parties created by the working class as tools of its emancipation are now no more than the "checks and balances" of the system. Their leaders have made these organizations their private property; their stepping stone to a role within the ruling class. The party program or the trade union statute may contain vestiges of revolutionary phraseology, but their practice is everywhere reformist—and doubly so now that official capitalist ideology mouths the same reformist slogans. Where the unions have seized power—in countries more backward than Russia in 1917—the Stalinist model of counter-revolutionary totalitarianism has been faithfully repro-duced.[1] Elsewhere, they have become a static complement to the self-regulation of managerial capitalism.[2] The official organizations have become the best guarantee of repression—without this "opposi-tion" the humanist-democratic façade of the system would collapse and its essential violence would be laid bare.

In the struggle with the militant proletariat, these organizations are the unfailing defenders of the bureaucratic counter-revolution, and the docile creatures of its foreign policy. They are the bearers of the most blatant falsehood in a world of lies, working diligently for the perennial and universal dictatorship of the State and the Economy. As the situationists put it, "a universally dominant social system, tending toward totalitarian self-regulation, is apparently being re-sisted—but only apparently—by false forms of opposition which re-main trapped on the battlefield ordained by the system itself. Such illusory resistance can only serve to reinforce what it pretends to attack. Bureaucratic pseudo-socialism is only the most grandiose of these guises of the old world of hierarchy and alienated labor."

---

[1] These countries have been industrialized on classic lines: primitive accumu-lation at the expense of the peasantry, accelerated by bureaucratic terror.

[2] For 45 years the French "Communist" Party has not taken a single step towards the conquest of power. The same situation applies in all advanced nations which have not fallen under the heel of the so-called Red Army.

As for student unionism, it is nothing but the travesty of a travesty, the useless burlesque of a trade unionism itself long totally degenerate.

The principal platitude of all future revolutionary organization must be the theoretical and practical denunciation of Stalinism in all its forms. In France at least, where economic backwardness has slowed down the consciousness of crisis, the only possible road is over the ruins of Stalinism. It must become the *delenda est Carthago* of the last revolution of prehistory.

Revolution must break with its past, and derive all its poetry from the future. Little groups of "militants" who claim to represent the authentic Bolshevik heritage are voices from beyond the grave. These angels who come to avenge the "betrayal" of the October Revolution will always support the defense of the USSR—if only "in the last instance." The "underdeveloped" nations are their promised land. They can scarcely sustain their illusions outside this context, where their objective role is to buttress theoretical underdevelopment. They struggle for the dead body of "Trotsky," invent a thousand variations on the same ideological theme, and end up with the same brand of practical and theoretical impotence. Forty years of counter-revolution separate these groups from the Revolution; since this is not 1920 they can only be wrong (and they were already wrong in 1920).

. . . The Scylla and Charybdis of present revolutionary action are the museum of revolutionary prehistory and the modernism of the system itself.

As for the various anarchist groups, they possess nothing beyond a pathetic and ideological faith in this label. They justify every kind of self-contradiction in liberal terms: freedom of speech, of opinion, and other such bric-a-brac. Since they tolerate each other, they would tolerate anything.

The predominant social system, which flatters itself on its modernization and its permanence, must now be confronted with a worthy enemy: the equally modern negative forces which it produces. Let the dead bury their dead. The advance of history has a practical demystifying effect—it helps exorcise the ghosts which haunt the revolutionary consciousness. Thus the revolution of everyday life comes face to face with the enormity of its task. The revolutionary project must be reinvented, as much as the life it announces. If the project is still essentially the *abolition of class society,* it is because the material conditions upon which revolution was based are still with us.

But revolution must be conceived with a new coherence and a new radicalism, starting with a clear grasp of the failure of those who first began it. Otherwise its *fragmentary* realization will bring about only a new division of society.

The fight between the powers-that-be and the new proletariat can only be in terms of the totality. And for this reason the future revolutionary movement must be purged of any tendency to reproduce within itself the alienation produced by the commodity system;[3] it must be the *living* critique of that system and the negation of it, carrying all the elements essential for its transcendence. As Lukacs correctly showed, revolutionary organization is this necessary mediation between theory and practice, between man and history, between the mass of workers and the proletariat *constituted as a class* (Lukacs' mistake was to believe that the Bolsheviks fulfilled this role). If they are to be realized in practice "theoretical" tendencies or differences must be translated into organizational problems. It is by its present organization that a new revolutionary movement will stand or fall. The final criterion of its coherence will be the compatibility of its actual form with its essential project—*the international and absolute power of Workers' Councils* as foreshadowed by the proletarian revolutions of the last hundred years. There can be no compromise with the foundations of existing society—the system of commodity production, ideology in all its guises, the State, and the imposed division of labor from leisure.

The rock on which the old revolutionary movement foundered was the separation of theory and practice. Only at the supreme moments of struggle did the proletariat supersede this division and attain their truth. As a rule the principle seems to have been *hic Rhodus hic non salta*. Ideology, however "revolutionary," always serves the ruling class; false consciousness is the alarm signal revealing the presence of the enemy fifth column. The lie is the essential produce of the world of alienation, and the most effective killer of revolutions: once an organization which claims the *social truth* adopts the lie as a tactic, its revolutionary career is finished.

All the positive aspects of the Workers' Councils must be already there in an organization which aims at their realization. All relics of

---

[3] Whose defining characteristic is the dominance of work *qua* commodity. Cf. in English our pamphlet "The Decline and Fall of the Spectacular Commodity-Economy."

the Leninist theory of organization must be fought and destroyed. The spontaneous creation of Soviets by the Russian workers in 1905 was in itself a practical critique of that baneful theory,[4] yet the Bolsheviks continued to claim that working-class spontaneity could not go beyond "trade union consciousness" and would be unable to grasp the "totality." This was no less than a decapitation of the proletariat so that the Party could place itself "at the head" of the Revolution. If once you dispute the proletariat's capacity to emancipate itself, as Lenin did so ruthlessly, then you deny its capacity to organize all aspects of a post-revolutionary society. In such a context, the slogan "All Power to the Soviets" meant nothing more than the subjection of the Soviets to the Party, and the installation of the Party State in place of the temporary "State" of the armed masses.

"All Power to the Soviets" is *still* the slogan, but this time without the Bolshevik afterthoughts. The proletariat can only play the *game* of revolution if the stakes are the whole world, for the only possible form of workers' power—generalized and complete autogestion—can be shared with nobody. Workers' control is the abolition of all authority: it can abide no limitation, geographical or otherwise: any compromise amounts to surrender. "Workers' control must be the means and the end of the struggle: it is at once the goal of that struggle and its adequate form." [5]

A *total* critique of the world is the guarantee of the realism and reality of a revolutionary organization. To tolerate the existence of an oppressive social system in one place or another, simply because it is packaged and sold as revolutionary, is to condone universal oppression. To accept alienation as inevitable in any one domain of social life is to resign oneself to reification in all its forms. It is not enough to favor Workers' Councils in the abstract; in concrete terms they mean the abolition of commodities and therefore of the proletariat. Despite their superficial disparities, all existing societies are governed by the logic of commodities—and the commodity is the basis of their dreams of self-regulation. This famous fetishism is still the *essential* obstacle to a total emancipation, to the free construction of social life. In the world of commodities, external and invisible forces direct men's actions; autonomous action directed towards clearly perceived goals is impossible. The strength of economic laws lies in

[4] Compare the theoretical critique of Rosa Luxemburg.
[5] "Les Luttes de Classes en Algérie," in *Internationale Situationniste 10*.

their ability to take on the appearance of natural ones, but it is also their weakness, for their effectiveness thus depends *only* on "the lack of consciousness of those who help create them."

The market has one central principle—the loss of self in the aimless and unconscious creation of a world beyond the control of its creators. The revolutionary core of autogestion is the attack on this principle. Autogestion *is* conscious direction by all of their whole existence. It is not some vision of a workers' control *of the market,* which is merely to choose one's own alienation, to program one's own survival ("squaring the capitalist circle"). The task of the Workers' Councils will not be the autogestion of the world which exists, but its continual qualitative transformation. The commodity and its laws (that vast detour in the history of man's production of himself) will be superseded by a new social form.

With autogestion ends one of the fundamental splits in modern society—between a labor which becomes increasingly reified and a "leisure" consumed in passivity. The death of the commodity naturally means the suppression of *work* and its replacement by a new type of free activity. . . . But it is work itself which must be called in question. Far from being a "Utopia," its suppression is the first condition for a break with the market. The everyday division between "free time" and "working hours," those complementary sectors of alienated life, is an *expression* of the internal contradiction between the use-value and exchange-value of the commodity. It has become the strongest point of the commodity ideology, the one contradiction which intensifies with the rise of the consumer. To destroy it, no strategy short of the abolition of work will do. It is only beyond the contradiction of use-value and exchange-value that history begins, that men make their activity an object of their will and their consciousness, and see themselves in the world they have created. The democracy of Workers' Councils is the resolution of all previous contradictions. It makes "everything which exists apart from individuals impossible."

What is the revolutionary project? The conscious domination of history by the men who make it. Modern history, like all past history, is the product of social praxis, the unconscious result of human action. In the epoch of totalitarian control, capitalism has produced its own religion: *the spectacle.* In the spectacle, ideology becomes flesh of our flesh, is realized here on earth. The world itself walks upside down. And like the "critique of religion" in Marx's day, the critique of the spectacle is now the essential precondition of any critique.

The problem of revolution is once again a concrete issue. On one side the grandiose structures of technology and material production; on the other a dissatisfaction which can only grow more profound. The bourgeoisie and its Eastern heirs, the bureaucracy, cannot devise the means to *use* their own overdevelopment, which will be the basis of the *poetry* of the future, simply because they both depend on the *preservation of the old order*. At most they harness overdevelopment to invent new repressions. For they know only one trick, the accumulation of *Capital* and hence of *the proletariat*—a proletarian being a man with no power over the use of his life, and who knows it. The new proletariat inherits the riches of the bourgeois world and this gives it its historical chance. Its task is to transform and destroy these riches, to constitute them as part of a human project: the total appropriation of nature and of human nature by man.

A realized human nature can only mean the infinite multiplication of *real desires* and their gratification. These real desires are the underlife of present society, crammed by the spectacle into the darkest corners of the revolutionary unconscious, realized by the spectacle only in the dreamlike delirium of its own publicity. We must destroy the spectacle itself, the whole apparatus of commodity society, if we are to realize human *needs*. We must abolish those pseudo-needs and false desires which the system manufactures daily in order to preserve its power.

The liberation of modern history, and the free use of its hoarded acquisition, can come only from the forces it represses. In the nineteenth century the proletariat was already the inheritor of philosophy; now it inherits modern art and the first conscious critique of everyday life. With the self-destruction of the working class art and philosophy shall be realized. To transform the world and to change the structure of life are one and the same thing for the proletariat—they are the passwords to its destruction as a class, its dissolution of the present reign of necessity, and its accession to the realm of liberty. As its maximum program it has the radical critique and free reconstruction of all the values and patterns of behavior imposed by an alienated reality. The only poetry it can acknowledge is the creativity released in the making of history, the free invention of each moment and each event: Lautreamont's *poesie faite par tous**—the beginning of the revolutionary celebration. For proletarian revolt is a festival or it is nothing; in revolution the road to excess leads once and for all to the palace of wisdom. A palace which knows only one rationality: the *game*. The rules are simple: to live instead of devising a lingering death, and to indulge untrammeled desire.

* Poetry made by everyone—*Ed.*

Murray Bookchin

Murray Bookchin is an anarchist theoretician and activist, who has attempted to produce a new synthesis of libertarian Marxist, ecological and anarcho-communist views. He has been deeply involved in the problems of ecology since the early fifties and is the author (under the pen name of Lewis Herber) of two books on the subject: *Our Synthetic Environment* (1962) and *Crisis in Our Cities* (1965). A founder of *Anarchos* magazine, he recently completed *The Spanish Anarchists* and is currently at work on *The Ecology of Freedom,* both of which are scheduled for publication in the autumn of 1970.

The following essay originally appeared in *Anarchos,* May, 1969, and has been widely discussed in New Left circles.

Bookchin's essay is at once a fiery polemic against the Marxism-Leninism of the New Left sect groups and a passionate defense of anarcho-communism. He argues that Marxism is not applicable to advanced capitalism, because the analytical categories of Marxism were formulated in response to a situation of economic scarcity which no longer exists and at a stage of technological development which has long since been superseded. He argues further that the Marxist notion of the industrial proletariat as the agency of revolutionary change is purely illusory and that the Leninist notion of a vanguard party is incorrigibly authoritarian and therefore counter-revolutionary. Although the language and tone of the essay are markedly similar to those of the Situationist manifesto, there are important differences between Bookchin and the Situationists. He explains these (in a personal letter to the editor) as follows: "The Situationists have retained very traditional notions about the workers' movement, Pannekoek's 'council communism,' almost Stalinist forms of internal organization (they are completely monolithic and authoritarian in their internal organization), and are surprisingly academic."

LISTEN, MARXIST!

All the old crap of the thirties is coming back again: the shit about the "class line," the "role of the working class," the "trained cadres," the "vanguard party," and the proletarian dictatorship." It's all back again, and in a more vulgarized form than ever. Progressive Labor is not the only example; it is merely the worst. One smells the same shit in the chapter meetings, labor committees, the National Office of S.D.S., in the various Marxist and Socialist clubs on campuses, not to speak of the "Militant Labor Forum," the Independent Socialist Clubs, and Youth Against War and Fascism.

In the thirties, at least, it was understandable. The United States was paralyzed by a chronic economic crisis, the deepest and longest in its history. The only living forces that seemed to be battering at the walls of capitalism were the great organizing drives of the C.I.O., with their dramatic sitdown strikes, their radical militancy, and their bloody clashes with the police. The political atmosphere throughout the entire world was charged by the electricity of the Spanish Civil War, the last of the classical workers' revolutions, when every radical sect in the American Left could identify with its own militia column in Madrid and Barcelona. That was thirty years ago. It was a time when anyone who cried out "Make Love, Not War" would have been regarded as a freak; the cry, then, was "Make Jobs, Not War"—the cry of an age burdened by unavoidable scarcity, when the achievement of socialism entailed "sacrifices" and a long "transition period" to an economy of material abundance. To an eighteen-year-old kid in 1937 the very concept of cybernation would have seemed like the wildest science fiction, a fantasy comparable to visions of space travel. That eighteen-year-old kid has now reached fifty years of age today, and his roots are planted in an era so remote as to differ *qualitatively* from the realities of the present period in the United States. Even capitalism itself has changed since then, taking on increasingly statified forms that could be anticipated only dimly thirty years ago. And now we are being asked to go back to the "class line," the "strategies," the "cadres"

Reprinted by permission of *Anarchos,* P.O. Box 466, Peter Stuyvesant Station, New York, N.Y. 10009.

and organizational forms of that distant period in almost blatant disregard of the new issues and possibilities that have emerged.

When the hell are we finally going to create a movement that looks to the future instead of to the past? When will we begin to learn from what is being born instead of what is dying? Marx, to his lasting credit, tried to do that in his own day; he tried to evoke a futuristic spirit in the revolutionary movement of the 1840's and 1850's. "The tradition of all the dead generations weighs like a nightmare on the brain of the living," he wrote in *The Eighteenth Brumaire of Louis Bonaparte*. "And just when they seem to be engaged in revolutionizing themselves and things, in creating something entirely new, precisely in such epochs of revolutionary crisis they anxiously conjure up the spirits of the past to their service and borrow from them names, battle slogans and costumes in order to present the new scene of world history in this time-honored disguise and borrowed language. Thus Luther donned the mask of the Apostle Paul, the Revolution of 1789 to 1814 draped itself alternately as the Roman Republic and the Roman Empire, and the Revolution of 1848 knew nothing better than to parody, in turn, 1789 and the tradition of 1793 to 1795. . . . The social revolution of the nineteenth century cannot draw its poetry from the past, but only from the future. It cannot begin with itself, before it has stripped off all superstition in regard to the past. . . . In order to arrive at its content, the revolution of the nineteenth century must let the dead bury their dead. There the phrase went beyond the content; here the content goes beyond the phrase."

Is the problem any different today, as we approach the twenty-first century? Once again the dead are walking in our midst—ironically, draped in the name of Marx, the man who tried to bury the dead of the nineteenth century. So the revolution of our own day can do nothing better than parody, in turn, the October Revolution of 1917 and the Civil War of 1918–1920, with its "class analysis," its Bolshevik Party, its "proletarian dictatorship," its puritanical morality, and even its slogan of "soviet power." The complete, all-sided revolution of our own day that can finally resolve the historic "social question," born of scarcity, domination, and hierarchy, follows the tradition of the partial, the incomplete, the one-sided revolutions of the past, which merely changed the form of the "social question," replacing one system of domination and hierarchy by another. At a time when bourgeois society itself is in the process of disintegrating the traditional social classes that once gave it stability, we hear the hollow echoes of the "class line." At a time when all the political institutions of hierarchical society are entering a period of profound decay, we hear the hollow echoes of the "political party" and the "workers' state." At a time when hierarchy as such is being brought into question, we hear the hollow echoes of "cadres," "vanguards," and "leaders." At a time when centralization and the State have been brought to the most explosive point of historical negativity, we hear the hollow echoes of a "centralized movement" and a "proletarian dictatorship."

This pursuit for security in the past, this attempt to find a haven in a fixed dogma and an organizational hierarchy—all as substitutes for creative thought and praxis—is bitter evidence of how little many "revolutionaries" are capable of "revolutionizing themselves and things," much less of revolutionizing society as a whole. The deep-rooted conservatism of the P.L. "revolutionaries" is almost painfully evident: the authoritarian Party replaces the authoritarian Family; the authoritarian Leader and Hierarchy replaces the Patriarch and School Bureaucracy; the Discipline of the Movement replaces the Discipline of Bourgeois Society; the authoritarian code of Political Obedience replaces the State; the credo of "Proletarian Morality" replaces the mores of Puritanism and the Work Ethic. The old substance of exploitative society reappears in new forms, draped in a red flag, decorated by portraits of Mao (or Castro or Che) and the little "Red Book" and other sacred litanies.

The majority of people who remain in P.L., today, deserve it. If they can live with a movement that cynically dubs its own slogans into photographs of DRUM pickets; if they can read a magazine that asks whether Marcuse is a "cop-out or cop"; if they can accept a "discipline" that reduces them to poker-faced, programmed automata; if they can use the most disgusting techniques (techniques borrowed from the cesspool of bourgeois business operations and parliamentarism) to manipulate other organizations; if they can parasitize virtually every action and situation to merely promote the growth of their Party —even if this means defeat for the action itself—they are beneath contempt. For these people to call themselves "Reds" and describe attacks upon them as "Red-Baiting" is a form of McCarthyism in reverse. To rephrase Trotsky's juicy description of Stalinism, they are the syphilis of the radical youth movement today. And for syphilis there is only one treatment—an antibiotic, not an argument.

Our concern, here, is with those honest revolutionaries who have turned to Marxism, Leninism, or Trotskyism because they earnestly seek a coherent social outlook and an effective strategy of revolution. We are also concerned with those who are awed by the theoretical armamentarium of Marxist ideology and are disposed to flirt with it in the absence of more systematic alternatives. To these people we address ourselves as brothers and sisters and ask for a serious discussion and comprehensive re-evaluation. We believe that Marxism has ceased to be applicable to our time not because it is too visionary or revolutionary, but because it is not visionary or revolutionary enough. We believe it was born of an era of scarcity and presented a brilliant critique of that era, specifically its industrial capitalist form; that a new era is in birth which Marxism does not adequately encompass and whose outlines it only partially and one-sidedly anticipated. We argue the problem is not so much to "abandon" Marxism or to "annul" it, but to dialectically transcend it, just as Marx transcended Hegelian philosophy, Ricardian economics, and Blanquist tactics and modes of organization. We shall argue that in a more advanced stage of capitalism than Marx dealt with a century ago and in a more advanced stage of technological development than Marx could have clearly anticipated, a new critique is necessary, which in turn yields new modes of struggle, of organization, of propaganda, and of life-style. Call these new modes of struggle, organization, propaganda, and life-style, whatever you will, even "Marxism" if the word hangs on your lips like a scab. We have chosen to call these new approaches Post-Scarcity Anarchy, for a number of compelling reasons which will become evident in the pages that follow.

The Historical Limits of Marxism

The idea that a man, whose greatest theoretical contributions were made between 1840 and 1880, could "foresee" the entire dialectic of capitalism is, on the face of it, utterly preposterous. If we can still learn much from Marx's insights, we can learn even more from the inescapable errors of any man who was limited temporally by an era of material scarcity and a technology that barely involved the use of electric power. We can learn how different our own era is from that of *all* past history, how qualitatively new are the potentialities that confront us, how unique are the issues, analyses, and praxis that stand before us if we are to make a revolution—and not another historical abortion.

The problem is not that Marxism is a "method" which must be re-applied to "new situations" or that a "neo-Marxism" has to be developed to overcome the limitations of "classical Marxism." The attempt to rescue the Marxian pedigree by emphasizing the method over the system or by adding "neo" to a sacred word is sheer mystification if all the *practical* conclusions of the system flatly contradict these efforts.* Yet this is precisely the state of affairs in Marxian exegesis today. Marxists lean on the fact that the system provides a brilliant interpretation of the past, while willfully ignoring its utterly misleading features in dealing with the present and future. They cite the coherence that historical materialism and the class analysis give to the interpretation of history, the economic insights *Capital* provides into the development of industrial capitalism, the brilliance of Marx's analysis of earlier revolutions and the tactical conclusions he established, without once recognizing that qualitatively new problems have arisen which never existed in his day. Is it conceivable that historical problems and methods of class analysis, based entirely on unavoidable scarcity, can be transplanted over to a new era of potential abundance, indeed, of overwhelming material superfluity? Is it conceivable that an economic analysis, focused primarily on a "freely competitive" system of industrial capitalism, can be transferred over to a managed system of capitalism, where State and monopoly combine to manipulate economic life? Is it conceivable that a strategic and tactical armamentarium, formulated in a period when coal and steel constituted the

---

* Marxism is above all a theory of praxis, or to place this relationship in its correct perspective, a praxis of theory. This is the very meaning of Marx's transformation of dialectics from the subjective dimension (to which the Young Hegelians still tried to confine Hegel's outlook) into the objective, from philosophical critique into social action. If theory and praxis become divorced, Marxism is not killed; it commits suicide. This is its most admirable and noble feature. The attempts of the cretins who follow in Marx's wake to keep the system alive with a patchwork of emendations, exegesis, and above all, a half-ass "scholarship" *à la* Maurice Dobb and George Novack, are degrading insults to Marx's name and a disgusting pollution of everything he stood for.

basis of industrial technology, can be transferred over to an age based on radically new sources of energy, on electronics, on cybernation?

The result is that a theoretical corpus which was liberating a century ago is turned into a straitjacket today. We are asked to focus on the working class as the "agent" of revolutionary change at a time when capitalism visibly antagonizes and produces revolutionaries in virtually all strata of society, particularly among the young. We are asked to guide our tactical methods by the vision of a "chronic economic crisis" despite the fact that no such crisis has been in the offing for thirty years.* We are asked to accept a "proletarian dictatorship"—a long "transitional period" whose function is not merely the suppression of counterrevolutionaries but above all the development of a technology of abundance—at a time when a technology of abundance is at hand. We are asked to orient our "strategies" and "tactics" around poverty and material immiseration at a time when revolutionary sentiment is being generated by the banality of life under conditions of relative material abundance. We are asked to establish political parties, centralized organizations, "revolutionary" hierarchies and elites, and a new State at a time when political institutions as such are decaying and when centralization, hierarchy, elitism, and the State are being brought into question on a scale that has never occurred before in the history of propertied society.

We are asked, in short, to return to the past, to diminish instead of grow, to force the throbbing reality of our times with its hopes and promises into the deadening preconceptions of an outlived age. We are asked to operate with principles that have been transcended not only theoretically but by the very development of society itself. History has not stood still since Marx, Engels, Lenin, and Trotsky died; nor has it followed the simplistic direction which was charted out by thinkers—however brilliant—whose minds were still rooted in the nineteenth century or the opening years of the twentieth. We have seen capitalism itself perform many of the tasks (the development of a technology of abundance) which were imputed to socialism; we have seen it "nationalize" property, merging the economy with the State wherever necessary. We have seen the working class neutralized

* It is fascinating to note that Marxists do very little talking about the "chronic [economic] crisis of capitalism" these days—despite the fact that this concept forms the focal point of Marx's economic theories.

as the "agent of revolutionary change," albeit still struggling within a *bourgeois* framework for more wages, shorter hours, and "fringe" benefits. The class struggle in the *classical* sense has not disappeared; it has suffered a more deadening fate by being co-opted into capitalism. The revolutionary struggle within the advanced capitalist countries has shifted to a historically new terrain: a struggle between a generation of youth that has known no chronic economic crisis and the culture, values, and institutions of an older, conservative generation whose perspective on life has been shaped by scarcity, guilt, renunciation, the work ethic, and the pursuit of material security. Our enemies are not only the visibly entrenched bourgeoisie and the State apparatus but also an outlook which finds its support in liberals, Social Democratic types, the minions of a corrupt mass media, the "revolutionary" parties of the past, and, painful as it may be to the acolytes of Marxism, the worker dominated by the factory hierarchy, by the industrial routine, and by the work ethic. The point is that the divisions now cut across virtually all the traditional class lines and they raise a spectrum of problems that none of the Marxists, leaning on analogies with scarcity societies, could foresee.

The Myth of the Proletariat

Let us cast aside all the ideological debris of the past and cut to the theoretical roots of the problem. For our age, Marx's greatest contribution to revolutionary thought is his dialectic of social development: the great movement from primitive communism, through private property, to communism in its highest form—a communal society resting on a liberatory technology. According to Marx, man thus passes from the domination of man by nature, to the domination of man by man, and finally to the domination of nature by man and the elimination of social domination as such.* Within this larger dialectic, Marx examines the dialectic of capitalism itself—a social system which constitutes the last historical "stage" in the domination of man by man. Here, Marx makes not only profound contributions to the thought of our time (particularly in his brilliant analysis of the commodity rela-

---

* For ecological reasons, we do not accept the notion of the "domination of nature by man" in the simplistic sense that it was passed on by Marx a century ago. For a discussion of this problem, see "Ecology and Revolutionary Thought" in *Anarchos* no. 1.

tionship) but also exhibits those limitations of time and place that play so confining a role in our own time.

The most serious of these limitations emerges from Marx's attempt to explain the transition from capitalism to socialism, from a class society to a classless society. It is vitally important to emphasize that this explanation was reasoned out almost entirely by analogy with the transition of feudalism to capitalism—that is, *from one class society to another class society,* indeed, from one system of property to another. Accordingly, Marx points out that just as the bourgeoisie developed within feudalism as a result of the split between town and country (more precisely, between crafts and agriculture), so the modern proletariat developed within capitalism with the advance of industrial technology. Both classes, we are told, develop social interests of their own —indeed, revolutionary social interests that throw them against the old society in which they were spawned. If the bourgeoisie gained control over economic life long before it overthrew feudal society, the proletariat, in turn, gains its own revolutionary power by the fact that it is "disciplined, united, organized" by the factory system.* In both cases, the development of the productive forces becomes incompatible with the traditional system of social relations. "The integument is burst asunder." The old society is replaced by the new.

The critical question we face is this: can we explain the transition from a class society to a classless society by means of the same dialectic that accounts for the transition of one class society to another? This is not a textbook problem that involves the juggling of logical abstractions but a very real and concrete issue for our time. There are pro-

---

* It is ironical that all the Marxists who talk about the "economic power" of the proletariat are actually echoing the position of the anarchosyndicalists, a position that Marx bitterly opposed. Marx was not concerned with the "economic power" of the proletariat but with its *political* power: notably, the fact that it would become the majority of the population. He was convinced that the *industrial* workers would be driven to revolution primarily by material destitution which would follow from the tendency of capitalist accumulation; that, *organized* by the factory system and disciplined by the industrial routine, they would be able to constitute trade unions and, above all, political parties, which in some countries would be obliged to use insurrectionary methods and in others (notably, England, the United States, and in later years Engels added France) might well come to power in elections and legislate socialism into existence. Characteristically, many Marxists have been as dishonest with their Marx and Engels as P.L. has been with the readers of "Challenge," leaving important observations untranslated or grossly distorting the meaning and reasons why Marx developed conclusions of this kind.

found differences between the development of the bourgeoisie under feudalism and of the proletariat under capitalism which Marx either failed to anticipate or never faced with clarity. The bourgeoisie controlled economic life long before it took State power; it had become the dominant class materially, culturally, and ideologically before it asserted its dominance politically. The proletariat does not control economic life. Despite its indispensable role in the industrial process, the industrial working class is not even the majority of the population and its strategic economic position is being eroded by cybernation and other technological advances.* Hence it requires an act of high consciousness for the proletariat to use the power it has to achieve a social revolution. Up to now, the achievement of this consciousness has been blocked continually by the fact that the factory milieu is one of the most entrenched arenas of the work ethic, of hierarchical systems of management, of obedience to leaders, and in recent times, of production committed to superfluous commodities and armaments. The factory serves not only to "discipline," "unite," and "organize" the workers, but to achieve this in a thoroughly bourgeois fashion. In the factory, capitalistic production not only renews the social relations of capitalism with each working day, as Marx observed, but it also renews the psyche, values, and ideology of capitalism.

Marx sensed this fact sufficiently to look for reasons more compelling than the mere fact of exploitation or conflicts over wages and hours to propel the proletariat into revolutionary action. In his general theory of capitalist accumulation he tried to delineate the harsh, objective laws that force the proletariat to assume a revolutionary role. Accordingly he developed his famous theory of immiseration: competition between capitalists compels them to undercut each other's prices, which in turn leads to a continual reduction of wages and the absolute impoverishment of the workers. The proletariat is compelled to revolt

* This is as good a place as any to dispose of the notion that a "proletarian" is reducible to anyone who has nothing to sell but his labor power. It is true that Marx defined the proletariat in these terms but he also worked out a historical dialectic in the development of the proletariat. The proletariat developed out of a propertyless, exploited class, reaching its most "mature" form in the *industrial* proletariat. This class, according to Marx, was the most advanced form, corresponding to the most advanced form of capital. In the late years of his life, Marx came to despise the Parisian workers, who were engaged preponderantly in the production of luxury goods, citing "our German workers"—the most robot-like in Europe—as the "model" proletariat of the world.

because with the process of competition and the centralization of capital "grows the mass of misery, oppression, slavery, degradation." *

But capitalism has not stood still since Marx's day. Writing in the
middle years of the 19th century, Marx could not be expected to grasp
the full consequences of his insights into the centralization of capital
and the development of technology. He could not be expected to foresee that capitalism would develop not only from mercantilism into the
dominant industrial form of his day, from State-aided trading monopolies into highly competitive industrial units; but further, that with the
centralization of capital it returns to its mercantilist origins on a higher
level of development and reassumes the State-aided monopolistic form.
The economy tends to merge with the State and capitalism begins to
"plan" its development instead of leaving it exclusively to the interplay
of competition and market forces. The system, to be sure, does not
abolish the class struggle but manages to contain it, using its immense
technological resources to assimilate the most strategic sections of the
working class.

Thus the full thrust of the immiseration theory is blunted and in the
United States the class struggle in the traditional sense fails to develop
into the class war. It remains entirely within a bourgeois dimension.
Marxism, in fact, becomes ideology. It is assimilated by the most advanced forms of the state capitalist development—notably, Russia. By
an incredible irony of history, Marxian "socialism" turns out to be in
large part the very state capitalism that Marx failed to anticipate in the
dialectic of capitalism.† The proletariat, instead of developing into a

---

* The attempt to describe Marx's immiseration theory in international terms
instead of national (as Marx did) is sheer subterfuge. In the first place, this
theoretical legerdemain simply tries to sidestep the reasons why immiseration
has not occurred within the industrial strongholds of capitalism, the *only areas
which form a technologically adequate point of departure for a classless society.*
If we are to pin our hopes on the colonial world as "the proletariat," this position conceals a very real danger: genocide. America and her recent ally,
Russia, have all the technical means to bomb the underdeveloped world into
submission. This threat lurks on the historical horizon—the development of
the United States into a truly fascist imperium of the Nazi type. It is sheer
rubbish to say that this country is a "paper tiger." It is a thermonuclear tiger
and the American ruling class, owing to the absence of any cultural restraints,
is capable of being even more vicious than the German.

† Lenin sensed this and described "socialism" as "nothing but state capitalist
monopoly *made to benefit the whole people."* (Cf. Lenin's "The Threatening
Catastrophe and How to Fight It," *Collected Works,* Vol. XXI, pg. 157.) This
is an extraordinary statement, if one thinks out its implications—and a mouth-
ful of contradictions.

revolutionary class within the womb of capitalism, turns out to be an organ within the body of bourgeois society.

The question we must ask at this late date in history is whether a social revolution that seeks to achieve a classless society can emerge from a conflict between traditional classes in a class society? Or whether such a social revolution can only emerge from the decomposition of the traditional classes, indeed, from the emergence of an entirely new "class" *whose very essence is that it is a non-class,* a growing stratum called the *revolutionary?* In trying to answer this question, we can learn more by returning to the broader dialectic which Marx developed for human society as a whole than by the model he borrowed from the passage of feudal into capitalist society. Just as primitive kinship clans began to differentiate into classes, so in our own day there is a *tendency* for classes to decompose into entirely new subcultures which bear a resemblance to noncapitalist forms of relationships. These are not strictly economic groups anymore; in fact, they reflect the tendency of the social development to transcend the economic categories of scarcity society. They constitute, in effect, a cultural preformation in an extremely crude, even ambiguous form, of the movement of scarcity society into post-scarcity phases.

The process of class decomposition must be understood in all its dimensions. The word "process" must be emphasized, here: the *traditional* classes do not disappear, nor for that matter does the class struggle. Only a social revolution can remove the prevailing class structure and the conflicts it engenders. The point is that the traditional class struggle ceases to have revolutionary implications; it reveals itself as the physiology of the prevailing society, not as the labor pains of birth. In fact, the traditional class struggle forms a precondition for the stability of capitalist society by "correcting" its abuses (wages, hours, inflation, employment, etc.). The unions constitute themselves into a counter-"monopoly" to the industrial monopolies and are incorporated into the neo-mercantilist, statified economy as an estate. Within this estate there are lesser or greater conflicts, but taken as a whole they strengthen the system and serve to perpetuate it.

To reinforce this class structure by babbling about the "role of the working class," to reinforce this traditional class struggle by imputing a "revolutionary" content to it, to infect the new, revolutionary movement of our time with "workeritis" is *reactionary to the core.* How often do the Marxian doctrinaires have to be reminded that the history of the class struggle is the history of a disease, of the wounds opened by the famous "social question," of man's one-sided development in trying to gain control over nature by dominating his fellow man? If the byproduct of this disease has been technological advance, the main product has been repression, a horrible shedding of human blood and a terrifying distortion of the human psyche.

As the disease approaches its end, as the wounds begin to heal in their deepest recesses, the process now unfolds toward wholeness; the *revolutionary* implications of the class struggle lose their meaning as a theoretical construct and social reality. The process of decomposition embraces not only the traditional class structure but also the patriarchal family, authoritarian modes of upbringing, the influence of religion, the institutions of the State, the mores built around toil, renunciation, guilt, and repressed sexuality. *The process of disintegration, in short, now becomes generalized and cuts across virtually all the traditional classes, values, and institutions. It creates entirely new issues, modes of struggle, forms of organization and calls for an entirely new approach to theory and praxis.*

What does this mean concretely? Let us contrast two approaches, the Marxian and the revolutionary. The Marxian doctrinaire would have us approach the worker—or better, "enter" the factory—and proselytize him in "preference" to anyone else. The purpose?—to make the worker "class conscious." To cite the most Neanderthal example (P.L.'s of course): one cuts one's hair, grooms oneself in conventional sports clothing, abandons pot for cigarettes and beer, dances conventionally, and affects "rough" mannerisms. In P.L., one develops a humorless, deadpan, and pompous mien.*

One becomes, in short, what the worker is at his most caricaturized worst: not a "petty bourgeois degenerate," to be sure, but a *bourgeois* degenerate. One becomes an imitation of the worker insofar as the worker is an imitation of his masters. Beneath this metamorphosis of the P.L. student into the P.L. "worker" lies a vicious cynicism. One tries to use the discipline inculcated by the factory milieu to discipline the worker to the Party milieu. One tries to use the worker's respect for the industrial hierarchy to wed the worker to the Party hierarchy. This disgusting process, which if successful could lead only to the sub-

---

* On this score, P.L. projects its own Neanderthal image on the American worker. Actually, this image more closely approximates the character of the union bureaucrat and Stalinist commissar.

stitution of one hierarchy by another, is achieved by pretending to be concerned with the worker's economic, day-to-day demands. Even Marxian theory is degraded to this debased image of the worker. (See almost any copy of "Challenge"—the "New York Inquirer" of the "left." Nothing bores the worker more than this kind of shit literature.) In the end, the worker is shrewd enough to know that he will get better results in the day-to-day class struggle through his union bureaucracy than through a Marxian party bureaucracy. The thirties revealed this so dramatically that within a year or two, unions succeeded in kicking out "Marxians" by the thousands (with hardly any protest from the rank-and-file) who had done spade-work in the labor movement for more than a decade, even rising to the top leadership of the C.I.O. internationals.

The worker becomes a *revolutionary* not by becoming more of a worker but by undoing his "workerness." And in this he is not alone; the same applies to the farmer, the student, the clerk, the soldier, the bureaucrat, the professional—and the Marxist. The worker is no less a "bourgeois" than the farmer, student, clerk, soldier, bureaucrat, professional—and Marxist. His "workerness" is the *disease* he is suffering from, the social affliction telescoped to individual dimensions. Lenin understood this in *What Is to Be Done?* but he smuggled in the old hierarchy under a red flag and revolutionary verbiage. The worker begins to become a revolutionary when he undoes his "workerness," when he comes to detest his class status here and now, when he begins to disgorge exactly those features which the Marxists most prize in him: his work ethic, his characterology derived from industrial discipline, his respect for hierarchy, his obedience to leaders, his consumerism, his vestiges of puritanism. In this sense, the worker becomes a revolutionary to the degree that he sheds his class status and achieves an *un*-class consciousness. He degenerates—and he degenerates magnificently. What he is shedding are precisely those *class* shackles that bind him to *all* systems of domination. He abandons those *class* interests that enslave him to consumerism, suburbia, and a bookkeeping conception of life.*

---

* The worker, in this sense, begins to approximate the socially transitional human types who provided history with its most revolutionary elements. Generally, the "proletariat" has been most revolutionary in transitional periods, when it was least "proletarianized" psychically by the industrial system. The great foci of the classical workers' revolutions were Petrograd and Barcelona, where the workers had been directly uprooted from a peasant background,

The most promising development in the factories today is the emergence of young workers who smoke pot, fuck-off on their jobs, drift into and out of factories, grow long or longish hair, demand more leisure time rather than more pay, steal, harass all authority figures, go on wildcats, and turn on their fellow workers. Even more promising is the emergence of this human type in trade schools and high schools, the reservoir of the industrial working class to come. To the degree that workers, vocational students, and high school students link their life-styles to various aspects of the anarchic youth culture, to that degree will the proletariat be transformed from a force for the conservation of the established order into a force for revolution.

A qualitatively new situation emerges when man is faced with a transformation from a repressive, class society, based on material scarcity, into a liberatory, classless society, based on material abundance. From the decomposing traditional class structure, a new human type is created in ever-increasing numbers: the *revolutionary*. This revolutionary begins to challenge not only the economic and political premises of hierarchical society, but hierarchy as such. He raises not only the need for social revolution but tries to *live* in a revolutionary manner to the degree that this is possible in the existing society.* He

---

and Paris, where they were still anchored in crafts or came directly from a craft background. These workers had the greatest difficulty in acclimating themselves to industrial domination and became a continual source of social and revolutionary unrest.

By contrast, the stable, hereditary working class tended to be surprisingly non-revolutionary. Even in the much-cited case of the German workers (which, as we know, had been cited by Marx and Engels as models for the European proletariat), the majority did not support the Spartacists in 1919. They returned large majorities of official Social Democrats to the Congress of Workers' Councils, to the Reichstag in later years, and rallied consistently behind the Social Democratic Party right up to 1933.

* This revolutionary life-style may develop in the factories as well as on the streets, in schools as well as in crashpads, in the suburbs as well as the Bay Area-East Side axis. Its essence is defiance, and a personal "propaganda of the deed" that erodes all the mores, institutions, and shibboleths of domination.

As society begins to approach the threshold of the revolutionary period, the factories, schools, and neighborhoods become the actual arena of revolutionary "play"—a "play" that has a very serious core. Strikes become a chronic condition and are called for their own sake, to break the veneer of routine, to defy the society on an almost hourly basis, to shatter the mood of bourgeois normality. This new mood of the workers, students, and neighborhood people is a vital precursor to the actual moment of revolutionary transformation. Its most conscious expression is the demand for "self-management"; the worker refuses to be a "managed" being, a *class* being. This is an eminently revolu-

attacks not only the forms created by the legacy of domination, but improvises new forms of liberation which take their poetry from the future.

This preparation for the future, this experimentation with liberatory, post-scarcity forms of social relations, may be illusory if the future involves a substitution of one class society by another; it is indispensable, however, if the future involves a classless society built on the *ruins* of a class society. What, then, will be the "agent" of revolutionary change? Literally, the great majority of society, drawn from all the different traditional classes and funded into a common revolutionary force by the decomposition of the institutions, social forms, values, and life-styles of the prevailing class structure. Typically, its most advanced elements are the youth—a generation, today, that has known no chronic economic crisis, that is less and less oriented toward the myth of material security so widespread among the generation of the thirties.

If it is true that a social revolution cannot be achieved without the active or passive support of the workers, it is no less true that it cannot be achieved without the active or passive support of the farmers, technicians, and professionals. Above all, a social revolution cannot be achieved without the support of the youth, from which the ruling class recruits its armed forces. If the ruling class retains its armed might, the revolution is lost *no matter how many workers rally to its support.* This has been vividly demonstrated not only by Spain in the thirties but by Hungary in the fifties and Czechoslovakia in the sixties. The revolution of today—by its very nature, indeed, in its *pursuit of wholeness*—wins not only the soldier and the worker, *but the very generation from which soldiers, workers, technicians, farmers, scientists, professionals, and even bureaucrats have been recruited.* Discarding the tactical handbooks of the past, the revolution of the future follows the path of least resistance, eating its way into the most susceptible areas of the population, irrespective of their "class position." It is nourished

_____

tionary demand even if it takes its point of departure from the factory, the economic arena of the arena of survival.

This process was most evident, historically, in the Paris Commune and especially in Spain, on the eve of the 1936 revolution, when workers in almost every city and town called strikes "for the hell of it"—to express their independence, their sense of awakening, their break with the social order and with bourgeois conditions of life. This was also an essential feature of the 1968 general strike in France.

by *all* the contradictions in bourgeois society, not by preconceived ones borrowed from the 1860's and 1917. Hence it attracts all those who feel the burdens of exploitation, poverty, racism, imperialism and, yes, those whose lives are frustrated by consumerism, suburbia, the mass media, the family, school, supermarket, and the prevailing system of repressed sexuality. Here the form of the revolution becomes as totalistic as its content: classless, propertyless, hierarchyless, and *wholly* liberating.

To barge into this revolutionary development with the worn recipes of Marxism, to babble about a "class line" and the "role of the working class," amounts to subverting the present and future by the past. To elaborate this deadening ideology by babbling about "cadres," a "vanguard party," "democratic centralism" and the "proletarian dictatorship" is sheer counterrevolution. It is this matter of the "organizational question"—this vital contribution of Leninism to Marxism— that we must now direct some attention.

The Myth of the Party

Social revolutions are not "made" by "parties," groups, or cadres; they occur as a result of deep-seated historic forces and contradictions that activate large sections of the population. They occur not merely (as Trotsky argued) because the "masses" find the existing society intolerable, but also because of the tension between the actual and the possible, between "what *is*" and "what *could* be." Abject misery alone does not produce revolutions; more often than not, it produces an aimless demoralization, or worse, a private, personalized struggle to survive.

The Russian Revolution of 1917 weighs on the brain of the living like a nightmare because it was largely a product of "intolerable conditions," of a devastating imperialistic war. Whatever dreams it had were pulverized by an even bloodier civil war, by famine, and by treachery. What emerged from the revolution were the ruins not of an *old* society but of whatever hopes existed to achieve a *new* one. The Russian Revolution failed miserably; it replaced Tsarism by state capitalism.* The Bolsheviks were the tragic victims of their ideology and

---

* A fact which Trotsky never understood. He never followed through the consequences of his own concept of "combined development" to its logical conclusions. He saw (quite correctly) that Tsarist Russia, the late-comer in

paid with their lives in great numbers during the purges of the thirties. To attempt to acquire any unique wisdom from this *scarcity* revolution is ridiculous. What we can learn from the revolutions of the past is what all revolutions have in common and their profound limitations compared with the enormous possibilities that are now open to us.

The most striking feature of the past revolutions is that they began spontaneously. Whether one chooses to examine the opening phases of the French Revolution of 1789, the revolutions of 1848, the Paris Commune, the 1905 revolution in Russia, the overthrow of the Tsar in 1917, the Hungarian Revolution of 1956, the French general strike of 1968, the opening stages are generally the same: a period of ferment that explodes spontaneously into a mass upsurge. Whether the upsurge is successful or not depends on its resoluteness and on whether the State can effectively exercise its armed power—that is, on whether the troops go over to the people.

The "glorious party," when there is one, almost invariably lags behind the events. In February, 1917, the Petrograd organization of the Bolsheviks opposed the calling of strikes precisely on the eve of the revolution which was destined to overthrow the Tsar. Fortunately, the workers ignored the Bolshevik "directives" and went on strike anyway. In the events which followed, no one was more surprised by the revolution than the "revolutionary" parties, including the Bolsheviks. As

---

the European bourgeois development, necessarily acquired the most advanced industrial and class forms instead of recapitulating the entire bourgeois development from its beginnings. He neglected to consider that Russia, torn by a tremendous internal upheaval, might even *run ahead* of the capitalist development elsewhere in Europe. Hypnotized by the formula, "nationalized property = socialism," he failed to recognize that monopoly capitalism itself *tends to amalgamate with the State by its own inner dialectic.*

The Bolsheviks, having cleared away the *traditional* forms of bourgeois social organization (which still act as a rein on the state capitalist development in Europe and America), inadvertently prepared the ground for a "pure" state capitalist development in which the State finally becomes the ruling class. Lacking support from a technologically advanced Europe, the Russian Revolution passed into an internal counterrevolution; Soviet Russia became a form of state capitalism that does not "benefit the whole people." Lenin's analogy between "socialism" and state capitalism became a terrifying reality under Stalin.

Despite its humanistic core, Marxism failed to comprehend how much its concept of "socialism" approximates a later stage of capitalism itself: the return to neo-mercantilist forms on a higher industrial level. To fail to understand this development is to create devastating theoretical confusion in the contemporary revolutionary movement, as witness the splits within the Trotskyist movement over this question.

the Bolshevik leader Kayurov recalled: "Absolutely no guiding initiatives from the party were felt . . . the Petrograd committee had been arrested and the representative from the Central Committee, Comrade Shliapnikov, was unable to give any directives for the coming day." Perhaps this was fortunate: before the Petrograd committee was arrested, its evaluation of the situation and its role were so dismal that, had the workers followed its guidance, it is doubtful if the revolution would have occurred when it did.

The same kind of stories could be told of the upsurges which preceded 1917 and those which followed. To cite only the most recent: the student uprising and general strike in France during May–June, 1968. There is a convenient tendency to forget that close to a dozen "tightly centralized" Bolshevik-type organizations existed in Paris at this time. It is rarely mentioned that *virtually every one of these "vanguard" groups were disdainful of the student uprising up to May 7th,* when the street fighting broke out in earnest. The Trotskyist J.C.R.[1] was a notable exception—and it merely coasted along, essentially following the initiatives of the March 22nd Movement.* Up to May 7th, all the Maoist groups criticized the student uprising as peripheral and unimportant; the Trotskyist F.E.R.[2] regarded it as "adventuristic" and tried to get the students to leave the barricades on May 10th; the Communist Party, of course, played a completely treacherous role. Far from leading the popular movement, they were its captives throughout. Ironically, most of these Bolshevik groups were to manipulate shamelessly in the Sorbonne student assembly in an effort to "control" it, introducing a disruptive atmosphere that demoralized the entire body. Finally, to complete the irony, all of these Bolshevik groups were to babble about the need for "centralized leadership" when the popular movement collapsed—a movement that occurred despite their directives and often in opposition to them.

Revolutions and uprisings worthy of any note not only have an initial phase that is magnificently anarchic but *also tend spontaneously to*

[1] Revolutionary Communist Youth—*Ed.*

* The March 22nd Movement functioned as a catalytic agent in the events, not as a leadership. It did not "command"; it instigated, leaving a free play to the events. This free play which allowed the students to push ahead on their own momentum was indispensable to the dialectic of the uprising, for without it there would have been no barricades on May 10th, which in turn triggered off the general strike of the workers.

[2] Federation of Revolutionary Students—*Ed.*

create their own forms of revolutionary self-management. The Parisian sections of 1793–94 were the most remarkable forms of self-management to be created by any of the social revolutions in history.* A more familiar form were the councils or "soviets," which the Petrograd workers established in 1905. Although less democratic than the sections, the council form was to reappear in a number of revolutions of later years. Still another form of revolutionary self-management were the factory committees which the anarchists established in the Spanish Revolution of 1936. Finally, the sections reappeared as student assemblies and action committees in the May–June uprising and general strike in Paris a year ago.†

* It is unfortunate that so little has been written about the Parisian sections in English. The sections were neighborhood associations based on face-to-face democracy, not on representation. These extraordinary bodies not only provided the real momentum of the Great French Revolution but they undertook the administration of the entire city. They policed their own neighborhoods, elected their own revolutionary tribunals, were responsible for the distribution of foodstuffs, provided public aid for the poor, and contributed to the maintenance of the National Guard. It must be borne in mind that this complex of extremely important activities was undertaken not by professional bureaucrats, but for the most part by ordinary shopkeepers, workers, and craftsmen. The bulk of sectional responsibilities were discharged after working hours, during the leisure time of the section members. The popular assemblies of the sections usually met during the evenings in neighborhood churches which had been expropriated for their use and were open to all citizens, without property qualifications after the summer of 1792. In periods of emergency, assembly meetings were held daily; normally, they could be called at the request of fifty members. Most administrative responsibilities were discharged by committees, but the popular assemblies established all the policies of the committees, reviewed and passed on their work, and replaced section officers at will. It is not too difficult to surmise why these sections have received very little attention by Marxist theoreticians; they were much too "anarchic" to please the pontiffs of the "Left."

† With a sublime arrogance that is accountable partly to ignorance, a number of Marxist groups were to dub virtually all of the above forms of self-management as "soviets." The attempt to bring all of these different forms under a single rubric is not only misleading but willfully obscurantist. The actual soviets were the least democratic of the revolutionary forms and the Bolsheviks shrewdly used them to transfer the power to their own party. The soviets were not based on face-to-face democracy, like the Parisian sections or like the Parisian student assemblies of 1968. Nor were they based on economic self-management, like the Spanish anarchist factory committees. The soviets were actually a workers' parliament, hierarchically organized, which drew their representation from factories, later military units and peasant villages. Despite its "class character," the Congress of Soviets was a geographic organism which structurally differed little from the House of Representatives and soon surrendered its power to an executive, staffed by the Bolshevik Party. In short, the soviets were a State which existed *over* the working class, not *of* it.

We must ask, at this point, what role the "revolutionary" party plays in all of these developments. In the beginning, as we have seen, it tends to have an inhibitory function, not a "vanguard" role. Where it exercises influence, it tends to slow down the flow of events, not "co-ordinate" the revolutionary forces. This is not accidental. The party is structured along hierarchical lines *that reflect the very society it professes to oppose.* Despite its theoretical pretensions, it is a bourgeois organism, a miniature State, with an apparatus and a cadre, whose function is to *seize* power, not *dissolve* power. Rooted in the pre-revolutionary period, it assimilates all the forms, techniques, and mentality of a bureaucracy. Its membership is schooled in obedience, in the preconceptions of a rigid dogma, and taught to revere the "leadership." The party's leadership, in turn, is schooled in habits born of command, authority, manipulation, and egomania. This situation is worsened when the party participates in parliamentary elections. Owing to the exigencies of election campaigns, the party now models itself completely on existing bourgeois forms and even acquires the paraphernalia of the electoral party. The situation assumes truly crucial proportions when the party acquires large presses, costly headquarters, and a large inventory of centrally controlled periodicals, and develops a paid "apparatus"—in short, a bureaucracy with vested material interests.

As the party expands, the distance between the leadership and the ranks invariably increases. Its leaders not only become "personages," but they lose contact with the living situation below. The local groups, which know their own immediate situation better than any remote leader, are obliged to subordinate their insights to directives from above. The leadership, lacking any direct knowledge of local problems, responds sluggishly and prudently. Although it stakes out a claim to the "larger view," to greater "theoretical competence," the competence of the leadership tends to diminish the higher one ascends the hierarchy of command. The more one approaches the level where the *real* decisions are made, the more conservative is the nature of the decision-making process, the more bureaucratic and extraneous are the factors which come into play, the more considerations of prestige and retrenchment supplant creativity, imagination, and a disinterested dedication to revolutionary goals.

The result is that the party becomes *less* efficient from a revolutionary point of view the more it seeks efficiency in hierarchy, cadres, and centralization. Although everyone marches in step, the orders are usually wrong, especially when events begin to move rapidly and take unexpected turns—as they do in all revolutions. The party is efficient in only one respect: in molding society in its own hierarchical image if the revolution is successful. It re-creates bureaucracy, centralization, and the State. It fosters the very social conditions which justify this kind of society. Hence instead of "withering away," the State controlled by the "glorious party" preserves the very conditions which "necessitate" the existence of a State—and a party to "guard it."

On the other hand, this kind of party is extremely vulnerable in periods of repression. The bourgeoisie has only to grab its leadership to virtually destroy the entire movement. With its leaders in prison or in hiding, the party becomes paralyzed; the obedient membership has no one to obey and tends to flounder. Demoralization sets in rapidly. The party decomposes not only because of its repressive atmosphere but also because of its poverty of inner resources.

The foregoing account is not a series of hypothetical inferences; it is a composite sketch of all the mass Marxian parties of the past century—the Social Democrats, the Communists, and the Trotskyist party of Ceylon, the only mass party of its kind. To claim that these parties ceased to take their Marxian principles seriously merely conceals another question: why did this happen in the first place? The fact is that these parties were co-opted into bourgeois society because they were structured along bourgeois lines. The germ of treachery existed in them from birth.

The Bolshevik Party was spared this fate between 1904 and 1917 for only one reason: it was an illegal organization during most of the years leading up to the revolution. The party was continually being shattered and reconstituted, with the result that until it took power it never really hardened into a fully centralized, bureaucratic, hierarchical machine. Moreover, it was riddled by factions. This intense factional atmosphere persisted throughout 1917 into the civil war. Nevertheless the Bolshevik leadership was ordinarily extremely conservative, a trait that Lenin had to fight throughout 1917—first, in his efforts to reorient the Central Committee against the Provisional Government (the famous conflict over the "April Theses"), later in driving this body into insurrection in October. In both cases, he threatened to resign from the Central Committee and bring his views to "the lower ranks of the party."

In 1918, factional disputes became so serious over the issue of the Brest-Litovsk Treaty that the Bolsheviks nearly split into two warring Communist parties. Oppositional Bolshevik groups like the Democratic Centralists and the Workers' opposition waged bitter struggles within the party throughout 1919 and 1920, not to speak of oppositional movements that developed within the Red Army over Trotsky's propensity for centralization. The complete centralization of the Bolshevik Party—the achievement of "Leninist unity," as it was to be called later—did not occur until 1921, when Lenin succeeded in persuading the Tenth Party Congress to ban factions. By this time, most of the White Guards had been crushed and the foreign interventionists had withdrawn their troops from Russia.

It cannot be stressed too strongly that the Bolsheviks tended to centralize their party to the degree that they became isolated from the working class. This relationship has rarely been investigated in latter-day Leninist circles, although Lenin was honest enough to admit it. The Russian Revolution is not merely the story of the Bolshevik Party and its supporters. Beneath the veneer of official events described by Soviet historians there was another, more basic development —the spontaneous movement of the workers and revolutionary peasants, which later clashed sharply with the bureaucratic policies of the Bolsheviks. With the overthrow of the Tsar in February, 1917, workers in virtually all the factories of Russia spontaneously established factory committees, staking out an increasing claim in industrial operations. In June, 1917, an all-Russian Conference of Factory Committees was held in Petrograd which called for the "organization of thorough control by labor over production and distribution." The demands of this Conference are rarely mentioned in Leninist accounts of the Russian Revolution, despite the fact that the Conference aligned itself with the Bolsheviks. Trotsky, who describes the factory committees as "the most direct and indubitable representation of the proletariat in the whole country," deals with them peripherally in his massive, three-volume history of the revolution. Yet so important were these spontaneous organisms of self-management that Lenin, despairing of winning the soviets in the summer of 1917, was prepared to jettison the slogan "All Power to the Soviets" for "All Power to the Factory Committees." This demand would have catapulted the

Bolsheviks into a completely anarchosyndicalist position, although it is doubtful that they would have remained there very long.

With the October Revolution, all the factory committees seized control of the plants, ousting the bourgeoisie and completely taking control of industrial operations. In accepting the concept of workers' control, Lenin's famous decree of November 14, 1917, merely acknowledged an accomplished fact; the Bolsheviks dared not oppose the workers at this early date. But they began to whittle down the power of the factory committees. In January, 1918, a scant two months after "decreeing" workers' control, the Bolsheviks shifted the administration of the factories from the committees to the bureaucratic trade unions. The story that the Bolsheviks "patiently" experimented with workers' control, only to find it "inefficient" and "chaotic," is a myth. Their "patience" did not last more than a few weeks. Not only did they end direct workers' control within a matter of weeks after the decree of November 14, but even union control came to an end shortly after it had been established. By the spring of 1918, virtually all Russian industry was placed under bourgeois forms of management. As Lenin put it, the "revolution demands . . . precisely in the interests of socialism that the masses *unquestionably obey the single will* of the leaders of the labor process." Workers' control was denounced not only as "inefficient," "chaotic," and "impractical," but as "petty bourgeois"!

The Left Communist Osinsky bitterly denounced all of these spurious claims and warned the party: "Socialism and socialist organization must be set up by the proletariat itself, or they will not be set up at all; something else will be set up—state capitalism." In the "interests of socialism," the Bolshevik Party elbowed the proletariat out of every domain it had conquered by its own efforts and initiative. The party did not coordinate the revolution or even lead it; it dominated it. First, workers' control, later union control, were replaced by an elaborate hierarchy, as monstrous as any structure that existed in pre-revolutionary times. As later years were to demonstrate, Osinsky's prophecy became bitter reality with a vengeance.

The problem of "who is to prevail"—the Bolsheviks or the Russian "masses"—was by no means limited to the factories. The issue reappeared in the countryside as well as the cities. A sweeping peasant war had buoyed up the movement of the workers. Contrary to official Leninist accounts, the agrarian upsurge was by no means limited to a redistribution of the land into private plots. In the Ukraine, peasants influenced by the anarchist militias of Nestor Makhno established a multitude of rural communes, guided by the communist maxim: "From each according to his ability; to each according to his needs." Elsewhere, in the north and in Soviet Asia, several thousands of these organisms were established partly on the initiative of the Left Social Revolutionaries and in large measure as a result of traditional collectivist impulses which stemmed from the Russian village, the *mir*. It matters little whether these communes were numerous or embraced large numbers of peasants; the point is that they were authentic popular organisms, the nuclei of a moral and social spirit that ranged far above the dehumanizing values of bourgeois society.

The Bolsheviks frowned upon these organisms from the very beginning and eventually condemned them. To Lenin, the preferred, the more "socialist" form of agricultural enterprise was represented by the State Farm: literally, an agricultural factory in which the State owned the land and farming equipment, appointing managers who hired peasants on a wage basis. One sees in these attitudes toward workers' control and agricultural communes the essentially *bourgeois* spirit and mentality that permeated the Bolshevik Party —a spirit and mentality that emanated not only from its theories, but from its corporate mode of organization. In December, 1918, Lenin launched an attack against the communes on the pretext that peasants were being "forced" to enter them. Actually, little if any coercion was used to organize these communistic forms of self-management. As Robert G. Wesson, who studied the Soviet communes in detail, concludes: "Those who went into communes must have done so largely of their own volition." The communes were not suppressed but their growth was discouraged until Stalin merged the entire development in the forced collectivization drives of the late twenties and early thirties.

By 1920, the Bolsheviks had isolated themselves from the Russian working class and peasantry. The elimination of workers' control, the suppression of the Makhnovtsy, the restrictive political atmosphere in the country, the inflated bureaucracy, the crushing material poverty inherited from the civil war years—all, taken together, generated a deep hostility toward Bolshevik rule. With the end of hostilities, a new movement surged up from the depths of Russian society for a "Third Revolution"—not a restoration of the past, but a deep-felt desire to realize the very goals of freedom, economic as well as political, that had rallied the "masses" around the Bolshevik program of 1917. The new movement found its most conscious form in the Petrograd proletariat and the Kronstadt sailors. It also found expression in the Party: the growth of anti-centralist and anarchosyndicalist tendencies among the Bolsheviks reached a point where a bloc of oppositional groups, oriented toward these issues, gained 124 seats at a Moscow provincial conference as against 154 for supporters of the Central Committee.

On March 2, 1921, the "Red sailors" of Kronstadt rose in open rebellion, raising the banner of a "Third Revolution of the toilers." The Kronstadt program centered around demands for free elections to the soviets, freedom of speech and press for the anarchists and Left Socialists parties, free trade unions, and the liberation of all prisoners who belonged to Socialist parties. The most shameless stories were fabricated by the Bolsheviks to account for this uprising, which in later years were acknowledged as brazen lies. The revolt was characterized as a "White Guard plot," this despite the fact that the great majority of Communist Party members in Kronstadt joined the sailors—*precisely as Communists*—denouncing the party leaders as betrayers of the October Revolution. As Robert Vincent Daniels observes in his study of Bolshevik oppositional movements: "Ordinary Communists were indeed so unreliable . . . that the government did not depend upon them, either in the assault on Kronstadt itself or in keeping order in Petrograd, where Kronstadt's hopes for support chiefly rested. The main body of troops employed were Chekists and officer cadets from Red Army training schools. The final assault on Kronstadt was led by the top officialdom of the Communist Party— a large group of delegates at the Tenth Party Congress was rushed from Moscow for this purpose." So weak was the regime internally that the elite had to do its own dirty work.

Even more significant than the Kronstadt revolt was the strike movement that developed among the Petrograd workers, a movement that sparked the uprising of the sailors. Leninist histories do not recount this critically important development. The first strikes broke out in the Troubotchny factory on February 23, 1921. Within a matter of days, the movement swept in one factory after another until, by

February 28, the famous Putilov works—the "crucible of the Revolution"—went on strike. Not only were economic demands raised but workers raised distinctly political ones, anticipating all the demands that were to be raised by the Kronstadt sailors a few days later. On February 24, the Bolsheviks declared a "state of siege" in Petrograd and arrested the strike leaders, suppressing the workers' demonstrations with officer cadets. The fact is that the Bolsheviks did not merely suppress a "sailors' mutiny"; they crushed by armed force the working class itself. It was at this point that Lenin demanded the banning of factions in the Russian Communist Party. Centralization of the party was now complete—and the way was paved for Stalin.

We have discussed these events in detail because they lead to a conclusion that our latest crop of Marxist-Leninists tend to avoid: the Bolshevik Party reached its maximum degree of centralization in Lenin's day *not to achieve a revolution or suppress a White Guard counterrevolution, but to effect a counterrevolution of its own against the very social forces it professed to represent.* Factions were prohibited and a monolithic party created not to prevent a "capitalist restoration" but to contain a mass movement of workers for soviet democracy and social freedom. The Lenin of 1921 stood opposed to the Lenin of October, 1917.

Thereafter, Lenin simply floundered. This man, who above all others sought to anchor the problems of his party in *social* contradictions, found himself literally playing an *organizational* "numbers game" in a last-ditch attempt to arrest the very bureaucratization he had himself created. There is nothing more pathetic and tragic than Lenin's last years. Paralyzed by a simplistic body of Marxist formulas, he can think of no better countermeasures than organizational ones. He proposes the formation of the Workers' and Peasants' Inspection to correct bureaucratic deformations in the Party and State—which body falls under Stalin's control and becomes highly bureaucratic in its own right. Lenin then suggests that the size of the Workers' and Peasants' Inspection be reduced and that it be merged with the Control Commission. He advocates enlarging the Central Committee. Thus it rolls along: this body to be enlarged, that one to be merged with another, still a third to be modified or abolished. The strange ballet of organizational forms continues up to his very death, as though the problem could be resolved by organizational means. As Mosche Lewin, an obvious admirer of Lenin, admits: the Bolshevik leader "approached the problems of government more like a chief executive of a strictly 'elitist' turn of mind. He did not apply methods of social analysis to the government and was content to consider it purely in terms of organizational methods."

If it is true that in the bourgeois revolutions that "phrase went beyond the content," in the Bolshevik revolution the forms replaced the content. The soviets replaced the workers and their factory committees, the Party replaced the soviets, the Central Committee replaced the Party, and the Political Bureau replaced the Central Committee. In short, means replaced ends. This incredible substitution of form for content is one of the most characteristic traits of Marxism-Leninism. In France, during the May–June events, all the Bolshevik organizations were prepared to destroy the Sorbonne student assembly in order to increase their influence and membership. Their principal concern was not for the revolution or the authentic social forms created by the students, but the growth of their own parties. In the United States, an identical situation exists in P.L.'s relationship with S.D.S.

Only one force could have arrested the growth of bureaucracy in Russia: a *social* force. Had the Russian proletariat and peasantry succeeded in increasing the domain of self-management through the development of viable factory committees, rural communes, and free soviets, the history of the country might have taken a dramatically different turn. There can be no question that the failure of socialist revolutions in Europe after the First World War led to the isolation of the revolution in Russia. The material poverty of Russia, coupled with the pressure of the surrounding capitalist world, clearly militated against the development of a consistently libertarian, indeed, a socialist society. But by no means was it ordained that Russia had to develop along state capitalist lines; contrary to Lenin's and Trotsky's expectations, the revolution was defeated by *internal* forces, not by the invasion of armies from abroad. Had the movement from below restored the initial achievements of the revolution in 1917, a multi-faceted social structure might have developed, based on workers' control of industry, on a freely developing peasant economy in agriculture, and on a living interplay of ideas, programs, and political movements. At the very least, Russia would have not been imprisoned in totalitarian chains and Stalinism would not have poisoned the world revolutionary movement, paving the way for fascism and World War II.

The development of the Bolshevik Party, however, precluded this development, Lenin's or Trotsky's "good intentions" aside. By destroying the power of the factory committees in industry and by crushing the Makhnovtsy, the Petrograd workers, and the Kronstadt sailors, the Bolsheviks virtually guaranteed the triumph of the Russian bureaucracy over Russian society. The centralized party—a completely bourgeois institution—become the refuge of counterrevolution in its most sinister form. This was the *covert* counterrevolution that draped itself in the red flag and the terminology of Marx. Ultimately, what the Bolsheviks suppressed in 1921 was not an "ideology" or a "White Guard conspiracy," but an elemental struggle of the Russian people to free themselves of their shackles and take control of their own destiny.* For Russia, this meant the nightmare of Stalinist dictatorship; for the generation of the thirties it meant the horror of fascism and the treachery of the Communist parties in Europe and the United States.

The Two Traditions

It would be incredibly naïve to suppose that Leninism was the aberrant product of a single man. The disease lies much deeper, not only in the limitations of Marxian theory but in the limitations of the social era that produced Marxism. If this is not clearly understood, we will remain as blind to the dialectic of events today as Marx, Engels, Lenin, and Trotsky were in their own day. For us, this blindness will be all the more reprehensible because behind us lies a wealth of experience that these men sorely lacked in developing their theories.

Karl Marx and Friedrich Engels were centralists—not only polit-

* In interpreting this elemental movement of the Russian workers and peasants as a series of "White Guard conspiracies," "acts of kulak resistance," and "plots of international capital," the Bolsheviks reached an incredible theoretical low and deceived no one but themselves. A spiritual erosion developed in the party that paved the way for the politics of the secret police, for character assassination, and finally for the Moscow Trials and the annihilation of the Old Bolshevik cadre. One sees the return of this odious mentality in P.L. articles like "Marcuse: Cop-Out or Cop?"—the theme of which is to establish Marcuse as an agent of the C.I.A. (See *Progressive Labor,* February, 1969.) The article has a caption under a photograph of demonstrating Parisians which reads: "Marcuse got to Paris too late to stop the May action." Opponents of P.L. are invariably described by this rag as "red-baiters" and "anti-worker." If the American Left does not repudiate this police approach and character assassination, it will pay bitterly in the years to come.

ically, but socially and economically. They never denied this fact and their writings are studded with gleaming encomiums to political, organizational, and economic centralization. As early as March, 1850, in the famous *Address of the Central Council to the Communist League,* they call upon the workers to strive not only for "the single and indivisible German republic, but also strive in it for the most decisive centralization of power in the hands of the state authority." Lest the demand be taken lightly, it is repeated continually in the same paragraph, which concludes: "As in France in 1793, so today in Germany the carrying through of the strictest centralization is the task of the really revolutionary party."

The theme reappears continually in later years. With the outbreak of the Franco-Prussian War, for example, Marx writes to Engels: "The French need a thrashing. If the Prussians win, the centralization of *state power* is useful to the centralization of the German working class."

Marx and Engels were not centralists, however, because they believed in the virtues of centralism per se. Quite to the contrary: both Marxism and anarchism have always agreed that a liberated, communist society entails sweeping decentralization, the dissolution of bureaucracy, the abolition of the State, and the break-up of the large cities. "Abolition of the antithesis between town and country is not merely possible," notes Engels in *Anti-Duhring.* "It has become a direct necessity . . . the present poisoning of the air, water and land can be put to an end only by the fusion of town and country. . . ." To Engels, this involves "As uniform a distribution of the population over the whole country"—in short, the physical decentralization of the cities.

The origins of Marxian centralism emerge from problems around the *formation of the national state.* Until well into the latter half of the 19th century, Germany and Italy were divided into a multitude of independent duchies, principalities, and kingdoms. The consolidation of these geographic units into unified nations, Marx and Engels believed, was a *sine qua non* for the development of modern industry and capitalism. Their praise of centralism is engendered not by any centralistic mystique but by the problems of the period in which they lived: the development of technology, trade, a unified working class and the national state. Their concern on this score, in short, is with the emergence of capitalism, with the tasks of the bourgeois revolution in an era of unavoidable material scarcity. Marx's approach to a "proletarian revolution," on the other hand, is markedly different. He enthusiastically praises the Paris Commune as a "model to all the industrial centers of France. This regime," he writes, "once established in Paris and the secondary centers, the old centralized government would in the provinces, too, have to give way to the *self-government of the producers*." [Our emphasis.] The unity of the nation, to be sure, would not disappear and a central government would exist during the transition to communism, but its functions would be limited.

Our object is not to bandy about quotations from Marx and Engels, but to emphasize how key tenets of Marxism—which are accepted so uncritically today—were in fact the product of a time that has long been transcended by the development of capitalism in the United States and western Europe. In his day, Marx was occupied not only with the problems of the "proletarian revolution" but also with the problems of the bourgeois revolution, particularly in Germany, Spain, Italy, and eastern Europe. He dealt not only with problems of transition from capitalism to socialism in capitalist countries which had not advanced much beyond the coal-steel technology of the Industrial Revolution; he was also concerned with the problems of transition from feudalism to capitalism in countries which had scarcely advanced much beyond handicrafts and the guild system. To state these concerns more broadly: Marx was occupied above all with the *preconditions* of freedom (technological development, national unification, material abundance) rather than the *conditions* of freedom (decentralization, the formation of communities, the human scale, direct democracy). His theories were still anchored in the realm of *survival*, not the realm of *life*.

Once this is grasped it is possible to place Marx's theoretical legacy in meaningful perspective—to separate its rich contributions from its historically limited, indeed, paralyzing shackles on our own time. The Marxian dialectic, the many seminal insights provided by historical materialism, the superb critique of the commodity relationship, many elements of the economic theories, the theory of alienation, and above all, the notion that freedom has material preconditions—these are lasting contributions to revolutionary thought.

By the same token, Marx's emphasis on the industrial proletariat as the "agent" of revolutionary change, his "class analysis" in explaining the transition from a class to a classless society, his concept of the proletarian dictatorship, his emphasis on centralism, his theory of the capitalist development which tends to jumble state capitalism with socialism, his advocacy of political action through electoral parties— these and many related concepts are false in the context of our time and were misleading, as we shall see, even in his own day. They emerge from the limitations of his vision, more properly, from the limitations of his time. They make sense only if one remembers that Marx regarded capitalism as historically progressive, as an indispensable stage to the development of socialism, and they have practical applicability only to a time when Germany in particular was confronted by bourgeois-democratic tasks and national unification. In taking this retrospective approach, we are not trying to say that Marx was correct in holding this approach—merely, that the approach makes sense when viewed in its time and place.

Just as the Russian Revolution included a subterranean movement of the "masses" which conflicted with Bolshevism, so there is a subterranean movement in history which has conflicted with all systems of authority. This movement has entered into our time under the name of "anarchism," although it has never been encompassed by a single ideology or body of sacred texts. Anarchism is a libidinal movement of humanity against coercion in any form, reaching back in time to the very emergence of propertied society, class rule, and the State. From this period onward, the oppressed have resisted all forms that seek to imprison the spontaneous development of social order. By whatever name men chose to call it, anarchism surged to the foreground of the social arena in periods of major transition from one historical era to another. The decline of the ancient and feudal world witnessed the upsurge of mass movements, in some cases, wildly Dionysian in character, that demanded an end to all systems of authority, privilege, and coercion.

The anarchic movements of the past failed largely because material scarcity, a function of the low level of technology, vitiated an organic harmonization of human interests. Any society that could promise little more materially than equality of poverty invariably engendered deep-seated tendencies to restore a new system of privilege. In the absence of a technology that could appreciably reduce the working day, the need to work vitiated social institutions based on self-management. The Girondins of the French Revolution shrewdly recognized that they could use the working day against revolutionary

Paris. To exclude radical elements from the sections, they tried to enact legislation which would end all assembly meetings before 9 P.M., the hour when Parisian workers returned from their jobs. Indeed, it was not only the manipulative techniques and the treachery of the "vanguard" organizations that brought the anarchic phase of past revolutions to an end; it was also the material limits of past eras. The "masses" were always compelled to return to a lifetime of toil and rarely were they free to establish organs of self-management that could last beyond the revolution.

Anarchists such as Bakunin and Kropotkin, however, were by no means wrong in criticizing Marx for his emphasis on centralism and his elitist notions of organization. Was centralism absolutely necessary for technological advances in the past? Was the nation-state indispensable to the expansion of commerce? Did the workers' movement benefit by the emergence of highly centralized economic enterprises and the "indivisible" State? We tend to accept these tenets of Marxism too uncritically, largely because capitalism developed within a centralized political arena. The anarchists of the last century warned that Marx's centralistic approach, insofar as it affected the events of the time, would so strengthen the bourgeoisie and the State apparatus that this development would make the overthrow of capitalism extremely difficult. The revolutionary party, by duplicating these centralistic, hierarchical features, would reproduce hierarchy and centralism in the post-revolutionary society.

Bakunin, Kropotkin, and Malatesta were not so naïve as to believe that anarchy could be established overnight. In imputing this notion to Bakunin, Marx and Engels willfully distorted the Russian anarchist's views. Nor did the anarchists of the last century believe that the abolition of the State involved "laying down arms" immediately after the revolution, to use Marx's obscurantist choice of terms, and which Lenin thoughtlessly repeated in *State and Revolution*. Indeed, much that passes for "Marxism" in *State and Revolution* is pure anarchism: the substitution of revolutionary militias for professional armed bodies, the substitution of organs of self-management for parliamentary bodies. What is authentically Marxist in Lenin's pamphlet is the demand for "strict centralism," the acceptance of a "new" bureaucracy, the identification of soviets with a State.

The anarchists of the last century were deeply preoccupied with the question of achieving industrialization without crushing the revolutionary spirit of the "masses" and rearing new obstacles to emancipation. They feared that centralization would reinforce the ability of the bourgeoisie to resist the revolution and instill in the workers a sense of obedience. They tried to rescue all those pre-capitalist communal forms (such as the Russian *mir* and the Spanish *pueblo*) which might provide a springboard to a free society, not only in a structural sense but also a spiritual one.

Hence they emphasized the need for decentralization even under capitalism. In contrast to the Marxian parties, their organizations gave considerable attention to what they called "integral education"—the development of the *whole* man—to counteract the debasing and banalizing influence of bourgeois society. The anarchists tried to live by the values of the future to the extent that this was possible under capitalism. They believed in direct action in order to foster the initiative of the "masses," to preserve the spirit of revolt, to encourage spontaneity. They tried to develop organizations based on mutual aid and brotherhood, in which control would be exercised from below upward, not from above downward.

We must pause, here, to examine the nature of anarchist organizational forms in some detail if only because the subject has been obscured by an appalling amount of rubbish. Anarchists, or at least anarchist communists, accept the need for organization.* It should be as absurd to have to repeat this point as to argue over whether Marx accepted the need for social revolution.

The real question at issue here is not organization versus nonorganization, but rather, what *kind* of organization the anarchist communists try to establish. What the different kinds of anarchist communist organizations have in common is that they are developed organically from below, not engineered into existence from above. They are social movements, combining a creative revolutionary life-style

---

* The term "anarchist" is a generic word, like the term "socialist" and there are probably as many different kinds of anarchists as there are socialists. In both cases, the spectrum ranges from individuals whose views derive from an extension of liberalism (the "individualist anarchists," the Social Democrats) to revolutionary communists (the anarchist communists, the revolutionary Marxists, Leninists, and Trotskyists). In speaking of anarchists, here, we refer to the anarchist communists, not followers of Max Stirner or admirers of Paul Goodman. The differences between anarchist communists and reformist or individualist schools are as sharp as those between reformist socialists and revolutionary communists.

with a creative revolutionary theory, not political parties, whose mode of life is indistinguishable from the surrounding bourgeois environment and whose ideology is reduced to rigid "tried and tested programs." They try to reflect as much as is humanly possible the liberated society they seek to achieve, not slavishly duplicate the prevailing system of hierarchy, class and authority. They are built around intimate groups of brothers and sisters—affinity groups—whose ability to act in common is based on initiative, on convictions freely arrived at and a deep personal involvement, not a bureaucratic apparatus fleshed out by a docile membership and manipulated from above by a handful of all-knowing leaders.

The anarchist communists do not deny the need for coordination between groups, for discipline, for meticulous planning, and unity in action. But they believe that coordination, discipline, planning and unity in action must be achieved *voluntarily,* by means of a self-discipline nourished by conviction and understanding, not by coercion and a mindless, unquestioning obedience to orders from above. They seek to achieve the effectiveness imputed to centralism by means of voluntarism and insight, not by establishing a hierarchical, centralized structure. Depending upon needs or circumstances, affinity groups can achieve this effectiveness through assemblies, action committees, and local, regional or national conferences. But they vigorously oppose the establishment of an organizational structure that becomes an end in itself, of committees that linger on after their practical tasks have been completed, of a "leadership" that reduces the "revolutionary" to a mindless robot.

These conclusions are not the result of flighty "individualistic" impulses; quite to the contrary, they emerge from an exacting study of past revolutions, of the impact centralized parties have had on the revolutionary process and the nature of social change in an era of potential material abundance. Anarchist communists *seek to preserve and extend the anarchic phase that opens all the great social revolutions.* Even more than Marxists, they recognize that revolutions are produced by deep historical processes. No Central Committee "makes" a social revolution; at best it can stage a *coup d'état,* replacing one hierarchy by another—or worse, arrest a revolutionary process if it exercises any widespread influence. A Central Committee is an organ for acquiring power, for *re-creating* power, for gathering to itself what the "masses" have achieved by their own revolutionary efforts. One must be blind to all that has happened over the past two centuries not to recognize these essential facts.

In the past, Marxists could make an intelligible, although not a valid, claim for the need for a centralized party, because the anarchic phase of the revolution was vitiated by material scarcity. Economically, the "masses" were always compelled to return to a daily life of toil. The revolution closed at "nine o'clock" quite aside from the reactionary intentions of the Girondins of 1793; it was arrested by the low level of technology. Today, even this excuse has been removed by the development of a post-scarcity technology notably in the U.S. and western Europe. A point has now been reached where the masses can begin, almost overnight, to expand drastically the "realm of freedom" in the Marxian sense—to acquire the leisure time needed to achieve the highest degree of self-management.

What the May–June events in France demonstrated was not the need for a centralized, Bolshevik-type party (these parties exist in profusion and they lagged behind the event) but the need for *greater consciousness* among the "masses." Paris demonstrated that an organization is needed to systematically propagate ideas—and not ideas alone, but *ideals* which *promote the concept of self-management.* What the French "masses" lacked was not a Central Committee or a Lenin to "organize" or "command" them, but the conviction that they could have *operated* the factories instead of merely occupying them. It is noteworthy that *not a single Bolshevik-type party in France raised the demand of self-management;* the demand was raised only by the anarchists and the Situationists.

There is a need for a revolutionary organization—but its function must always be kept clearly in mind. Its first task is propaganda, to "patiently explain" as Lenin put it. In a revolutionary situation, the revolutionary organization presents the most advanced demands: it is prepared at every turn of events to formulate—in the most concrete fashion—the immediate task that should be performed to advance the revolutionary process. It provides the boldest elements in action and in the decision-making organs of the revolution.

In what way then, do anarchist communist groups differ from the Bolshevik-type party? Certainly not on such issues as the need for organization, planning, coordination, propaganda in all its forms or the need for a social program. Fundamentally, they differ from the

Bolshevik-type party in their belief that genuine revolutionaries must function *within the framework of the forms created by the revolution,* not within the forms created by the party. What this means is that their commitment is to the revolutionary organs of self-management, not the revolutionary "organization"; to the *social* forms, not the *political* forms. Anarchist communists seek to persuade the factory committees, assemblies, or soviets, to make themselves into *genuine organs of popular self-management,* not dominate them, manipulate them, and hitch them to an all-knowing political party. Anarchist communists do not seek to rear a state structure over these popular revolutionary organs but, on the contrary, to dissolve all the organizational forms developed in the pre-revolutionary period (including their own) into these genuine revolutionary organs.

These differences with the Bolshevik-type parties are decisive. Despite their rhetoric and slogans, the Russian Bolsheviks never believed in the soviets; they regarded them as instruments of the Bolshevik Party, an attitude which the French Trotskyists faithfully duplicated in their relations with the Sorbonne students' assembly, the French Maoists with the C.G.T.,[1] and P.L. with S.D.S. By 1921, the soviets were virtually dead and all decisions were made by the Bolshevik Central Committee and Political Bureau. Not only do anarchist communists seek to prevent Marxist parties from repeating this again; they also wish to prevent their own organization from playing a similar role. Accordingly, they have tried to prevent bureaucracy, hierarchy, and elites from emerging in their midst. No less important, they attempt to *remake themselves;* to root out from their own personalities those authoritarian traits and elitist propensities that are assimilated in propertied society almost from birth. The concern of the anarchist movement with life-style is not merely a preoccupation with its own integrity, but with the integrity of the revolution itself.*

[1] General Confederation of Work; the largest trade union in France, affiliated with the French Communist Party.

* It is this goal, we may add, that motivates anarchist Dadaism—the "anarchist flipout"—that produces the creases of consternation on the wooden faces of P.L. types. The "anarchist flipout" attempts to shatter the internal values inherited from hierarchical society, to explode the rigidities instilled by the bourgeois socialization process. In short it is an attempt to break down the superego that exercises such a paralyzing effect upon spontaneity, imagination, and sensibility; indeed to restore a sense of desire, possibility, the marvelous—of revolution as a liberating joyous festival.

In the midst of all the confusing ideological cross-currents of our time, one question must always remain in the foreground: what the hell are we trying to make a revolution for? Are we trying to make a revolution to re-create hierarchy again, dangling a shadowy dream of future freedom before the eyes of humanity? Is it to promote further technological advance, to create an even greater abundance of goods than exists today? Is it to "get even" with the bourgeoisie? Is it to bring P.L. to power? Or the Communist Party? Or the Socialist Workers Party? Is it to emancipate abstractions such as "The Proletariat," "The People," "History," "Society"?

Or is it to finally dissolve hierarchy, class rule, coercion—*to make it possible for each individual to gain control of his everyday life?* Is it to make each moment as marvelous as it could be and the life span of each individual an utterly fulfilling experience? If the true purpose of revolution is to bring the Neanderthal men of P.L. to power, it is not worth making. We need hardly argue the inane questions of whether individual development can be severed from social and communal development; obviously the two go together. The basis for the whole man is a rounded society; the basis for the free man is the free society.

These issues aside, however, we are still faced with the question that Marx raised in 1850: when will we begin to take our poetry from the future instead of the past? The dead must be permitted to bury the dead. Marxism is dead because it was rooted in an era of material scarcity, limited in its possibilities by material want. The most important social message of Marxism is that freedom has material preconditions; we must survive in order to live. With the development of a technology that could not have been conceived by the wildest science-fiction of Marx's day, the possibilities of a post-scarcity society now lie before us. All the institutions of propertied society— class rule, hierarchy, the patriarchal family, bureaucracy, the city, the state—have been exhausted. Today, decentralization is not only desirable as a means of restoring the human scale; it becomes necessary to re-create a viable ecology, to preserve life on this planet from destructive pollutants, soil erosion, the perpetuation of a breathable atmosphere, the balance of nature. The promotion of spontaneity is necessary if the social revolution is to place each individual in control of his everyday life.

The old forms of struggle do not totally disappear but they are being transcended in the decomposition of class society by the issues of a classless society. There can be no social revolution without winning the workers; hence, they must have our active solidarity in every struggle they wage against exploitation. We fight against social crimes wherever they appear—and industrial exploitation is a profound social crime.

But so are racism, the denial of a people's right to self-determination, imperialism, and poverty profound social crimes—and for that matter pollution, rampant urbanization, the malignant socialization of the young, and sexual repression. We do not make "alliances"; to the contrary, we try to destroy the very barriers—be they class, cultural, institutional, or psychological—that make alliances a necessity. The preconditions for the existence of the bourgeoisie is the development of the proletariat. Capitalism as a social system presupposes the existence of *both* classes and is perpetuated by the development of both classes. We begin to undermine the premises of class rule to the degree that we foster the declassifying of the non-bourgeois classes, at least institutionally, psychologically, and culturally.

For the first time in history, the anarchic phase that opened all the great revolutions of the past can be preserved as a permanent condition by the advanced technology of our time. The anarchic institutions of that phase—the assemblies, the factory committees, the action committees—can be stabilized as the elements of a liberated society, as the elements of a new system of self-management. Will we build a movement that can defend them? Can we create an organization of affinity groups that is capable of dissolving into these revolutionary institutions? Or will we build a hierarchical, centralized, bureaucratic party that will try to dominate them, supplant them and finally destroy them?

Listen, Marxist: the organization we try to build is the kind of society our revolution will create. Either we will shed the past—in ourselves, as well as in our groups—or there will simply be no future to win.

Part II

Culture and Advanced Capitalism

Fredy Perlman

Fredy Perlman is a founder of the New Left journal *Black and Rèd* and is the author of a number of important articles and pamphlets on New Left politics. Born in Czechoslovakia, he grew up in Bolivia and then studied economics at the University of Belgrade in Yugoslavia, where he obtained a PhD.

The following essay was originally published as a *Black and Red* pamphlet, January, 1969, and has recently been republished conjointly by *Black and Red* and *Radical America*.

Perlman's aim in this essay is "to make the reproduction of the social form of capitalist activity visible within people's daily activities." He attacks the bourgeois economic thesis that capital is a "natural force," arguing that it is "a set of activities performed by people every day," "a form of daily life." The "power" of capital, he claims, "consists of the disposition of people to sell their daily activities in exchange for money, and to give up control over the products of their own activity and of the activity of earlier generations." Having unveiled the process by which wage earners reproduce the social form of capitalism, Perlman argues that the viability of capital depends only on "the disposition of people to continue to alienate their working lives." The implication is clear: Workers must stop reproducing "the capitalist form of daily life."

THE REPRODUCTION OF DAILY LIFE

The everyday practical activity of tribesmen reproduces, or perpetuates, a tribe. This reproduction is not merely physical, but social as well. Through their daily activities the tribesmen do not merely reproduce a group of human beings; they reproduce a tribe, namely a particular *social form* within which this group of human beings performs *specific* activities in a *specific* manner. The specific activities of the

Reprinted by permission of Fredy Perlman.

tribesmen are not the outcome of "natural" characteristics of the men who perform them, the way the production of honey is an outcome of the "nature" of a bee. The daily life enacted and perpetuated by the tribesman is a specific *social* response to particular material and historical conditions.

The everyday activity of slaves reproduces slavery. Through their daily activities, slaves do not merely reproduce themselves and their masters physically; they also reproduce the instruments with which the master represses them, and their own habits of submission to the master's authority. To men who live in a slave society, the master-slave relation seems like a natural and eternal relation. However, men are not born masters or slaves. Slavery is a specific social form, and men submit to it only in very particular material and historical conditions.

The practical everyday activity of wage-workers reproduces wage labor and capital. Through their daily activities, "modern" men, like tribesmen and slaves, reproduce the inhabitants, the social relations and the ideas of their society; they reproduce the *social form* of daily life. Like the tribe and the slave system, the capitalist system is neither the natural nor the final form of human society; like the earlier social forms, capitalism is a specific response to material and historical conditions.

Unlike earlier forms of social activity, everyday life in capitalist society *systematically* transforms the material conditions to which capitalism originally responded. Some of the material limits to human activity come gradually under human control. At a high level of industrialization, practical activity creates its own material conditions as well as its social form. Thus the subject of analysis is not only how practical activity in capitalist society reproduces capitalist society, but also how this activity itself eliminates the material conditions to which capitalism is a response.

Daily Life in Capitalist Society

The social form of people's regular activities under capitalism is a response to a certain material and historical situation. The material and historical conditions explain the origin of the capitalist form, but do not explain why this form continues after the initial situation disappears. A concept of "cultural lag" is not an explanation of the continuity of a social form after the disappearance of the initial conditions to which it responded. This concept is merely a name for the continuity of the social form. When the concept of "cultural lag" parades as a name for a "social force" which determines human activity, it is an obfuscation which presents the outcome of people's activities as an external force beyond their control. This is not only true of a concept like "cultural lag." Many of the terms used by Marx to describe people's activities have been raised to the status of external and even "natural" forces which determine people's activity; thus concepts like "class struggle," "production relations" and particularly "The Dialectic," play the same role in the theories of some "Marxists" that "Original Sin," "Fate" and "The Hand of Destiny" played in the theories of medieval mystifiers.

In the performance of their daily activities, the members of capitalist society simultaneously carry out two processes: they reproduce the form of their activities, and they eliminate the material conditions to which this form of activity initially responded. But they do not know they carry out these processes; their own activities are not transparent to them. They are under the illusion that their activities are responses to natural conditions beyond their control, and do not see that they are themselves authors of those conditions. The task of capitalist ideology is to maintain the veil which keeps people from seeing that their own activities reproduce the form of their daily life; the task of critical theory is to unveil the activities of daily life, to render them transparent, to make the reproduction of the social form of capitalist activity visible within people's daily activities.

Under capitalism, daily life consists of related activities which reproduce and expand the capitalist form of social activity. The sale of labor-time for a price (a wage), the embodiment of labor-time in commodities (salable goods, both tangible and intangible), the consumption of tangible and intangible commodities (such as consumer goods and spectacles)—these activities which characterize daily life under capitalism are not manifestations of "human nature," nor are they imposed on men by forces beyond their control.

If it is held that man is "by nature" an uninventive tribesman and an inventive businessman, a submissive slave and a proud craftsman, an independent hunter and a dependent wage-worker, then either man's "nature" is an empty concept, or man's "nature" depends on material and historical conditions, and is in fact a response to those conditions.

Alienation of Living Activity

In capitalist society, creative activity takes the form of commodity production, namely production of marketable goods, and the results of human activity take the form of commodities. Marketability or salability is the universal characteristic of all practical activity and all products.

The products of human activity which are necessary for survival have the form of salable goods: they are only available in exchange for money. And money is only available in exchange for commodities. If a large number of men accept the legitimacy of these conventions, if they accept the convention that commodities are a prerequisite for money, and that money is a prerequisite for survival, then they find themselves locked into a vicious circle. Since they have no commodities, their only exit from this circle is to regard themselves, or parts of themselves, as commodities. And this is, in fact, the peculiar "solution" which men impose on themselves in the face of specific material and historical conditions. They do not exchange their bodies or parts of their bodies for money. They exchange the creative content of their lives, their practical daily activity, for money.

As soon as men accept money as an equivalent for life, the sale of living activity becomes a condition for their physical and social survival. Life is exchanged for survival. Creation and production come to mean sold activity. A man's activity is "productive," useful to society, only when it is sold activity. And the man himself is a productive member of society only if the activities of his daily life are sold activities. As soon as people accept the terms of this exchange, daily activity takes the form of universal prostitution.

The sold creative power, or sold daily activity, takes the form of *labor*. Labor is a historically specific form of human activity. Labor is abstract activity which has only one property: it is marketable, it can be sold for a given quantity of money. Labor is *indifferent* activity: indifferent to the particular task performed and indifferent to the particular subject to which the task is directed. Digging, printing and carving are different activities, but all three are *labor* in capitalist society. Labor is simply "earning money." Living activity which takes the form of labor is a means to earn money. Life becomes a *means of survival*.

This ironic reversal is not the dramatic climax of an imaginative novel; it is a fact of daily life in capitalist society. Survival, namely self-preservation and reproduction, is not the means to creative practical activity, but precisely the other way around. Creative activity in the form of *labor,* namely *sold activity,* is a *painful necessity* for survival; labor is the means to self-preservation and reproduction.

The sale of living activity brings about another reversal. Through sale, the labor of an individual becomes the "property" of another, it is appropriated by another, it comes under the control of another. In other words, a person's activity becomes the activity of another, the activity of its owner; it becomes *alien* to the person who performs it. Thus one's *life,* the accomplishments of an individual in the world, the difference which his life makes in the life of humanity, are not only transformed into *labor,* a painful condition for survival; they are transformed into *alien* activity, activity performed by the buyer of that labor. In capitalist society, the architects, the engineers, the laborers, are not builders; the man who buys their labor is the builder; their projects, calculations and motions are alien to them; their living activity, their accomplishments, are his.

Academic sociologists, who take the sale of labor for granted, understand this alienation of labor as a feeling: the worker's activity "appears" alien to the worker, it "seems" to be controlled by another. However, any worker can explain to the academic sociologists that the alienation is neither a feeling nor an idea in the worker's head, but a real fact about the worker's daily life. The sold activity is *in fact* alien to the worker; his labor is *in fact* controlled by its buyer.

In exchange for his sold activity, the worker gets money, the conventionally accepted means of survival in capitalist society. With this money he can buy commodities, things, but he cannot buy back his activity. This reveals a peculiar "gap" in money as the "universal equivalent." A person can sell commodities for money, and he can buy the same commodities with money. He can sell his living activity for money, but he cannot buy his living activity for money.

The things the worker buys with his wages are first of all consumer goods which enable him to survive, to reproduce his labor-power so as to be able to continue selling it; and they are spectacles, objects for passive admiration. He consumes and admires the products of human activity passively. He does not exist in the world as an active agent who transforms it, but as a helpless, impotent spectator; he may call this state of powerless admiration "happiness," and since labor is *painful,* he may desire to be "happy," namely inactive, all his life (a condition similar to being born dead). The commodities, the spectacles, *consume him;* he uses up living energy in passive admiration; he is consumed by things. In this sense, the more he has, the less he is. (An individual can surmount this death-in-life through marginal creative activity; but the population cannot, except by abolishing the capitalist form of practical activity, by abolishing wage-labor and thus de-alienating creative activity.)

The Fetishism of Commodities

By alienating their activity and embodying it in commodities, in material receptacles of human labor, people reproduce themselves and create Capital.

From the standpoint of capitalist ideology, and particularly of academic Economics, this statement is untrue: commodities are "not the product of labor alone"; they are produced by the primordial "factors of production," Land, Labor and Capital, the capitalist Holy Trinity, and the main "factor" is obviously the hero of the piece, Capital.

The purpose of this superficial Trinity is not analysis, since analysis is not what these Experts are paid for. They are paid to obfuscate, to mask the social form of practical activity under capitalism, to veil the fact that producers reproduce themselves, their exploiters, as well as the instruments with which they're exploited. The Trinity formula does not succeed in convincing. It is obvious that *land* is no more of a commodity producer than water, air, or the sun. Furthermore *Capital,* which is at once a name for a social relation between workers and capitalists, for the instruments of production owned by a capitalist, and for the money-equivalent of his instruments and "intangibles," does not produce anything more than the ejaculations shaped into publishable form by the academic Economists. Even the instruments of production which are the capital of one capitalist are primordial "factors of production" only if one's blinders limit his view to an isolated capitalist firm, since a view of the entire economy reveals that the capital of one capitalist is the material receptacle of the labor alienated to another capitalist. However, though the Trinity formula does not convince, it does accomplish the task of obfuscation by shifting the subject of the question: instead of asking why the activity of people under capitalism takes the form of wage-labor, potential analysts of capitalist daily life are transformed into academic house-Marxists who ask whether or not labor is the only "factor of production."

Thus Economics (and capitalist ideology in general) treats land, money, and the products of labor, as things which have the power to produce, to create value, to work for their owners, to transform the world. This is what Marx called the *fetishism* which characterizes people's everyday conceptions, and which is raised to the level of dogma by Economics. For the economist, living people are *things* ("factors of production"), and things *live* (money "works," Capital "produces").

The fetish worshipper attributes the product of his own activity to his fetish. As a result, he ceases to exert his own power (the power to transform nature, the power to determine the form and content of his daily life); he exerts only those "powers" which he attributes to his fetish (the "power" to buy commodities). In other words, the fetish worshipper emasculates himself and attributes virility to his fetish.

But the fetish is a dead thing, not a living being; it has no virility. The fetish is no more than a thing for which, and through which, capitalist relations are maintained. The mysterious power of Capital, its "power" to produce, its virility, does not reside in itself, but in the fact that people alienate their creative activity, that they sell their labor to capitalists, that they materialize or reify their alienated labor in commodities. In other words, people are bought with the products of their own activity, yet they see their own activity as the activity of Capital, and their own products as the products of Capital. By attributing creative power to Capital and not to their own activity, they renounce their living activity, their everyday life, to Capital, which means that people *give themselves,* daily, to the personification of Capital, the capitalist.

By selling their labor, by alienating their activity, people daily reproduce the personifications of the dominant forms of activity under capitalism, they reproduce the wage-laborer and the capitalist. They do not merely reproduce the individuals physically, but socially as well; they reproduce individuals who are sellers of labor-power, and individuals who are owners of means of production; they reproduce the individuals as well as the specific activities, the sale as well as the ownership.

Every time people perform an activity they have not themselves defined and do not control, every time they pay for goods they produced with money they received in exchange for their alienated activity, every time they passively admire the products of their own activity as alien objects procured by their money, they give new life to Capital and annihilate their own lives.

The aim of the process is the reproduction of the relation between the worker and the capitalist. However, this is not the aim of the individual agents engaged in it. Their activities are not transparent to them; their eyes are fixed on the *fetish* that stands between the act and its result. The individual agents keep their eyes fixed on *things,* precisely those things for which capitalist relations are established. The worker as producer aims to exchange his daily labor for money-wages, he aims precisely for the thing through which his relation to the capitalist is re-established, the thing through which he reproduces himself as a wage-worker and the other as a capitalist. The worker as consumer exchanges his money for products of labor, precisely the things which the capitalist has to sell in order to realize his Capital.

The daily transformation of living activity into Capital is *mediated* by things, it is not *carried out by* the things. The fetish worshipper does not know this; for him labor and land, instruments and money, entrepreneurs and bankers, are all "factors" and "agents." When a hunter wearing an amulet downs a deer with a stone, he may consider the amulet an essential "factor" in downing the deer and even in providing the deer as an object to be downed. If he is a responsible and well-educated fetish worshipper, he will devote his attention to his amulet, nourishing it with care and admiration; in order to improve the material conditions of his life, he will improve the way he wears his fetish, not the way he throws the stone; in a bind, he may even send his amulet to "hunt" for him. His own daily activities are not transparent to him: when he eats well, he fails to see that it is his own action of throwing the stone, and not the action of the amulet, that provided his food; when he starves, he fails to see that it is his own action of worshipping the amulet instead of hunting, and not the wrath of his fetish, that causes his starvation.

The fetishism of commodities and money, the mystification of one's own daily activities, the religion of everyday life which attributes living activity to inanimate things, is not a mental caprice born in men's imaginations; it has its origin in the character of social relations under capitalism. Men do in fact relate to each other through things; the fetish is in fact the occasion for which they act collectively, and through which they reproduce their activity. But it is not the fetish that performs the activity. It is not Capital that transforms raw materials, nor Capital that produces goods. If living activity did not transform the materials, these would remain untransformed, inert, dead matter. If men were not disposed to continue selling their living activity, the impotence of Capital would be revealed; Capital would cease to exist; its last remaining potency would be the power to remind people of a bypassed form of everyday life characterized by daily universal prostitution.

The worker alienates his life in order to preserve his life. If he did not sell his living activity he would not get a wage and could not survive. However, it is not the wage that makes alienation the condition for survival. If men were collectively not disposed to sell their lives, if they were disposed to take control over their own activities, universal prostitution would not be a condition for survival. It is people's disposition to continue selling their labor, and not the *things* for which they sell it, that makes the alienation of living activity necessary for the preservation of life.

The living activity sold by the worker is bought by the capitalist. And it is only this living activity that breathes life into Capital and makes it "productive." The capitalist, an "owner" of raw materials and instruments of production, presents natural objects and products of other people's labor as his own "private property." But it is not the mysterious power of Capital that creates the capitalist's "private property"; living activity is what creates the "property," and the form of that activity is what keeps it "private."

Transformation of Living Activity into Capital

The transformation of living activity into Capital takes place *through* things, daily, but is not carried out *by* things. Things which are products of human activity *seem* to be active agents because activities and contacts are established for and through things, and because people's activities are not transparent to them; they confuse the mediating object with the cause.

In the capitalist process of production, the worker embodies or materializes his alienated living energy in an inert object by using instruments which are embodiments of other people's activity. (Sophisticated industrial instruments embody the intellectual and manual activity of countless generations of inventors, improvers and producers from all corners of the globe and from varied forms of society.) The instruments in themselves are inert objects; they are material embodiments of living activity, but are not themselves alive. The only active agent in the production process is the living laborer. He uses the products of other people's labor and infuses them with life, so to speak, but the life is his own; he is not able to resurrect the individuals who stored their living activity in his instrument. The instrument may enable him to do more during a given time period, and in this sense it may raise his productivity. But only the living labor which is able to produce can be productive.

For example, when an industrial worker runs an electric lathe, he uses products of the labor of generations of physicists, inventors, electrical engineers, lathe makers. He is obviously more productive than a craftsman who carves the same object by hand. But it is in no sense the "Capital" at the disposal of the industrial worker which is more "productive" than the "Capital" of the craftsman. If generations of intellectual and manual activity had not been embodied in the electric lathe, if the industrial worker had to invent the lathe, electricity, and the electric lathe, then it would take him numerous lifetimes to turn a single object on an electric lathe, and no amount of Capital could raise his productivity above that of the craftsman who carves the object by hand.

The notion of the "productivity of capital," and particularly the detailed measurement of that "productivity," are inventions of the "science" of Economics, that religion of capitalist daily life which uses up people's energy in the worship, admiration and flattery of the central fetish of capitalist society. Medieval colleagues of these "scientists" performed detailed measurements of the height and width of angels in Heaven, without ever asking what angels or Heaven were, and taking for granted the existence of both.

The result of the worker's sold activity is a product which does not belong to him. This product is an embodiment of his labor, a materialization of a part of his life, a receptacle which contains his living activity, but it is not his; it is as alien to him as his labor. He did not decide to make it, and when it is made he does not dispose of it. If he wants it, he has to buy it. What he has made is not simply a product with certain useful properties; for that he did not need to sell his labor to a capitalist in exchange for a wage; he need only have picked the necessary materials and the available tools, he need only have shaped the materials guided by his goals and limited by his knowledge and ability. (It is obvious that an individual can only do this marginally; men's appropriation and use of the materials and tools available to them can only take place after the overthrow of the capitalist form of activity.)

What the worker produces under capitalist conditions is a product with a very specific property, the property of salability. What his alienated activity produces is a *commodity*.

Because capitalist production is commodity production, the statement that the goal of the process is the satisfaction of human needs is false; it is a rationalization and an apology. The "satisfaction of human needs" is not the goal of the capitalist or of the worker engaged in production, nor is it a result of the process. The worker sells his labor in order to get a wage; the specific content of the labor is indifferent to him; he does not alienate his labor to a capitalist who does not give him a wage in exchange for it, no matter how many human needs this capitalist's products may satisfy. The capitalist buys labor and engages it in production in order to emerge with commodities which can be sold. He is indifferent to the specific properties of the product, just as he is indifferent to people's needs; all that interests him about the product is how much it will sell for, and all that interests him about people's needs is how much they "need" to buy and how they can be coerced, through propaganda and psychological conditioning, to "need" more. The capitalist's goal is to satisfy *his* need to reproduce and enlarge Capital, and the result of the process is the expanded reproduction of wage labor and Capital (which are not "human needs").

The commodity produced by the worker is exchanged by the capitalist for a specific quantity of money; the commodity is a *value* which is exchanged for an equivalent *value*. In other words, the living and past labor materialized in the product can exist in two distinct yet equivalent forms, in commodities and in money, or in what is common to both, *value*. This does not mean that value is labor. Value is the social *form* of reified (materialized) labor in capitalist society.

Under capitalism, social relations are not established directly;

they are established through value. Everyday activity is not exchanged directly; it is exchanged *in the form of value*. Consequently, what happens to living activity under capitalism cannot be traced by observing the activity itself, but only by following the metamorphoses of value.

When the living activity of people takes the form of *labor* (alienated activity), it acquires the property of exchangeability; it acquires the form of value. In other words, the labor can be exchanged for an "equivalent" quantity of money (wages). The deliberate alienation of living activity, which is perceived as necessary for survival by the members of capitalist society, itself reproduces the capitalist form within which alienation is necessary for survival. Because of the fact that living activity has the form of value, the products of that activity must also have the form of value: they must be exchangeable for money. This is obvious since, if the products of labor did not take the form of value, but for example the form of useful objects at the disposal of society, then they would either remain in the factory or they would be taken freely by the members of society whenever a need for them arose; in either case, the money-wages received by the workers would have no *value*, and living activity could not be *sold* for an "equivalent" quantity of money; living activity could not be alienated. Consequently, as soon as living activity takes the form of value, the products of that activity take the form of value, and the reproduction of everyday life takes place through changes or metamorphoses of value.

The capitalist sells the products of labor on a market; he exchanges them for an equivalent sum of money; he realizes a determined value. The specific magnitude of this value on a particular market is the *price* of the commodities. For the academic Economist, Price is St. Peter's key to the gates of Heaven. Like Capital itself, Price moves within a wonderful world which consists entirely of objects; the objects have human relations with each other, and are alive; they transform each other, communicate with each other; they marry and have children. And of course it is only through the grace of these intelligent, powerful and creative objects that people can be so happy in capitalist society.

In the Economist's pictorial representations of the workings of Heaven, the angels do everything and men do nothing at all; men simply enjoy what these superior beings do for them. Not only does

Capital produce and money work; other mysterious beings have similar virtues. Thus Supply, a quantity of things which are sold, and Demand, a quantity of things which are bought, together determine Price, a quantity of money; when Supply and Demand marry on a particular point of the diagram, they give birth to Equilibrium Price, which corresponds to a universal state of bliss. The activities of everyday life are played out by things, and people are reduced to things ("factors of production") during their "productive" hours, and to passive spectators of things during their "leisure time." The virtue of the Economic Scientist consists of his ability to attribute the outcome of people's everyday activities to things, and of his inability to see the living activity of people underneath the antics of the things. For the Economist, the things *through* which the activity of people is regulated under capitalism are themselves the mothers and sons, the causes and consequences of their own activity.

The magnitude of value, namely the price of a commodity, the quantity of money for which it exchanges, is not determined by things, but by the daily activities of people. Supply and demand, perfect and imperfect competition, are nothing more than social forms of products and activities in capitalist society; they have no life of their own. The fact that activity is alienated, namely that labor-time is sold for a specific sum of money, that it has a certain value, has several consequences for the magnitude of the value of the products of that labor. The value of the sold commodities must *at least* be equal to the value of the labor-time. This is obvious both from the standpoint of the individual capitalist firm, and from the standpoint of society as a whole. If the value of the commodities sold by the individual capitalist were smaller than the value of the labor he hired, then his labor expenditures alone would be larger than his earnings, and he would quickly go bankrupt. Socially, if the value of the laborers' production were smaller than the value of their consumption, then the labor force could not even reproduce itself, not to speak of a class of capitalists. However, if the value of the commodities were merely equal to the value of the labor-time expanded on them, the commodity producers would merely reproduce themselves, and their society would not be a capitalist society; their activity might still consist of commodity production, but it would not be capitalist commodity production.

For labor to create Capital, the value of the products of labor must be larger than the value of the labor. In other words, the labor force must produce a *surplus product,* a quantity of goods which it does not consume, and this surplus product must be transformed into *surplus value,* a form of value which is not appropriated by workers as wages, but by capitalists as profit. Furthermore, the value of the products of labor must be larger still, since living labor is not the only kind of labor materialized in them. In the production process, workers expend their own energy, but they also use up the stored labor of others as instruments, and they shape materials on which labor was previously expended.

This leads to the strange result that the value of the laborer's products and the value of his wage are different magnitudes, namely that the sum of money received by the capitalist when he sells the commodities produced by his hired laborers is different from the sum he pays the laborers. This difference is not explained by the fact that the used-up materials and tools must be paid for. If the value of the sold commodities were equal to the value of the living labor and the instruments, there would still be no room for capitalists. The fact is that the difference between the two magnitudes must be large enough to support a class of capitalists—not only the individuals, but also the specific activity that these individuals engage in, namely the purchase of labor. The difference between the total value of the products and the value of the labor spent on their production is surplus value, the seed of Capital.

In order to locate the origin of surplus value, it is necessary to examine why the value of the labor is smaller than the value of the commodities produced by it. The alienated activity of the worker transforms materials with the aid of instruments, and produces a certain quantity of commodities. However, when these commodities are sold and the used-up materials and instruments are paid for, the workers are not given the remaining value of their products as their wages; they are given less. In other words, during every working day, the workers perform a certain quantity of unpaid labor, *forced labor,* for which they receive no equivalent.

The performance of this unpaid labor, this forced labor, is another "condition for survival" in capitalist society. However, like alienation, this condition is not imposed by nature, but by the collective practice of people, by their everyday activities. Before the existence of unions, an individual worker accepted whatever forced labor was available, since rejection of the labor would have meant that other workers would accept the available terms of exchange, and the individual worker would receive no wage. Workers competed with each other for the wages offered by capitalists; if a worker quit because the wage was unacceptably low, an unemployed worker was willing to replace him, since for the unemployed a small wage is higher than no wage at all. This competition among workers was called "free labor" by capitalists, who made great sacrifices to maintain the freedom of workers, since it was precisely this freedom that preserved the surplus value of the capitalist and made it possible for him to accumulate Capital. It was not any worker's aim to produce more goods than he was paid for. His aim was to get a wage which was as large as possible. However, the existence of workers who got no wage at all, and whose conception of a large wage was consequently more modest than that of an employed worker, made it possible for the capitalist to hire labor at a lower wage. In fact, the existence of unemployed workers made it possible for the capitalist to pay the lowest wage that workers were willing to work for. Thus the result of the collective daily activity of the workers, each striving individually for the largest possible wage, was to lower the wages of all; the effect of the competition of each against all was that all got the smallest possible wage, and the capitalist got the largest possible surplus.

The daily practice of all annuls the goals of each. But the workers did not know that their situation was a product of their own daily behavior; their own activities were not transparent to them. To the workers it seemed that low wages were simply a natural part of life, like illness and death, and that falling wages were a natural catastrophe, like a flood or a hard winter. The critiques of socialists and the analyses of Marx, as well as an increase in industrial development which afforded more time for reflection, stripped away some of the veils and made it possible for workers to see through their activities to some extent. However, in Western Europe and the United States, workers did not get rid of the capitalist form of daily life; they formed unions. And in the different material conditions of the Soviet Union and Eastern Europe, workers (and peasants) replaced the capitalist class with a state bureaucracy that purchases alienated labor and accumulates Capital in the name of Marx.

With unions, daily life is similar to what it was before unions. In fact, it is almost the same. Daily life continues to consist of labor, of alienated activity, and of unpaid labor, or forced labor. The unionized worker no longer settles the terms of his alienation; union functionaries do this for him. The terms on which the worker's activity is alienated are no longer guided by the individual worker's need to accept what is available; they are now guided by the union bureaucrat's need to maintain his position as pimp between the sellers of labor and the buyers.

With or without unions, surplus value is neither a product of nature nor of Capital; it is created by the daily activities of people. In the performance of their daily activities, people are not only disposed to alienate these activities, they are also disposed to reproduce the conditions which force them to alienate their activities, to reproduce Capital and thus the power of Capital to purchase labor. This is not because they do not know "what the alternative is." A person who is incapacitated by chronic indigestion because he eats too much grease does not continue eating grease because he does not know what the alternative is. Either he prefers being incapacitated to giving up grease, or else it is not clear to him that his daily consumption of grease causes his incapacity. And if his doctor, preacher, teacher and politician tell him, first, that the grease is what keeps him alive, and secondly that they already do for him everything he would do if he were well, then it is not surprising that his activity is not transparent to him and that he makes no great effort to render it transparent.

The production of surplus value is a condition of survival, not for the population, but for the capitalist system. Surplus value is the portion of the value of commodities produced by labor which is not returned to the laborers. It can be expressed either in commodities or in money (just as Capital can be expressed either as a quantity of things or of money), but this does not alter the fact that it is an expression for the materialized labor which is stored in a given quantity of products. Since the products can be exchanged for an "equivalent" quantity of money, the money "stands for," or represents, the same value as the products. The money can, in turn, be exchanged for another quantity of products of "equivalent" value. The ensemble of these exchanges, which take place simultaneously during the performance of capitalist daily life, constitutes the capitalist process of circulation. It is through this process that the metamorphosis of surplus value into Capital takes place.

The portion of value which does not return to labor, namely surplus value, allows the capitalist to exist, and it also allows him to do much more than simply exist. The capitalist invests a portion of this surplus value; he hires new workers and buys new means of production; he expands his dominion. What this means is that the capitalist *accumulates new labor*, both in the form of the living labor he hires and of the past labor (paid and unpaid) which is stored in the materials and machines he buys.

The capitalist class as a whole accumulates the surplus labor of society, but this process takes place on a social scale and consequently cannot be seen if one observes only the activities of an individual capitalist. It must be remembered that the products bought by a given capitalist as instruments have the same characteristics as the products he sells. A first capitalist sells instruments to a second capitalist for a given sum of value, and only a part of this value is returned to workers as wages; the remaining part is surplus value, with which the first capitalist buys new instruments and labor. The second capitalist buys the instruments for the given value, which means that he pays for the total quantity of labor rendered to the first capitalist, the quantity of labor which was remunerated as well as the quantity performed free of charge. This means that the instruments accumulated by the second capitalist contain the unpaid labor performed for the first. The second capitalist, in turn, sells his products for a given value, and returns only a portion of this value to his laborers; he uses the remainder for new instruments and labor.

If the whole process were squeezed into a single time period, and if all the capitalists were aggregated into one, it would be seen that the value with which the capitalist acquires new instruments and labor is equal to the value of the products which he did not return to the producers. This accumulated surplus labor is *Capital*.

In terms of capitalist society as a whole, the total Capital is equal to the sum of unpaid labor performed by generations of human beings whose lives consisted of the daily alienation of their living activity. In other words Capital, in the face of which men sell their living days, is the product of the sold activity of men, and is reproduced and expanded every day a man sells another working day, every moment he decides to continue living the capitalist form of daily life.

Storage and Accumulation of Human Activity

The transformation of surplus labor into Capital is a specific historical form of a more general process, the process of industrialization, the permanent transformation of man's material environment.

Certain essential characteristics of this consequence of human activity under capitalism can be grasped by means of a simplified illustration. In an imaginary society, people spend most of their active time producing food and other necessities; only part of their time is "surplus time" in the sense that it is exempted from the production of necessities. This surplus activity may be devoted to the production of food for priests and warriors who do not themselves produce; it may be used to produce goods which are burned for sacred occasions; it may be used up in the performance of ceremonies or gymnastic exercises. In any of these cases, the material conditions of these people are not likely to change, from one generation to another, as a result of their daily activities. However, one generation of people of this imaginary society may store their surplus time instead of using it up. For example, they may spend this surplus time winding up springs. The next generation may unwind the energy stored in the springs to perform necessary tasks, or may simply use the energy of the springs to wind new springs. In either case, the stored surplus labor of the earlier generation will provide the new generation with a larger quantity of surplus working time. The new generation may also store this surplus in springs and in other receptacles. In a relatively short period, the labor stored in the springs will exceed the labor time available to any living generation; with the expenditure of relatively little energy, the people of this imaginary society will be able to harness the springs to most of their necessary tasks, and also to the task of winding new springs for coming generations. Most of the living hours which they previously spent producing necessities will now be available for activities which are not dictated by necessity but projected by the imagination.

At first glance it seems unlikely that people would devote living hours to the bizarre task of winding springs. It seems just as unlikely, even if they wound the springs, that they would store them for future generations, since the unwinding of the springs might provide, for example, a marvelous spectacle on festive days.

However, if people did not dispose of their own lives, if their working activity were not their own, if their practical activity consisted of *forced labor,* then human activity might well be harnessed to the task of winding springs, the task of storing surplus working time in material receptacles. The historical role of Capitalism, a role which was performed by people who accepted the legitimacy of others to dispose of their lives, consisted precisely of storing human activity in material receptacles by means of forced labor.

As soon as people submit to the "power" of money to buy stored labor as well as living activity, as soon as they accept the fictional "right" of money-holders to control and dispose of the stored as well as the living activity of society, they transform money into Capital and the owners of money into Capitalists.

This double alienation, the alienation of living activity in the form of wage labor, and the alienation of the activity of past generations in the form of stored labor (means of production), is not a single act which took place sometime in history. The relation between workers and capitalists is not a thing which imposed itself on society at some point in the past, once and for all. At no time did men sign a contract, or even make a verbal agreement, in which they gave up the power over their living activity, and in which they gave up the power over the living activity of all future generations on all parts of the globe.

Capital wears the mask of a natural force; it seems as solid as the earth itself; its movements appear as irreversible as tides; its crises seem as unavoidable as earthquakes and floods. Even when it is admitted that the power of Capital is created by men, this admission may merely be the occasion for the invention of an even more imposing mask, the mask of a man-made force, a Frankenstein monster, whose power inspires more awe than that of any natural force.

However, Capital is neither a natural force nor a man-made monster which was created sometime in the past and which dominated human life ever since.

The power of Capital does not reside in money, since money is a social convention which has no more "power" than men are willing to grant it; when men refuse to sell their labor, money cannot perform even the simplest tasks, because money does not "work."

Nor does the power of Capital reside in the material receptacles in which the labor of past generations is stored, since the potential energy stored in these receptacles can be liberated by the activity of living people whether or not the receptacles are Capital, namely alien "property." Without living activity, the collection of objects which constitute society's Capital would merely be a scattered heap of assorted artifacts with no life of their own, and the "owners" of Capital would merely be a scattered assortment of uncommonly uncreative people (by training) who surround themselves with bits of paper in a vain attempt to resuscitate memories of past grandeur. The only "power" of Capital resides in the daily activities of living people; this "power" consists of the disposition of people to sell their daily activities in exchange for money, and to give up control over the products of their own activity and of the activity of earlier generations.

As soon as a person sells his labor to a capitalist and accepts only a part of his product as payment for that labor, he creates conditions for the purchase and exploitation of other people. No man would willingly give his arm or his child in exchange for money; yet when a man deliberately and consciously sells his working life in order to acquire the necessities for life, he not only reproduces the conditions which continue to make the sale of his life a necessity for its preservation; he also creates conditions which make the sale of life a necessity for other people. Later generations may of course refuse to sell their working lives for the same reason that he refused to sell his arm; however each failure to refuse alienated and forced labor enlarges the stock of stored labor with which Capital can buy working lives.

In order to transform surplus labor into Capital, the capitalist has to find a way to store it in material receptacles, in new means of production, and he must hire new laborers to activate the new means of production. In other words, he must enlarge his enterprise, or start a new enterprise in a different branch of production. This presupposes or requires the existence of materials that can be shaped into new salable commodities, the existence of buyers of the new products, and the existence of people who are poor enough to be willing to sell their labor. These requirements are themselves created by capitalist activity, and capitalists recognize no limits or obstacles to their activity; the democracy of Capital demands absolute freedom.

Imperialism is not merely the "last stage" of Capitalism; it is also the first.

Anything which can be transformed into a marketable good is grist for Capital's mill, whether it lies on the capitalist's land or on the neighbor's, whether it lies above ground or under, floats on the sea or crawls on its floor; whether it is confined to other continents or other planets. All of humanity's explorations of nature, from Alchemy to Physics, are mobilized to search for new materials in which to store labor, to find new objects that someone can be taught to buy.

Buyers for old and new products are created by any and all available means, and new means are constantly discovered. "Open markets" and "open doors" are established by force and fraud. If people lack the means to buy the capitalists' products, they are hired by capitalists and are paid for producing the goods they wish to buy; if local craftsmen already produce what the capitalists have to sell, the craftsmen are ruined or bought-out; if laws or traditions ban the use of certain products, the laws and the traditions are destroyed; if people lack the objects on which to use the capitalists' products, they are taught to buy these objects; if people run out of physical or biological wants, then capitalists "satisfy" their "spiritual wants" and hire psychologists to create them; if people are so satiated with the products of capitalists that they can no longer use new objects, they are taught to buy objects and spectacles which have no use but can simply be observed and admired.

Poor people are found in pre-agrarian and agrarian societies on every continent; if they are not poor enough to be willing to sell their labor when the capitalists arrive, they are impoverished by the activities of the capitalists themselves. The lands of hunters gradually become the "private property" of "owners" who use state violence to restrict the hunters to "reservations" which do not contain enough food to keep them alive. The tools of peasants gradually become available only from the same merchant who generously lends them the money with which to buy the tools, until the peasants' "debts" are so large that they are forced to sell land which neither they nor any of their ancestors had ever bought. The buyers of craftsmen's products gradually become reduced to the merchants who market the products, until the day comes when a merchant decides to house "his craftsmen" under the same roof, and provides them with the instruments which will enable all of them to concentrate their activity on the production of the most profitable items. Independent as well as dependent hunters, peasants and craftsmen, free men as well as slaves, are transformed into hired laborers. Those who previously disposed of their own lives in the face of harsh material conditions cease to dispose of their own lives precisely when they take up the task of modifying their material conditions; those who were previously conscious creators of their own meager existence become unconscious victims of their own activity even while abolishing the meagerness of their existence. Men who were much but had little now have much but are little.

The production of new commodities, the "opening" of new markets, the creation of new workers, are not three separate activities; they are three aspects of the same activity. A new labor force is created precisely in order to produce the new commodities; the wages received by these laborers are themselves the new market; their unpaid labor is the source of new expansion. Neither natural nor cultural barriers halt the spread of Capital, the transformation of people's daily activity into alienated labor, the transformation of their surplus labor into the "private property" of capitalists. However, Capital is not a natural force; it is a set of activities performed by people every day; it is a form of daily life; its continued existence and expansion presuppose only one essential condition: the disposition of people to continue to alienate their working lives and thus reproduce the capitalist form of daily life.

André Gorz

André Gorz is a member of the editorial board of the French journal *Les Temps Modernes* and is a regular contributor to the French journal *Le Nouvel Observateur* (under the pen name, Michel Bosquet).

His best-known works are *Strategy for Labor* (1964), *Le Socialisme Difficile* (1967), and *Réforme et Révolution* (1969).

The following essay was originally prepared for delivery at a conference on modern European capitalism held under the auspices of the Gramsci Institute in Rome at the end of June, 1965. It appeared in the *International Socialist Journal,* Year 2, Number 10, August, 1945.

Gorz argues that "the development of the productive forces" in the advanced capitalist countries has produced qualitatively new changes in the socially necessary labor force, which in turn have generated new contradictions within the capitalist social system. He shows why "atomistic learning" and "atomized men" are functional to the capitalist social system and why the "despotism of capital" requires alienated labor and hierarchical work relations. Gorz assigns to a working class party the task of rendering explicit "the objective contradiction between capitalist relations of production and the character of the labor force." The concept of a working class party is, however, only briefly discussed in this essay. For a systematic analysis of this concept the reader should consult Gorz's essay, "The Way Forward," in Part III. That Gorz's essay was written in 1965 in no way diminishes the cogency of his argument since the contradictions he discusses would appear to be endemic to capitalism in its later stages and, if anything, have only sharpened since 1965.

Reprinted by permission of the *International Socialist Journal.*

CAPITALIST RELATIONS OF PRODUCTION AND THE SOCIALLY NECESSARY LABOR FORCE

During the last twenty years, the development of the productive forces in the advanced capitalist economies has led, apparently at an accelerating pace, to a qualitative change in the character of the labor force which, at every level, is socially necessary to the advance of the social process of production.

I hope, very briefly and rather schematically, to pinpoint some of the contradictions—dormant or explosive—which this current change has created for European capitalism and the way in which it attempts to disguise them, defuse them and prevent them. Put very shortly, these contradictions can be listed under the following heads:

1. The contradiction between the growing cost of production of the socially necessary labour force (principally, the increasing length and cost of the training required) and the tendency for society to try and avoid responsibility for this social cost as far as possible.

2. The contradiction between the character and level of the training required by the development of the productive forces *and* the character and level of the training required, from the management's point of view, to perpetuate hierarchic relations in the factory and, more generally, the existing relations of production in society.

3. The contradiction between the growing—latent or actual—autonomy of productive work for an increasing number of workers and its plainly social character *and* the situation of work within the factory and within capitalist society. Or, in fact, in other words, the contradiction, in a particular context, between the nature of the productive forces *and* capitalist relations of production.

I

The shortage of skilled labor is acknowledged, in all the leading European capitalist countries, as one of the chief bottlenecks holding back monopolistic expansion. In France, the Fifth Plan explicitly mentions the scarcity of skilled workers, technicians and engineers as a reason for postponing any reduction at all in working hours till 1970.

Despite the fact that there is definite short-term under-employment in several industries and increasing structural unemployment in certain regions, the French government felt, in May 1965, that no reduction of working hours was possible, on the grounds that this would mean, if it were applied without discrimination to jobs where labour was in short supply, a general falling-off in economic activity and a slowing-down of expansion.

In this way, it was unconsciously revealed that full employment and a reduction in working hours would lead to a tightening of the bottleneck in skilled labour and that, hence, campaigns on employment and working hours can only be successfully concluded if there is a massive training programme for skilled workers. But, according to French government statements, a programme of this kind is quite incompatible with the present policy of monopolistic accumulation: by 1970, the number of skilled workers leaving job training centres each year will only have gone up by about 50% over 1964. Yet this number amounts to *less than one third* of the skilled workers annually required by industry.[1]

Thus, as in other capitalist countries (though to a lesser extent than in Italy), the shortage of skilled labour leads, in France, to the continued existence of both an excessively long working week and, particularly among school-leavers, a considerable degree of unemployment and under-employment.

The wretched state of professional training cannot be directly blamed on the calculations of management. Indeed, the biggest employers are quite aware of the urgent need for extended training programmes, both bigger and better, in order to improve the "competitivity" of the national industry. The reason why investment in training programmes is nevertheless so scanty (the 4th Plan only met its targets for professional training by about 40%) is evidently that, since the development of education falls under the general head of growing collective needs produced by monopolistic expansion and since the government is bound to respect the spontaneous process of *private* accumulation (restricting itself to ad hoc measures of "cor-

---

[1] The situation is no better in West Germany: most apprentices are still trained in craft or semi-craft conditions and receive no instruction in advanced technology. One out of three learn a trade they will never use. Efforts to give apprentices at least a theoretical minimum have come to nothing, because of lack of personnel and management hostility. (Cf. Leo Bauer, *Der Stern,* 50/51, 1964).

rective programming"), it is impossible to divert the resources necessary for meeting collective needs into *public* investment.

Thus, what happens is that monopolistic expansion, separating immediate costs from long-run social costs, transfers responsibility for
meeting its more and more burdensome requirements to the collectivity
and, at the same time refuses the collectivity the necessary funds.[2]

When we come to consider education, we find that current technological developments have produced the following collective needs: a
longer period of school and university study; an increased number of
grammar-school and university graduates and post-graduates; a corresponding increase in teachers. And, in their turn, these needs can
only be satisfied if there is a very rapid growth in the number of students and the possibility of attracting them into teaching by commensurate salaries: in fine, a transfer of resources from the private
to the public sector.

Now, on most of these points, the short-term interests of the
capitalist sector are in contradiction with their long-term interests.
In the first place, the problem of finance is utterly insoluble without
a programme which attacks the "spontaneous" process of private
accumulation. The trend of private accumulation, by creating collective needs whose social costs cannot be met by the resources
permitted the State, produces dramatic bottlenecks which, eventually,
will make it very difficult for expansion to continue.

The fact that the bourgeois system of education is quite unable
to train enough actual teachers and hence enough skilled workers
and technical and scientific graduates, is due not only to the economic
structure but also to the social structure.[3] Besides the lack of buildings
and equipment, there is a process of social selection for secondary
and higher education.

What happens is that, leaving aside some marginal corrections,
the cost of socially necessary education is carried by individual
families, which amounts to leaving professional training to the private
enterprise of individuals. Except for the minimum period of education prescribed by law, the pursuit of studies is considered a minority
privilege, through which entry into "active life" is postponed by

[2] French planning is a consistently flagrant example of this; it has never been
able to subordinate private investments to social needs.

[3] In West Germany, if there are to be enough teachers in 1970, the whole
graduate outflow would have to be recruited. Cf. *Die Deutsche Bildungskata-
strophe*, Freiburg, 1964.

parental wealth. The time spent on education and professional training is consequently thought of as *"unproductive."*

This system was thrown into crisis when the development of the
productive forces began to require "a reproduction of the labour
force on a more extended scale"[4]; in other words, the acquisition by
each successive generation of students of more advanced and expensive
professional skills than those of their parents. The European capitalist
economies cannot obtain the quality and quantity of labour now
socially necessary unless they socialize at least a part of the cost,
since the number of families capable of meeting the expense on their
own account is quite inadequate.

From this arises the objective trend, somewhat fragmentary though
it is, towards including the cost of extended education in the cost
of labour power itself: in various kinds of occult ways (scholarships,
family allowances, grants, etc.) the work of learning, of extending
and transforming professional skills, is implicitly recognized as
socially necessary and productive work, through which the individual
produces *himself* according to the needs of society and hence acquires
rights over society.

These rights, which have been principally stated by student movements, chiefly comprise: 1. Right to payment for the socially necessary
work of training and study; 2. Right to the collectively necessary
equipment for carrying out this work; 3. Right to an education of
sufficient quality for a young worker to dominate technico-scientific
developments instead of being dominated and downgraded by them
and having his professional career cut short by the initial inadequacy
of his education.

These three demands, common to the French and Italian students
and to the German SDS,[5] are responses to the institutional crisis of
the bourgeois educational system and, especially of the universities,
by linking it explicitly with the crisis of capitalism. The first of these
demands, on the subject of paid study *for all,* deserves more detailed
discussion.

It is often argued, both on the right and the left, that it is pre-
mature to demand payment for *all* students for their work of self-
production while the immense majority of students still come from
middle-class backgrounds and that, instead of subsidizing the priv-

[4] Cf. A. Gorz, *Stratégie ouvrière et néo-capitalisme,* pp. 95–122, Seuil, 1964.
[5] Sozialistischer Deutscher Studentenbund.

ileged classes who send their children to university by socializing the cost, it would be more logical to increase the number of scholarships reserved for students of working-class origin, in order to thereby "democratize" higher education.

The student vanguard (UNEF in France, SDS in Germany) counters this argument in the following way:

1. We must take advantage of the necessity for capitalism to enlarge the social base of university entrance by exploiting to the full the anti-capitalist implications of this necessity. We must fight, in future, for the most advanced democratic solution, making it a principle that the State should be responsible for the cost of socially necessary education and acknowledge that all students who are accomplishing socially useful work are young workers, entitled to a public allowance.

There is no unavoidable fate which compels the student of middle-class origin to have a middle-class conception of his future professional work. Indeed, the status of the young worker, endorsed by pay, and the struggle for this status will enable the student to defend himself against the hold of his family and the temptation to think of his studies as a "private venture," foreshadowing a lucrative career.[6]

If the principle of the social and socially productive character of study is not insisted on today and if the student—and workers'—movements allow capitalism to bring in piecemeal measures to create class discrimination among students, by treating some as young workers but not others, then the social character of study and the right of every student to a public salary will have been abnegated and could only be reimposed with great difficulty.

2. Instead of guaranteeing freedom of study (and independence of the University), the scholarship system (both public and private), by acting on social criteria, tends to accentuate the dependence of students either on their parents (non-scholarship holders) or on the State or private patrons (scholarship holders).

In fact, both systems of aid—parental and governmental—tend to subordinate student work to two outside systems of priorities:

a) State scholars (and private scholars) are or will be under pressure to exhibit out of the ordinary talents, industry and discipline

[6] Cf. *Manifeste pour une Réforme Démocratique de l'Enseignement*, UNEF, 1964.

and hence unwavering ideological conformism, whereas non-scholars will usually enjoy much more freedom regarding the choice and duration of their studies.

b) Scholarships decided by social criteria allow the State to funnel students of working-class origins into frankly utilitarian studies, while non-scholars are pressured by their parents to take up the studies with the greatest "social prestige" and those associated with the traditional bourgeois elite (in France, the *Grandes Ecoles*). These can only be entered by scholars with some difficulty[7-8], whereas others meet nothing but encouragement. The fact that there are more scholarships does not mean that there is less class discrimination at the University.

c) While scholars are dependent on the State—which gets rights over them by giving them grants, which it could not get by a system of salaries for all—non-scholars are dependent on their parents' goodwill and are effectively wards even after they have reached their legal maturity (which most of them have).[9]

Thus, the demand that all students should be paid, according to university rather than class criteria, as urged by the UNEF since 1964, is a consciously "synthetic" response to the crisis in bourgeois education and the piecemeal measures proposed by the capitalist State. Student unionism encompasses in this demand the following other points:

i) It demonstrates how only a socialization of the costs of study can liberate the students from bourgeois criteria of education, of culture, of careers and of the "elite"; from capitalist criteria of the utility and profitability of study; from the various pressures brought to bear by parents, State and industry; from the shortage of time and of resources.

It further demonstrates that this alone guarantees freedom of work and of intellectual, cultural and professional formation and hence the independence of the University itself. And that this alone guarantees, by removing discriminations of entrance, the end of the divorce between theory and practice, between science and technology and between elite and utilitarian culture.

[7] In West Germany, according to their "mental maturity" and "understanding of the world around them".

[8] Cf. Pierre Bourdieu & André Passeron, *Les Héritiers,* Minuit, 1965.

[9] A recent survey in France showed that students had to provide 24% of their income through outside work.

ii) It situates the body of students in society as young workers and thus induces them to understand the meaning of their demands for independence and intellectual and cultural development in the actual historical situation—free from ideological and mercenary degradation —and become aware of their contradictions with the needs of monopoly capital and of the impossibility of any satisfaction except through alliance with the working class.

Or, put in another way, student unionism is attempting to carry out the same struggle, for the emancipation and valorization of labour power, in the field of education, which the working class is waging in the field of production. But, as far as can be seen, this struggle can only be and remain socialist and avoid the pitfalls of subservient reformism and corporative action, if it is prolonged and sustained by the action of a strong workers' and revolutionary movement.[10] Left to itself, student unionism, however socialist its ideas and goals, cannot transcend the limits of corporativism; it is fatally restricted if the working class party does not take up its demands and insert them into an overall social struggle, saving the student movement from its peculiar mythologies and idiosyncracies.[11]

II

I have concentrated on showing how the increasing cost and time required to produce the socially necessary labour force has thrown the whole system of bourgeois education into crisis. The development of the productive forces provides an objective basis for the need to democratize higher education, to pay public allowances to those engaged in study and professional training and to reform the Universities root-and-branch.

This reform does not only involve university entrance and payment of students. The objective necessity to increase university entrance from the working class also implies the downfall and death of the traditional methods and content of university teaching, which has been looked on up till now as training the "elite" of

[10] Cf. Marc Kravets, *Naissance d'un syndicalisme étudiant, Les Temps Modernes,* February, 1964.

[11] Cf. Antoine Griset & Marc Kravets, *Critique du syndicalisme étudiant, Les Temps Modernes,* May, 1965.

bourgeois society. In the past, Universities have provided a bogus mixture of high-table wit, bookworming and *belle-lettrisme,* designed to produce "superior minds," above (or, at least, apart from) reality, whose job is to supply an ideological justification for current social practice; but industry expects the universities to produce swarms of skilled workers, who can be put directly to work in production, applied research and management. However, the monopolies are perfectly well aware of the danger for the existing order of a general upgrading of educational standards. For, once a certain level of culture has been reached, highly skilled workers feel the vital need for professional, intellectual and existential independence as much as workers in old-fashioned industry feel or felt the gnawing need for material satisfaction.

It is for this reason that the monopolies, although they are constantly clamouring for education "more in touch with real life," attempt to cut back the quality of higher education and the number of students enjoying it. For example, the chairman of Kodak-Pathé recently remarked: "It is a bad thing to be in a country where there is a surplus of highly skilled personnel, since, should a crisis arise, young people who have spent a long time in studying but without being able to get a suitable post at the end, are not merely a pointblank loss, from the point of view of wasted investment, but also a threat to the established order." [12] The most extraordinary thing in this particular line of management argument is not only the expressed wish to restrict the number of "highly skilled personnel" to the number of "suitable posts . . . should a crisis arise," but also the utilitarian concept of culture (which is a "pointblank loss" if it does not lead to a "suitable post") and the cultural malthusianism motivated by fright at the thought that too much and too widespread culture might imperil "the established order" or, as we might choose to put it, the capitalist relations of production and the hierarchic relations of the firm.

In fine, the problem for big management is to harmonize two contradictory necessities: the necessity of developing human capabilities, imposed by modern processes of production and the—political —necessity of ensuring that this kind of development of capabilities

[12] From *Humanisme et Entreprise,* employers' propaganda journal for students.

does not bring in its wake any augmentation of the independence of the individual, provoking him to challenge the present division of social labour and distribution of power.

A solution is sought for—as we can see quite clearly in the French Fouchet reform—by backing specialization: educational reforms aim to set up, in contrast with traditional elite education, a stunted, utilitarian alternative, heavily biassed towards technology. Frightened that an "over-rich" fostering of talents could lead to non-acceptance of discipline to work routines, an effort is made at initial mutilation: the end-product must be competent, but blinkered; zestful but docile; intelligent as far as his immediate functions are concerned, but stupid about everything else.

The cry is for specialists, for people who are not able to situate their knowledge in the general movement of science or their limited activity in the overall process of social praxis. It is with this in mind that the Fouchet reform splits education into two: the great majority of *lycée* and college students will receive a technical education, completely shorn of any advanced theoretical studies, such as philosophy, and—conversely—the teaching of philosophy, unaccompanied by any mathematics or science, will be nothing but an intellectual pastime; the point seems to be to deny access by people with a philosophical training to any jobs in which their critical turn of mind might endanger the established order. In other words, higher professional training will be separated off from authentic culture—by which I mean familiarity with the methods and proceedings of creative activity in the sciences and technology—and "culture" will be cut off from social praxis and knowledge of productive work.[13] It ought to be pointed out that this choice really bears no relation to technological advance: indeed, it actually militates against it. It is completely untrue that modern technology demands specialization: quite the reverse. It demands a basic "polyvalent" education, comprising not a fragmentary, pre-digested and specialized knowledge, but an initiation—or, put more precisely, a faculty of self-initiation—into methods of scientifico-technological research and discovery. There is no purpose in cramming the student with immediately useful information and set-pieces; the important thing is to teach

---

[13] Cf. H. Tanaka, *L'Enseignement au Japon, Recherches Internationales,* 28, 1961. Also A. Minucci, *Sul rapporto classe operaia-società, Critica Marxista,* 1, 1965.

him to learn, to inquire and to develop his knowledge in an independent way, to dominate a whole field of activity and knowledge conceptually and synthetically in its connexions with adjacent fields. Only an education of this kind would enable the worker to maintain his standard of skills or, put another way, to master innovations which, given the rapid turnover of scientific and technological developments, will threaten him—more than once in his productive life—with the redundancy of his store of knowledge and force him completely to overhaul and renovate his learning in order to avoid its depreciation and, in the last resort, his own loss of employment.

Hence, objectively technological development demands a solid and polyvalent education encompassing both methodology and theory and stimulating independence, which presupposes a total recasting of educational curricula and pedagogical methods.[14] Management is against this not just because of the social cost of this kind of education—the rapid production of specialists is less burdensome and their loss of skills has to be carried by themselves—but also because specialists, pre-deprived of any true professional independence, will be more tame and ready to submit to the current division of labour and distribution of power.

It is instructive to examine the precedent of the United States in order to get some estimate of the chances of success of this education policy espoused by monopoly capitalism. The remedies adopted by European capitalism to cope with the crisis in bourgeois education are in many ways parallel to those essayed during the thirties in America, whose rotten fruits William H. Whyte described ten years ago—from a bourgeois humanist point of view, it must be admitted—in *The Organization Man*. He recounted there how theoretical studies, particularly in the natural sciences, were allowed to fall into discredit and decadence, while simultaneously, with monopoly encouragement, specialized studies (management, public relations, marketing, etc.) flourished handsomely, their curricula rigidly utilitarian and adjusted to the immediate needs of industry, attracting the great majority of students and teaching them "know-how" rather than a coherent complex of knowledge.

The advantages of this system for big business seemed astonishing: secondary schools kept piping in a labour force which was not only

---

[14] Jean-Pierre Milbergue, *La Signification politique des rapports pédagogiques, Les Temps Modernes,* April 1965.

directly utilizable but actually pre-conditioned and pre-integrated in the sense that the education given encouraged careerist ambition and discouraged habits of criticism. While the traditional universities of Europe stick to their old academic and mandarin ways, they too are leaving the field open to free enterprise in education, to private specialized schools, mushrooming everywhere, which give no proper technico-scientific or practico-theoretic culture but only formulae for making a successful career.

Yet, at the time when Whyte published his book, the educational system he denounced was already virtually over and done with. A report compiled by Allen Dulles, head of the CIA, on the comparative number of scientists and researchers in the USA and the Soviet Union, witnessed to Americans that they were in danger of building up a time-lag and provoked the government into taking measures to develop theoretical studies right across the board, through massive injections of funds and a vast programme of scholarships.

The fruits of this development programme are already visible: over-crowded universities, dispensing mass instruction to an unprecedented number of students, cut off from overloaded staff, seething in revolt, often with staff backing, protesting the lack of proper teaching; demands for a voice in creating curricula, in organizing courses, in fixing work methods and conditions; protests against authoritarian university administration; protests, more or less explicit, against the whole policy of American imperialism and the American way of life.

The general trend of this revolt, rather reminiscent of others in Italy (architectural students, for instance) or in France (at the Sorbonne or the IDES), is that, once a certain level of education has been reached, it becomes out of the question to try and limit the need for independence: it is impossible to teach knowledge and ignorance in the same breath, without those taught finally grasping how they are being stunted; it is impossible to contain the independence inherent in cognitive praxis within tight limits, even by early specialization. In fine, it is impossible, in the long run, to bottle up independence. Monopoly capital dreams of a particular kind of specialized technician, recognizable by the co-existence in one and the same person of zest for his job and indifference about its purpose, professional enterprise and social submission, power and responsibility over technical questions and impotence and irresponsibility over questions of economic and social management. It is the task of the workers' movement to ensure that this dream really does prove a delusion, to bring the contradictions involved into the daylight and to counter the repressive and mystifying ideology of organization capitalism with the possibility, through struggle on every level, of a total alternative and a reconquest of man.

III

During the era of Taylorism, capitalist relations of production found their natural extension and confirmation in work relations. For the vast majority of workers, labour power was merely a quantity of physiological energy, undifferentiatable between workers, and without any value in itself: it had value only when combined and utilized outside itself with other quantities of human energy. In other words, it was valorized only by management *fiat* and by being alienated into a product and production whose ultimate finality remained foreign to the worker. The worker was supposed to "work", not "think"; other people had the job of thinking his work, and that of others, for him. In short, his dehumanization and the alienation of his labour found their natural basis in the division of labour and the process of production.

But, for a growing number of workers, this objective basis for the dehumanization of the worker by capital—and for its single possible form of negation: violent suppression of unhumanizable labour—is tending to disappear.[15] I am not claiming that new techniques, such as automation, are producing a new working class and a generally greater amount of individual autonomy at work. The process is, in fact, very much more complex: previous individual grades of skill are being rendered obsolete—a new kind of semi-skilled worker is ousting the old, who is required on account of his technical responsibilities to have some qualification and, most important, a general level of education higher than that immediately required by his tasks. His tasks, though they require a lesser degree of individual qualification and direct initiative, demand a much

[15] Cf. Gorz, *op. cit.,* Minucci, *op. cit.*

broader spectrum of knowledge and involve control over a much more extensive section of the production process.[16] The personal involvement of a worker supervising a multiple semi-automatic lathe, for instance, is less than that of a worker using a precision lathe, but his position in the production process is less restricted and he can gain a much more extensive understanding of it. The same thing applies to a worker supervising an automated line or a technician in a refinery or a petro-chemical or atomic energy plant, etc. Individual skill and job qualification are supplanted by more directly social functions and qualifications. Qualifications are no longer centred round man's relations with inorganic nature but round social collaboration with others—that is to say, harmonious group action, collective team work, etc. Briefly, the labor force is socially qualified as a whole[17]; relations are no longer the solitary relations of the individual worker with his material, mediated by his tools, but relations of groups of workers to the industrial process, emerging from the conscious combination of human actions.[18] Production no longer requires combination imposed from outside, by a third party—the combination of labour as a quantity of raw physiological energy; more and more, it is coming to require the reciprocal combination of those who actually accomplish production—in other words, cooperation within work-teams, in which traditional divisions between worker, technician and engineer have disappeared.

Additionally, the natural basis of the industrial hierarchy tends to be dissolved in a number of advanced sectors and the whole traditional system of wages and grades, based on individual work, productivity and qualification, is thrown into crisis. The technical or scientific worker in automated industry is consigned to permanent under-employment as far as his individual tasks go, and hence, as far as his level of consciousness allows, he tends to transfer his interest from his purely individual work to his social function and from his purely individual role in production to the social significance and purposes of management.

Furthermore, in scientific industries stimulated by automation (electronics, heavy machinery, research, etc.) the work itself takes

[16] Cf. Pierre Rolle, *Automation, ISJ,* April 1965.
[17] Cf. Gorz, *op. cit.,* Minucci, *op. cit.*
[18] K. Marx, *Grundrisse der Kritik der politischen Ökonomie,* Dietz, Berlin, 1953, pp. 593–4.

on a potentially—or even actually—creative character and there is
a latent conflict between the teams of scientific and technical workers,
conscious of their abilities and eager to valorize their labour power,
and the capitalist management of the firm, whose policy subordinates
—and often sacrifices—this valorization to criteria of short or long-
run profitability. In France, an interesting example of this was the
Neyrpic affair and, even more striking, the vanguard role played by
the employees at Bull-Gambetta (technicians and engineers) who
drew attention to management errors and foresaw the 1964 crisis
more than a year in advance, and whose struggle ascended from the
issue of the firm to general political issues, denunciation of the
management and demands for nationalization and the socialization of
research, since the development of the productive forces and the
valorization of "human capital" had proved impossible under the
system of capital management.*

In a key group of industries, scientific and economic pacesetters,
the character of work—either on account of its social or its creative aspects—increasingly tends to enter into contradiction with
capitalist management criteria and decision-making powers. It is
more or less openly felt that tasks should be re-organized and re-
shuffled, that the command system should be re-cast and workers'
control over the process of production be introduced, and that all this
is quite within the bounds of possibility. And, at the same stroke,
this very possibility demonstrates the true despotism of capital: it
reveals that the alienation and mutilation of the worker has never
been the necessary conclusion of the technology employed, but that
capitalism actually needs shattered and atomized men and that, as
long as it sustains the old system of traditional centralized and military
hierarchies, arbitrarily limiting tasks and responsibilities even against
the interests of greater productivity, it needs them, above all, in
order to perpetuate its domination over men, not only as workers,
but also as consumers and citizens. The natural basis of enslavement
and dehumanization is replaced by deliberate techniques, gleaming
with scientific chrome and dubbed "human engineering," "public
relations," "management psychology" and so on. Oppression through
the necessary division of labour is replaced, wherever it is on the way
out, by indoctrination, ideological repression, smooth grimness and

* Still more striking examples are provided by the May, 1968, events in
France—*Ed.*

"cultural" conditioning, which starts at school, in the content and method of teaching, and which is prolonged and projected into public life through the degradation and diversion of genuine cultural needs in order to benefit needs (and merchandise) of personal consumption, comfort and escape.

It would be unrealistic to imagine that the objective contradiction between capitalist relations of production and the character of the labour force—its cost of production and reproduction, its mode of training and employment—will necessarily become conscious and explode. In reality, this contradiction is, as a rule, disguised in advanced capitalist societies, able to engage an enormous armoury of repression, conditioning and stupefaction; it will only explode at special moments of crisis. The importance of political and *cultural* work by the working class party must be kept in the forefront, to make these contradictions explicit and to weld together the scientific and technical neo-proletariat, the students and the teachers with the working class, by demonstrating the character and prospects of the solutions to which their own specific problems will lead them, while taking the greatest care to respect them in their specificity and relative independence. This respect need not mean a nurturing of corporative or sectional interests. Quite the reverse:

"A socialist party can only successfully pose its candidature to the direction of a society, when it is the bearer of *universal values,* which are recognized and experienced as such by a majority of all whose humanity is denied and dislocated by the social order.

These social forces must find their truth in a socialist party for it to be capable of victory over the universe of capitalism. The task of the party is to unite them in *a new historical bloc.* The concept of a bloc is radically different from that of a coalition, which remains the normal type of political combination on the Left today. In such heterogeneous coalitions, with their atmosphere of a promiscuous populism . . . a process of dilution occurs, in which the political programme of the party—catering as it does for every different group in the coalition—reduces the aspirations and demands of each *downwards* to the lowest common denominator on which they can all agree, in a kind of *descending integration.* This is what makes these parties, despite appearances, inert and conservative organizations, incapable of changing their societies in any significant way.

The structure of a historical bloc, as Gramsci conceived it, is diametrically opposed to this system of alliances. The unity of the bloc rests on an *ascending integration,* which fuses together different hopes and demands on a higher level. Partial and sectional demands are inserted into a coherent and articulated vision of the world, which confers on them a common meaning and goal. The bloc is thus a synthesis of the aspirations and identities of different groups in a global project which exceeds them all. Its critique of capitalism is the truth of each particular claim . . . The vocation of the hegemonic party is thus manifestly universal: it is the dynamic unity of all the forces and ideals in the society which are premonitions of a new human order." [19]

[19] Perry Anderson, *Problems of Socialist Strategy, Towards Socialism,* Fontana & New Left Review, 1965. Cf. also Minucci, *op. cit.*

Margaret Benston

Margaret Benston is a member of the Chemistry Department faculty at Simon Fraser University.

The following essay originally appeared in *Monthly Review*, Vol. 21, No. 4, September, 1969. Since its publication it has stirred wide controversy in radical political circles. For further discussion of the issues raised by Miss Benston, the reader should consult Mickey and John Rowntree's article "More on the Political Economy of Women's Liberation," *Monthly Review*, Vol. 21, No. 8, January, 1970, and the exchange between L. Hornstra and Bobbye Ortiz on the nuclear family in *Monthly Review*, Vol. 22, No. 1, May, 1970.

Miss Benston argues that until women's special relation to the means of production is defined, no analysis of "the women's question" will fit into a class analysis of society. The bulk of her essay is devoted to defining that special relation and to explicating the material basis of the inferior status of women under neo-capitalism. She argues that changing that special relation is a necessary condition for changing the personal and psychological factors of women's oppression, which, she maintains, are parasitic upon women's special relation to the means of production. This special relation is defined tentatively as "the production of simple use-values in those activities associated with the home and family." Since the production of use-values remains outside the money economy, women are not just discriminated against, but are also exploited. Having explained the material basis for women's oppression under neo-capitalism, Miss Benston discusses some of the prerequisites of women's liberation, most notably the industrialization of housework. She argues that work in the home should not be a matter of private production and the responsibility of women. She also analyzes the function of the nuclear family, arguing that it is not primarily a source of emotional satisfaction, as bourgeois social scientists claim, but rather a production unit for housework and child-rearing.

Reprinted by permission of *Monthly Review*.

THE POLITICAL ECONOMY
OF WOMEN'S LIBERATION

The position of women rests, as everything in our complex society, on an economic base.
                    —*Eleanor Marx and Edward Aveling*

The "woman question" is generally ignored in analyses of the class structure of society. This is so because, on the one hand, classes are generally defined by their relation to the means of production and, on the other hand, women are not supposed to have any unique relation to the means of production. The category seems instead to cut across all classes; one speaks of working-class women, middle-class women, etc. The status of women is clearly inferior to that of men,*[1] but analysis of this condition usually falls into discussing socialization, psychology, interpersonal relations, or the role of marriage as a social institution.[2] Are these, however, the primary factors? In arguing that the roots of the secondary status of women are in fact economic, it can be shown that women as a group do indeed have a definite relation to the means of production and that this is different from that of men. The personal and psychological factors then follow from this special relation to production, and a change in the latter will be a necessary (but not sufficient) condition for changing the former.[3] If this special relation of women to production is accepted, the analysis of the situation of women fits naturally into a class analysis of society.

The starting point for discussion of classes in a capitalist society is the distinction between those who own the means of production and those who sell their labor power for a wage. As Ernest Mandel says:

> The proletarian condition is, in a nutshell, the lack of access to the means of production or means of subsistence which, in a society of generalized commodity production, forces the proletarian to sell his labor power. In exchange for this labor power he receives a wage which then enables him to acquire the means of consumption necessary for satisfying his own needs and those of his family.

* Notes will be found at the end of the article.

This is the structural definition of wage earner, the proletarian. From it necessarily flows a certain relationship to his work, to the products of his work, and to his overall situation in society, which can be summarized by the catchword alienation. But there does not follow from this structural definition any necessary conclusions as to the level of his consumption . . . the extent of his needs, or the degree to which he can satisfy them.[4]

We lack a corresponding structural definition of women. What is needed first is not a complete examination of the symptoms of the second status of women, but instead a statement of the material conditions in capitalist (and other) societies which define the group "women." Upon these conditions are built the specific superstructures which we know. An interesting passage from Mandel points the way to such a definition:

The commodity . . . is a product created to be exchanged on the market, as opposed to one which has been made for direct consumption. *Every commodity must have both a use-value and an exchange-value.*

It must have a use-value or else nobody would buy it. . . . A commodity without a use-value to anyone would consequently be unsalable, would constitute useless production, would have no exchange-value precisely because it had no use-value.

On the other hand, every product which has use-value does not necessarily have exchange-value. It has an exchange-value only to the extent that the society itself, in which the commodity is produced, is founded on exchange, is a society where exchange is a common practice. . . .

In capitalist society, commodity production, the production of exchange-values, has reached its greatest development. It is the first society in human history where the major part of production consists of commodities. It is not true, however, that all production under capitalism is commodity production. Two classes of products still remain simple use-value.

The first group consists of all things produced by the peasantry for its own consumption, everything directly consumed on the farms where it is produced. . . .

The second group of products in capitalist society which are not commodities but remain simple use-value consists of all things produced in the home. Despite the fact that considerable human labor goes into this type of household production, it still remains a production of use-values and not of commodities. Every time a soup is made or a button sewn on a garment, it constitutes production, but it is not production for the market.

The appearance of commodity production and its subsequent regularization and generalization have radically transformed the way men labor and how they organize society.[5]

What Mandel may not have noticed is that his last paragraph is precisely correct. The appearance of commodity production has indeed transformed the way that *men* labor. As he points out, most household labor in capitalist society (and in the existing socialist societies, for that matter) remains in the pre-market stage. This is the work which is reserved for women and it is in this fact that we can find the basis for a definition of women.

In sheer quantity, household labor, including child care, constitutes a huge amount of socially necessary production. Nevertheless, in a society based on commodity production, it is not usually considered "real work" since it is outside of trade and the market place. It is pre-capitalist in a very real sense. This assignment of household work as the function of a special category "women" means that this group *does* stand in a different relation to production than the group "men." We will tentatively define women, then, as that group of people who are responsible for the production of simple use-values in those activities associated with the home and family.

Since men carry no responsibility for such production, the difference between the two groups lies here. Notice that women are not excluded from commodity production. Their participation in wage labor occurs but, as a group, they have no structural responsibility in this area and such participation is ordinarily regarded as transient. Men, on the other hand, are responsible for commodity production; they are not, in principle, given any role in household labor. For example, when they do participate in household production, it is regarded as more than simply exceptional; it is demoralizing, emasculating, even harmful to health. (A story on the front page of the *Vancouver Sun* in January 1969 reported that men in Britain were having their health endangered because they had to do too much housework!)

The material basis for the inferior status of women is to be found in just this definition of women. In a society in which money determines value, women are a group who work outside the money economy. Their work is not worth money, is therefore valueless, is therefore not even real work. And women themselves, who do this valueless work, can hardly be expected to be worth as much as men, who work for money. In structural terms, the closest thing to the condition of women is the condition of others who are or were also outside of commodity production, i.e., serfs and peasants.

In her recent paper on women, Juliet Mitchell introduces the subject as follows: "In advanced industrial society, women's work is only marginal to the total economy. Yet it is through work that man changes natural conditions and thereby produces society. Until there is a revolution in production, the labor situation will prescribe women's situation within the world of men." [6] The statement of the marginality of women's work is an unanalyzed recognition that the work women do is *different* from the work that men do. Such work is not marginal, however; it is just not wage labor and so is not counted. She even says later in the same article, "Domestic labor, even today, is enormous if quantified in terms of productive labor." She gives some figures to illustrate: In Sweden, 2,340 million hours a year are spent by women in housework compared with 1,290 million hours spent by women in industry. And the Chase Manhattan Bank estimates a woman's overall work week at 99.6 hours.

However, Mitchell gives little emphasis to the basic economic factors (in fact she condemns most Marxists for being "overly economist") and moves on hastily to superstructural factors, because she notices that "the advent of industrialization has not so far freed women." What she fails to see is that no society has thus far industrialized housework. Engels points out that the "first premise for the emancipation of women is the reintroduction of the entire female sex into public industry. . . . And this has become possible not only as a result of modern large-scale industry, which not only permits the participation of women in production in large numbers, but actually calls for it and, moreover, strives to convert private domestic work also into a public industry." [7] And later in the same passage: "Here we see already that the emancipation of women and their equality with men are impossible and must remain so as long as women are excluded from socially productive work and restricted to housework, which is private." What Mitchell has not taken into account is that the problem is not simply one of getting women into *existing* industrial production but the more complex one of converting private production of household work into public production.

For most North Americans, domestic work as "public production" brings immediate images of Brave New World or of a vast institution —a cross between a home for orphans and an army barracks—where we would all be forced to live. For this reason, it is probably just as well to outline here, schematically and simplistically, the nature of industrialization.

A pre-industrial production unit is one in which production is small-scale and reduplicative; i.e., there are a great number of little units, each complete and just like all the others. Ordinarily such production units are in some way kin-based and they are multi-purpose, fulfilling religious, recreational, educational, and sexual functions along with the economic function. In such a situation, desirable attributes of an individual, those which give prestige, are judged by more than purely economic criteria: for example, among approved character traits are proper behavior to kin or readiness to fulfill obligations.

Such production is originally not for exchange. But if exchange of commodities becomes important enough, then increased efficiency of production becomes necessary. Such efficiency is provided by the transition to industrialized production which involves the elimination of the kin-based production unit. A large-scale, non-reduplicative production unit is substituted which has only one function, the economic one, and where prestige or status is attained by economic skills. Production is rationalized, made vastly more efficient, and becomes more and more public—part of an integrated social network. An enormous expansion of man's productive potential takes place. Under capitalism such social productive forces are utilized almost exclusively for private profit. These can be thought of as *capitalized* forms of production.

If we apply the above to housework and child rearing, it is evident that each family, each household, constitutes an individual production unit, a pre-industrial entity, in the same way that peasant farmers or cottage weavers constitute pre-industrial production units. The main features are clear, with the reduplicative, kin-based, private nature of the work being the most important. (It is interesting to notice the other features: the multipurpose functions of the family, the fact that desirable attributes for women do not center on economic prowess, etc.) The rationalization of production effected by a transition to large-scale production has not taken place in this area.

Industrialization is, in itself, a great force for human good; exploitation and dehumanization go with capitalism and not necessarily with industrialization. To advocate the conversion of private domestic labor into a public industry under capitalism is quite a different thing from advocating such conversion in a socialist society. In the latter case the forces of production would operate for human welfare, not private profit, and the result should be liberation, not dehumanization. In this case we can speak of *socialized* forms of production.

These definitions are not meant to be technical but rather to differentiate between two important aspects of industrialization. Thus the fear of the barracks-like result of introducing housekeeping into the public economy is most realistic under capitalism. With socialized production and the removal of the profit motive and its attendant alienated labor, there is no reason why, *in an industrialized society,* industrialization of housework should not result in better production, i.e., better food, more comfortable surroundings, more intelligent and loving child-care, etc., than in the present nuclear family.

The argument is often advanced that, under neocapitalism, the work in the home has been much reduced. Even if this is true, it is not structurally relevant. Except for the very rich, who can hire someone to do it, there is for most women, an irreducible minimum of necessary labor involved in caring for home, husband, and children. For a married woman without children this irreducible minimum of work probably takes fifteen to twenty hours a week; for a woman with small children the minimum is probably seventy or eighty hours a week.[8] (There is some resistance to regarding child-rearing as a job. That labor is involved, i.e., the production of use-value, can be clearly seen when exchange-value is also involved—when the work is done by baby sitters, nurses, child-care centers, or teachers. An economist has already pointed out the paradox that if a man marries his housekeeper, he reduces the national income, since the money he gives her is no longer counted as wages.) The reduction of housework to the minimums given is also expensive; for low-income families more labor is required. In any case, household work remains structurally the same —a matter of private production.

One function of the family, the one taught to us in school and the one which is popularly accepted, is the satisfaction of emotional needs: the needs for closeness, community, and warm secure relationships. This society provides few other ways of satisfying such needs; for example, work relationships or friendships are not expected to be nearly as important as a man-woman-with-children relationship. Even other ties of kinship are increasingly secondary. This function of the family is important in stabilizing it so that it can fulfill the second, purely economic, function discussed above. The wage earner, the husband-father, whose earnings support himself, also "pays for" the labor done by the mother-wife and supports the children. The wages of a man buy the labor of two people. The crucial importance of this second function of the family can be seen when the family unit breaks down in divorce. The continuation of the economic function is the major concern where children are involved; the man must continue to pay for the labor of the woman. His wage is very often insufficient to enable him to support a second family. In this case his emotional needs are sacrificed to the necessity to support his ex-wife and children. That is, when there is a conflict the economic function of the family very often takes precedence over the emotional one. And this in a society which teaches that the major function of the family is the satisfaction of emotional needs.[9]

As an economic unit, the nuclear family is a valuable stabilizing force in capitalist society. Since the production which is done in the home is paid for by the husband-father's earnings, his ability to withhold his labor from the market is much reduced. Even his flexibility in changing jobs is limited. The woman, denied an active place in the market, has little control over the conditions that govern her life. Her economic dependence is reflected in emotional dependence, passivity, and other "typical" female personality traits. She is conservative, fearful, supportive of the status quo.

Furthermore, the structure of this family is such that it is an ideal consumption unit. But this fact, which is widely noted in Women's Liberation literature, should not be taken to mean that this is its primary function. If the above analysis is correct, the family should be seen primarily as a production unit for housework and child-rearing. *Everyone* in capitalist society is a consumer; the structure of the family simply means that it is particularly well suited to encourage consumption. Women in particular *are* good consumers; this follows naturally from their responsibility for matters in the home. Also, the inferior status of women, their general lack of a strong sense of worth and identity, make them more exploitable than men and hence better consumers.

The history of women in the industrialized sector of the economy has depended simply on the labor needs of that sector. Women function as a massive reserve army of labor. When labor is scarce (early industrialization, the two world wars, etc.) then women form an important part of the labor force. When there is less demand for labor (as now under neocapitalism) women become a surplus labor force— but one for which their husbands and not society are economically responsible. The "cult of the home" makes its reappearance during times of labor surplus and is used to channel women out of the market economy. This is relatively easy since the pervading ideology ensures that no one, man or woman, takes women's participation in the labor force very seriously. Women's real work, we are taught, is in the home; this holds whether or not they are married, single, or the heads of households.

At all times household work is the responsibility of women. When they are working outside the home they must somehow manage to get both outside job and housework done (or they supervise a substitute for the housework). Women, particularly married women with children, who work outside the home simply do two jobs; their participation in the labor force is only allowed if they continue to fulfill their first responsibility in the home. This is particularly evident in countries like Russia and those in Eastern Europe where expanded opportunities for women in the labor force have not brought about a corresponding expansion in their liberty. Equal access to jobs outside the home, while one of the preconditions for women's liberation, will not in itself be sufficient to give equality for women; as long as work in the home remains a matter of private production and is the responsibility of women, they will simply carry a double work-load.

A second prerequisite for women's liberation which follows from the above analysis is the conversion of the work now done in the home as private production into work to be done in the public economy.[10] To be more specific, this means that child-rearing should no longer be the responsibility solely of the parents. Society must begin to take responsibility for children; the economic dependence of women and children on the husband-father must be ended. The other work that goes on in the home must also be changed—communal eating places and laundries for example. When such work is moved into the public sector, then the material basis for discrimination against women will be gone.

These are only preconditions. The idea of the inferior status of women is deeply rooted in the society and will take a great deal of effort to eradicate. But once the structures which produce and support that idea are changed then, and only then, can we hope to make progress. It is possible, for example, that a change to communal eating places would simply mean that women are moved from a home kitchen to a communal one. This *would* be an advance, to be sure, particularly in a socialist society where work would not have the inherently exploitative nature it does now. Once women are freed from private production in the home, it will probably be very difficult to maintain for any long period of time a rigid definition of jobs by sex. This illustrates the interrelation between the two preconditions given above: true equality in job opportunity is probably impossible without freedom from housework, and the industrialization of housework is unlikely unless women are leaving the home for jobs.

The changes in production necessary to get women out of the home might seem to be, in theory, possible under capitalism. One of the sources of women's liberation movements may be the fact that alternative capitalized forms of home production now exist. Day care is available, even if inadequate and perhaps expensive; convenience foods, home delivery of meals, and take-out meals are widespread; laundries and cleaners offer bulk rates. However, cost usually prohibits a complete dependence on such facilities, and they are not available everywhere, even in North America. These should probably then be regarded as embryonic forms rather than completed structures. However, they clearly stand as alternatives to the present system of getting such work done. Particularly in North America, where the growth of "service industries" is important in maintaining the growth of the economy, the contradictions between these alternatives and the need to keep women in the home will grow.

The need to keep women in the home arises from two major aspects of the present system. First, the amount of unpaid labor performed by women is very large and very profitable to those who own the means of production. To pay women for their work, even at minimum wage scales, would imply a massive redistribution of wealth. At present, the support of a family is a hidden tax on the wage earner—his wage buys the labor power of two people. And second, there is the problem of whether the economy can expand enough to put all women to work as a part of the normally employed labor force. The war economy has been adequate to draw women partially into the economy but not adequate to establish a need for all or most of them. If it is argued that the jobs created by the industrialization of housework will create this need, then one can counter by pointing to (1) the strong economic forces operating for the status quo and against capitalization discussed above, and (2) the fact that the present service industries, which somewhat counter these forces, have not been able to keep up with the growth of the labor force as presently constituted. The present trends in the service industries simply create "underemployment" in the home; they do not create new jobs for women. So long as this situation exists, women remain a very convenient and elastic part of the industrial reserve army. Their incorporation into the labor force on terms of equality—which would create pressure for capitalization of housework—is possible only with an economic expansion so far achieved by neocapitalism only under conditions of full-scale war mobilization.

In addition, such structural changes imply the complete breakdown of the present nuclear family. The stabilizing consuming functions of the family, plus the ability of the cult of the home to keep women out of the labor market, serve neocapitalism too well to be easily dispensed with. And, on a less fundamental level, even if these necessary changes in the nature of household production were achieved under capitalism it would have the unpleasant consequence of including *all* human relations in the cash nexus. The atomization and isolation of people in Western society is already sufficiently advanced to make it doubtful if such complete psychic isolation could be tolerated. It is likely in fact that one of the major negative emotional responses to women's liberation movements may be exactly such a fear. If this is the case, then possible alternatives—cooperatives, the kibbutz, etc.—can be cited to show that psychic needs for community and warmth can in fact be better satisfied if other structures are substituted for the nuclear family.

At best the change to capitalization of housework would only give women the same limited freedom given most men in capitalist society. This does not mean, however, that women should wait to demand freedom from discrimination. There *is* a material basis for women's status; we are not merely discriminated against, we are exploited. At present, our unpaid labor in the home is necessary if the entire system is to function. Pressure created by women who challenge their role will reduce the effectiveness of this exploitation. In addition, such challenges will impede the functioning of the family and may make the channeling of women out of the labor force less effective. All of these will hopefully make quicker the transition to a society in which the necessary structural changes in production can actually be made. That such a transition will require a revolution I have no doubt; our task is to make sure that revolutionary changes in the society do in fact end women's oppression.

BIBLIOGRAPHY AND NOTES

1. Marlene Dixon, "Secondary Social Status of Women." (Available from U.S. Voice of Women's Liberation Movement, 1940 Bissell, Chicago, Illinois 60614.)

2. The biological argument is, of course, the first one used, but it is not usually taken seriously by socialist writers. Margaret Mead's *Sex and Temperament* is an early statement of the importance of culture instead of biology.

3. This applies to the group or category as a whole. Women as individuals can and do free themselves from their socialization to a great degree (and they can even come to terms with the economic situation in favorable cases), but the majority of women have no chance to do so.

4. Ernest Mandel, "Workers Under Neocapitalism," paper delivered at Simon Fraser University. (Available through the Department of Political Science, Sociology and Anthropology, Simon Fraser University, Burnaby, B.C., Canada.)

5. Ernest Mandel, *An Introduction to Marxist Economic Theory* (New York: Merit Publishers, 1967), pp. 10–11.

6. Juliet Mitchell, "Women: The Longest Revolution," *New Left Review,* December 1966.

7. Frederick Engels, *Origin of the Family, Private Property and the State* (Moscow: Progress Publishers, 1968), Chapter IX, p. 158. The anthropological evidence known to Engels indicated primitive woman's dominance over man. Modern anthropology disputes this dominance but provides evidence for a more nearly equal position of women in the matrilineal societies used by Engels as examples. The arguments in this work of Engels do not require the former dominance of women but merely their former equality, and so the conclusions remain unchanged.

8. Such figures can easily be estimated. For example, a married woman without children is expected each week to cook and wash up (10 hours), clean house (4 hours), do laundry (1 hour), and shop for food (1 hour). The figures are *minimum* times required each week for such work. The total, 16 hours, is probably unrealistically low; even so, it is close to half of a regular work week. A mother with young children must spend at least six or seven days a week working close to 12 hours.

9. For evidence of such teaching, see any high school text on the family.

10. This is stated clearly by early Marxist writers besides Engels. . . .

David Horowitz

David Horowitz is a senior editor of *Ramparts* magazine and the author of *The Free World Colossus* (1965) and *Empire and Revolution* (1969), among other books. He is also the editor of *Containment and Revolution* (1967), *Marx and Modern Economics* (1968), and *Corporations and the Cold War* (1970). From 1963 to 1965 he was director of research for the Bertrand Russell Peace Foundation in London.

The following essay has not been published before.

Horowitz argues that the present crisis in American society is a "specific phase of the general crisis of world capitalism." He claims that the failure of liberalism to understand the global economic and political basis of the American social crisis is due to its blindness to the *class* structure of American society, to "the link between social power, social distribution, and social investment." He then shows why advanced capitalism suffers "the fate of Midas"—that is, why the abundance of wealth produced by capitalism is "no more usable than the riches created by the touch of Midas." He argues that advanced capitalism's so-called Keynesian solution to the problem of surplus capital absorption—and thus to the problems of stagnation, unemployment, and depression—is not a welfare state, as the liberals suggest, but a warfare state, and he shows why this is so. Horowitz's conclusion is that the technical-economic power needed to liberate America and all mankind is already available but must first be liberated from the corporate ruling class.

THE FATE OF MIDAS: A Marxist Interpretation of the American Social Crisis*

. . . of two equal communities, having the same technique but different stocks of capital, the community with the smaller stock of capital may be

* I wish to thank Paul Sweezy and Harry Magdoff for helpful criticisms of earlier versions of this essay.

able for the time being to enjoy a higher standard of life than the community with the larger stock; though when the poorer community has caught up with the rich—as, presumably, it eventually will—then both alike will suffer the fate of Midas. This disturbing conclusion depends, of course, on the assumption that the propensity to consume and the rate of investment are not deliberately controlled in the social interest but are mainly left to the influences of laissez-faire.

JOHN MAYNARD KEYNES, *The General Theory*

Liberal Prophecy and Illusion

America is now in the grip of a profound and pervasive crisis, unprecedented in its history. "Consider what has happened," commented *Fortune,* surveying the events of spring, 1968, from a vantage situated at the gold-plated top of the American social structure: "the U.S. for the first time in its history has found itself committed to a war to which it can find no military solution . . . ; a sizable and vocal body of American youth have refused to support their country in time of war; a minority race has demanded immediate end to its inferior status and the leader of that race has been murdered; dozens of American cities have been torn by riots, . . . the national capital has been occupied by troops and the seat of government protected by machine guns; a group of political scientists gathering recently at Princeton has felt justified in concluding that for the first time an American administration has been "toppled" in the European sense: a major American university has been paralyzed and almost taken over by student radicals and other campuses have been disrupted by riots; various economic prophets have stated that we are in the most dangerous fiscal crisis since the early Thirties; and now the brother of our recently assassinated President has been shot down at a climactic moment in his drive to unseat the ruling powers in his own party." These events, *Fortune* judged, had "shaken American society to its roots." Moreover, it is clear, they were neither the beginning nor the end of the increasingly insistent historical trend.

Surely one of the impressive ironies of the American crisis is that it has emerged in a period of unparalleled economic prosperity and at a time when the United States is at the very pinnacle of its career as a world power. This irony has not been overlooked by those seeking to understand events in the dominant liberal perspective of the day, but it has thus far been left unexplained. It is even questionable whether one can speak of an American crisis at all in connection with the liberal perspective, if one means to imply by that an integrated phenomenon rooted in the very structure of the American social and economic order. In the liberal view, the current disturbance of the status quo appears to be merely the cumulative result of a series of fragmented and only tenuously related troubles: a Vietnam "problem" here, a race and poverty problem there, a problem of domestic "law and order" over all.

Not only has liberalism shrunk from a confrontation with the structural nature of the crisis, but it has been surprised by the appearance of the crisis itself. The intensification of the conflicts generated by the social "problem areas" and their eruption in civil violence at the very surface of America's domestic order fly in the face of the liberal myth of slow but steady progress and come as wholly unexpected and inexplicable events. And this has led to a crisis in liberalism itself.

One has only to read the "consensus" pundits of the fifties—writers like Daniel Bell, Seymour Martin Lipset and John Kenneth Galbraith —to realize that the very assumptions of the postwar liberal faith— the transcendence of old-fashioned capitalism and capitalist class conflict, the "end of ideology" and the emergence of an allegedly pluralistic planned "new industrial state"—rule out the very crisis which is now irrevocably upon us. If this were the first time that liberalism had banged its head so firmly against the rock of historical events, the necessity of turning to other modes of analysis would not be so self-evident. However, the history of liberalism indicates that its incapacity is chronic and that the roots of its failure lie in the unshakable commitment of its spokesmen to the social and economic status quo.

Liberals of the Victorian era, basking in the sun of *Pax Britannica,* natural evolution and the free market economy, viewed their future as a golden age, promising Peace, Progress, and Increasing Social Sanity. A few souls among them, it is true, joined with the socialists in condemning the "residual" evils of industrial exploitation and the new barbarism of colonial expansion, but even among these, the inevitability of reform in white Christian democracy and the eventual, if gradual, elimination of these unwanted blemishes was regarded as inevitable, an article of faith. Marxist unbelievers might warn against the mounting tide of capitalist monopolization and militarism and the inevitable catastrophe of global warfare foreshadowed in the intensified struggle for world markets, but their "doctrinaire" clamorings could be safely ignored.

Until 1914, that is. In that inaugural year of the European slaughter the great white hope of nineteenth-century liberal civilization was shattered forever. But while the old complacency was shaken, the sustaining system, with its comforts, benefits, and privileges for chosen strata, survived, and with it the necessity for renewed (and refurbished) rationalization. Thus the liberal mind emerged from the war with a doctrine whose thesis, if not basically different in terms of power and program, had nonetheless undergone a change.

For the first time, liberals were compelled to recognize that the basic features of the capitalist system, the great inequalities of wealth and power, the anarchic structure of the macroeconomic system, the cyclical spells of boom and bust, and the unchecked scramble for international markets were in fact grave menaces to social progress and order. Yet, however much the preceding disasters might have underscored the necessity of revolution, the liberal middle classes were no more willing to pay the price of such a revolution than they had been before. The impressive, if deceptive, performance of the economy under wartime planning and the equally deceptive postwar boom further helped prepare the ground in which a new faith could bloom. As the expansion of the twenties accelerated, the new liberals began to propound the notion of *an already achieved social transformation* and to hail the advent of a "new capitalism" in which wealth was alleged to be increasingly shared, production increasingly planned for social needs, and prosperity a permanent feature of economic life. As one prominent spokesman for this emergent ruling ideology proclaimed in a tract published on the very eve of the Great Depression: "Not merely will prosperity (soon) be stabilized, but the rule of class will for the first time disappear." *

The precipitous crash from the heights of this giddy optimism into the depths of the deepest abyss in capitalist economic history ought to have dispelled once and for all any illusions about the possibility for rational and humane social development under such a fundamentally

---

* For a collection of such statements by prominent figures and groups of the twenties from Secretary of the Treasury Andrew Mellon to the President's Committee on Recent Economic Changes, see Lewis Corey, *The Decline of American Capitalism* (Lane, 1935).

188 THE FATE OF MIDAS

flawed system. But while some liberals may have been tempted to abandon ship (even such apostles of "free enterprise" capitalism as Keynes began to talk about the necessity of a "somewhat comprehensive socialization of investment"), the mainstream of liberalism remained true to its faith. Indeed, the very voices that had heralded the phantom transformation of the twenties now began to praise the mild reforms and tinkerings of the New Deal as yet another substitute revolution. In fact, the most salient characteristic of the New Deal was its utter failure to stimulate demand on the scale necessary to reflate the economy to its predepression levels. The very attempt to do so by government means had been abandoned by the Roosevelt administration when, with 8,000,000 still unemployed, the demand for war orders and the institution of wartime planning lifted the economy by its bootstraps to hitherto unattainable heights. Meanwhile, the pastiche of partial reforms, mildly ameliorative social legislation (all of which had been projected earlier by the farsighted business executives of the National Civic Federation),* and war prosperity were built by liberal imaginations into a new revolutionary order. It was not long before the promise of permanently increasing economic affluence and perpetual social harmony that had apparently been laid to rest in 1929 was being resurrected in the cold war fifties in an outpouring of ill-conceived enthusiasm which C. W. Mills sarcastically dubbed the Great American Celebration.

Like its predecessor, however, this celebration was short-lived. The civil rebellions of the sixties in the black ghettos, the threatening prospect of price inflation and world monetary crisis, and the escalation of the genocidal war against the peasantry of Vietnam abruptly dissolved the consensual order of American politics, deflated the Panglossian platitudes of the new liberalism, and prepared a shift politically toward the right and a further sharpening of social antagonism and conflicts.

Liberalism, Marxism, and the Capitalist World System

Despite these repeated debacles of its world vision, liberalism remains in the current crisis the analytic framework in which all socially

* Cf. James Weinstein, *The Corporate Ideal in the Liberal State* (Boston, Beacon, 1968).

respectable (and academically "professional") interpretations of the social impasse must be set. An alternative approach exists in Marxism, but it is forced to lead an embattled existence underground—except in its official, ideological, and therefore safe varieties.*

The contrast between the Marxist and liberal perspectives on twentieth-century capitalist development and the nature of the current crisis could not be more complete. To Marxists, the present crisis in American society comes as no isolated or unexpected event. It appears rather as a specific phase of the general crisis of world capitalism, which began with the monopolization and colonization movements at the turn of the century, erupted first in the barbarism of the first European World War and has since established its permanent and pervasive character through the economic and political collapses of the interwar decades, their issue in the bloody engagements of World War II, and the emergence of the postwar cold war.

One of the chief features of this last phase has been the rise of the United States to preeminence in the capitalist world system, replacing England (and to a lesser extent France) as the guardian power of the international status quo. In this role Washington has necessarily emerged as the leader of a worldwide conservative coalition aiming to contain the anticapitalist revolution, which took root in 1917 in one of the most exploited and underdeveloped regions of the globe, and has been gaining ground in those regions ever since. It is this inheritance of a mortally challenged world system that explains more than anything else the paradox of America's present power and ultimate impotence, as so fatefully symbolized in the struggle over the destiny of Vietnam. In the two postwar decades the effort to contain revolution has cost the United States alone more than a *trillion* dollars of the national income. It has also resulted in the little noted deaths of more than 4,000,000 peasants in the exploited and awakening areas of the world at the hands of U.S. and U.S.-Allied forces. The sheer magnitude of these figures indicates that they are not only symbols of the

---

* The percentage of economists and sociologists familiar with the work of Marxists like Maurice Dobb, Paul Sweezy, Paul Baran, Lewis Corey, Ernest Mandel, Harry Magdoff, Perry Anderson, and André Gorz is surely infinitesimal. A major theoretical work on economic development like Baran's *Political Economy of Growth,* Monthly Review Press, 1957, is virtually censored from the bibliographies of academic works on development, though its author was a highly respected professor at Stanford and well known to other economists.

crisis in general, but expressions of its deepest causes, and that the crisis in American society is not separable from the crisis of its *world* system.

This "world system" is of course more extensive (and more complex) than the U.S. economic stake in it, but that stake is itself an impressive index of the increasingly international basis of the American order. U.S. direct overseas investments now exceed the figure of $60 billion. The sales of this overseas system is equal to 40 percent of the U.S. domestic output of mines, factories, and farms and accounts for more than 20 percent of the profits of U.S. nonfinancial corporations. The U.S. overseas economic empire is, in fact, the third largest economic unit in the world after the domestic economies of the United States and Russia.* In regions like the Middle East, Southeast Asia, and Latin America, the locus of a good many "international" crises, U.S. interests constitute *the* dominant economic unit; in other key areas, like the Indian subcontinent and southern Africa, U.S. interests share dominance with the corporations and financial institutions of other NATO powers, as the increasingly primary joint partners. It is not necessary, of course, that U.S. investments be the direct target of a revolutionary upheaval for U.S. investments to be threatened. Thus, what is at stake for American capital in Vietnam and in similar revolutionary areas is not simply the specific markets and resources of the countries in question, but the international status quo order—*i.e.,* the whole structural environment, embracing economic, political, and social policies and institutions, that make it possible for U.S. capital to expand and grow throughout the region and the world.

So manifest is the importance of the U.S. overseas system to the emergence of international crises in the postwar period (and to the crises besetting American society at home) that it would seem to require no emphasis. Yet in the contemporary liberal perspective this system has hardly even begun to exist. Consider, for example, John Kenneth Galbraith's latest best-selling effort at a definitive analysis of what he calls "the new industrial state." Not *one* of the thirty-five chapters of his highly praised book even mentions, let alone analyzes, the U.S. overseas system or attempts to assess its ramifications. In other words, the most far-reaching postwar development in the American social structure, the globalization of American business, is simply

* Harry Magdoff, *The Age of Imperialism* (New York, Monthly Review Press, 1969).

ignored by the most widely acclaimed apostle of critical realism toward the corporate society. The American imperium is apparently not a subject for respectable discourse.

Non-Marxist social science in the United States, however, was not always so willfully ignorant or so crudely apologetic toward American imperialism as it has come to be in the cold war years. In the thirties the distinguished (but now patronized) American historian Charles Beard had already drawn attention to the political implications of the stepped-up expansion of American capital overseas following the First World War. For just as "trade" had followed the flag in the course of previous American overseas expansion, so the "flag" was invariably put at the services of American financial and corporate interests abroad. If the historical record was any indication, the risk of future overseas capital investments would be underwritten by the United States government itself and by the blood of its citizens pressed into service to defend them.* "The United States," Beard wrote, "through the investment of capital, has become a silent partner in the fate of every established order in the world." † And so it has.

Capitalism and the Crisis of Abundance

The failure of liberalism to recognize the overriding significance of the American economic empire stems from its unwillingness to open its eyes to the *class* nature of American society. Similarly, its failure to understand the domestic roots of the crisis lies in a failure to see that the basic power division of society is indeed a class division and that this class division is tied to the social processes of accumulation,

* Cf. the studies of American expansion and foreign policy by Beard (*The Idea of National Interest;* New York, Macmillan, 1934) and William A. Williams (*The Tragedy of American Diplomacy;* New York, World, 1959). One important reason (but not the only one) why this should be so is that the State Department is run by businessmen and their protégés. The last three Secretaries of State, spanning sixteen critical years of office, were John Foster Dulles, a Wall Street lawyer intimately associated with the Rockefeller Standard Oil interests; Christian Herter, who married into one of the original Standard Oil families; and Dean Rusk, a protégé of Dulles' who came to the post from the presidency of the Rockefeller Foundation—the largest stockholder in Standard Oil. The fact that the Standard Oil Company was the first of the truly world-oriented U.S. corporations (it now has subsidiaries and investments in more than fifty countries) accounts in large part for its affinity for this particular Cabinet post.

† Beard, *The Economic Basis of Politics* (New York, Knopf, 1922).

resource allocation, and the distribution of goods and services. It is because liberalism doesn't see the link between social power, social distribution, and social investment that it can fragment the facets of the current crisis, isolate them as "problems," and project a solution that depends on the correction of errors of judgment and the reform of technical structures, rather than the root-and-branch overthrow of a basically maleficent, undemocratic, and obsolescent social system.

In attempting to outline an alternative analysis to liberalism, one that is based on a recognition of the structural foundations of the capitalist system, let us begin with a historical perspective.* For a long time an industrial economy is engaged in the process of industrialization, *i.e.,* in the transition from noncapital-using to capital-using methods of production. During this transition, society's overall rate of consumption is low; its rate of saving for investment in yet more instruments of production is high. "Society," of course, is no homogeneous community where each labors for the benefit of all and takes his share according to some equitable principle of distribution and reward. Capitalist society is divided in a fundamental way into those who work for a wage and those who possess the capital to hire them (where "capital" means both surplus money and the instruments of production at which to work). During industrialization, it is the laboring class that tightens its belt, receiving a bare consumption minimum for survival, while the capital-owning class plows its surplus income (derived from profits) into new means of production and yet greater future income for itself. It is, thus, the unequal distribution of income which forces a low consumption rate on the great mass of the population, while providing the privileged few with a surplus (even after their lavish consumption requirements are met) to reinvest.

During the early stages of industrialization, demand for this investment surplus is generated primarily in the capital goods sector (plant, machinery, equipment, etc.) for yet more capital goods. As the productive powers of the economy increase and the period of industrialization draws to an end, however, the demand for further expansion naturally tends to slacken. As basic industries and communication systems come into being, the productive apparatus gradually becomes large enough to supply all the expansion and replacement demands of

* The following argument draws heavily on Paul Sweezy's "A Crucial Difference Between Capitalism and Socialism" in Horowitz, ed., *Marx and Modern Economics* (New York, Monthly Review Press, 1968).

the industries in the consumption sector, while its own expansion demand diminishes to the vanishing point. The natural overall tendency of this development is toward what Keynes once called a "quasi-stationary community," where change "would result only from changes in technique, taste, population and institutions" rather than from the classical accumulation and industrialization process, involving saving and net investment.* There would still be progress in such a community—in the accepted sense of better quality techniques, better quality goods, and increased productivity—but such progress would take place as the result of the *replacement* of machines already in existence rather than as the result of *net* additions to the stock of capital (*net* investment).†

The significance of the achievement of this stage in development—it might be called "full industrialization"—is that all the social energies and resources that went into accumulation (or investment in future production) could go into the realization of a humane and humanly wealthy social order in the present. The maldistribution of income, which restricted consumption for the many and generated an income surplus for the few would no longer serve any social function,** as there would be no need for a net surplus, since the increase in production to cover population increases would result from the march of technical progress. Thus not only could the whole population be raised to decent standards of living, but there would be more time for leisure, for education, culture, and politics in the Aristotelian sense. "Given social production," wrote Marx, "the allocation of time naturally remains of the essence. . . . Just as in the case of a single individual, the all-sidedness of society's development, of its enjoyment, and of its activity depends on the saving of time. The economy

* The inevitability of such a development is systematically argued in A. Murad, "Net Investment and Industrial Progress," in K. Kurihara, ed. *Post-Keynesian Economics* (New Brunswick, Rutgers University Press, 1954). The statistical evidence of a decline in net capital formation in the United States as an already existent trend is also discussed in this essay. Cf. also Magdoff, *op. cit.*

† In the United States it is estimated that somewhere between one-third and three-quarters of the increase in per capita income of Americans in the postwar period was the result of technological progress rather than increased savings and investment. Cf. Edward Denison, *The Sources of Economic Growth in the U.S. and the Alternatives Before the U.S.*, Committee for Economic Development, New York, 1962.

** Of course, industrialization, theoretically, could have been accomplished by other, less inequitable means.

of time, this is what all economy dissolves itself into—in the last analysis." In terms of our model, social income previously "saved" and "invested" in future production would be "consumed" in education and culture (in its broadest sense), environmental reconstruction and the uplifting of the social underclasses.*

In the advanced industrial countries, as a result of the previous accumulation of capital and the development of scientific technologies, human liberation, in the sense of a comprehensive redirection of social energies from the production of necessities and the struggle for existence to the realization of a truly human culture has become a real, practical historical prospect. But this prospect of liberation is foreclosed as a possibility by the class structure of capitalist society.

Already this is painfully visible in the United States. For the incredible powers of the productive organism in this richest of all countries make the problems of poverty, of environmental pollution and underdevelopment, of the disadvantaged underclasses and blighted cities fully solvable with existing resources *within the present generation*. Not only would the $30 billion per year that has been made available for the slaughter of peasants in Vietnam accomplish much of the required program in a decade or two, but the utilization of existing capacity that is kept idle by the monopolistic structure of American capitalism would, on a conservative estimate,† more than double that sum, and with it the potential tempo of reconstruction. Moreover, this has been an unseized option for the past forty years.

The basic reason for capitalism's inability to make a rational and socially progressive adjustment to the onset of abundance is that under capitalist economic organization the end of production is not the

* Education and culture, of course, can be regarded from a social point of view as forms of investment. However, in a capitalist society, education and culture are financed not out of the net profits (income surplus) of the capitalists, thence not out of society's accumulation fund, but out of taxed income accruing to the government and the consumption income of individuals in the form of tuition, etc.

† According to Leon Keyserling, former chairman of the President's Council of Economic Advisers, the amount of output lost between 1953 and 1964 as a result of unemployment and underutilized plant facilities was $550 billion. This is a conservative estimate. An economist writing in the Marxist magazine *Monthly Review*, for example, analyzed idle capacity in the American economy and concluded that "American industry has enough idle capacity today to permit an almost instantaneous doubling of manufacturing output." "Idle Machines," *MR* (June, 1962).

fulfillment of human needs, but the expansion of private capital. Social accumulation is private accumulation. In other words, the investment surplus (profit) which society no longer needs (or needs redistributed) is also the income of the capital-owning class, the economic foundation of its very existence. Accordingly, any pressure to reduce and redistribute that income and reallocate the social resources which it commands is passionately and fiercely resisted. Indeed, this resistance has been historically built by the capital-owning class into the very economic, ideological, and institutional structure of the society which it dominates.

This resistance, of course, does not manifest itself directly as an opposition to the liberating program outlined above. A minority class which set itself in opposition to the raising of living standards, the eradication of poverty, the building of livable cities, the redirection of social energies to human cultural pursuits would be swept into oblivion. Nor is there a conscious conspiracy on the part of capital owners to conceal their opposition to social liberation. As individuals, many would probably invite it. Their opposition as a class is not a conscious decision, but a function of the social mechanism. For it is a central feature of capitalism that the decisions about the overall allocation of social resources are ones that can never be directly confronted. There is no social economic plan, but the integration of a multitude of private "plans" through the market. An "invisible hand" organizes production and determines the allocation and distribution of social resources, so that in capitalism it appears as though the economy made decisions and ruled individual men. This is what Marx characterized as fetishism, where men are ruled (as in religion) by their own creation.

Capitalism's adjustment to the onset of abundance should, therefore, take place through the mediation of the market. The offset to the decline in demand for continued *net* additions to the stock of capital would be accomplished through the price mechanism. As demand began to slacken, prices would fall; this in turn would bring about a falling rate of profit (or interest). The share of wage and salary earners in personal income would increase at the expense of the share of investors (capital owners) at the same time as the inducement to invest would decrease. These two influences would result in a reduction in the proportion of income going into savings (investment surplus) and an immediate rise in the real living standards of the wage earning classes.

In practice, however, the price system in advanced capitalism does not work this way. As a result of monopolistic and oligopolistic concentrations of capital, prices are downwardly rigid: They rise, but in general, they do not fall. Now, as Paul Sweezy has pointed out, "what is often called the degree of monopoly (in the economy as a whole) is little more than a reflection of capitalists' success in putting up economic, institutional and legal fences around their profits." In fact, so preponderant has been the economic, social, and political power of capital in defense of its profits in all the capitalist countries that income shares have been kept remarkably constant since the end of the nineteenth century in the face of all redistributive forces.

The macroeconomic result of this resistance is that capitalism, as it approaches abundance, is threatened, as Keynes put it, with "the fate of Midas." The richer a capitalist society becomes, the more it is faced with a critical problem of surplus capital absorption and hence with the prospect of stagnation, unemployment, and depression. What happens to an economy which generates an investment surplus that cannot be utilized is vividly recorded in the history of the American thirties. If profitable investment outlets cannot be found for the surplus, if society, *whatever its real needs,* cannot utilize its savings, returning them to the market as demand for yet more productive capacity and hence more consumption goods, then total income will contract, and unemployment grow until savings fall to the level of investment. The monopolization of the economy intensifies the overall problem, not only by artificially maintaining the level of savings, but by retarding the introduction of innovations and thereby reducing the available number of profitable investment outlets.* Moreover, because of the expanding labor force and increasing labor productivity, the level of output and income at which there will be full employment is constantly increasing. Here the liberating promise of automation is converted into a boundless menace: To avoid *rising* secular unemployment, market demand must *increase* in proportion to the rate of increase of labor productivity plus the rate of increase of the labor force. Thus, the system is caught ever deeper in its web of contradictions, because the inducement to invest at a constant, let alone an expanding rate, no longer exists.

* Cf. Joan Robinson, *The Accumulation of Capital* (London, Macmillan, 1936), p. 407.

The Crisis and the Keynesian State I: Theory

During the whole postwar period, of course, the threat of stagnation on the scale of the thirties has never materialized. This is because the system has managed to generate counteracting forces to maintain the rate of surplus absorption at prosperity levels. These counteracting forces, however, have necessarily operated within the framework created by capitalist class relations. The solution which they pose to the crisis of capitalist abundance is therefore no solution at all, but the crisis itself in a new form.

Private capital attempts to counteract the tendency to stagnation, viewed as a threat to profit margins, by *expanding* its normal domestic and foreign markets. The fruits of this latter effort can be seen in the phenomenal postwar expansion of U.S. capital abroad.* While generating investment outlets and a vital export surplus,† it has also produced an interventionist and destructive foreign policy and in effect internationalized the American crisis. As for the expansion of domestic markets, the rigid and unequal distribution of income, which precludes a widening of the domestic consumption base (and an end to existing deprivation), makes it necessary, instead, for private capital to induce those who already can afford to buy what they want to want more and, if possible, to waste what they have already bought. This obscene objective is achieved primarily via the sales effort (underpinned by a vast credit liberalization and expansion of consumer debt). The immensely consequential nature of this enterprise can hardly be overstressed. Taking the whole of the sales effort into account, including, for example, the cost of annual style changes in the automobile industry, more money is spent on making Americans into "voracious, wasteful, compulsive consumers" than is spent on their entire education through the university levels. Not the fulfillment of need, but the

* For other factors in this expansion, see my *Empire and Revolution* (New York, Random House, 1969).

† An export surplus has the same expansionary effect on the economy and on profits as a budget deficit. Without foreign markets "profits are conditioned by the ability of capitalists to consume or to undertake capital investment. It is the export surplus and the budget deficit which enable the capitalists to make profits over and above their own purchases of goods and services."— M. Kalecki, *Theory of Economic Dynamics* (MR Press, 1968) pp. 50–52. Purchases by the foreign affiliates of U.S. corporations account for 23 percent of all U.S. exports. See Magdoff, *op. cit.*

artificial creation of new desires, not education but miseducation at once moronizing and degrading appear as the chief cultural contributions of advanced capitalism to human civilization.

The effort of private capital artificially to expand its domestic markets and to enlarge forcefully its international presence is not only socially wasteful, culturally pernicious, and politically destructive, but also economically insufficient. Consequently, the economic intervention of the state is required on an extensive scale to deal with the growing problem of "abundance." In this effort, the state theoretically has several options. It could, for example, dramatically shift purchasing power to the lower income units via progressive taxes and transfer payments and thus make effective the very real but powerless demand of the poverty-stricken, deprived two-fifths of the nation's population. Such tax laws exist, but in practice, the tax system is widely recognized to function regressively,* and no significant income redistribution from capital owners to wageworkers and the poor has occurred as a result of state policies in any capitalist country. The reason, of course, is not difficult to divine. This kind of redistribution means a shift in wealth from a class which wields predominant political power —and in practice sets the guidelines for all state-administered socio-economic reform†—to classes which wield virtually no power.

Moreover, the mainspring of the economic system—hence of the prosperity on which the survival of governments depends—is private investment. Thus, any injury to business confidence, such as would be caused by the enforcement of redistributive tax measures, would have a deleterious effect on the overall economic situation. In other words, assaults on the privileged sanctuaries of private capital (and generally property income) inevitably provoke spontaneous "retaliations" via a decline in current investment, a general shrinkage of demand and a corresponding drop in national income. As a result, across-the-board attempts to restrict corporate privileges and the prerogatives of wealth are not even attempted by governments except in times of exceptional national crisis. (When the crisis passes, needless to say, capital mounts its counterattack and restores an equilibrium more to its liking.)

* See Philip Stern, *The Great Treasury Raid* (New York, Random House, 1964); F. Lundberg, *The Rich and the Super-Rich* (New York, Lyle Stuart, 1968).

† Cf. James Weinstein, *The Corporate Ideal in the Liberal State* (Beacon, 1968); Gabriel Kolko, *The Triumph of Conservatism* (Quadrangle, 1963).

The same reasoning applies to the whole range of possible government purchases of the private product to meet needs in education, health, housing, culture, and recreation. A significant part of the payment for these goods and services must come from taxation of the wealthy, to whom they are already available, and thus would represent a recutting of the national income pie. Any attempt to correct the misallocation of resources and the resultant blight of the social environment on a truly significant scale would run head on into the resistance of those forces whose own life-style with all its privileges depends on the maintenance of the status quo. In short, any attempt by the government to make up for the deficiency of demand which results from the inequalities generated by capitalist production relations must collide with the fact that these inequalities have their origin in an inequality of power which runs all through capitalist society and cannot be altered by any one set of institutions within it.

Striking confirmation of this analysis is provided by the experience of the welfare state in postwar England, where the expansion of welfare services has not brought with it any significant redistribution of income. This is because "the great mass of the working class and of the population as a whole receive back in services no more than they pay in taxes." * In the United States, resistance to welfare spending is certainly no less intense, and despite a dramatic expansion of federal expenditures, there has been no comparable increase in the realm of federal welfare. In 1939, 42.5 percent of federal expenditures was for education, health, labor, welfare, housing, and community development, whereas in 1965 the figure was only 7 percent.†

There is, however, one kind of government expenditure which performs the same economic function as consumption expenditures (thus sustaining total demand) and does *not* meet with resistance from the corporate interests, indeed is supported by them.** This is *military* spending, which has the dual advantage of providing a

* Anderson & Blackburn, *Towards Socialism* (Ithaca, Cornell University Press, 1965).

† Melman, *Our Depleted Society* (New York, Holt, Rinehart and Winston, 1965).

** Actually, there is another form of federal spending—highway construction—which is supported for obvious reasons by a powerful bloc of corporate interests.

virtually limitless market for the private product and also of performing a necessary service to the corporations which they could not provide for themselves—namely, the protection of their expanding investments and markets overseas.* The huge arms budget is in fact *the* vital difference between America's economic performance since 1950 and the stagnation and depression of the 1930's accounting for as much as 60 percent of gross investment in the pre-Vietnam war of 1961. (It is, therefore, the vital difference for the *global* capitalist system.†)

Baran and Sweezy have constructed an illustrative index of this much-disparaged but indubitable relation. In 1939, they point out, the number of unemployed was 17.2 percent and the number of persons employed as a consequence of the military budget was 1.4 percent, or a total of 18.6 percent. In a comparable year 1961 the respective figures were 6.7 percent and 9.4 percent for a total of 16.1 percent either unemployed or dependent for employment on military spending.

In other words, the so-called Keynesian solution to the stagnation and depression-bound system of the thirties in practice turns out to be not a welfare state, as liberal ideology proclaims, but a warfare state. A moment's reflection, moreover, will indicate why this should be so. Keynes showed that there is a natural tendency for capitalism to run into chronic stagnation, with permanent unemployment, and that capitalism is, by nature, highly unstable. In order to make up for private capital's failure to maintain the level of investment, Keynes argued that governments must undertake compensatory expenditures. But high rates of socially useful investment undertaken by the government may lead to a decline in the profitability of further investment in private enterprise. Thus "wasteful" government spending is more acceptable to investors than useful spending: "Two pyramids, two masses for the dead, are twice as good as one; but not so two railways from London to York" (Keynes). This explains the readiness

* That U.S. foreign policy is designed to contain revolution, not national expansion, is extensively argued in *The Free World Colossus,* especially Chapter 25.

† This is because effective demand is interlinked through trade and finance, and the United States accounts for about half the economy of the so-called free world. On the role of arms spending in the Western world, see M. Kidron, *Western Capitalism Since the War,* Weidenfeld and Nicolson, 1968; in the United States see Baran and Sweezy, *Monopoly Capital* (Monthly Review Press, 1966).

of capitalist governments to spend money on armaments. For as the eminent Keynesian Joan Robinson has noted: "If there were no need for armaments, it would be necessary to make (socially) useful investments and so to encroach upon the power and independence of the capitalists [financial as well as industrial]. The capitalists therefore prefer a situation in which armaments do seem necessary. This cure, most of us would agree, is even worse than the disease, and on the basis of Keynes' reasoning it can be argued that capitalism will not save itself from the tendency to unemployment by any other means." *

Thus, in advanced capitalism, the rate of military spending has a strong, even irresistible, tendency to rise, first, because given the relative saturation of profitable markets and the stake of society's dominant class in maintaining its power, "wasteful" expenditures must be undertaken by the state on an ever-increasing scale to absorb the economic surplus (savings) and maintain a high level of output and employment; second, because as a result of the new technological level of the forces of production—and the complex and expensive nature of the research required to develop them—and of the monopolistic corporations' increasing control over the expanding Keynesian state, the military-industrial complex has become the focal point for the country's research and development funds;† and third, because the compelling pressure to expand overseas investment requires a vast network of bases, alliances, and generally mobile military forces for the dominant imperial power.**

In sum, the matrix of class power and interest which determines the normal path of capitalist social and economic development also exerts a formative influence over any attempts by the state to alter that path. For the state is not an institution suspended above society, but is itself a social institution, and the power relations generated by the existing economic order and its class structure may be modified, but not fundamentally altered by the state.‡

* "Marx, Marshall and Keynes," in Joan Robinson, *Collected Economic Papers, II* (Blackwell Oxford, 1960).

† Nieburg, *In the Name of Science* (Quadrangle, 1965).

** This is an important point. The U.S. military umbrella makes it less necessary for a capitalist power like Britain to maintain a maximum level of forces; similarly the military-powered U.S. economic expansion buoys up the British economy at lower levels of British military spending.

‡ On upper-class control of Washington in the postwar period, see G. William Domhoff, *Who Rules America?* (Prentice-Hall, 1967).

The Crisis and the Keynesian State II: Practice

A series of key economic decisions which illustrate these general observations and illuminate the specific way in which the structural relations manifest themselves at the political surface were taken at the threshold of the present phase of the American crisis.

In 1961 a new administration calling itself the New Frontier had taken office in Washington. This was self-consciously put forward as a socially aware administration, informed with idealism and sensitive as its predecessor had not been to the "other" Americas, the plight of the poverty-stricken underclasses, the suffering of the oppressed black communities, and the general blight of the social and human environment, which decades of unplanned urbanization and industrialization had wrought. Moreover, this administration was heralded as being the first to accept officially the Keynesian analysis and to acknowledge the power and responsibility of the state to deal with the demand problem via its own spending policies. The stage seemed set for a much-needed program of social reform, a beginning of the long-deferred and desperately overdue harnessing of the forces of the postwar prosperity to the task of promoting something like the general welfare.

It was not very long after its inaugural "honeymoon" that the Kennedy administration was faced with the necessity of making some hard political choices and laying its fine rhetoric on the line. A slackening of the economy on top of almost a decade of stagnation and sluggish growth made it imperative to take expansionary economic measures. The political question confronting the New Frontiersmen was what kind of measure it was to be. Initially the answer seemed to be a tax reform, which was to be combined either with a tax cut or an expanded program of federal expenditures to produce the required expansionary budget.

On the allocation side, the plugging of some of the more notorious tax loopholes which allow the very rich to escape the progressive intent of the existing tax laws would divert social resources away from the luxury sectors of the economy and society and make them available for those social areas and social groupings which lacked the necessities and amenities for a decent existence.

The second of the possible measures, a tax cut, would, if biased toward the lower income groups, broaden the consumption bases and make goods from the private sector available to those in need of them. An increase in federal nondefense spending (the third possibility) would initiate the massive task of social reconstruction and rehabilitation made necessary by the past misallocation of resources under a system of production organized for private profit rather than social need.

The course actually taken by the New Frontier was simple and instructive. Under pressure centering within the administration in the person of Secretary of the Treasury C. Douglas Dillon (in private life one of Wall Street's leading investment bankers) and outside the administration in a committee headed by Stuart Saunders (head of the largest railroad in the country) and Henry Ford II, the promised tax reform was abandoned. Also rejected was any substantial expansion of federal expenditures on housing, urban development, conservation, environmental purification, education, and welfare. According to banker Dillon, in a speech presenting the administration's viewpoint, such expenditure might prove inflationary and could not be "justified on its own merit"!

The measure decided on by the administration, as being in the best interests of the nation, was the measure supported from the outset by Dillon and his friends: a tax cut. This was no across-the-board tax cut, however. As if to gild the lily, the Dillon-Ford interests pressed through a tax reduction sharply biased toward the corporate rich, since, they argued, if production were to be expanded, incentives must be given to the controllers of the means of production. (On the other hand, when the tax surcharge was put through four years later to stem inflation, it was an across-the-board surcharge, affecting all income categories equally.)

As a result of the tax cut, a family of four with a $3,000-a-year income received $60 extra to spend, while a similar family with a $200,000-a-year income received $32,000 extra. Nor was this the end of the story. A series of steps to grant more liberalized depreciation measures to corporations, effectively reduced corporate taxes from 16 to 23 percent with the result that in the first five years of the Kennedy-Johnson administrations corporate profits (savings income) rose 76.5 percent, while wages (consumption income) rose only 18 percent. The whole series of New Frontier measures represented a massive distribution of income from the poor to the rich, from consumers to savers, and while it inevitably put some immediate steam into the economy, it promised to deepen and complicate the economy's long-term problem and crisis.

By 1965 slack was again being felt in the economy, and an imminent end to the long boom was being predicted in respected quarters when the escalation of the Vietnam War and the expansion of war expenditures from $2 billion to $30 billion annually spelled a temporary end to the recessionary forces. The war in Vietnam, symbolizing the global military effort, is not at all peripheral to this story. When Dillon proclaimed that expanded federal expenditures on welfare might prove inflationary and could not be justified on their own merits, the Kennedy administration had already increased the military budget by 16 percent or more than $7 billion. And this at a time, when U.S. missile and military superiority vis-à-vis the Soviet Union was overwhelming (*i.e.*, according to Pentagon estimates between 5 and 10 to 1).*

The priorities expressed in the New Frontier spending and tax policies were as characteristic of the dominant forces of American society as was Dillon himself. Scion of the investment banking house of Dillon, Read & Co. and a director of the Chase Manhattan Bank, Dillon personified the most globally oriented interests of U.S. capital. There is certainly no mystery about why the interests represented by Dillon, Read & Co. and Chase, with investments from Southeast Asia to South Africa, from the Middle East to the Cape of Good Hope, should regard the $30 billion (of public money) allocated for the counterinsurgency operation in Vietnam a justifiable expense a year or so after they had considered less than a third of that sum "too much" to spend for the rehabilitation of the most exploited and oppressed layers of American society.

However, these priorities could hardly be shared by the great mass of the American people. The black uprisings in the ghettos of the American cities, the antidraft resistance, and the student rebellions are but the initial shock waves in what must become a popular earthquake against an intolerable social system: one that is richer than any in history, but cannot eliminate poverty or build a decent environment or provide equality of opportunity for its citizens; a social system that can spend hundreds of billions to dominate the nonwhite peoples of the underdeveloped world and their resources

* *The Free World Colossus,* Chapters 23–25.

and raw materials, but only pennies for the general welfare at home.

Because capitalism is by nature an exploitative system and the motive force of its development is not provision for social need, but the expansion of business profits, and because this expansion inevitably comes at the expense of the vast majority of the population and of the environment itself, the task of coping with the growing social catastrophe which its "progress" engenders is inevitably a Sisyphean labor. Indeed, even, as capitalism's reaction to the revolutionary pressures generated by its exploitation of populations abroad is military violence, so at home, the most basic and consistent response of the ruling powers to the social chaos which the system produces and to the revolt which its criminal priorities inspire is the extension of the mechanisms of repression and control. The democratic order itself threatens to become the first major victim of intensified class struggle.

Thus, the fabulous riches created by capitalism prove to be no more humanly usable than the riches created by the touch of Midas. To turn raw materials and human labor into capitalist gold requires the blood of millions of nonwhite peoples in the imperial realms and thousands of black and white Americans who have no stake in the imperial system and no real say in its governance and who receive no essential benefits from its operation. This situation has already inspired an unprecedented revolutionary resistance among America's younger generations. For the technical-economic power to liberate America and all mankind is already available, and Americans are for the first time beginning to realize it. Before this liberation can take place, the technical-economic power to liberate must itself be liberated from the class that owns and controls it. To convert the menace of too much wealth and power for the few into the promise of enough for all, it is only necessary that the democratic principle be extended to the corporate and financial institutions of the social order. To do that is the task of the social revolution.

James O'Connor

James O'Connor is an associate professor of economics at San Jose State College. He is a former associate editor of *Studies on the Left* and an editor of the new radical journal *Socialist Revolution*. Professor O'Connor is the author of *The Origins of Socialism in Cuba* (1970) and is a member of the Bay Area Collective of Socialist Economists.

The following essay is a section from *The Meaning of Economic Imperialism,* a pamphlet published by the Radical Education Project (Box 625, Ann Arbor, Michigan 48107). The footnotes are omitted here.

O'Connor's essay is a systematic analysis of the meaning of economic imperialism and neo-colonialism. The concept of the economic surplus is defined, and the surplus absorption capacity of the advanced capitalist countries, especially the United States, is explained. Imperialism is then analyzed as a mode of surplus utilization, and the mechanics of contemporary imperialism are carefully elucidated. Finally, the foreign policy of the modern imperialist state is analyzed, and the economic and political problems facing the latter, especially the United States, are delineated.

THE MEANING OF ECONOMIC IMPERIALISM

The definition of economic imperialism which we employ is the economic domination of one region or country over another—specifically, the formal or informal control over local economic resources in a manner advantageous to the metropolitan power, and at the expense of the local economy. Economic control assumes different forms and is exercised in a number of ways. The main form of economic domination has always been control by the advanced capitalist countries over the liquid and real economic resources of

Reprinted by permission of James O'Connor.

economically backward areas. The main liquid resources are foreign exchange and public and private savings, and real resources consist of agricultural, mineral, transportation, communication, manufacturing, and commercial facilities and other assets. The most characteristic modes of domination today can be illuminated by way of contrast with examples drawn from the colonial period.

Control over Money

Examples of control over foreign exchange assets are numerous. In the colonial era the metropolitan powers established currency boards to issue and redeem local circulating medium against sterling and other metropolitan currencies. In its purest form, the currency board system required 100 percent backing of sterling for local currency. The East African Currency Board, for example, was established in 1919, staffed by British civil servants appointed by the Colonial Office, and at one time exercised financial domination over Ethiopia, British and Italian Somaliland, and Aden, as well as the East African countries. The Board did not have the authority to expand or contract local credit, and therefore expenditures on local projects which required imported materials or machinery were limited to current export earnings, less outlays for essential consumer goods, debt service and other fixed expenses. Measures to expand exports were thus necessary pre-conditions of local initiatives toward economic progress. In this way, British imperialism indirectly controlled the allocation of real resources.

This mode of control still survives in modified form in the Commonwealth Caribbean economies and elsewhere. The Jamaican central bank, for example, has limited power to influence the domestic money supply, but sterling and local currency are automatically convertible in unlimited amounts at fixed rates of exchange. The local government is thus prohibited from financing investment projects by inflation, or forced savings, nor are exchange controls and related financial instruments of national economic policy permitted. The structure and organization of the commercial banking system aggravates the situation. Local banks are branches of foreign-owned banks whose headquarters are located in the overseas financial centers and are more responsive to economic and monetary changes abroad than in the local economy; specifically, local banks have contracted credit at times when foreign exchange assets have been accumulating. This combination of monetary and financial dependence has caused artificial shortages of funds and prevented the Jamaican government from allocating local financial resources in a rational manner.

A more characteristic form of control over foreign exchange today is private direct investment. In the 19th and early 20th centuries, backward countries were often able to attract portfolio investments and local governments and capitalists were thus able to exercise some control over the use of foreign exchange made available by long-term foreign investment. Today direct investment constitutes the great mass of long-term capital exported on private account by the metropolitan countries. Foreign exchange receipts typically take the form of branch plants and other facilities of the multi-national corporations—facilities which are difficult or impossible to integrate into the structure of the local economy. What is more, satellite countries which depend on direct investment ordinarily provide free currency convertibility and hence foreign-owned enterprises which produce for local markets have privileged access to foreign exchange earned in other sectors of the economy.

Another feature of economic domination is the control of local savings, which assumes two forms. First, economic rule means that local government revenues, or *public* savings, are mortgaged to loans received from the metropolitan powers. An extreme example is Liberia—a country with an open door policy with regard to foreign capital—which in 1963 expended 94 percent of its annual revenues to repay foreign loans. In the 19th century, persuasion, coercion, and outright conquest often insured that tariffs and other taxes were turned over to foreign bondholders. In the absence of direct colonial rule, however, foreign lending was frequently a precarious undertaking. Latin American countries, for example, had an uneven history of bond payments. Foreign loans today are secured in more peaceful and more effective ways. The international capital market is highly centralized and dominated by the agencies of the main imperialist powers—the International Bank for Reconstruction and Development, the International Monetary Fund, and other financial institutions. No longer is it possible for borrowing countries to play one lending country off against another, or to default on their obligations or unilaterally scale down their debt without shutting the door on future loans. That no country has ever defaulted on a World Bank loan, or failed to amortize a loan on schedule, is eloquent testimony to the ability of the advanced capitalist countries to mortgage local tax receipts to foreign loans.

Secondly, *private* savings are mobilized by foreign corporations and governments in order to advance the interests of foreign capital. Foreign companies float local bond issues, raise equity capital, and generally attempt to monopolize available liquid resources in order to extend their field of operations and maximize profits. World Bank affiliates finance local Development Banks which scour the country for small and medium size savings to funnel into local and foreign enterprise. The United States government acquires a significant portion of the money supply of India and other countries through its policy of selling surplus foodstuffs for local currencies which it makes available to United States corporations. In these and other ways foreign interests today exercise control of local private savings.

A final feature of economic domination is the control of mineral, agricultural, manufacturing, and other real assets, and the organization and management of trade by foreign corporations. In Africa, for example, French bulk-buying companies in the ex-colonies monopolize the purchase and sale of coffee, peanuts, palm-oil products, and other commodities produced by small and medium-sized growers. In Mexico, one foreign corporation organizes the great part of cotton production and exportation. Frequently control of commerce necessitates financial domination. The United States, for example, has penetrated Mexico's financial structure with the aim of restricting Mexican-Latin American trade in order to insure control of Latin American markets for itself. Control of iron, copper, tin, oil, bauxite, and other mineral resources is in the hands of a handful of giant corporations. In some countries, foreign interests dominate the commanding heights of the economy—transportation, power, communication, and the leading manufacturing industries. These examples should suffice to show that foreign control of real, as well as of liquid, assets extends into all branches of local economies and penetrates every economically backward region in the world capitalist system.

The Main Features of Contemporary Imperialism

These examples of specific kinds of economic domination illustrate most of the main features of contemporary imperialism which can be summarized as follows:

First, the further concentration and centralization of capital, and the integration of the world capitalist economy into the structures of the giant United States-based multi-national corporations, or integrated conglomerate monopolistic enterprises; and the acceleration of technological change under the auspices of these corporations.

Second, the abandonment of the "free" international market, and the substitution of administered prices in commodity trade and investment; and the determination of profit margins through adjustments in the internal accounting schemes of the multi-national corporations.

Third, the active participation of state capital in international investment; subsidies and guarantees to private investment; and a global foreign policy which corresponds to the global interests and perspective of the multi-national corporation.

Fourth, the consolidation of an international ruling class constituted on the basis of ownership and control of the multi-national corporations, and the concomitant decline of national rivalries initiated by the national power elites in the advanced capitalist countries; and the internationalization of the world capital market by the World Bank and other agencies of the international ruling class.

Fifth, the intensification of all of these tendencies arising from the threat of world socialism to the world capitalist system.

Why Imperialism?

The general features of contemporary imperialism are much better understood than the sources of economic expansion, the specific contradictions in the metropolitan economies which drive the multi-national corporations to extend their scale of operations over the entire globe. As we have seen, Hobson explained 19th century British imperialism by way of reference to inequalities in the distribution of income, while Lenin rested his case on the declining rate of profit in the home economy. Neither of these explanations are very useful today, at least in the form which they have come down to us. In the first place, the advanced capitalist economies have become mass consumption societies; secondly, savings have become concentrated in the hands of the government, financial intermediaries, and trust funds, as well as a relatively few giant corporations; thirdly, the concept of "the" rate of profit is out-of-date. In the overcrowded competitive sector of the advanced capitalist economies the profit rate remains a datum, a given, but in the oligopolistic sector profit margins are themselves determined by corporate price, output, and investment policies.

ECONOMIC SURPLUS

Some contemporary Marxist economists have proposed an alternative approach to the problem of identifying the important economic contradictions in advanced capitalist societies. These approaches are based on the elementary concept of economic surplus, which Baran and Sweezy define as the difference between total national product and socially necessary costs of production. Total product is the aggregate value of all commodities and services produced in a given period of time, or, alternatively, total business, worker, and government expenditures. Nowhere in the literature is there a satisfactory discussion of the meaning of socially necessary costs. A working definition is the outlays which are required to maintain the labor force and society's productive capacity in their present state of productivity or efficiency.

Economic surplus consists of outlays which either augment productive capacity and increase labor skills and efficiency, or are used for economically wasteful or destructive ends. Any specific expenditure item which can be reallocated from one use to another without affecting total production (e.g. military expenditures to foreign gifts) falls into the general category of economic surplus. An expenditure item which cannot be reallocated from one employment to another (e.g. wages of workers in basic food industries to military expenditures) without reducing total production can be defined as a necessary cost. Unlike total output, neither necessary costs nor surplus is easily quantifiable, particularly since many outlays, highway expenditures for example, comprise both costs and surplus. Hence it is not possible to calculate with any great precision the proportion of total product which is constituted by surplus, nor can the relation between total product and surplus over a span of time be known with absolute certainty. Nevertheless, there is powerful indirect evidence that the surplus in relation to total product in the advanced capitalist countries tends to increase historically.

Provisionally identifying surplus corporate profits, sales expenditures, and taxes, Baran and Sweezy demonstrate easily that corporate price and cost policies result in an absolute and relative increase in the surplus. In a nutshell, the corporations stabilize prices around an upward secular trend, while constantly seeking to increase efficiency by reducing production costs. Cost reductions are not transmitted to consumers in the form of lower prices, but rather are channeled into new investment, sales expenditures, and taxes.

The questions thus arise: What are the various ways available to advanced capitalist countries to absorb the increasing economic surplus, or raise the level of demand? and, What are the limits on their absorptive capacity? These are obviously large and complex questions the answers to which we can do no more than suggest here.

Within the metropolitan economy the economic surplus is absorbed in three distinctive ways. Expenditures on productive investment in both physical and human capital are the first, and historically most important, mode of surplus utilization. Investment outlays are made on both private and government account. In the private sector of the economy, investment opportunities are available in two distinct spheres, oligopolistic industries, dominated by the giant conglomerate corporation, and competitive industries, characterized by relatively inefficient, small-scale enterprise. In the former, technological change, which was at one time the most important outlet for investment-seeking funds, no longer can be relied upon to absorb more than a tiny fraction of the surplus. In the first place, in the few older, stabilized industries where competition between firms for larger shares of the market is at a minimum, there is a tendency to suppress new technologies in order to preserve the value of the existing productive capacity. There is, in [Maurice] Dobb's words, "an increasing danger of the ossification of an existing industrial structure owing to the reluctance or inability of entrepreneurs to face the cost and the risks attendant upon such large-scale change."

Secondly, Baran and Sweezy have shown that in industries in which firms struggle to increase their share of the market and hence are under considerable pressure to lower costs, the rate of introduction of new technology is reduced, thus limiting the amount of investment-seeking funds which can be profitably absorbed during any given period. Lastly, as Gillman and others have demonstrated, there has been a historic rise in fixed capital stock per employed worker, and a decline in business fixed investment and producer durable equipment expenditures in relation to total national product. Thus technological change—independent of the rate at which it is introduced into the production processes—tends increasingly to be capital-saving. To put it another way, oligopolistic enterprises favor input-saving, rather than output-increasing innovations when (and if) the industrial structure becomes relatively stabilized and a provisional market-sharing plan has been agreed upon. For their part, competitive industries are overcrowded, the turnover rate is high, profit margins are minimal, and they offer few incentives to corporations with investment-seeking funds.

Productive investment outlays are also made on government, or state account, but most of these are merely special forms of private investment and hence are determined by the rhythm of capital accumulation in the private sector. The costs of these complementary investments—water investments in agricultural districts, for example—are borne by the taxpayer, while the benefits are appropriated by private capitalists. The state also finances investments which aim to create future profitable opportunities for private capital—examples are industrial development parks—but these discretionary investments are limited by the need on the part of the state bureaucracy to justify the extra tax burden (due to the absence of long-term investment horizons generally shared by capitalist class and state officials), as well as by the lack of new markets for final commodities.

Consumption-Related Use of Surplus

Expenditures on private and social consumption over and above economic needs, or in excess of outlays on necessary costs, constitute the second mode of surplus utilization. These expenditures, like all economically wasteful outlays, are limited to the degree that they can be rationalized within the logic of capitalist economy—that is to say, in so far as they lead to greater profits. The proportion of current earnings which the corporation can channel into advertising expenditures, product differentiation, forced obsolescence, and other selling expenses, as well as other socially wasteful uses of the surplus, is limited to the extent to which these outlays increase commodity demand, sales, and profits. There are also limits on the absorption of the surplus via borrowing private consumption demand from the future—that is, by the expansion of consumer credit—which are determined by the relation of current consumer income to loan repayments.*

Consumption outlays are also made by local, state, and Federal government bodies. A greater or lesser portion of education, transportation, recreational, and cultural expenditures—in general, spending on social amenities—constitutes social consumption, a special form of private consumption. Socially necessary costs make up a large part of social consumption, while much of the remainder comprises economic waste. Again, government expenditures are limited by the ability of the political authority to rationalize waste within the framework of private profit-making. In addition, there are political limits on the expansion of spending destined for public housing, health, and other socio-economic activities which are inconsistent with the hierarchy of rank and privileges in a capitalist society, or which compete with private capital. The same conclusion can be drawn in connection with the possibilites of redistributing income with the aim of raising the wage and salary share of total product— and hence private consumption expenditures—at the expense of private profits. The only major type of discretionary state expenditure consistent with private ownership of the means of production, social and economic inequality, and other central features of a capitalist society is military spending.

IMPERIALISM AS USE OF SURPLUS

The preceding sketch in no sense substitutes for a full-dress analysis of the surplus absorption capacity of the advanced capitalist countries, in particular the United States, but rather provides a general background for the detailed exploration of the possibilities of utilizing the economic surplus in the backward capitalist countries and the other advanced capitalist societies. Our general conclusions are two-fold: First, the multi-national corporations are under unceasing pressure to extend their field of operations outside the United States. Economic prosperity in the United States during the two decades since World War II has increasingly depended on military expenditures

---

* In general, a consumer will not be able to borrow in order to finance new consumption when economically necessary outlays (or costs), together with loan repayments, equal current income.

and overseas expansion. Between 1950 and 1964, United States commodity exports, including the sales of overseas facilities of United States corporations, rose nearly 270 percent, while commodity sales at home increased only 126 percent. Expectedly, earnings on foreign investments make up a rising portion of after-tax corporate profits—10 percent in 1950, and 22 percent in 1964. In the strategic capital goods sector of the United States economy, military and foreign purchases account for a surprisingly large share of total output—between 20 and 50 percent in twenty-one of twenty-five industries, and over 80 percent in two industries. Our second general conclusion is that overseas expansion since World War II has not weakened, but intensified the antagonism between the generation and absorption of the economic surplus.

Close examination of the two modes of surplus utilization overseas is required to substantiate these claims. Foreign commodity trade is the first, and, until the era of monopoly capitalism, the only important way of absorbing the surplus abroad. Contemporary state policies which seek to promote commodity trade encounter a number of crippling handicaps. For one thing, low-cost supplier credits and other forms of export subsidies provided by state agencies such as the Import-Export Bank merely export the surplus absorption problem abroad and hence meet with resistance from other advanced capitalist countries. A comprehensive system of export subsidies is almost guaranteed to result in retaliation in kind. The widely adopted "most favored nation" clause in international trade agreements was an expression of the willingness to "give and take" on the part of the advanced capitalist countries in the immediate post-war period. Second, in recent decades United States commodity exports have run consistently ahead of imports, limiting the ability of the United States to wring tariff concessions from other countries without offering even greater reductions in return. Third, United States penetration of Europe, regions in the sphere of influence of the European imperialist powers, and the semi-independent backward capitalist countries which employ tariffs, import quotas, and exchange controls to conserve foreign exchange by reducing imports is increasingly restricted by a revival of economic nationalism, as well as by the birth of a new economic regionalism—that is, by what Joan Robinson has termed The New Mercantilism.

Private foreign investments and state loans and grants constitute the second, and today far and away the most important, mode of surplus absorption. Capital exports may increase demand in one of two ways: first, by borrowing demand from the future and directly expanding the market for capital goods; second, by raising production and income abroad and therefore indirectly increasing imports in the recipient country or in third countries.

In recent years there have been three new tendencies in capital exporting which support the conclusion that it will become increasingly difficult to find outlets abroad for the investment-seeking surplus generated by the multi-national corporations. These tendencies are: first, increased collaboration between foreign and local capital; second, the shift in the composition of foreign investments against primary commodity sectors and in favor of manufacturing and related activities; and third, the shift in the composition of capital exports against private investment and in favor of state loans and grants. All three tendencies are related to the development of anti-colonial and national independence movements in the backward capitalist countries. A brief review of the general implications of national independence for foreign investment opportunities is therefore in order.

Political Independence and Foreign Capital

Gillman and others have put forward two arguments which support the view that national independence reduces opportunities for the penetration of foreign capital. In the first place, it is asserted that public ownership of the means of production in the ex-colonies encroaches on the traditional territory of private capital and limits investment opportunities available to the international monopolies. This line of reasoning is not only at odds with the facts—in the backward capitalist countries joint state-private ventures are more characteristic than state enterprise—but also pushes aside the critical question of the control of capital. In a number of countries, including many European capitalist nations, the state is the nominal owner of many heavy industrial and infra-structure facilities, but control rests with an autonomous bureaucracy which is highly responsive to the needs of private capital. The vast majority of state and joint enterprises in the backward countries are market-oriented, integrated into the structure of the private market. Far from discouraging foreign investors, one task of state enterprise in many countries is to attract new private investment.

Secondly, there is the argument that anti-colonial sentiment and the urge for an independent field of economic action lead to exchange controls, restrictions on profit remittances, higher business taxes, more costly social legislation, and other policies which are repugnant to foreign capital. Against this view it should be stressed that the economic autonomy of politically independent countries is itself a question for analysis. Military coups in Brazil, Indonesia, and Ghana, to cite only three recent counter-revolutionary movements, provide dramatic evidence for the view that political autonomy must be insured by economic autonomy. Again seven long-independent Latin American countries with such disparate attitudes toward foreign capital as Chile and Peru—historically the former has been less permissive than the latter—collectively signed the Treaty of Montevideo (1960) which favored foreign investment, and recognized the need for foreign capital in economic development. On the other side, China, Cuba, and other countries which have abandoned the world capitalist system obviously hold little promise for foreign capital.

In reality, there are a number of reasons to believe that politically independent, economically under-exploited countries will continue to welcome private foreign capital. First, and perhaps most important, local financiers and industrialists are eager to participate in profitable economic activities initiated by the multi-national corporations based in the advanced countries. Joint ventures and other partnership arrangements are looked upon with great favor by local business interests. Tariff policy is designed to encourage assembly, packaging, and other final manufacturing investments not only to promote the development of national industry but also to increase the flow of foreign capital and open up profit opportunities for the local bourgeoisie.

Secondly, the Latin American countries, as well as the ex-colonies in Asia and Africa, are under great pressure from the masses to initiate and promote economic and social development. In these non-socialist countries local sources of capital are dissipated in luxury consumption and other wasteful expenditures, or cannot be mobilized in the absence of fundamental agrarian and other economic reforms, and hence local governments increasingly depend on foreign capital, private as well as public. Most ex-colonial governments are desperately searching for ways to conserve foreign exchange and actively seek foreign investments and loans. Third, British and French foreign investments are welcome in backward countries which belong to one or the other of these metropoles' currency blocs— where exchange controls are minimal or entirely absent—because there are few if any ways to acquire private foreign capital from other advanced capitalist countries. British investments, for example, are more and more oriented to Sterling Area countries. Fourth, backward countries which have no ambition beyond expanding exports of primary commodities require active foreign participation in the export sector because of the difficulties of independently acquiring and maintaining distribution channels and marketing outlets. After Bolivia nationalized the tin mines, for example, planning of production and sales was partly thwarted because the government "remained beholden to the same big companies for processing and sale."

On the other side, there are at least two reasons for believing that political independence has discouraged some foreign investment, although it is difficult to even guess how much. In the first place, foreign corporations hesitate to invest in the absence of political controls which prevent local firms from using unpatented production processes to invade third-country markets or to pass on to competitors. Second, the ex-colonies have eliminated or reduced in many spheres of the economy the special privileges and exclusive rights which corporations based in the colonial power once took for granted. The increased risk and uncertainty which face foreign capital have discouraged investments by small-scale enterprises which are unable to finance multi-plant, multi-country operations.

The Reduction of Surplus Absorption Capacity:
Use of Local Savings . . .

Anti-colonialism, political independence, and the elimination of the colonial powers from many formal economic command posts have contributed to three new tendencies in foreign investment which reduce the surplus absorption capacity of the backward capitalist countries. There is overwhelming evidence of the first tendency, the growing mobilization of local savings and capital by foreign corporations which diminishes the need for capital exports from the advanced countries. In Latin America, local capital is the most important source of financing for wholly-owned subsidiaries of United States corporations. One-half of American and Foreign Power Company's $400 million post-war expansion program in eleven countries was financed from local savings, the other half from retained earnings. A $72 million investment in Argentina by five oil companies illustrates the character of modern overseas finance; the corporations' investment amounted to only $18 million; debentures raised $30 million in Argentina; and the United States government and local investment corporations supplied the remainder. In the capitalist world as a whole, roughly one-third of total U.S. corporate financing overseas in 1964 comprised foreign borrowing or equity financing, and foreign supplies of capital made up two-thirds of the increase in financing over 1963 levels.

The multi-national corporations mobilize local savings and capital in a variety of ways: bonds and equities are sold in local capital markets; joint ventures and mixed enterprises mobilize private and state capital, respectively; local development and investment banks acquire local savings directly, and indirectly via local governments; foreign and domestic banks, insurance companies and other financial intermediaries have access to pools of local savings. To cite one example, Morgan Guarantee Trust Company's 16 correspondent banks in Venezuela hold 55 percent of privately-owned commercial bank resources, and help foreign firms raise local funds. Morgan is also part-owner of a large Spanish investment bank which in a two-year period raised $40 million for local and foreign companies. The World Bank pioneered in the organization and contributes to the financing of local development banks, develops and integrates capital markets in countries where monetary institutions are weak, and acts as a wedge for private foreign capital into established capital markets.*

The growing demand by the international monopolies for local capital is prompted by both political and economic factors. First, and probably most important, both the multi-national corporations

* Industrial finance institutions in East Africa are typical. "National Development Corporations" were established before political independence to promote and direct new ventures and to participate in existing enterprises by subscribing to equity capital issues. "Development Finance Corporations," in which British and German capital are deeply involved, were established more recently, specialize in loans and grants, and promote partnerships between African and European capital.

and local bourgeoisies are eager to form partnership arrangements, the former to exercise indirect control over, and politically neutralize, the latter, the latter in order to share in the profits of the former. In Nigeria, for example, "foreign investors are beginning to realize that their presence constitutes a political problem and that it is in their interest to encourage Nigerian participation in the structure of their firms to enhance acceptability." Joint ventures and partnerships are up-to-date versions of the colonial policy of creating a dependent, passive local bourgeoisie; British capital, to cite perhaps the most important instance, allied itself with the largest and best organized Indian monopolies, such as those dominated by the Tatas and Birlas, as a hedge against possible discriminatory action by the Indian government.

Second, the alliance between foreign and local capital inhibits potential economic competition and paves the way for the diversification of the foreign operations of the international monopolies, and extends their control over related product fields in the local economy. Even in countries such as Mexico, where the government refuses to extend its cooperation to foreign corporations which compete with local business or displace local capital, foreigners often have "decisive influence" over company policy because domestic equity ownership is dispersed and minority stock ownership is concentrated in the hands of one or two United States corporations. Extending the sphere of corporate operations opens up opportunities for increased profits in the form of royalties and fees for technical services, patents, and brand names. What is more, the use of local capital reduces the risk of conducting operations in foreign countries; local capital is smaller and less diversified than foreign capital and therefore is more vulnerable and assumes a disproportionate risk. In addition, local businessmen are valuable for their knowledge of domestic product and labor markets, government contacts, and other information which insures secure and profitable operations overseas. Finally, the international monopolies profit by spreading their capital thin in branches of production characterized by economies of large-scale production.

. . . Growth of Investment in Manufacturing . . .

The growth of private foreign investment in manufacturing industries, and the relative decline of agricultural and mining investments, is the second new tendency in capital exporting. The development of synthetic fibers, the rise in agricultural productivity in the advanced countries, the inelastic demand for foodstuffs, the reduction in the mineral component in production (e.g. non-ferrous metals), and tariff walls erected by the advanced capitalist countries against imports of primary commodities have reduced the demand for investment funds abroad in mining and agriculture. Tariffs, quotas, and other measures to protect manufacturing industries in the backward countries and regional marketing arrangements in Europe and elsewhere have compelled the large corporations in the United States to construct or purchase manufacturing facilities abroad to retain traditional markets. In turn, the expansive impulses of the multinational corporation have affected world-wide capital flows and the production and distribution of commodities.

Accurate comparable statistics covering long spans of time are not available, but the benchmark data shown in Table I below suggest the general order of magnitude of change.

Between 1940 and 1964 United States direct manufacturing investments in Latin America (which absorbs about 60 percent of U.S.

TABLE I

BOOK VALUE OF UNITED STATES DIRECT FOREIGN
INVESTMENT BY INDUSTRY (millions of dollars)

	1929	1940	1946	1950	1955	1959
Total	7,528	7,002	8,854	11,787	19,313	29,735
Agriculture	880	435	545	589	725	662
Mining and Smelting	1,185	782	1,062	1,129	2,209	2,858
Petroleum	1,117	1,278	1,769	3,390	5,849	10,423
Manufacturing	1,813	1,926	2,854	3,831	6,349	9,692
Public Utilities, Comm. & Transportation	1,610	1,514	1,277	1,425	1,614	2,413
Trade	368	523	740	762	1,282	2,039
Other (excludes Insurance in 1929)	555	544	607	661	1,285	1,648

Source: Raymond Mikesell, "US Postwar Investment Abroad: A Statistical Analysis," in Mikesell, ed., *Public International Lending for Development*, 1966, p. 54, citing: US Dept. of Commerce, Office of Business Economics, Washington, DC, *Balance of Payments Statistical Supplement;* US Dept. of Commerce, US Business Investments in Foreign Countries, 1960 (for 1959 figures); *Survey of Current Business,* December 1951, p. 13 (for 1946 figures).

manufacturing investments in all backward regions) increased from $210 million to $2,340 million, or from 10 percent to 25 percent of total Latin American holdings. In the same period, agricultural investments remained unchanged, mining investments doubled, and the value of petroleum holdings rose from $572 million to $3,142 million. A similar trend is visible in connection with British investments in India. In 1911, about three-quarters of all direct private investments were in extractive industries, utilities and transportation accounted for roughly one-fifth, and the remainder was divided between commerce and manufacturing. In 1956, manufacturing investments made up over one-third of the total, commerce another one-fourth, and plantation investments only one-fifth. As Hamza Alavi has written, "this is a complete contrast from the old pattern" of investment holdings. Of all British direct foreign investments (excluding oil) in 1965, Kemp has estimated that manufacturing investments constituted about one-half, the great part located in other advanced capitalist countries.

Turning again to the United States, Table II below summarizes the distribution of direct investments by region and industry in 1964.

Most United States manufacturing investments in backward countries are concentrated in consumer goods fabrication, assembly and

TABLE II

VALUE OF DIRECT INVESTMENTS ABROAD
BY REGION AND INDUSTRY, 1964 (preliminary)
(millions of dollars)

	Total	Mining/ Smelt.	Pe-troleum	Manu-facturing	Pub. Util.	Trade	Other
Total	44,343	3,564	14,350	16,861	2,023	3,730	3,808
Canada	13,820	1,671	3,228	6,191	467	805	1,458
Latin America	8,932	1,098	3,142	2,340	568	951	832
Other Western Hemisphere	1,386	250	569	166	49	89	263
Common Market	5,398	13	1,511	3,098	45	551	180
Other Europe	6,669	43	1,575	3,449	8	921	674
Africa	1,629	356	830	225	2	93	122
Asia	3,062	34	2,014	535	55	238	186
Oceania	1,582	100	444	856	2	87	93
International	1,865	—	1,038	—	827	—	—

Source: US Dept. of Commerce, *Survey of Current Business*, Vol. 45, No. 9, September 1965, Table 2, p. 22.

packaging, and light chemicals. The pattern is roughly the same in the advanced capitalist economies, with the single exception that investments in industrial equipment facilities are more common. During 1958–1959, of 164 U.S. investments in new or expanded manufacturing enterprises in Latin America, 106 were located in the chemical and consumer good sectors; in other backward regions, the number of facilities were 34 and 24, respectively.

In connection with opportunities for capital exporting, and the significance of capital exports for absorbing the economic surplus, 19th century and mid-20th century imperialism differ in a number of profound respects. In the earlier period, foreign investments were concentrated in raw material and mineral production, and the economic satellites were no more than extensions of the metropolitan economies. Overseas capital expenditures opened up cheap sources of productive inputs, and lowered the costs of production in manufacturing industries in the metropoles. In turn, home and foreign demand for manufactured goods increased, prompting an expansion of output and fresh rounds of foreign investment. To the degree that capital exports were channeled into railroad and other transportation facilities, there were favorable indirect effects on the availability of raw materials, and hence manufacturing costs in the metropoles. For 19th century Great Britain, this cumulative, expansive system worked to perfection. Income generated in the satellites by the inflow of capital was expended on British manufactured exports. During periods of rising foreign investment, British exports rose faster than imports, and a consistently favorable balance of payments was maintained.

To be sure, contemporary imperialist powers continue to import many raw materials, and petroleum needs expand at a rapid pace. The economic relationships between the metropolitan economies and their satellites, however, differ in important respects. Petroleum production is concentrated in the hands of a few oligopolists which maintain rigid price structures and fail to pass on reductions in exploration, drilling, and production costs to consumers. The same conclusion can be drawn with regard to other raw materials (iron and copper, for example) for which the ratio of imports to U.S. production is higher than in the pre-war era. Moreover, in comparison with other regions, imports have increased more rapidly from Latin American countries, which have met the expansion of demand for copper, tin, manganese, cocoa, and other commodities largely by diverting sales from other markets, rather than by expanding supplies. The basic reason is that Latin American raw material production is today highly monopolized, and, in addition, operates, under conditions of decreasing returns to large-scale production. Thus neither new capital outlays nor modernization investments have significantly reduced the costs of production of primary commodities, and, unlike investments in the earlier period, are not self-perpetuating. What is more, international commodity agreements and regional marketing arrangements reduce competition between raw material producing countries, and tend to maintain prices at relatively high levels.

Manufacturing investments in backward countries fall into one of two categories. Tariff-hopping investments, quantitatively most significant, are defensive moves which enable the international corporations to retain established export markets, and merely change the locale of investment from the metropole to the satellite. These outlays fail to expand commodity demand, and hence do not provide growing outlets for the economic surplus. Opportunities for other manufacturing investments in backward countries are also generally limited to import-substitute activities because domestic markets are typically oriented toward middle and upper class consumption patterns which are imitative of those in the advanced countries. Export markets for satellite manufactured goods are weak because national and regional monopolies operate behind high tariff walls, and, in addition, monopoly controls which the multi-national corporations exercise over international distribution systems and marketing outlets place insurmountable barriers to large-scale satellite manufacturing exports. For these reasons, the United States has shown a growing interest in new regional marketing groupings such as the Latin American Free Trade Area and the Central American Common Market. One of the chief objectives of the Common Market during its formative period (1958–1962) was to attract fresh supplies of foreign capital. There are two important barriers, however, to flourishing regional marketing arrangements in economically backward areas. First, less productive, entrenched local monopolies put up a tenacious struggle to retain their privileged market positions—in comparison with the giant, integrated European cartels and monopolies which promoted the European Common Market. Secondly, the new preferential trading areas in backward regions are too small to compete effectively with Britain's Sterling Area or the European Economic Community. In sharp contrast to the upsurge of United States investment in Canada after the expansion of the Imperial Preference System in 1932, to cite one example, dollar flows of fresh investment to the new trading areas will be limited.

We have finally to consider opportunities for manufacturing investments in other advanced economies. As we have seen, in recent years the great mass of United States manufacturing investments have been in Europe and Canada. Most of these investments have been tariff-hopping operations, or have been channeled into the purchase of existing facilities. Moreover, United States corporations have increasingly been compelled to penetrate lines of production which are competitive with United States exports. Similar to the effect of British reconstruction investments in Europe following World War I, United States capital flows to other advanced capitalist countries tend to be self-defeating in the long run. An excellent illustration is provided by one study of the impact of 112 British subsidiary companies in Europe on British exports; only 5.6 percent of the subsidiaries' capital outlays was expended on British capital goods. Only investments in distribution facilities, specifically motivated to expand foreign sales, can be expected to significantly increase commodity exports.

These lines of analysis suggest that the surplus absorption capacity of both the advanced and backward countries—in both traditional and newer branches of the economy—will in the future be limited to replacement demand, together with the modest flow of new investments necessary to keep pace with expanding incomes abroad. Reflecting the marginal impact of foreign investments on United States commodity exports is the continuing, although muted, crisis in the United States' balance of payments.

. . . State Loans Replace Private

Roughly the same conclusion can be drawn in connection with public and international loans. The third, and perhaps most striking, tendency in capital exporting is the substitution of state loans for private capital outflows. About two-thirds of all capital exports are on state or international (public) account. As Table III shows, nearly three-quarters of all loans and investments destined for backward capitalist countries originate in the public or international sector. In 1964, the net outflow of resources to satellite countries and multi-national agencies (which in turn loans funds to the satellites) amounted to nearly $8 billion, of which less than $2 billion was private.

TABLE III

NET OUTFLOW OF RESOURCES TO BACKWARD COUNTRIES
AND MULTINATIONAL AGENCIES, 1964
(millions of dollars)

		State Flows			Private Flows		
	Total	Total	Bi-lateral	Multi-lateral Agencies	Total	Bi-lateral	Multi-lateral Agencies
1960	7,177	4,572	3,982	590	2,605	2,420	185
1961	8,109	5,617	4,803	814	2,492	2,390	102
1962	7,533	5,676	5,031	645	1,857	1,627	230
1963	7,351	5,704	5,294	410	1,647	1,685	−38
1964	7,854	5,698	5,271	427	2,156	1,999	157

Source: United Nations, Department of Economic and Social Affairs, *The Financing of Economic Development, World Economic Survey*, 1956, Part 1, New York, 1966, Table II-1, p. 45.

The relationship between private and public capital flows is highly complex, and a brief analysis inevitably runs the risk of over-simplification. Reduced to essentials, however, state loans serve two main purposes. First, public funds which build up the infra-structure of backward countries frequently complement private capital flows and represent merely a special form of private investment, the costs of which are borne by taxpayers in the lending country. With regard to surplus absorption capactiy within the infra-structure sectors of backward countries, the same conclusion reached in our discussion of private investment can be applied a fortiori.

Second, the character of United States "aid" programs underlines their growing importance as projected points of entry for private capital. Many Export-Import Bank loans are made with the purpose of encouraging the flow of private investment—since 1960 the Bank has offered long-term loans of up to five years. Provisions of Public Law 480, the "Food for Peace" program, are "designed almost entirely for the purpose of stimulating the flow of U.S. private investment to the less-developed countries." Under this program, the United

States government loans local currencies acquired from the sale of surplus agricultural commodities to American corporations in order to finance the local costs of investment projects. The greatest portion of both the interest and principal is reloaned either to private investors or local governments. "How useful to our own foreign aid and foreign development programs could it be," the president of one multinational corporation has written, "if these funds, in local currencies, were to be loaned on an increasing scale to competitive private borrowers—either Americans or others—for local investment. . . ." Finally, the United States' Agency for International Development grants survey loans to American corporations, paying one-half of the cost of feasibility studies in the event it is decided not to proceed with the investment.

The international agencies, in particular, the World Bank, are also beacon lights for private investment. Originally regarded by the leading imperialist nations as a way to restore private international capital movements by guaranteeing private loans, the World Bank has been compelled to centralize and rationalize the world capital market. The Bank has eliminated many of the anarchic features of international capital movements, supervises vast amounts of capital which penetrate the backward countries, and acts as a funnel for private capital in search of safe, profitable returns—banks and investment houses participate in World Bank loans, and the Bank frequently floats bond issues in United States and European money markets. In part dependent on private money market conditions, most Bank activities are financed by subscribed or borrowed government funds. The Bank is thus relatively autonomous, and allocates vast amounts of capital for large-scale infra-structure projects in order to clear the way for private investment flows.

MODERN IMPERIALISM'S FOREIGN POLICY

Whether or not private capital responds to the incentives held out by national governments and international agencies depends on a host of factors, chief among which are the investment "climate" in the satellite economies and the character of other state political-economic policies. . . . Suffice it for now to note some of the major differences between imperialist foreign policy in the 19th and mid-20th centuries.

First, and most obvious, modern imperialism attempts to substitute informal for formal modes of political control of countries in the backwash of world capitalism. The methods of establishing political control are varied. The use of old economic and political ties is practiced whenever possible; these include the relationships formed within the British Commonwealth and the French Community, closed currency zones, preferential trading systems, military alliances, and political-military pacts. Economic, political, and cultural missions, labor union delegations, joint military training programs, military grants, bribes to local ruling classes in the form of economic "aid," substitute for direct colonial rule. Only when indirect policies fail are the older instruments of coercion and force brought into play, and the principle of continuity in change applies. An excellent example is the United States-instigated and supported counter-revolution in Guatemala in 1954, the accomplishments of which the State Department listed under four headings:

1. "The conclusion of an agreement with a United Fruit Company subsidiary providing for the return of property expropriated by the Arbenz Government."
2. "The repeal of the law affecting remittances and taxation of earnings from foreign capital."
3. "The signing of an Investment Guarantee Agreement with the United States."
4. "The promulgation of a new and more favorable petroleum law." (*State Department Bulletin,* No. 6465, April 1, 1957.)

Within Guatemala, the Armas regime in the post-1954 period was maintained in office via contracts with United Fruit, Bond and Share, and other monopolies.

Secondly, contemporary imperialist states enjoy relatively more financial, and hence political, autonomy. In the 19th century, imperialist countries regarded themselves as dependent on the private capital market for raising funds for discretionary state expenditures and were compelled to pursue economic and fiscal policies designed to make it possible for their colonies to meet their private debt service. The dominant state capitalist countries today are financially independent and can follow a more flexible policy toward their satellites. The reason is that both the potential and actual economic surplus are comparatively large. The potential surplus is large because the normal tendency of monopoly capitalist economies is stagnation and unemployment of labor and capital, attributable to a deficiency of aggregate demand. State expenditures—including military expenditures and foreign loans and grants—normally increase not only aggregate demand but also real income and output, and hence the tax base. A rise in expenditures thus increases revenues, even if tax rates remain unchanged. State expenditures are partly self-financing and virtually costless in terms of the real resources utilized. The actual economic surplus constitutes a relatively large portion of national product because of technological and productivity advances. For these reasons, taxes (and state expenditures) make up a large share of national product with few serious adverse effects on economic incentives, and thus on total production itself.

The significance of the financial independence of the contemporary imperialist state for foreign policy lies in its ability to export capital— or absorb the surplus overseas—without a quid pro quo. The Marshall Plan, the extensive program of military aid and grants, and the low-cost loans extended to backward countries by AID are the main examples of this mode of surplus absorption. The surplus absorption capacity of satellite countries which are closely tied to the United States political-military bloc is for practical purposes unlimited. Two factors, however, circumscribe state grants without a quid pro quo. First, low-cost state loans and grants-in-aid, or capital exports which are not extended on normal commercial principles, compete "unfairly" with private loans and are resisted by private capitalist interests in the metropolitan economy. Second, metropolitan governments are unable to discipline their satellites effectively unless there are economic strings attached to international loans. Moreover, state bilateral and multilateral loans financed in private capital markets in the advanced countries must earn a return sufficient to cover the cost of borrowing and administration. Opportunities for capital exports extended on commercial principles are limited by the availability of profitable investment projects.

19th century and mid-20th century imperialism depart in a third important respect. In the 19th century there were few important antagonisms between Great Britain's role as the leading national capitalist power on the one hand, and as the dominant imperialist power on the other. Policies designed to expand Britain's home economy extended capitalist modes of production and organization to the three under-exploited continents, directly and indirectly strengthening the growing British imperial system.* For this reason, foreign policy ordinarily served private foreign investors and other private foreign investors and other private interests oriented to overseas activity. Only occasionally—as in the case of Disraeli's decision to purchase Suez Canal shares in 1875—was foreign investment employed as a "weapon" of British foreign policy. Even less frequently did Britain promote private foreign investments with the purpose of aiding global foreign policy objectives.†

By way of contrast, the national and international ambitions of the United States in the mid-20th century are continually in conflict. In the context of the limited absorption capacity of the backward capitalist world and international competition from other advanced capitalist economies and the socialist countries, the United States is compelled to employ a wide range of policies to expand trade and investment. To further national ends, a "partnership" between "public lending institutions" and "private lenders"—with the former "leading the way" for the latter—has been formed. Underlining the role of the state in the service of the multi-national corporations, in 1962 Secretary of State Rusk described the newer government policies which extend beyond state loan programs—investment guarantee programs in 46 backward capitalist countries which cover currency inconvertibility, expropriation, war, revolution, and insurrection; instructions to local embassies to support business interests by making "necessary representations to the host governments . . ."; the creation of a new Special Assistant for International Business in the State Department in order to insure that private business interests receive "prompt representation" in the government ("Trade, Investment, and U.S. Foreign Policy," *State Department Bulletin,* November 5, 1962.) Especially when public loans are disguised as special forms of private loans (see above), the commitment of the United States government

* The argument that Britain's home economy suffered because it was deprived of capital which was absorbed abroad is fallacious. On the one hand, given the prevailing distribution of income and industrial organization, there were few profitable opportunities to absorb the surplus at home; on the other hand, the return flow on foreign investments more than offset the original capital exports.

† It has been suggested by one expert, however, that private investments were made to serve specific foreign policy objectives more frequently than it is ordinarily believed.

to national capitalist interests inhibits state policies which seek to strengthen the industrial bourgeoisie and ruling classes in other advanced countries and the national bourgeoisie in the backward nations. Perhaps this is the most important limit on capital exports on public account.

As the leading international power, the United States is under constant and growing pressure to strengthen world capitalism as a system, including each of its specific parts. Policies which aim to recruit new members for local comprador groups, stimulate the development of capitalist agriculture and the middle farmers, reinforce the dominance of local financial and commercial classes, and reinvigorate local manufacturing activities—these general policies pose a potential or real threat to the interests of United States national capital. Alliance for Progress funds destined for the middle sectors of Latin American agriculture, Export-Import bank loans to foreign commercialists, loans and grants to foreign governments dominated by the urban bourgeoisie, loans and subsidies to the Indian iron and steel industry, Mexican industry and agriculture, and other branches of production in countries which are slowly industrializing—these and other stop-gap and long-range measures help to keep the backward countries in the imperialist camp in the short run, but directly or indirectly create local capitalist interests which may demand their independence from United States capital in the long run.

United States private capital increasingly requires the aid of the state, and the state enlists more and more private and public capital in its crusade to maintain world capitalism intact. Specific and general capitalist interests serve each other, finally merging into one phenomenon, a certain one-ness emerges between them. This must have, finally, its institutional reflection. The multi-national corporation has become the instrument for the creation and consolidation of an international ruling class, the only hope for reconciling the antagonisms between national and international interests.

SURPLUS ABSORPTION OR SURPLUS CREATION?

The preceding analysis supports the conclusion that the surplus absorption capacity of the backward countries, and, probably to a lesser degree, the other advanced economies, and hence opportunities for utilizing investment-seeking funds overseas, are circumscribed in a variety of ways. Opportunities for "enterprise," or profit-making, however, show few signs of weakening. We have touched on some of the reasons: First, the multi-national corporations increasingly mobilize and utilize local and state savings and capital, undertake more ambitious investment projects, and profit from economies of large-scale production and more efficient intra-corporate planning. Second, a larger share of the retained earnings of corporation branch plants and subsidiaries is absorbed by modernization investments, which reduce costs and raise profits. Third, the multi-national corporations monopolize patents, brand names, and production processes in the greatest demand, and are able to establish control over national and international markets via licensing and similar agreements which require relatively small capital outlays. Fourth, the giant international corporations are more and more integrated and diversified, and production and sales are subject to less risk and uncertainty. Lastly, the international monopolies can count on the active participation and aid of the state.

For these reasons, the multi-national corporations command growing profit margins on their overseas operations. Small amounts of capital are sufficient to penetrate, control, and dominate the weaker, less productive national economies. The price of disposing of a given amount of economic surplus this year is the creation of even more surplus next year—hardly a high price for the individual corporation to pay, but from the standpoint of the metropolitan economy as a whole, the problem of surplus absorption becomes increasingly severe.

The United States government, the European powers, and the United States-dominated international agencies are thus under growing pressure by the international monopolies to formulate and implement political-economic policies which will create an "attractive" investment climate abroad, in particular in the under-exploited countries. Looked at from another angle, the imperialist powers are increasingly compelled to "promote economic development" overseas or, to put it differently, to integrate the backward areas even more closely into the structure of world capitalism. In effect, the advanced countries are desperately seeking to expand outlets for the economic surplus. To be sure, the imperialist powers view the problem as one of surplus creation (or profit-realization), rather than of surplus absorption—their line of vision generally corresponds in this respect with the perspective of the corporations themselves. These are merely different sides to the same coin: by promoting profitable opportunities abroad for private capital, the state lays the basis for the absorption of a portion of this year's surplus, and, simultaneously, for the creation of additional surplus next year.

For United States economic, political and foreign policy this line of analysis has a number of important consequences. In the first place, national economic development programs in the backward countries which seek the participation of the socialist countries and other advanced capitalist countries have been and will continue to be opposed by the United States. Secondly, investments in lines of industry which are non-competitive with United States products, especially those which increase demand for United States products, have been and will continue to be encouraged.

Thirdly, the participation of United States capital in the European economy (as well as the participation of European capital in the backward countries) will increasingly be discouraged because these investments will eventually compete with United States commodity exports. Fourth, the United States will continue to initiate anti-socialist, anti-communist military and political pacts and alliances with both backward and advanced capitalist countries—for the international monopolies the basic importance of state loans and aid lies in the long-run impact on the demand for arms, capital equipment, and consumer goods in those satellites which have developed intimate political and military bonds with the United States.

More generally, because the expansion of commodity exports, as well as capital exports, generate even more surplus in the future— because the process of surplus creation and absorption is a cumulative one—the United States is increasingly compelled to follow the policies of a militant, expansive imperialist power, all in the name of economic development for the underdeveloped countries. The task facing the United States in relation to the backward countries is truly Herculean.

At one and the same time, the United States must convince the backward countries that the growing penetration of United States capital, and the growing control of the multi-national companies over local economies, are useful and necessary for their economic growth and development, at a time when politically oppressive policies which aim to create more favorable conditions for private investment are followed. Thus economic development is oriented by the multi-national companies, and where there are national development plans which on paper assign a certain limited role to private investment, in fact private investment assigns a role to the plan. The underdeveloped world becomes bound up even more closely in a new imperialist system in which investments in consumer goods industries replace investments in raw materials and minerals; in which the backward countries are compelled to deal with a unified private capital-state capital axis; in which political control by the World Bank and the other international agencies, together with the political arm of the official labor movement, the giant foundations, and other quasi-private political agencies, replace colonial rule; and in which the national middle classes in the underdeveloped countries are slowly but surely transformed into a new class of clients and compradors, in every important respect equivalent to the old class of traders, bankers, and landlords which for centuries bowed and scraped before their imperial rulers in China, India, Latin America and elsewhere. A new era of imperialism is just beginning, an era which holds out contradictory promises to the imperial powers and their clusters of satellites. Whether or not the advanced capitalist countries can deal with this crisis of their own making depends on two basic factors: first, the power of peoples in the under-exploited continents to resist; and, secondly, the flexibility of the structure of the imperialist system.

Göran Therborn

Göran Therborn is the editor of the Swedish socialist review *Zenit*. He is the author of many important articles on New Left politics in European radical journals.
The following essay is reprinted from *New Left Review* 48, March/April, 1968.

Therborn analyzes the meaning of the Vietnamese War in the context of the world socialist revolution. He compares the Vietnamese War to "the classical phase of the Cold War," arguing that the historical circumstances under which the cold war was waged necessarily resulted in the "political and ideological consolidation of capitalism in the West." Unlike the cold war, which was "a fundamentally unequal conflict" but which "was presented and experienced on both sides as equal," and which "*blocked* the contradictions within capitalism," the Vietnamese War "is a conflict between unequal forces presented and lived as unequal," which has "*reactivated* its [capitalism's] internal contradictions." Since the Vietnamese War "is the *natural* product of the *normal* regime of the *centre* of the world capitalist system," it explodes the contradictions within advanced capitalism which necessitate imperialist aggression in Vietnam. Furthermore, the fact that the Vietnamese Revolution is "led by Marxists and supported by a Communist State," prevents opposition to American imperialism in Vietnam from degenerating into a pallid pacifism and "logically implies" support of revolutionary socialism. More generally, Therborn argues that the Vietnamese Revolution has radically redefined the "international contradiction" between capitalism and socialism.

FROM PETROGRAD TO SAIGON

The staggering blows that the National Liberation Front has now dealt the American military expedition in Vietnam have changed

Reprinted by permission of the *New Left Review*.

history. When some half a million American troops with enormous technological superiority are no longer capable of keeping even the U.S. Embassy in Saigon safe, the most rabid spokesmen of imperialism have temporarily lapsed into a stunned silence. The incredible heroism of the Vietnamese militants has awed the world. They have proved, once and for all, that revolutionary peoples, not imperialism, are invincible. Socialists everywhere owe them an immense homage.

It is now a truism that Vietnam dominates the whole international political situation, and that solidarity with the Vietnamese Revolution is today the duty that solidarity with the October Revolution was in 1917. Every Marxist knows this instinctively. What we now need is some initial theoretical analysis of the *significance* of the Vietnamese War for the world socialist movement. Le Duan, Secretary-General of the North Vietnamese Communist Party, has recently reminded us, in an important article commemorating the 50th anniversary of the October Revolution, that: "The Vietnamese Revolution is part of the world revolution and its success cannot be dissociated from that of the world revolution." [1] What is the exact nature of the relationship between the two? This brief contribution is intended only as a first step to the elucidation of the problem.

A social conflict is not just a clash of two or more forces on a flat plane. It has a complex, multi-dimensional structure, which determines its prospects and limits. Some exponents of bourgeois political science have recently advanced the concept of the international political system, but they have mostly confined themselves to such formalistic categories as bipolarity, multipolarity, antagonism, complementarity, or co-operation. Marxist analysis naturally replaces this empty labyrinth with a concrete historical theory, centered on the dialectical concept of contradiction.

To understand the meaning and consequences of the Vietnamese War today, a comparison of it and the classical phase of the Cold War, above all in Europe, is essential. This is the fundamental context in which it emerges with all its explosive force. For American imperialism is fighting the Vietnamese Revolution today with the identical ideological banner—Anti-Communism—under which it trampled on the Greek Revolution 20 years ago. Yet the outcome and impact of the conflict has been totally different. Why?

[1] Le Duan, *Forward Under the Magnificent Red Banner of the October Revolution.*

1. The Structure of the Cold War

No properly constituted theory of the Cold War exists. But its essential political character is clear. *The Cold War was a fundamentally unequal conflict, that was presented and experienced on both sides as being equal.* The Soviet Union was put forward as a direct alternative model of society to that of the Western capitalist countries. The conflict was seen, both within the Communist movement and within capitalism, as a struggle as to which was the better society, compared at a single moment of time. Posed like this, the conflict was inevitably detrimental to the advance of socialism everywhere. For Russia in no way represented an equivalent economic base to that of Western Europe or the United States. It was still a society marked by poverty and scarcity, aggravated by the tremendous losses and devastations of the Second World War, and engaged in the inhuman imperatives of isolated primitive accumulation. (This condition naturally determined its relationship to the countries of Eastern Europe.) The affluent and advanced West was never deeply challenged from within by this social model. Russia was manifestly authoritarian and violent, whereas Western capitalist societies had in most cases a long bourgeois-democratic tradition. But politically, violence and bureaucracy was pitted, without historical mediations, against the bland parliamentarianism of the West, in a world where socialism was an encircled enclave within the world imperialist economy. This was the meaning and genesis of the Cold War. The specific form taken by the contradiction between socialism and capitalism thus determined an internal neutralization of the contradictions within capitalism. The working-class was by and large mobilized in the anti-Communist crusade, because of its fear of the Soviet model, symbolized by a regime of shortages and repression. Both economic and political "competition" between the blocs was, under these circumstances, to the advantage of the West. Neither, in the form they took, threatened bourgeois rationality. While the USSR, anyway a vastly poorer society, was shattered by the German invasion, the USA— already much the wealthiest society in the world—emerged not merely unscathed but actually economically assisted by the war. It was thus able to pour a profusion of dollars into Western Europe (while the USSR was securing reparations from Eastern Europe), and get it on the path of a successful capitalist restoration and reconstruction, greatly strengthened by the armaments boom of the fifties. Saturated with Cold War ideology, the working-class in the West was by and large enlisted in the cause of the Truman Doctrine and Nato, the defenders of both freedom (parliament) and prosperity (free enterprise) from the evils of international Communism. The Communists in Italy, France, Finland and elsewhere retrenched themselves in isolated enclaves, and waited for the international situation to change. The non-Communist Left was crushed or compromised. The Cold War, fought out as a competitive conflict between the USSR and the USA in Europe, resulted in the massive political and ideological consolidation of capitalism in the West. *An unequal conflict fought as equal redoubles the inequality.* The Cold War was a long penalization of socialism.

2. The Structure of the War of National Liberation: Vietnam

The contemporary conflict between imperialism and national liberation, of which the war in Vietnam is the principal aspect today, is totally different in structure. *It is a conflict between unequal forces presented and lived as unequal.* There is no question of any comparison between the desperately deprived and rebellious workers and peasants of Asia, Africa and Latin America and the wealthy capitalist societies of the West which sends its praetorians to obliterate them. The very essence of the struggle between them is their incommensurability. This, indeed, is the meaning of the military form of the conflict. The Cold War was a struggle on the same plane between two forces at different levels. The protracted war of a guerrilla army against an imperialist military expedition is the armed expression of a conflict where the inequality of the parties is matched by a struggle on disparate planes—each party fighting on different terrain. All of Mao's writings on guerrilla warfare are concerned with this fundamental *strategic asymmetry*. The rule is, of course, that normally there is only a one-way connection between the two planes. Successfully fought and led, the guerrilla army can erode and eventually disintegrate the social, political and military position of its cumbersome conventional enemy, while the latter unavailingly unleashes its technological fury on the population—before being decisively defeated.

But this strategic asymmetry reflects a deeper historical relationship. The struggle in Vietnam today and Cuba yesterday is for liberation from imperialist exploitation and oppression. Given the global structure of capitalism, this means not merely secession from, but a frontal attack on, capitalism as a system and the bourgeois rationality that integrates it. Two social models are now in a quite new relationship with each other. Socialist liberation in Vietnam does not compete with US capitalism, it focuses a diamond light on the internal structure of the rich capitalist societies which compels their negation of the freedom and development of other societies. Thus whereas the "competitive" contradiction between socialism and capitalism during the Cold War *blocked* the contradictions within capitalism, the Vietnamese conflict has *detonated* the contradictions within US capitalism itself. For there is now no question of comparing a scarcity political model with the affluent societies of the West—the ideological device which successfully mystified a generation of the Western proletariat.[2] On the contrary, the ideologies of imperialism and racism with which the USA is fighting the war in Vietnam have recoiled on it. The war in Asia has triggered a war in the ghettoes. For the young in the West, the examples of dedication and heroism are now drawn from the movements of liberation in Asia, Africa and Latin America.

Socialism here is no longer a dull, harsh austerity threatening the consumers of the West, but a heroic fight by exploited and starving peoples for a human existence, denied them by imperialism and its lackeys. It is no longer an alien social mode, but an immediate ideological inspiration—a source of emulation. The Vietnamese Revolution has thus done what no other economic or political force in the world has achieved for 30 years—it has shattered the cemented unity of American society and at last *reactivated* its internal contradictions. The potential shift in the international class struggle that this represents is enormous, and may still not be perceived by those whose political horizons have become habituated to a world in which the citadel of imperialism was itself an undivided monolith. The emergence of a militant, revolutionary Left in the USA—no matter how quanti-

[2] It might be added that the abandonment of the comparison of socialist accumulation with capitalist affluence has been accompanied, in China, Cuba, and North Vietnam, by a new theoretical and political insistence on economic egalitarianism (criticized in the USSR during the thirties). The Cultural Revolution, the "simultaneous construction of socialism and communism" in Cuba, and the war-time practice of the DRV share this preoccupation.

tatively limited as yet—is a tremendous change in world politics. The most lucid spokesmen of imperialism are aware of this today, and they fear more than anything else the impact of the Vietnamese War at home.

The Vietnamese War, then, shows that *an unequal struggle waged as unequal equalizes the inequality*. All the political and ideological consequences in the world at large are reversed. Imperialism today is on the defensive. The social peace installed by the Cold War is disintegrating in the vortex of the Vietnamese War. The tranquil conscience of 1949 has become the brutalized demoralization of 1968. The mass defection of hitherto conventionally anti-Communist American intelligentsia from the Johnson administration and its war is the most evident sign today of this extraordinary transformation.

3. The Nature of the Aggressor: USA

The nature of the two parties to the conflict must now be considered. The Spanish War of 1936–39 is often invoked by militants in the West, when they prosecute the campaign against the Vietnamese War. This is an argument designed to appeal to liberal opponents of the war, *enroute* to radicalization. There is every justification for this, of course, if the focus of the argument is the precedent of Guernica—mass bombing of civilians as a deliberate instrument of terror. The US atrocities in Vietnam may obviously be compared to those of fascism. Jean-Paul Sartre has provided an explanation of the nature of the genocide they institute. But the argument is in other respects misleading. In particular, it implies that the USA in Vietnam today *only* plays the role of Germany or Italy. This is manifestly not so. Franco had a considerable social base in Spain, and was not a mere creature of Hitler or Mussolini. He was the leader of a broad counter-revolutionary coalition, although he was aided by them. Thieu and Ky, of course, are puppets with no social basis whatever: the Americans are the sole reason for their existence. The war in Vietnam today is not a civil war, it is an imperialist war: Americans against Vietnamese. The ARVEN troops are mere looters in the interludes.

It is thus incorrect in a number of important ways to speak of America's role in Vietnam as fascist. Polemical insistence here is actually counter-productive: if anything, it minimizes the implications of the US aggression. For fascism was an *abnormal* form of capitalist society. It was the response of the crisis-threatened German and Italian bourgeoisies to economic chaos and political disorder. These were second-echelon capitalist countries, in the last analysis, and fascist ideology even conceived them as the "proletarian" nations of Europe in their day. The irrationality of fascism followed from its genesis. It is thus important to emphasize that the United States is *not* a fascist country, like Germany or Italy. Nor is it a declining colonial power like France, when it waged its ruthless war against the Algerian Revolution in the fifties. It is the richest capitalist society in history, the leader of the "Free World" and a functioning democracy. Yet in Vietnam it is committing many of the same crimes as fascism. Why? Because that is the inner logic of imperialism as a social system. *The very bourgeois democracy that adorned capitalism during the Cold War today stands indicted with it.* The Vietnamese War is not the exceptional product of an exceptional regime: it is the *natural* product of the *normal* regime of the *center* of the world capitalist system. The truth of US society has been blown open by the Vietnamese mortars that circle Saigon. It is there for all to see, above all the Americans.[3]

4. The Nature of the Resistance: NLF and DRV

The crimes committed in Vietnam today are not committed by a Nazi Germany or a colonial France. They are committed by the "Land of the Free," the world's premier bourgeois democracy. They thus lead, without any confusion or side-issue, straight to the political core of the system that perpetrates them: capitalism. The Vietnamese War has produced a parallel unprecedented focusing of the essential

[3] Discussing possible exits from the Vietnamese War, Mary McCarthy writes sarcastically of the electoral solution: "In national election years, you are free to choose between Johnson and Goldwater or Johnson and Romney or Reagan, which is the same as choosing between a Chevrolet and a Ford—there is a marginal difference in styling. Just as in American hotel rooms you can decide whether or not to turn on the air conditioner (that is *your* business), but you cannot open the window." (*Vietnam.*) The importance of such statements— they have become a general cry in the last year—is not the novelty of the thought, but the evolution of the author. Before the Vietnamese War, Mary McCarthy was a prominent representative of the conventionally anti-Communist intelligentsia. Today, she writes publicly that the Communist societies have more promising futures than the United States.

conflicts on the other side. The Cold War did not pass uninterruptedly into the Vietnamese conflict, of course. There was a considerable intermediary phase, during which détente developed in Europe. Destalinization and polycentrism greatly modified the Communist world. Abroad, "neutralism" had become the official doctrine of many ex-colonial countries within the capitalist system, while sentimentalism about underdevelopment often replaced aggressive Cold War liberalism. In the West, some important internal anomalies began to be rediscovered by the Left. The myths of social equality and the abolition of poverty were exploded; structural unemployment and urban neglect re-emerged as major political issues. In this context, identification with the cause of the oppressed peoples of the three continents became increasingly frequent among the young on the Left—but often still in the form of a well-meaning anti-colonialism dissociated from any understanding of the concrete dynamics of class struggle, in the age of imperialism. An important example of this new phenomenon was the anti-nuclear movement (CND) in Britain. We know that CND never theoretically and strategically assumed the challenge it constituted to the "whole contemporary teleology of British society." [4] It rebelled against the ideological positions of both East and West, but it never developed any other articulated theory and ideology at all. It was quite natural that the anti-nuclear and neutralist movements should never have done so, because such a theory would have undermined the whole ideological rationale of the movements, showing the inevitability of the Cold War, given the irreconcilability of capitalism and socialism and the current structure of that conflict. But in the absence of such a theory, the movements soon collapsed, leaving a very modest inheritance indeed. The Cuban Revolution, with its decisive option for Marxism and Leninism, had already rendered this tendency obsolete.

Today, the Vietnamese Revolution has radically changed the co-ordinates of the situation. For just as it is the world's major bourgeois democracy which is waging an imperialist war in Vietnam, so the Vietnamese Revolution is organized and led—superbly—by Communist revolutionaries. The Vietnamese Revolution is not inspired by any cloudy "Third World" doctrines, but by the ideas of Marx and Lenin. There is thus no room for any ambiguity on the central issue. Opposition to the American War in Vietnam sooner or later logically

⁴ Perry Anderson, "The Left in the Fifties," *New Left Review* 29.

implies support for a socialist revolution led by Marxists and supported by a Communist State. Increasingly, even one-time Cold War liberals in the USA have admitted this logic and publicly affirmed their support for the NLF.

The political lesson, of course, is that only such a Marxist-Leninist ideology and organization today can prevail over the juggernaut of American imperialism: resistance movements all over the world will remember this from now on. But within the West, the lesson is no less salutary. The most sacred beliefs of the Cold War are being widely rejected by the young. The anti-nuclear movement was an opposition against a conflictual relationship between the capitalist and socialist Big Powers, stressing what united them, the threat of nuclear annihilation. The Vietnam movement, on the other hand, is based on opposition against an imperialist war waged by the leading capitalist state against a socialist country and a movement sustained by Communists. It necessarily produces solidarity with the latter. The rupture with bourgeois society is much sharper and deeper than with the anti-nuclear movement, no longer just drop-out but active support of the enemy. It is an index of the changed situation that the Vietnam movement has to fight, not so much systematic ideologies (as did the anti-nuclear movement), as anti-scientific and *ad hoc* "explanations" of the war in terms of the ignorance, errors and misjudgments of the Johnson administration. Against this, there is no reason why a theory of imperialism and a theory of advanced capitalism should not at last emerge on the Left. It is evident that it can only come from within Marxism. The dialectic of the war has transferred the ideology of the guerrillas into the culture of the metropolis.

5. The New Dialectic: From Petrograd to Saigon

The international contradiction between socialism and capitalism has thus been radically redefined by the Vietnamese Revolution. After a long and inescapable detour, it has been restored to a direct and unequivocal confrontation. This is the decisive meaning of this unequal war. Its reverberations have already shaken the world. A generation is now being formed in the homelands of imperialism which has experienced the truth of their own "democratic" and "affluent" societies. It is no accident that all over the advanced capitalist world—in the USA, Japan, Germany, Sweden, France, Italy and England—the new social force which has been the vanguard of the struggle against American imperialism is the student, high-school and youth population. For it is precisely their age which divides them from the myths of the bygone era of the Cold War. They no longer constitute a selected elite with a secure future status in the ruling class, but a young generation massed together in crowded and bureaucratic institutions adapted to the needs of private industry and the politico-military apparatus. For traditional cultural reasons, they are the social group that is most influenced by international issues, and they have been most affected by the de-Westernization of their conception of the world. In all capitalist countries, their numbers have grown enormously in the last decade. Set apart from the established society, in conflict with bourgeois morality and bureaucratic routines, deriving —and rapidly departing—from the spirit and methods of left-wing liberalism (the anti-nuclear campaign, the campaign against apartheid and, in the USA, the Civil Rights movement) the students have constituted the vanguard of the Vietnam movement.

In doing so, they have opened a new phase in international socialist solidarity. For many decades, this essential duty was conceived as an unconditional support for the "workers' fatherland"—a constituted socialist state, which commanded the loyalty, and often the actions, of revolutionaries abroad. The adverse effects of this form of solidarity are now indisputable. During Stalin's life, the relationship of socialist state to socialist opposition (abroad) was paramount—one of complete loyalty of the latter to the former. During Khrushchev's tenure in office, the stress of peaceful coexistence was a state relationship between socialist and capitalist powers—one of economic competition and diplomatic negotiation. Today, however, the Vietnamese have not imposed or requested any determinate form of solidarity whatever.[5] They have welcomed the solidarity movements, but have not organized or guided them. The Vietnam movements in the West have often spontaneously developed from below, without any *a priori* directions. In the process, they have—especially in the USA, Japan and Germany, the "vanguard" countries—discovered the violence and coer-

[5] These very incomplete reflections do not discuss, of course, the impact of the Vietnamese Revolution within the Communist world. Reasons of space dictated omission of this important subject, but all socialists should read Le Duan's report, referred to earlier. Russian and Chinese aid, of course, is vital to both NLF and DRV.

cion of Western societies behind the veils of consumer affluence and parliamentary institutions. Imperialism is not a peripheral phenomenon: it is inseparable from contemporary capitalism. The Vietnamese War has sent a searchlight to the core of the West. The result has been a *simultaneous* multiplication and radicalization of the resistance to it. The cause of Republican Spain and the Popular Fronts rallied even liberals to anti-fascism; but it did not often make socialists of them. The Vietnamese have welcomed any form of opposition to the American aggression, no matter what its political character. But the course of the war itself, the example of the Vietnamese struggle, has shifted the whole axis of the Vietnam movements in the West towards revolutionary socialism, among its main driving force—students and young people. There has been no incompatibility between this and the broadening of opposition to the war, as the great US mobilizations in Washington and New York have shown. On the contrary, the one has had a crucial impact on the other, by radicalizing a whole spectrum of intermediate opinion. The fundamental job of mobilizing the working-class of the USA, England, Germany and other countries—only marginally affected outside Japan—has, of course, yet to be done. It is obviously the strategic priority of the Vietnam movement. But the longer the war goes on, the more difficult it will be for anachronistic Cold War anti-communism to mystify the Western working-class. Already, large sectors of the Negro population of the USA have thrown off this degrading opiate. The future is now once again open, as the whole moral and ideological bases of Western imperialist society are increasingly widely questioned. The deepest fear of American capitalism is not of the Vietnamese peasants, but of the drugged and gagged American population. Its morale has never been lower than today, for the war is raging on its own territory.

The crisis of the world-wide capitalist system, which first matured in backward and peripheral Russia, is now penetrating the United States. The Vietnamese War will probably become its first serious, direct military and political defeat. This will mean peace and independence to the Vietnamese, at least. But the general political crisis of a starving world fettered by capitalist relations of production will not disappear. The internal contradictions and conflicts of the rich capitalist countries will doubtless be aggravated. Other revolutions will follow. The end of the Vietnamese War will not be the end of imperialism, but it may herald the beginning of the end. For something unprecedented has happened. The socialist revolution in a poor Asian country has liberated the dialectic in its oppressor. Internationalism has passed into the facts.

Donald Wells

Donald Wells is chairman of the Department of Philosophy at the University of Illinois, Chicago Circle. He is the author of *The War Myth* (1967), among other works, and is a well-known pacifist.

The following essay was written especially for this book.

Wells analyzes with painstaking care the medieval criteria for "justifying" war and various contemporary revisions of the same. He argues that when applied by belligerents in war, the traditional criteria can be made to justify any practice and so serve only to legitimize whatever practices the state wishes to follow. Wells concludes that the "just war" theorist does not succeed in demonstrating the "radical distinction" between killing in war and killing under any other circumstance—that is, that "war is a potentially moral means at all."

CAN ANY WAR BE "JUST"?

In ordinary problems concerning matters of fact, inductive or deductive justification resolves all the empirical questions that might be raised. There are no relevant psychological surds remaining. This means, simply, that if a man accepted the evidence for biological evolution, it would make no empirical sense for him to add: "but I do not like biological evolution." Normative questions, on the other hand, exhibit exactly this kind of response. Even those who accept the "case" for the dropping of the bomb on Hiroshima, commonly add: "but I do not approve of this act."

In a footnote to his cosmological argument, St. Thomas noted that arguments to prove the existence of a God neither would nor should persuade an unbeliever. The believer, though possibly reassured that belief in God is reasonable, does not otherwise need the arguments. Moral arguments share this tendency to be psychically otiose. More

247

than a shrewd argument is needed before men will create and operate a Belsen, and more than a logical inference is needed before these same men will cease their acts of genocide. It is in this context that moral "justification" tends to smack of casuistry, especially when the impression is given that the argument alone will suffice for moral persuasion. This state of affairs is clearly exhibited in the history of arguments for a "just" war.

In the ordinary course of logical justification, a claim is resolved when it is inferred validly from some axioms. Consistency within the given system is a necessary, if not sufficient, criterion of proof. The rules for testing these inferences are clear, cognitive, objective, and univocal enough so that there is a community of what might be called "competent judges." In normative discourse, however, even where the axioms are clear, cognitive, objective, and univocal, there seem to be no "competent judges." It appears that moral justification involves an exercise of heart, as well as of head. There appear to be no defensible criteria favoring one man's sensitivity over that of another. Ordinarily it is understood that to show that the German Jews were exterminated consistently with some rules would not make a sufficient case for the action. What is less clear is whose sentiments are to be used for the norm of moral repugnance. This is the psychic surd in all defenses of Belsen, Hiroshima, Nagasaki, and Dresden.

John Rawls discussed this issue in his essay "Outline of a Decision Procedure for Ethics." [1] His analysis included assessment of the idea of "competent judge" and of the conditions under which such a judge may be said to be operating justifiably. Judges are competent by virtue of ordinary capacities of intelligence, imagination, and sympathy. To make justifiable decisions, such judges must be free from the rewards of their decisions, as well as from the penalties for misdeciding a case. They must not be one of the litigants in the case, since it would be a contradiction of the meaning of a judge for any man to judge his own case. Judges, furthermore, make decisions only on actual cases. It is not their province to pass judgment on hypothetical or counterfactual instances.

All these modest suggestions have an application to the current interest in justifying war and may shed some insight on the dilemmas we face. Since there is a current revival of the medieval "just war" doc-

[1] John Rawls, "Outline of a Decision Procedure for Ethics," *Philosophical Review*, 66: pp. 177–97.

trine and since claims are being made about its capacity to justify modern war, let us assemble the case, identify the presuppositions, state the axioms, check the inferences, and poll the competent judges to see whether modern war can be justified by these medieval systems.

There are obviously some presuppositions that make such an analysis plausible. There are also presuppositions that would make such an analysis absurd:

1. If life taking were an intrinsic evil, then no war could be justified.
2. If human life were like garbage, then no justification of war would ever be necessary. The military, like garbage collectors, would need no defense.
3. If human life were considered to be only one of the elements in the justification of war, then these other goods would need to be made explicit, and their relative values assessed.
4. If the survival of the nation state were assumed to be "given," then the justification of war could consist merely in showing that the war in question saves the nation state in question. If this were all there were to justifying war, then the only unjust wars would be the unsuccessful ones.
5. What makes the justification of war a problem is that both the survival of the nation and the preservation of human life are accepted as important. War is a conflict situation in which we are asked to judge two kinds of apparently unresolvable issues:
   a. Where the survival of two nations is in conflict, such that only one can survive, which nation has the better justification?
   b. Where the price for national survival is human death, what constitute the criteria of a justification for killing persons?

A brief look at the history of the "just war" concepts illustrates how these presuppositions either make plausible or make absurd the entire exercise. The first- and second-century Christian churches considered human life to be intrinsically sacred, and they made no concessions to the support of Caesar. Hence, for them the terms "just" and "war" were contradictions. War involves men in immoral actions, and the concept of the "just war" would constitute an attempt to justify immoral actions and evil consequences. For such persons, "just war" would be like "just genocide," "just murder," or "just immorality." This single-minded commitment to the sacredness of human life precludes any attempt to justify war. From the seventeenth to the nineteenth century national survival was the nonnegotiable item, and thus the justification of war seemed irrelevant. Wars might be unnecessary, wastefully waged, hastily declared, or needlessly destructive of human life, but if the nation were preserved, they would always be justified. It was in the interim period from St. Augustine to Grotius that the attempt was made to salvage both items: nations and people.

The defenses of the "just war" have traditionally exhibited a friction or tension between the ethical ideal of nonkilling and the political practice of killing in the service of the state. In his essay "Politics as a Vocation," Max Weber distinguished these two basic concerns as contrary. They were formulated in two maxims:

1. *The ethics of ultimate ends.* According to this maxim, Christians have an obligation to act rightly and leave the outcome to God. It is sufficient that they comply with the universal rule.
2. *The ethics of responsibility.* According to this maxim, the politician or head of state accepts the survival of the state as the supreme goal, and he rejects, therefore, any idea that there are limits to permissible action. While the former refuses to sacrifice persons for any end, the latter refuses to sacrifice the state for any end.

While Weber did not intend to give the statesman carte blanche to perform any act at all which would secure the state, he did intend to permit the statesman to perform any act necessary to preserve the state. We have here a battle between two opposing ends, and as we noted at the outset, if we posit the supreme value of human life, then no war can be just even though we may confront paradoxes, while if we posit the state's survival as the nonnegotiable end, then no consideration of human life alone can take away from the "right" of the state to survive at any cost necessary.

What we need to do at the outset is to grant both the survival of the state and the survival of people as goods that need to be conserved and then determine whether the medieval criteria of the "just war" enable some justification to be performed. Historically, this is what the criteria were intended to do. They were to set limits to the so-called reasons of state without at the same time denying to the state the right to survive. The criteria set hypothetical limits to the actions of state, but at no point do they appear to require states to surrender or perish over humane considerations. The rules aimed to curb excessively destructive war practice. To accomplish this end, the rules had to be general enough to cover exigencies and to discourage the impermissible maneuver of leaving practice up to private whim.

We need to determine whether the criteria for a "just war" served to curb excessively inhumane war practice, to reduce the number of declared wars, and to assure that the means of war bore some proportionality to the ends of war. In part, of course, we need to assess the claim that wars can be justified at all. This, however, will be decided by a consideration of the rules of war and the means of waging war. As in the Middle Ages, the considerations will be prudential, and the discussion will center on such issues as the time, place, and issues at stake in a war. In a time when capital punishment is being generally rejected as "unjust" it may appear a little atavistic to attempt to defend war. What prompts our concern here, however, is that there is a current revival of interest in the "just war." We wish to know whether the medieval criteria are adequate for the task.

The Criteria of St. Thomas

In order for a war to be just three general conditions have to be met:

1. An authoritative sovereign has to declare the war.
2. A just cause is required.
3. The men who wage the war must have good intentions to use the means most moderately proportionate to the end in view. The good that results from war must be greater by some magnitude than the evil that is produced by the waging of war.

In their medieval application very few wars were criticized as unjust, suggesting that princes were remarkably wise and beneficent both in their declarations of war and in the ways in which they waged them.

In addition to the paucity of criticism, what critique there was came from persons not officially in government, with the result that their protest was a kind of academic baying at the moon. George Fox, for example, challenged the wars of Cromwell, but then Fox was a pacifist who rejected all wars as immoral, so that the injustice of wars followed from the definitions of the terms. Franciscus de Victoria, a theological professor at the University of Salamanca in the sixteenth century, chastised his Spanish superiors for their wars against the American Indians.[2] University professors, however, were no more influential in effecting changes in foreign policy in the sixteenth century than they appear to be in the twentieth. Thus such remarks as these are dismissed as a kind of irrelevant campus protest.

More recently, Joseph McKenna[3] has revived the "just war" doctrine with an expanded list of seven conditions. They are:

1. The war must be declared by the duly constituted authority.
2. The seriousness of the injury inflicted on the enemy, as well as on one's own citizens, must be proportional to the injuries that are suffered by the virtuous.
3. The injury to the aggressor must be immediate.
4. There must be a reasonable chance of winning the war.
5. The use of war must be a last resort.
6. The participants on the just side must intend harm only to belligerents or to evil people.
7. The means used to accomplish the ends of war must be moral. There are, in this sense, immoral weapons or means that ought never to be used.

In all these criteria it is presumed that the justice of a war is a function both of the means by which it is waged and the ends for which it is waged. It appears, on the face of it, that just ends do not warrant every means, nor do just means warrant every ends. Obviously all the criteria need to apply for the war to be just. A war which satisfies only the first condition obviously should not qualify as a just one. But what about a war which satisfies most, but not all, of the criteria? Here

[2] Franciscus de Victoria, *On the Law of War* (Washington, D.C., The Carnegie Institute, 1917), Section 22.
[3] Joseph McKenna, "Ethics and War: A Catholic View," *American Political Science Review* (September, 1960), pp. 647–658.

the medieval and modern versions exhibit a limitation in what they can establish. Let us look first at the criteria individually.

A Just War Is One Declared
by the Duly Constituted Authority

For both St. Augustine and St. Thomas the duly constituted authority was the prince or ruler. If they could imagine some ameliorating influence from the Christian principles, they might have imagined that Christian prelates would not declare wars for shallow reasons. Since both worthy saints accepted heathen princes as duly constituted, it was not obvious how this Christian influence was supposed to work. In the context of a Roman Empire, they might also have imagined a relatively small number of duly constituted authorities. By the sixteenth century rising nationalism had scores of litigants, each duly constituted, and the proliferation of princes raised issues that neither Thomas nor Augustine had in mind. By the time the "reasons of state," as Machiavelli elaborated them, permitted wars to be waged whenever the state was threatened, it ceased to be clear that the limitation of wars to those duly declared actually eliminated any wars at all. By the eighteenth century wars were the "sport of kings," and it became clear that duly constituted authorities had no obvious claim save that of office to defend their decisions.

The very minimum criteria for the "competent judge" as listed by Rawls[4] fail to be satisfied by this notion of duly constituted authority. The prince is expected to adjudicate his own case, assess his own motives, evaluate his own means, and sit in judgment against his enemies. While the rule did permit determination of whether a war existed, hence of whether the rules of war applied, the rule did nothing for distinguishing the relative merits of the litigants when each was duly constituted. Thus, war could be justly declared by both sides, since this could be determined solely by the office held by the declaimant.

In the conventional legal context, the judge is not one of the litigants in the dispute which he is asked to adjudicate. Nor, in addition, is the victim or the assailant put in the position as the judge of the other. A competent judge must be removed from the consequences of the judgment. He cannot stand to gain or lose by the decision. Seen in

[4] *Op. cit.,* pp. 183–184.

this context of competent judge, the prince of any state is incompetent, save by virtue of his office. And office, as is generally conceded, is not a badge of competence, although it may be a badge of authority. Unjust wars would be those declared by someone other than the prince. Whenever the prince failed to make any declaration of war, then no matter what was happening between nations or persons, war simply did not exist by definition.

If we could assume that princes were saints or scholars, then there might be some reason for supposing that their judgments on war were better at least than those of the unintelligent, unimaginative, and unsympathetic laymen who might wish to pass some judgment on the declaration of war. At least two obstacles lay in the way of such an assumption:

1. The permissible reasons which were given to princes for declaring a war were so inclusive that virtually any princely inclination was given sanction. In addition to wars for territory, glory, punishment of wrongdoers, retribution, and the like, wars of prevention were also allowed. The permissible reasons for war were so inclusive that the most vivid imagination failed to come up with an impermissible reason save sadism.

2. The nature of the selection processes by which princes were elevated to office gave no assurance that leaders had either intentions of sufficient warmth and sympathy or intelligence of sufficient quality that their decisions would meet even minimal standards of justice. Competent judges were, after all, supposed to be possessed of intelligence, imagination, and sympathy. The office of the prince contained no assurances that men of such talents would even be considered. We do not need to consider Hitler, Mussolini, or Thieu alone to recognize that this is so. There is nothing in the selection processes by which leaders are selected in France, England, or the United States to give assurance that persons of imagination and empathy even as good as the average citizen will be chosen. The loyal opposition normally recognizes this for domestic issues, where the lives of our own citizens are at stake. In international affairs, where the casualties are strangers, competence is even more unlikely.

Office is rarely a criterion of competence. Even the churches exhibit this fact. Witness, for example, the stand of Archbishop Groeber of Freiburgim Breisgau who rejected Christian pacifism for German Catholics on the grounds that Hitler was the duly constituted authority. Pope Pius XII was no more reassuring on this point when he rejected the right of conscientious objection for German Catholics at the time of the formation of NATO and for the same reasons. If competence to declare war is a function of office, then the sensitivities of the citizens will always be subservient to such princely office.

As a criterion of the "justness" of war, the first requisite that the war be declared by the right office serves no normative distinction at all. Such a criterion fails to satisfy the minimal notions of competence to adjudicate—namely, that the judge not be a litigant in the dispute and that his decisions follow from universal rules, rather than from his own inclinations. A World Court or a comparable body in the UN might serve competently, but princes in a world of nation-states are, by virtue of their office, incompetent.

A Just War Uses Means Proportional to the Ends

The medieval duly constituted authority was expected to satisfy this second criterion, and like the first criterion, the issue hinges on the notion of competent judge. Who was to determine, and by what yardstick, that the means of any war were proportional to the ends? Furthermore, who was to decide which ends were worthy of means of any sort at all? Franciscus de Victoria (1480–1546) had noted that if to retake a piece of territory would expose a people to "intolerable ills and heavy woes," [5] then it would not be just to retake it. We must be sure, the theologian argued, that the evils we commit in war do not exceed the evils we claim to be averting. This is surely appropriate advice, but in the absence of any specific suggestions on how to make such measurement of relative ills, it is not even a helpful counsel of perfection.

This was the point at which Mill first qualified Bentham's dictum: that each person counts for one and no one counts for more than one. If we were merely to count dead bodies, then, since the Allies in both world wars took more lives than they gave, we would conclude that

[5] Victoria, *op. cit.*, Sections 33, 37.

justice lay on the other side. If the present ABM arms race between Russia and the United States were assessed on this Benthamite measure, then at the last ditch before the buttons are pushed on doomsday, it should be noted that since there are more Russians than Americans, the American nation should be the one expended. But even where the number of potential dead was the same, who was the competent Solomon to decide that 100,000 Japanese were less valuable than 100,000 Americans? Obviously, such a Solomon could not be either American or Japanese, or a relative of either, or a dependent on either. As a matter of fact, such decisions are made by the litigants, and thus again the minimal requisite of competent judge fails to be satisfied.

The rubric of "military necessity" was most commonly appealed to as the decision procedure, and thus competence in office and competence in the assessment of proportionality were determined by those people least fit, by virtue of their interests, to make an imaginative and sympathetic ruling. Since Victoria granted to princes the right to despoil innocent children, if military necessity required it, it was clear that some explicit notion of proportionality needed to be announced. Furthermore, an explicit account of the nature and limits of military necessity was also required.

In a recent paper on this matter Father John A. Connery[6] stated that the morality of violence depends on the proportionality of this violence to that of the aggression. What Connery lacked, however, was precisely this measure. Both the medieval and the modern "just war" theorist wanes incoherent on this crucial question. John Courtney Murray, SJ, exhibited this recourse of refuge in semantic obfuscation. In a pamphlet, *Morality and Modern War,* he proposed the famous principle of proportion, but subtracted from its interpretation the obvious measurements that such a criterion requires:[7]

> The standard is not a "eudaemonism and utilitarianism of materialist origin," which would avoid war merely because it is uncomfortable, or connive at injustice simply because its repression would be costly. The question of proportion must be evaluated in more tough-minded fashion, from the viewpoint of the hierarchy of strictly moral values. It is not enough simply to

[6] "Morality and Nuclear Armament," in William J. Nagle, ed., *Morality and Modern Warfare* (Baltimore, Helicon, 1960), p. 92.

[7] John Courtney Murray, *Morality and Modern War* (New York, The Council on Religion and International Affairs, 1959), p. 12.

consider the "sorrows and evils that flow from war." There are greater evils than the physical death and destruction wrought in war. And there are human goods of so high an order that immense sacrifices may have to be borne in their defense.

Obviously the citizens who are about to be cremated under the mushroom-shaped cloud have a right to be confronted with the list of "greater evils than the physical death and destruction wrought in war." Neither a religious nor a secular ethical system possesses such a list.

In a paper read to Vatican II, the Reverend George Andrew Beck, Archbishop of Liverpool, berated the Catholics in attendance for their opposition to the use of nuclear weapons since it was deducible from this position that nuclear weapons could never be used proportionally. Furthermore, the archbishop remarked: "We must remember that responsibility for the use of nuclear weapons and for all decisions concerning peace and war rests with those who exercise supreme authority in the State." [8] As everyone understands, the duly constituted authorities have no objective interest in proportionality at all, and thus the decisions of justice are to be made by those who reject the criteria by which such decisions are traditionally measured. He adds, parenthetically, that the council make clear that it does not expect government to reject nuclear weapons "merely because of the very real and possibly proximate danger that these weapons may be used in an unjust and immoral way." [9] But this conclusion, then, rejects the notion of proportionality altogether and, in effect, takes the position that war is beyond judgments of justice. The same conclusion has been formulated in the context of the separation of moral versus legal wrong. Thus both Beck and Murray[10] propose that while such weapons constitute a crime in the moral order, they do not constitute one in the legal order. With this distinction, however, the second criterion becomes inapplicable at the very point where it is needed most—namely, in the judgments of war by duly constituted authorities.

Proportionality is a slippery term unless there is some measure. The Hague Declarations of 1899 and 1907 enumerated a long list of unacceptable or disproportionate military actions, all of which are

[8] George Andrew Beck, "The Use of Nuclear Weapons," in *Third Session Council Speeches of Vatican II* (New Jersey, Deus Books, 1966), p. 254.
[9] *Ibid.,* p. 255.
[10] Murray, *op. cit.,* p. 10.

now included by "just war" theorists in the class of permissible actions. Indeed, the same offenses for which Germans were sentenced at the War Crimes Trials at Nuremberg are now permissible when performed by the Americans in Vietnam.[11] Shortly before World War II Jacques Maritain[12] put bombing from the air in the category of an absolutely proscribed act. But how were such determinations of proportionality made? Both the lack of any explicitly announced measure and the fact of the striking changes in assessment suggest that proportionality is a function of one's sensitivity at the moment, and yesterday's painful actions become today's pleasurable ones. In the early period of World War II, for example, "saturation bombing" was considered to be too inhumane for American citizens to accept. Our military practiced, instead, what was euphemistically called precision bombing. But even here where precision of measurement would appear to be the most plausible, the distinction was empty. This was illustrated when the Air Force announced, at the time of the first test shot of the Atlas missile, that a bomb that lands within fifty miles of its target is considered accurate.[13]

During that same War the English writer Vera Brittain attacked both England and America for the bombing of civilians in her book *Massacre by Bombing.* Here was an opportunity to determine whether the supporters of the bombing could defend it on the basis of some measure of proportionality. Mrs. Brittain had claimed that the widespread bombing of civilians was not proportional to the end and that such a practice was, in addition, a traditionally proscribed one, especially by "just war" theorists. The Protestant journal *The Christian Century* saw no disproportion in the bombing of civilians. The *Saturday Evening Post,* which probably represented the majority of ordinary citizens, editorialized that it was a sign of "instability" to question the need for bombing civilians. Orthodox clergymen, the Reverend Carl McIntyre and the Reverend H. J. Ockenga, called her position "un-American and pro-Fascist."

The fact is that "military necessity" comes to the defense of any weapon and any use of such weapons, whenever the alternative appears, however remotely, to run the risk of national inconvenience,

[11] Cf. *In the Name of America,* Seymour Melman (ed.). Clergy and Laymen Concerned About Vietnam, 1968, *passim.*

[12] Jacques Maritain, "War and the Bombardment of Cities," *Commonweal* (September 2, 1938), *passim.*

[13] Nagle, *op. cit.,* p. 107.

let alone, national surrender. Increasing escalation goes hand in hand with decreasing concern. Every barbarity gets protection from the icon of national defense. John Courtney Murray, SJ, who might have been expected, by virtue of his theological commitments, to have sensitivities a notch above those of a Secretary of State,[14] defended the survival of "American culture" and the American state on the grounds that they were without peer in any moral system. Furthermore, he saw Communism as a kind of Antichrist, so evil and so destructive of the values of the American outlook that he defended any means necessary to "deter" them. Any amount of human destruction appeared preferable to the surrender of the "American Way." Innocent III thought that the use of the cross and long bows too disproportionate for Christians to endorse. John XXIII said the same for thermonuclear weapons. Unless there is some compelling case that modern states are infinitely more valuable than medieval states, it seems obvious that if there could be too much crossbow, there could never be a proportionate use of a megabomb.

The current discussion of what is called "thinking the unthinkable," under the rubric of "rational nuclear armament," has made of this criterion of proportionality a moral farce. Dr. Herman Kahn, famed for his insistence that we learn to think the unthinkable, recommended in the interests of proportionality that megabombs be limited to the half-megaton class. Since this is fifty times greater than the bombs dropped on Hiroshima and Nagasaki, it ceases to be clear what proportionality means. A similar Alice-in-Wonderland logic surrounds the missile race between America and Russia. If we have enough bombs to overkill every person in the enemy country by a factor of two, what proportional sense could it make to speak of the reduction of bombs to precisely enough to kill every person "once"? There is, to be sure, a mathematical difference here, but is there any moral difference? The use of too much firepower is an economic waste, not a superfluity of immorality.

We confront the same lacuna here as in the first criterion—namely, we have no competent judge. It surely makes no legal sense to permit the assailant to judge the appropriateness of his weapons. Nor is it any more helpful to decide international proportionality by "free enterprise" moral distinctions. Lacking a World Court with a world

[14] Nagle, *op. cit.,* pp. 69–73. See also Paul Ramsey, *The Just War* (New York, Scribner's, 1968), pp. 532–36.

judge, lacking even a role for the UN Commission of Human Rights, no nation can assume the prerogatives of competent judge without making a farce of the notion of judgment.

War May Justly Be Taken Only as a Last Resort

The intent of this criterion was not simply to identify the *kairos* of the war declaration, but, more important, to indicate that war was a recourse which, if avoidable, ought not to be a resort at all. In the conventional discussions of the notion of last resort it was presumed that there were viable first resorts. Thus, unless a nation could show that it had indeed exhausted meaningful first resorts, it would make no sense for it to claim any right to war as a last resort. First resorts might be such alternatives as economic, social, or political boycott, negotiations either through the UN or by unilateral arrangement. Of course, surrender is a first resort. Now let us assume that all the first resorts have been attempted, and there appear to be no nonviolent alternatives or any violent options less destructive than war. Wouldn't we still need to show that the last resort of war ought to be taken in this case? To permit war as a last resort is not equivalent to requiring that war be a resort in every instance. The permission of war as a last resort, if at all, is not the same as granting the right to go to war when all else fails.

It is consistent with the caution that war be taken only as a last resort—that is, if it is taken at all—that the first resorts of negotiation are the only ones that are proper in justice in the particular case. This is simple to observe in the case of the Nazi treatment of the Jews. Could the Germans have defended the following on the grounds of "last resort"? "Having exhausted every other resort to remove the threat of the Jews to Aryan supremacy, may we now as a last resort, open the gas chambers?" The only confusing element in the German case appears to have been the contingent fact that the Jews were German citizens. German theologians showed little concern over the extermination of the Jews in the early period of Nazi power. Since other countries, including the United States, used gas chambers on their citizens for domestic crimes, it wasn't obvious why the Germans should not be permitted the same option. Was the problem simply that the gas chambers had not been used as a last resort? Was the problem that the German Jews did not appear to be guilty by American standards? Suppose all the Jews had been guilty by the standards of American laws, such that they would have been sent to an American gas chamber had they been here. Would Belsen, Buchenwald, and Maidanek now have been proper last resorts?

Once again the problem of the competent judge arises. Who is to make the assessment that we have arrived at the state of last resort? Who is to determine, for the particular case, that war is a resort at all? To permit every nation to make this decision for its own case would merely assure that war would always be a resort that was taken sooner or later. Part of the notion of last resort seems to be the suspicion that war is so questionable as a method at all that perhaps it should be handled like domestic killing. While there are sound prudential reasons for timing war strategically, the notion of last resort appeared to mean more than this. There was a lingering suspicion that war was a kind of murder and that one should, therefore, be cautious about the application of "just" to the practice. Under ordinary circumstances we would not speak of "just murder," "just genocide," or "just annihilation of innocents." For the same reasons, we do not wish to use the expression "just war" carelessly.

Part of the implication of the War Crimes Trials in Nuremberg was that if war ever did become genocide or a "crime against humanity," then it could not be justified. That is to say, there comes a point when war acts are disproportional as a resort at all, and this would hold the case no matter how final the moment was when the resort to war was taken. What genuinely complicates the task of a putatively competent judge is the determination of the moment when the nation confronts the last resort. What we lack is any appropriate calculation that is even close in approximation to the domestic rule of a "clear and present danger." As Rawls had noted,[15] there must be an actual threat, a present problem, not a hypothetical one. Nowhere is this more difficult than in the preventive acts of military action. Could any judge show that the bombing of Dresden saved lives? Could any tactician make a real and present case that if the bombs had not been dropped on Hiroshima and Nagasaki, then some human catastrophe of greater magnitude would have occurred? Who decides that Hiroshima was bombed as a last resort? Who decides that the bombing of Hiroshima should be a resort at all? To say that war should not be undertaken, save as a last resort, is not to give carte blanche to gen-

[15] Rawls, *op. cit.,* pp. 183–184.

erals. Indeed, generals see acts of war as first resorts. Negotiations are the military last resorts.

In this day of mega-kill and of massive retaliation, the justification of the resort to war at all requires a defense which the medieval criteria neither anticipate nor allow. If human life was important enough for medieval theologians to be uneasy about the crossbow, then the sheer scope of modern mega-weapons should produce a cosmic uneasiness with the argument that Hiroshima was the lesser of two evils and thus an appropriate last resort. Here again "military necessity" has come to the rescue of theological generals. The last resort has arrived when military necessity calls. How can we assess the endorsement of Paul Ramsey, the distinguished Protestant advocate of the "just war," of the use of thermonuclear bombs on civilians because military men are at their wits' end? Shouldn't those who are about to die be consulted? Indeed, doesn't it seem plausible that the case for "better dead than Red," for example, requires the vote of Reds? Perhaps if there were some impartial judge who decided to sacrifice 150,-000 Japanese to save some unspecified number of Americans, we could feel less uneasy about the problem. As it is, however, the American decision to sacrifice Japanese scarcely satisfies the requisites of a competent judgment.

Since this criterion of last resort is the verbal tool of moral warriors or of theological tacticians, no one seriously considers that surrender might be the only moral option. Clearly, the discussants of last resort are speaking to nations that win wars, not to those that lose them. In retrospect, would we advise the Germans and Japanese that surrender should have been their first and last resort? If we had been possessed of omniscience, would we have encouraged the Allies to have taken the resort to war far sooner than they did? Since politicians and military strategists argue from premises of national sovereignty and the right of national self-defense, rather than from concerns with justice, the entire thesis of the "just war" is a kind of theological irrelevancy. The notion of surrender is not included in the military vocabulary, even as a last resort. This was illustrated by the vote in August, 1958, when the Senate of the United States voted 82 to 2 to deny government funds to any person or institution that proposed or actually conducted any study regarding the possible results of the surrender of the United States as an alternative to war.

Modern language of warfare has made this criterion otiose. In wars of mega-weapons no warrior can afford to speculate about whether he has exhausted the first resorts before he pushes the button, and our contemporary theorists of war endorse the strategy of the "first strike." Indeed, in guerrilla war the question of resorts is not germane, and thus, once again the criteria fail to operate. Actually, this was recognized as far back as Grotius, who rejected all the medieval sophistries on timing with this comment: "So true is this that we may destroy an enemy though he be unarmed, and for this purpose we may employ poison, an assassin, or incendiary bombs, though he is not provided with such things: in short everything is legitimate against an enemy." [16]

A Just War Must Be Waged with Right Intentions

On the assumption that war can be a resort to which duly constituted authorities can in justice turn, and on the assumption that the acts of war are proportional to the threat, it still remained to show that the actual consequences bore some appropriate relation to what the litigants intended. Since the derivative results of acts of war may extend far beyond what was immediately done, some notion of responsibility needed to be established. What ought a person to have foreseen? Can a reasonably intelligent calculator assign antecedent probabilities to the occurrences of the esential consequential effects? When is it a defensible excuse to say that we did not realize how disastrous the consequences would be? It is in the context of this criterion also that the princely presumption concerning the ultimacy of the survival of the nation commonly provides the excuse around the difficulties. Vatican II gave this escape when it noted: "As long as the danger of war remains and there is no competent and sufficiently powerful authority at the international level, governments cannot be denied the right to legitimate defense once every means of peaceful settlement has been exhausted." [17] What are the limits of "legitimate" defense? If we assume that there are some built-in notions of proportionality, are there some excuses provided by the doctrine that we are not responsible for what we produced unintentionally, where the consequences in question could not have been foreseen by intelligently

[16] Grotius, Hugo, *On the Law of War and Peace,* I.1:2,1. See also Cicero, *On Duties,* Book I, Section XI. New York, E. P. Dutton, 1942.
[17] *Pastoral Constitution on the Church in the Modern World,* Part II, Chap. V. National Catholic Welfare Conference, 1966.

addressing ourselves to the issue? What about the possibility of illegitimate defense or the cases where defense of any kind is illegitimate? Or is it intended that the survival of nations transcends any limitations raised by moral considerations? Thus, Nazi Germany had the right to defend itself, as does Thieu's South Vietnam, the Spain of Franco, or contemporary Greece. Are there instances where national leaders have no right to intend any consequences on behalf of national survival? We have already noted that national leaders are not competent judges on such questions, indeed, that there do not appear to be any such judges in a position to perform competently.

Much of the medieval controversy over intentionality revolved around the doctrine of the double effect. A just belligerent intended only as much killing as was proportional to the threat, and he was responsible only for the deaths he intended to cause. Innocent bystanders who were killed "by accident" were not the moral responsibility of the warrior. This assumed, of course, that the warrior did not intend to kill noncombatants. The attempt to fulfill this requisite explained in part the prohibition against firing on unfortified cities, a prohibition that still survived in the Hague Declarations, even though it had been observed more often in the breach than in the practice. That this was a counsel of perfection, hence expendable, was borne out by the concessions of theologians from St. Thomas to Victoria that military necessity would justify even the intentional despoiling of innocents.

In spite of this failure to take intentionality seriously, there was a general and pervading concern by church councils with the deaths of the innocents. The early Peace of God and Truce of God itemized the people who ought to be exempt from war acts, and it was presumed here that no just act could intend to slay these protected people. In 1076 at a council in Winchester, England, the cases of men who had fought with William the Conqueror at the Battle of Hastings were considered. Many of the soldiers were troubled by the memory of people whom they had slain and, in the case of archers, with the thought that they had slain innocents unknowingly. Archers, in these instances, were assigned the penance of daily prayers for the rest of their lives for the unknown deaths they might have caused. The absence of such contemporary concerns suggests that "out of sight, out of mind" also operates. Yet now when our weapons make our intentions to no avail, we cling to the mega-weapons and adjust our intentions to our moral yardstick. At least the medieval concern with unintended death was one that could be implemented. Their weapons made such concern practical. Although an archer might shoot his arrow into the air and not be too clear as to where it landed, he was not in serious doubt about where he was aiming it. He might miss a small barn, but he did hit the right city. Modern weapons, on the other hand, make such a concern with innocents inoperable and unfeasible. In the first place, the scope of the devastation caused by modern bombs inevitably includes as casualties many noncombatants. No warrior can choose his bombs to fit the size of the enemy emplacement. In the second place, the fact that in current wars more civilians than soldiers are slain suggests that the nature of guerrilla warfare (*i.e.,* from the point of view of the Americans who are fighting against guerrillas) makes the death of innocents inescapable. And finally, modern military tactics has excluded the class of noncombatants or at least made it a null class. Modern war is total in the sense that there are no innocents. Thus, intentionality is an irrelevant consideration. The medieval man might pardonably weep for the accidentally slain women and children. Modern man, however, could not weep for the Hiroshima victims since he intended the death of every one.

In every age the attempt has been made to keep alive the concept of intentionality by proscribing those weapons whose use made intentions of no effect. The discriminating weapons were frequently called "humane" to distinguish them from those that slew without distinction. William Paley eschewed poison.[18] J. G. Fichte considered the use of hidden snipers to be "downright illegal." [19] Pope Pius XII added his anathema to poison gas.[20] By the time Hitler declaimed against attack from the air as too inhumane to be tolerated by Christians,[21] it should have occurred to all that this Philistine breast-beating was mere genuflection. The Hague Declarations of 1899 and 1907 made "prohibited" the discharge of projectiles from the air, the use of asphyxiating gases, expanding bullets, contact mines, and torpedoes that remained

[18] William Paley, *Moral Philosophy* (London, C. and J. Rivington, 1825), Vol. IV, p. 531.
[19] J. G. Fichte, *The Science of Rights* (Philadelphia, J. B. Lippincott, 1869), p. 484.
[20] "C'est une Vive Satisfaction," radio talk, September 14, 1939.
[21] Adolf Hitler, *My New Order* (New York, Reynal and Hitchcock, 1941), p. 951.

dangerous after they had missed their mark.[22] Little remained for soldiers to do save to joust in knightly fashion like sensitive gentlemen. The absurdity of this exercise of disavowing weapons on the supposed grounds of humanitarianism was illustrated by the remarks of a medical doctor to the Berlin Military Medical Society in 1885 on the discovery of a high-speed nonexpanding bullet. "I welcome the new bullet with great joy and believe that if it were generally adopted by international consent, all humanity would have cause to rejoice." [23] He called this new type of bullet "humane." Hiram Maxim followed suit and named his newly invented machine gun "the greatest life-saving instrument ever invented." [24] The displacement of civilian populations, for which the Nazis were tried as criminals, is now part of established civilized warfare under the euphemism "pacification programs." Does this mean that good intentions can make evil a good? Or isn't it rather that the "double effect" is pointless unless we have criteria of inadmissible ends.

It is surely more than a little odd that while medieval men were troubled by misdirected arrows, modern men get squeamish only with the use of mega-bombs. The entire range of lesser weapons has been reconciled into the moral scheme. Contemporaries may argue that while chemical bombs are moral, biological bombs are not.[25] Part of this reasoning appears to rest on the difficulty of control in the case of biological weapons, but the fear is less that innocents will be slain than that our own soldiers will be slain. In addition, there is a long religious-psychic association between germs and evil. Thus napalm, antipersonnel shrapnel, and expanding bullets now pose no moral dilemmas of intentionality gone astray.

Two of the most discussed instances of heinous intentionality in the twentieth century are the German extermination of the Jews and the American extermination of the citizens of Hiroshima and Nagasaki. The gas chamber has become the symbol of the former event. Yet since Americans still use the gas chamber for their domestic offenders

[22] *The Proceedings of the Hague Peace Conferences.* Carnegie Endowment for International Peace. New York, Oxford University Press, 1920, pp. 235–267.

[23] I. S. Bloch, *The Future of War* (New York, Doubleday, 1902), p. 150.

[24] Hiram Maxim, *Defenseless America* (New York, Hearst, 1915), p. 83.

[25] Richard J. Krickus, "On the Morality of Chemical/Biological War," *Journal of Conflict Resolution* (June, 1965), pp. 200–10.

(although rarely to be sure), it must have been something other than the tool itself that led to the War Crimes Trials against the Nazis. Perhaps it was that the Germans gassed the wrong persons. Would the deed have been just if they had killed only soldiers and had left civilian women, men, and children alone? Was it that the Nazis killed the Jews for the wrong reasons? If the Jews had gassed the Nazis, would there have been no moral problem? Or was it simply that the Nazis intended the death of the Jews, so that they could not plead the extenuating circumstances of the double effect? The latter event poses much the same questions. Could the Americans claim that they did not intend to kill so many "innocents"? Was the fact that the killing was done remotely—*e.g.,* from a distance—germane? Germans, after all, might be found to have been sadistic in their direct tortures, while American pilots killed without quite being aware of it. In a kind of self-forgetful sense, pilots are always psychically blind to their deeds. Is there any viable way that the doctrine of intentionality can be applied to indict the former while praising the latter?

Once more we confront the unresolved problem of the competent judge. Surely if Americans were permitted to judge the Germans, we ought to permit the Japanese to judge the Americans. While this would not satisfy the conditions of competency, the procedure whereby Americans make both assessments is legally and morally preposterous.

Our problem throughout has been one of calculating the relative evils of war with the relative evils of the alternatives. What is worse, to kill 20 children or to lose the franchise? What is proportional to the threat of loss of freedom of speech? If the speech is lost by 50,000,000, then is the death of 3,000,000 to save that speech in proportion? These are precisely the kinds of questions that the "just war" theorist must answer, and yet his criteria do not allow of answers. Equally important, no competent judge who could make the needed assessments exists in the world presently constituted. When we recall that the ends for which the medievalist justified some wars were no different from those that now "justify" war and add to this fact the immense disparity in scope of weapons from the bow to the mega-bomb, something surely must seem to be missing. If there could be an excessive use of the spear, how could there be a permissible use of napalm? The criteria of the Middle Ages fail utterly to make modern warfare just, even if we once granted that these criteria could do so for medieval warfare.

Conclusion

We are back to our starting point and the problem of establishing "just wars" using the contemporary revisions of the medieval criteria. Not only do these criteria fail to make the necessary distinctions, but they fail for lack of any competent judges to apply them. If we accept the medieval criteria of the just war, then modern war could never be just. It is also clear that "justice" is only one of many possible criteria by which war could be judged. What is seriously lacking in the notions of justice entailed in the medieval and modern assessments is the entire range of "humane," "loving," "kindly," interpersonal qualities traditionally associated with moral actions. If wars are just, then it seems necessary to raise these other humanitarian considerations as so overriding as to take precedence over justice.

There is a legal distinction between killing done by private citizens (called murder), killing done by the state to its criminals (called capital punishment), killing done by individuals whose lives are threatened by some thug (called self-defense), and killing done by soldiers in the name of the state (called war). In each of the instances, short of "war," there are laws that assist in making the assignments of praise and blame. It is not that the former cases raise no problems, but rather, that for them there is a prototype of the competent judge. Obviously there are serious questions that deserve to be raised where the citizen shoots a thief for stealing his radio, but at least neither the thief nor the victim has to serve as judge.

Even with these formal distinctions, however, it probably makes no difference to the one who is slain whether the deed is called murder or war. This was what the ancient commandment "Thou shalt not kill" once intended to note. Since men hold their lives supremely valuable, taking these lives is a supreme disvalue, no matter what semantic distinctions are drawn. Furthermore, the killing done in war is so immense in quantity and so indiscriminating in application that what has not been established is: Are there any real goods so great that this kind of havoc can be "justified"?

This was part of the heinousness of the Nazi actions against the Jews: there were so many slain, and they were slain indiscriminatingly —*i.e.,* women and children, as well as men—and no Jew appeared to be "guilty." Imagine that some Nazi leader was attempting to justify the extermination program against the Jews and that he served as judge and used the medieval criteria, in the same way as modern princes do for their wars. He would probably reason as follows: "We Aryan Germans are confronted by the real possibility of 'mongrelization' by the Jews. Purity of race is a supreme value, and self-defense is, after all, an inalienable right. Let our leader declare the pogrom and that will make the pogrom just according to the first criterion. Furthermore, the death camps will be constructed and managed proportional to the threat of 'mongrelization.' We will, for example, take special care not to kill the innocent (non-Jews). Prior to taking this pogrom step, we will exhaust every other resort to resolve the problem. Thus, our pogrom will be just as a last resort. Finally, we will take special care of intentions. Jews must be killed because they are Jews, and not for other reasons of a financial or political nature. In all this, the innocent bystanders will be protected." Isn't this what the medieval criteria entail when they are applied by belligerents in war? With no more effort than now expended by "just war" theorists, the Germans may justly "contain the Jews," "prevent the spread of creeping Judaism," and save the Aryan nation from defeat. The entire enterprise will be carried out in accordance with the "laws of pogroms." With the same pretense of pure hearts they could march to Armageddon with "just pogrom" emblazoned on their banners.

There are several presuppositions with which war theorists approach their justification problem that preclude any resolution, short of ultimate annihilation under a mushroom-shaped cloud. We noted these at the outset, but it is helpful to make them explicit again.

1. Given a world of sovereign nation states, with no international adjudicating power and given the "right" of each state to defend itself without question, then no amount of moralizing will ever be able to deny to states the recourse to war.
2. If it is granted at the outset of the discussion that war as a method is, under some conditions, "just," then the discussion can only become an exercise in sensitivity. It will be a question of the amount of human death one can stomach. If war is seen as a neutral process, then denying nations the right to war will be equated with denying the surgeon the use of his scalpel. The metaphor, however, misses a crucial difference:

The surgeon aims to save the patient with his tools, while the warrior aims to kill the enemy.

3. If it is presumed at the outset that the life of the state transcends that of the individual in value, indeed, that the state is more important than all the citizens, then the fact of human death, on even a cosmic scale, will prove to be irrelevant as an argument against war.

At least the medievalist appeared to admit the coequal significance of the state and human life. In his context, his criteria intended to emphasize this tension. Modern theorists of war exhibit no such tension. National defense or military necessity justifies every war deed, and the loss of human life is not a datum in the problem. The medieval criteria fail utterly to enable contemporaries to determine how long it is proper for war to be waged, how great a human price it is proportional to pay, what subsidiary losses in property, culture, or manner of living it is reasonable to suffer, and what "military necessity" consists of.

With these limitations, discussion of the "just war" raises merely trivial questions of consistency with a set of axioms too ambiguous to be differentiating. The application of these trivial axioms, furthermore, will always be at the hands of the incompetent judge. What then can the "just war" justify? Obviously, it all depends on what we imagine this kind of argument is designed to accomplish. In its use by princes, the doctrine has given *ad hoc* warrant to whatever they happened to be doing. Since every prince was judge and jury of his own case, the result was a kind of Alice-in-Wonderland fantasy in which every nation was always "justified" in promoting what the "enemy" nations were "justified" in assailing. The enterprise became a kind of national therapy so that all the patients could feel secure. Thus the "just war" argument ends up defending doomsday. In those cases where military casuists make their defense for the "justice" of the deed at Hiroshima or Nagasaki, at the very least, this indicates that "justice" is only one of several bases on which human actions may be judged, and it may turn out not to be anywhere near the most important.

Part III

The Revolution of the Future:
Tactics and Goals

Herbert Marcuse

Herbert Marcuse is professor of philosophy at the University of California at San Diego. His major publications include *Reason and Revolution* (1941), *Eros and Civilization* (1955), *Soviet Marxism* (1958), *One Dimensional Man* (1964), *Negations* (1968), *An Essay on Liberation* (1969), and *Five Lectures* (1970). He is also the author with Robert Paul Wolff and Barrington Moore, Jr., of *A Critique of Pure Tolerance* (1965).

The following essay originally appeared in *New Left Review* 56, July/August, 1969.

Marcuse argues that the Marxian concept of revolution must be rethought in terms of the new global contradictions of advanced capitalism. He locates the negating forces within advanced capitalism in the "two opposite poles" of society—in the ghetto population and in the middle-class intelligentsia (the students). He argues that the national liberation movements in the Third World also express the new global contradictions of advanced capitalism and therefore also constitute a major threat to the political and economic stability of the advanced capitalist countries. Marcuse points out, however, that there are counterbalancing forces within corporate capitalism which could prevent the detonation of the internal contradictions within the global capitalist system and produce alternatively a mass base for neo-fascism or barbarism.

RE-EXAMINATION OF THE CONCEPT OF REVOLUTION

The concept of revolution in Marxian theory telescopes an entire historical period: the final stage of capitalism; the transitional period of proletarian dictatorship, and the initial stage of socialism. It is in a strict sense a historical concept, projecting actual tendencies in

Reprinted by permission of *New Left Review*.

the society; and it is a dialectical concept, projecting the counter-tendencies within the respective historical period, in as much as they are inherent in this period. These tendencies and counter-tendencies are manifestations of which Marxian theory and practice themselves are essential elements. Marxian theory itself is a power in the historical struggle, and to the degree to which its concepts, "translated" into practice, become forces of resistance, change and reconstruction, they are subject to the vicissitudes of the struggle, which they reflect and comprehend, but do not dominate. "Re-examination" is therefore an element of the concept of revolution, part of its internal development.

This paper* can raise only some of the problems involved in such a re-examination. I shall start with a brief recapitulation of the Marxian concepts. The revolution is:

1. a socialist revolution, overthrowing the capitalist system, introducing collective ownership of the means of production and control by the "immediate producers";

2. initiated in the advanced industrial societies (because of the magnitude of the internal contradictions at this stage of capitalism, and because of the possible realization of the socialist principle "to each according to his needs"); the shortening of the first phase is essential, otherwise repression would be perpetuated;

3. to occur in an economic crisis, which weakens the established state apparatus;

4. to be carried out by large-scale (organized) mass action of the working class, leading to the dictatorship of the proletariat as a transitory stage.

The concept contains the following democratic presuppositions:

a) the revolution is a majority affair; and

b) democracy offers the most favorable conditions for organization and for education to class consciousness.

This presupposition underlines the importance of the "subjective factor": awareness of the facts of exploitation, and of the ways to undo them; experience of intolerable conditions and of the vital need for change are pre-conditions of the revolution.

But the Marxian concept of revolution also implies continuity in change: development of the productive forces contained by capitalism,

* The paper was written before the May–June events in France. Marcuse has added only a few lines to indicate their historical significance.

taking over of the technology and of the technical apparatus by the new producers.

What is at stake in the re-examination is not only the identification and enumeration of those presuppositions invalidated by the actual development, but also the concept of the revolution *as a whole,* because all its elements are interrelated. This involves a re-examination of the Marxian concept of the structural relation between capitalism and socialism under the following aspects:

1. the problem of "transition": socialism in coexistence with, or as successor (heir) to capitalism;

2. the *"redefinition" of socialism,* in accordance with the new historical stage of the global development: namely, what is the *qualitative difference* of socialism as definite negation of capitalism?

The *scope* of this re-examination is *defined by Marxian theory itself,* i.e., by the inherent necessity to unfold the dialectical intent of its concepts in the analysis of the social reality. To the degree to which corporate capitalism is different from the previous stages of capitalism, which guided the Marxian concept, and to the degree to which the development of capitalism has "deflected" that of socialism, and vice versa, the concept of revolution will be a "new" concept.

But, inasmuch as the stage reached by capitalism and socialism is the result of the economic and political forces which determined the preceding stages, the new concept will be the internal development of the old one.

The following sections merely propose some guidelines for the elaboration of the new concept.

Global Context

Perhaps the most general aspect of the re-examination is the *change in the theoretical framework,* reflecting the *change in,* and the *extension of the social basis for the potential revolution,* or for the possible containment and defeat of the revolution.

This theoretical framework—and that of the subversive activity—has become a *global* one: no concept, no action, no strategy which does not have to be projected and evaluated, as element and chance and choice in the international constellation. Just as Vietnam is an integral part of the system of corporate capitalism, so are the national liberation movements an integral part of the potential socialist revolution. And the liberation movements in the Third World depend, for their subversive power, on the internal weakening of the capitalist metropoles.

It may be objected that Marxian theory has always been "international," also on the organizational level. True, but this "internationalism" was orientated on the industrial working classes as a counterforce within industrial capitalism; today, they are not a subversive force. Marxian theory paid attention to the peoples in the colonial and backward areas, but they appeared mainly as adjunct, ally, *"réservoir"* (Lenin's term) for the primary historical agent of revolution. The Third World obtained full theoretical and strategic recognition only in the wake of the Second World War, but then the pendulum swung to the other extreme. Today there is a strong tendency to regard the national liberation movements as the principal, if not as the sole revolutionary force, or a (seemingly opposite) tendency to impose upon these movements the theoretical and organizational pattern elaborated for and applied to the strategy in metropolitan areas (i.e., city-based leadership; centralized party control; alliances with groups of the national bourgeoisie; coalitions).

In reality, the global situation militates against a mechanistic division into the Third World and the others. Rather we are confronted with a *tripartite division* of historical forces *which cut across the division into the First, Second, and Third World*. The contest between capitalism and socialism divides the Third World too and, as a new historical force, there appears what may be called (and what is thus called by the New Left) an alternative to the capitalist as well as to the established socialist societies, namely, the struggle for a different way of socialist construction, a construction "from below," but from a "new below" not integrated into the value system of the old societies—a socialism of co-operation and solidarity, where men and women determine collectively their needs and goals, their priorities, and the method and pace of "modernization."

Opposition in the Metropoles

And this potential alternative (the chance of avoiding the indefinitely extended "first phase," the chance of breaking the continuum of repression and domination) has sparked and intensified the radical opposition in the advanced industrial countries (East and West), and especially in the center of the capitalist empire. This opposition may well be the catalyst of change. The Marxian concept is geared to the development in the advanced capitalist countries, and, in spite of the apparent evidence to the contrary, the fate of the revolution (as global revolution) may well be decided in the metropoles. Only if the strongest link in the chain becomes the weakest link can the liberation movements gain the momentum of a global revolutionary force.

The character of the opposition in the center of corporate capitalism is concentrated in the two opposite poles of the society: in the ghetto population (itself not homogeneous), and in the middle-class intelligentsia, especially among the students.

Common to these different and even conflicting groups is the total character of the refusal and rebellion:

1. insistence on a break with the continuity of domination and exploitation—no matter in what name; insistence not only on new institutions, but on self-determination;

2. distrust of all ideologies, including socialism made into an ideology;

3. rejection of the pseudo-democratic process sustaining the dominion of corporate capitalism.

This "unorthodox" character of the opposition is itself expressive of the structure of corporate capitalism (the "integration" of the majority of the underlying population). Neither of the two oppositional groups constitutes the "human basis" of the social process of production—for Marx a decisive condition for the historical agent of the revolution.

They do not make up the majority of the population.

They are faced with hostility (and resentment) among organized labor (still the human basis of capitalist production and the source of surplus value, and therefore still the potential agent of a possible revolution) and they are not effectively organized, neither on the national nor on the international level.

Working Class and Revolution

By itself, this opposition cannot be regarded as agent of radical change; it can become such an agent only if it is sustained by a working class which is no longer the prisoner of its own integration and of a bureaucratic trade-union and party apparatus supporting this integration. If this alliance between the new opposition and the working classes does not materialize, the latter may well become, in part at least, the mass basis of a neo-fascist regime.

Conclusion: the *Marxian concept of a revolution* carried by the majority of the exploited masses, culminating in the "seizure of power" and in the setting up of a proletarian dictatorship which initiates socialization, *is "overtaken" by the historical development:* it pertains to a stage of capitalist productivity and organization which has been overtaken; it does not project the higher stage of capitalist productivity, including the productivity of destruction, and the terrifying concentration of the instruments of annihilation and of indoctrination in the hands of the powers that be.

However, this "invalidation" of the Marxian concept is an authentic and accurate *Aufhebung;** the truth of the concept is preserved and reaffirmed on the level actually attained by the historical development. The revolutionary proletariat becomes an agent of change where it still is the human basis of the social process of production, namely, in the predominantly agrarian areas of the Third World, where it provides the popular support for the national liberation fronts.

And these areas and these forces are not external to the capitalist system. They are an essential part of its global space of exploitation, they are areas and forces which this system cannot allow to go and shift into that other orbit (of socialism or communism), because it can survive only if its expansion is not blocked by any superior power. The national liberation movements are expressive of the *internal contradictions* of the global capitalist system.

But precisely because of this relation between the revolutions abroad and the metropoles, the fateful link persists between the prospects of the liberation movements and the prospects of radical change in the metropoles. The "negating" forces abroad must be *"synchronized"* with those at home, and this synchronization can never be the result of organization alone, it must have its *objective basis* in the economic and political process of corporate capitalism. The objective factors announce themselves in the strains and stresses of the corporate economy:

1. the necessity of competition, and the threat of progressive auto-

---

* Annulment, preservation and supercession in one motion. Traditionally translated as sublation in Hegel—*Ed.*

mation, with the ensuing unemployment, demand ever enlarged absorption of labor by non-productive, parasitarian jobs and services;

2. the cost of neo-colonial wars, or controls over corrupt dictatorships, increase more and more;

3. as a result of the increasing reduction of human labor power in the process of production, the margin of profit declines;

4. society requires the creation of needs the satisfaction of which tends to conflict with the morale and discipline necessary for work under capitalism; the realm of necessity is invaded by the non-necessary, gadgets and luxury devices exist side by side with continuing poverty and misery, "luxuries" become necessities in the competitive struggle for existence.

If these tendencies continue to operate, the ever more blatant contradiction between the vast social wealth and its wasteful and destructive use, between the potential of freedom and the actuality of repression, between the possible abolition of alienated labor and the capitalist need to sustain it, may well lead to a gradual dysfunction of the society, a decline of the morale which normally assures the day-to-day performance and the compliance with the required pattern of behavior, at work and at leisure. This may awaken the consciousness of the use of technical progress as instrument of domination.

The events of May and June in France have shown to what extent these tensions in the established society can loosen the grip of capitalist and trade union integration, and promote the alliance between working class groups and the militant intelligentsia.

The concept of revolution must take into account this eventuality of the diffuse, apparently "spontaneous," disintegration of the system, the general loosening of its cohesion—an expression of the objective obsolescence of alienated labor, of the pressure for the liberation of man from his function as agent (and servant) of the process of production: the revolution may be seen as a crisis of the system in "affluence" and superfluity.

The Agents of Change

In such a crisis, the historical agents of change would emerge—and they would not be identical with any of the traditional classes. But the "qualification" of these agents can be gauged if we recall the perhaps most decisive element in the Marxian concept, namely, that the historical subject of revolution must be the "definite negation" also in the sense that this subject is a social class free from, that is, not contaminated by the exploitative needs and interests of man under capitalism, that it is the subject of essentially different, "humanistic" needs and values.

This is the notion of the rupture with the continuum of domination, the qualitative difference of socialism as a new form and way of life, not only rational development of the productive forces, but also the redirection of progress toward the ending of the competitive struggle for existence, not only abolition of poverty and toil, but also reconstruction of the social and natural environment as a peaceful, beautiful universe: *total transvaluation of values, transformation of needs and goals.* This implies *still another change in the concept of revolution,* a break with the continuity of the technical apparatus of productivity which, for Marx, would extend (freed from capitalist abuse) to the socialist society. Such *"technological" continuity* would *constitute a fateful link between capitalism and socialism,* because this technical apparatus has, in its very structure and scope, become an apparatus of control and domination. *Cutting this link* would mean, not to regress in the technical progress, but to reconstruct the technical apparatus in accordance with the needs of free men, guided by their own consciousness and sensibility, by their autonomy. This autonomy would call for a decentralized apparatus of rational control on a reduced basis—reduced because no longer inflated by the requirements of exploitation, aggressive expansion, and competition, held together by *solidarity* in co-operation.

Now is *this apparently "utopian" notion applicable to existing social and political forces,* which could thus be regarded as agents of qualitative change?

The Marxian concept of revolution is neither a utopian nor a romantic concept, it insists on the real basis of power, on the objective and subjective factors which can alone elevate the idea of qualitative change above the level of wishful thinking, and this basis is still in the advanced industrial countries.

In the capitalist countries, the force of the alternative appears today only in the "marginal" groups mentioned above: the opposition among the intelligentsia, especially the students, and among the politically articulate and active groups among the working classes.

Both reject not only the system as a whole and any transformation of the system "within the existing structures"; they also profess their adherence to a new and qualitatively different system of values and aspirations.

The weakness of these groups is expressive of the new historical constellation which defines the concept of the revolution:

1. against the majority of the integrated population, including that of the "immediate producers";

2. against a well-functioning, prosperous society, which is neither in a revolutionary nor a pre-revolutionary situation.

In accord with this situation, the role of this opposition is a strictly preparatory one: their task is radical enlightenment, in theory and by practice, and the development of cadres and nuclei for the struggle against the global structure of capitalism.

For it is precisely in its global structure where the internal contradictions assert themselves: in the sustained resistance against neo-colonial domination; in the emergence of new powerful efforts to construct a qualitatively different society in Cuba, in China's cultural revolution; and, last but not least, in the more or less "peaceful" co-existence with the Soviet Union. Here too, the dynamic of two antagonistic tendencies:

1. the common interest of the "have-nations" in the race of international upheavals in the precarious balance of power;

2. the conflicting interests of different social systems, both securing and defending their respective political and strategic orbits.

Conclusion

The Marxian concept of revolution must comprehend the changes in the scope and social structure of advanced capitalism, and the new forms of the contradictions characteristic of the latest stage of capitalism in its global framework. The modifications of the Marxian concept then appear, not as extraneous additions or adjustments, but rather as the elaboration of Marxian theory itself.

One aspect, however, seems to be incompatible with this interpretation. There is in Marx a strain that may be called a rationalistic, even positivistic prejudice, namely, his belief in the inexorable necessity of the transition to a "higher stage of human development," and in the final success of this transition. Although Marx was much aware of the possibility of failure, defeat, or betrayal, the alternative *"socialism or* *barbarism"* was not an integral part of his concept of revolution. It must become such a part: the subordination of man to the instruments of his labor, to the total, overwhelming apparatus of production and destruction, has reached the point of an all but incontrollable power: objectified, *verdinglicht** behind the technological veil, and behind the mobilized national interest, this power seems to be self-propelling, and to carry the indoctrinated and integrated people along. It may strike the fatal blow before the counter-forces are strong enough to prevent it: an explosion of the internal contradiction which would make a re-examination of the concept of revolution a merely abstract and speculative undertaking. The awareness of this possibility should strengthen and solidify the opposition in all its manifestations—it is the only hope.

* Thingified, reified—*Ed.*

Jean-Paul Sartre

Jean-Paul Sartre is the French existentialist philosopher and writer. His political writings include *Communists and Peace* (1952), *The Ghost of Stalin* (1956), *Critique de la raison dialectique* (1960; only Volume I has been published, and only the prefatory essay, *Search for a Method,* has been translated into English), and *On Genocide* (1968).

The following interview was conducted in Rome on August 27, 1969, by Rossana Rossanda, the co-editor of the new radical journal *Il Manifesto* and was published in Italian in *Il Manifesto* and then in English in *Telos,* Number 4, Fall, 1969. The subsequent polemics it has generated has led to, among other things, the expulsion of the editors of the journal (Lucio Magri and Rossana Rossanda) from the Italian Communist Party. The translation was done by Paul Piccone and Maria Coles, with revisions added by Arthur S. Lothstein.

In the interview, Sartre discusses—à propos of the May, 1968, events in France—the concept of a revolutionary party and the problematic relationship between working-class spontaneity and an institutionalized party structure. Sartre argues that while a revolutionary party is needed (for generalizing the struggle, for mediating between the struggle and culture, for developing post-revolutionary strategy, etc.), the party must continually fight against its own institutionalization in order to remain in working touch with ongoing social experience.

THE RISK OF SPONTANEITY AND THE LOGIC OF THE INSTITUTION

INTERVIEWER: One of the results of the May events in France and of the recent struggle in general has been a criticism of the Communist Party involving not only its decisions, but also its structure.

Reprinted by permission of *Telos*.

It is not only its degeneration that has been attacked, but its very nature—*i.e.,* the very concept of the party as a political organization. This polemic has not been fruitful. It has generally led the movement to impotence and ultimately, as in the present, to backward tendencies, *i.e.,* to a rediscovery of a Leninist theory of the party in its original purity and, subsequently, to the reiteration of it. This tendency seems as fruitless as the former. We believe that "spontaneity" can and, in fact, should be criticized, in terms of what was learned in 1968, *i.e.,* that the present struggle demands a new form of revolutionary organization commensurate with advanced capitalism.

We would like to pose the theoretical premises of this problem as the topic of our conversation. They have a space and a history within your thought, starting with the now classical polemics of 1952 (*Les Communistes et la Paix*) to the subsequent arguments with Lefort and Merleau-Ponty, on to 1956 (*Le Fantôme de Staline*), and finally to the *Critique de la Raison Dialectique.* In 1952 you were accused of hypersubjectivism, *i.e.,* viewing the working class as existing only within the party; in 1956, however, this accusation was reversed, and you were charged with an objectivism that attempted to explain Stalinism wholly as the inevitable product of a historical situation. Actually, this does not appear to us as a reversal; they both are based on the concept of *rareté* (scarcity), on the structural backwardness of the situation in which the October Revolution took place, on the subsequent necessities posed by an "immaturity" of the revolution, and, finally, on the building of Socialism in a context of primitive accumulation. It was against this general background that, at one time, you justified the need for a party superimposing itself on the masses, since the masses had not yet quite reached a state of full political consciousness. Do you think that your former concept of the party should be reconsidered since things have changed? Or do you think that it had been theoretically inadequate all along—an inadequacy much more evident today?

SARTRE: When I wrote *Les Communistes et la Paix* in 1952, the main task was to defend the French Communist Party and, above all, the USSR, which was being accused of imperialism. It was crucial to reject this accusation, so as not to wind up on the side of the Americans. Subsequent events revealed that the Soviet Union had become an imperialist power. It intervened in Budapest and sub-sequently invaded Czechoslovakia. It did precisely what Stalin did not do in Yugoslavia in 1948, because of political foresight or whatever other reasons. By saying this, I don't mean to make a moral judgment. I am merely asserting that the Soviet Union's foreign policy appears to be essentially motivated by the priority it ascribes to its antagonistic relationship with the United States, and not by the principle of respect for and equality with other socialist states. This is what led to my position of 1956. At this point I had to indicate the contradiction between my new position and that of 1952. Consequently, I sought to explain this in *Critique de la Raison Dialectique.* My solution was merely formal. It should have been followed by a historical analysis of the USSR in Stalin's era, an analysis which I had already outlined and which is part of the second volume of the *Critique,* which will probably never be published.

In sum, I have attempted to deal with such matters as mass, party, spontaneity, serialization, groups, etc., all of which represent a preliminary answer to this problem. What I attempted to show is that in relationship to the masses, the party is a necessary reality, insofar as the masses themselves do not have spontaneity. When the masses are left to themselves, they remain serialized. On the other hand, once the party becomes an institution, it invariably becomes, with minor exceptions, reactionary in relation to what it seeks to create or help develop, *i.e.,* the fusion of the group. In other words, the contraposition of spontaneity and the party is a pseudo problem. In terms of self-consciousness, the working class does not appear homogeneous, but a conglomeration of elements and groups which ultimately become "fused." If we examine con-cretely the situation of workers in plants where a struggle is being waged, we will always find certain groups in fusion. In the course of the struggle individual workers establish a certain relationship and respect toward one another. They experience what I have referred to as primitive liberty and attain a certain class con-sciousness. Alongside these fusing groups, however, there are other workers who are not bound by a struggle and who, therefore, re-main in a serial relationship to other workers and are actually incapable of spontaneity. Their connection to other workers is a mere relationship of reifications—a serial relationship. They are constantly other than themselves, because they are determined only through a relationship to someone else, who himself is also determined only through a relationship to someone else, and so on. Even a fusing group—*e.g.,* in a striking plant—is constantly under pressure from interfering serial elements. The same worker who at work is within a fusing group could very well be totally serialized at home or in certain other aspects of his life. Thus, we are confronted here with various forms of class consciousness. On the one hand, we have an advanced consciousness, while on the other, a practically nonexistent consciousness, and between these, a series of mediations. It is for this reason that I think we cannot speak of class spontaneity. It is correct to speak only of groups produced by circumstances which create themselves according to particular situations. In this process, the groups do not regain some kind of profound spontaneity. They do, however, experience similar situations as a result of specific conditions of exploitation and specific wage demands. In so doing, they see themselves in a more or less correct perspective.

Having said this, what is the party's relationship to the series? Clearly, it plays a positive role, because it prevents a lapse into complete serialization. If the party did not bring them together into a group by means of an organic link—which connects the Milanese Communist with every other Communist worker of every other country—the members of a Communist Party would themselves remain isolated and serialized individuals. Furthermore, as a result of communications facilitated by the party, many groups are formed in the course of the struggle. Nevertheless, the party usually finds itself confronted with either absorbing or repudiating those very groups it has helped create. The party is much more structured than the group, whose structure is never more than some kind of loose agreement. A group forms under stress, *e.g.,* around objectives, such as "The Bastille must be taken." Immediately after the action, the members of that group have a feeling of uncertainty toward one another. As such, they attempt to establish within their individual freedom an immediate bond replacing that which had been previously provided by the action. They try to establish some kind of pact or oath which would constitute an embryonic series and which somehow establishes among them a reified and contiguous relationship. This was my argument in

Fraternité et Terreur. The group goes no further. On the other hand, the party grows as a conglomerate of institutions and, therefore, as a closed system with sclerotic tendencies. Thus, it is always out of step with the fusing masses, even when it tries to lead them. This occurs because the party at best impoverishes the masses in its attempts to subordinate them, while at worst it rejects and negates them.

This is why the thinking of a fusing group which originated in the heat of a specific situation and which is not "spontaneous" has a stronger function, a much more critical and original function, than that of a structured group. The thinking and actions of groups reflect their structural makeup. Insofar as the party is an institution and its main concern is its own organization, it thinks as an institution and thus becomes removed from reality. It becomes an ideology and degenerates in the same way as does the experience of the struggle. On the other hand, the fusing group thinks about the experience as it occurs, without any institutionalized mediations. This is the reason why the thinking of a particular group can be vague and impossible to put into theory, *e.g.,* the students' ideas in 1968. This represents, however, a truer kind of reflection, since there is no institution acting as a filter between the experience and the reflection on that experience.

We are obviously faced here with a contradiction which is inherent in the very function of the party. The party comes into existence in order to free the working class from the serialization of which it is itself a reflection. Yet it is a special kind of reflection, insofar as the party comes into existence to abolish the very serialization and massification of the masses on which it operates. Its institutionality is a reflection of the serialization of the masses. Because it is forced to come in contact with that serialization, it too becomes, to some extent, idle and serial. In order to protect itself, the party ultimately contraposes itself to the fusing groups, which are one aspect of the very working class which it would like to represent, the very groups whose growth the party has very often helped nurture. This is the basic contradiction of the party. It comes into existence to free the masses from serialization but in so doing it becomes institutionalized. As such, it becomes passive (here I am not referring to bureaucracy or to other types of degeneration, but to its very institutionalized structure, which is not necessarily bureaucratic). This passivity will always lead it to *de facto* opposition to all new forces, both those it wants to use and those it rejects. Note the different attitudes which the French and Italian Communist parties have adopted in relation to the students: The FCP has rejected them, whereas the ICP tactfully attempts to bring them back into the fold by channeling their activities through contact and dialogue. A party can only do one or the other; this is its basic contradiction. Consider also the classical question of democratic centralization. As long as the party is in a transitional context—*e.g.,* during the clandestine buildup of the struggle in Russia, when Lenin was formulating a theoretical basis for it— it remains a viable force. At one time there was both a centralizing and a democratic moment, for the people discussed things and decisions were made jointly. As soon as the party became institutionalized, however, as has happened with all Communist parties, centralization took precedence over democracy. Consequently, even its democracy has become "institutionalized" and subject to its own kind of inertia. This is why there is such a thing as the "right of speech." However, the very fact that it is nothing but a right empties it of all substance and turns it into an actual "nonright." The real problem of unification, then, is how to go beyond the contradiction inherent in the very nature of the party, so that this very act (not only in relation to the enemy and its role within the struggle, which is a broader problem, but also in relation to the class which it represents) could become an active mediation among the elements of massification and serialization. In so doing, it would become capable of receiving the impetus which originates from the movement, and instead of pretending to direct this impetus, it would interpret it both for its own benefit and for that of the movement.

INTERVIEWER: You are saying, then, that true revolutionary consciousness is not to be found in the working class or in the party, but within the struggle. The party is viable as long as it is an instrument of struggle, but as soon as it becomes institutionalized, it takes the means for the end, and it itself becomes the end. On the other hand, the working class does not attain self-consciousness unless it constitutes itself as a group, and this is possible only if the working class outlines a political project. The contradiction which you have outlined could probably be resolved only by attempting to go beyond a mere general posing of the problem and ultimately by bringing it down to the immediacy of individual situations. In other words, a metahistorical solution does not seem possible. We must point out those objective contradictions in which the dilemma could from time to time find a solution. It appears to us that two conditions are necessary: (1) that the working class go beyond its serialization in order to actually and fully become a subject of collective action, capable of hegemony. . . .

SARTRE: That is an impossible condition. The working class could never entirely express itself as an active, political subject. There will always be zones or regions or outskirts which, for reasons of historical development, will remain serialized, massified, or on an unconscious level. There will always be some residue. At present, the generalization of the concepts of class consciousness and class struggle is commonly used as preexisting, a priori elements in relationship to the struggle. What is a priori, however, is only the objective state of exploitation of the working class. Consciousness comes into existence only through the struggle, and class struggle exists only insofar as there are places where there actually is a fight. It is true that the proletariat entails the death of the bourgeoisie. It is also true that the capitalist system is mined with antagonistic and structural contradictions. This does not necessarily entail, however, the existence of a class consciousness or the consciousness of a class struggle. In order for consciousness and struggle to exist, someone must be waging a fight. In other words, class struggle is virtually possible everywhere within the capitalist system. In reality, however, it exists only where it is being fought. Even where fights are being waged, conditions differ from place to place. *E.g.,* in France, conditions and types of struggle are very different from one place to another; the workers' struggles in St.-Nazaire are extremely violent and resemble those of the past century. In more mature capitalist sections, however, the struggles assume a different character; the articulation of demands is perhaps richer, but the context is more moderate. The outcome is that even that portion of the working class which is actually waging a struggle can express itself only if it is unified. The twenty-four-hour strikes dictated by the CGT do not add up to a unified struggle, but are merely symbols of the same.

INTERVIEWER: Isn't this a period of growing unification for capitalist society, both in the base and in the superstructure (patterns of consumption, patterns of life, language, and massification)? Isn't it true that corresponding to the fragmentation of individual situations there is an increasingly more evident "totality" of the capitalist system. Isn't it also true that what should follow from this is a material and objective base for the unification of the working class and for class consciousness?

SARTRE: In reality, the base remains very differentiated and unbalanced.

INTERVIEWER: But isn't there the tendency toward unification?

SARTRE: Yes and no. For example, in France, though economic rationality proscribes it, capitalism keeps thousands of small firms artificially alive. These small firms come in handy, however, because they represent a politically conservative belt (they are the section which consistently votes for De Gaulle and Pompidou). Furthermore, notwithstanding the increase in productivity, they allow capitalism to pile on them its cost of production. In other words, the tendencies toward integration do not eliminate the deep-seated diversifications of the structural situations. As far as the consciousness of one's own situation is concerned, advanced capitalism is always able to satisfy, despite the great imbalance of payments, the basic subsistence needs of the majority of the working class. This majority, of course, does not include marginal groups, i.e., 25 percent of the workers in the United States (i.e., blacks and immigrants). It does not include that segment composed of the older members of the working class, and on a worldwide level, it does not include the Third World. Capitalism fulfills basic needs. But it also fulfills certain false needs which it itself creates, e.g., the need of an automobile, of going to the movies, or of following its own fads. This has led me to reexamine my theory of needs. In advanced capitalism, these needs are no longer naturally contraposed to the system. On the contrary, they have become, to some extent, one of the means by which advanced capitalism injects into the proletariat mechanisms which are generated and induced by the profit motive. The worker wears himself out in the actual production of the automobile in order to earn the salary to buy one. It is the buying which satisfies one of his "needs." The very system which obviously exploits him also offers him a way of life and the possibility of satisfying it.

Awareness of the intolerability of the system, then, is no longer found in its inability to provide either for the elementary necessities of life or for the more general ones. It is to be found in the awareness of alienation within this system, *i.e.,* in the fact that this kind of life makes no sense and is not worth living, that this system is deceitful, that these needs are artificially created (they are false needs), and that they wear out one's existence and serve only the interests of capital. Now the unification of the working class along these lines is much more difficult to accomplish. For this reason, I am not in agreement with the optimistic vision of Communist parties and of left-wing movements—a vision which assumes that capitalism is really undergoing a crisis. On the contrary, it is still able to control the working class; it is not on the defensive. A revolutionary development still necessitates a long and patient effort toward the attainment of consciousness.

INTERVIEWER: However, during the May events in France this unification seemed immediate and obvious.

SARTRE: Yes. That was one of the few cases in which everyone saw his own struggle as similar to that being waged in the next plant. A similarly widespread phenomenon took place in 1936. At that time, however, the workers' institutions played a determining role. The movement unleashed itself when the socialist and the communist forces were in power, thus offering the working class a model for the quick development of consciousness, for fusion into groups, and for subsequent unification. In May, 1968, not only were the left-wing parties and trade unions not in power, but they played an altogether different role. The unifying factor of the struggle was something which, I think, came from the outside. It was an idea which came from Vietnam and which the students have expressed in the formula *"l'imagination au pouvoir."* * In other words, the universe of possibilities is much more vast than the one which the dominant class had led us to accept. Who would have ever believed that a people of 14,000,000 peasants could have ever held its own against the biggest industrial and military power in the world? Yet this has happened. Vietnam has taught us that the realm of possibilities is enormous and that we must not give up. This has been the springboard of the student revolt, and the workers have understood it. This idea suddenly became prevalent

* Imagination to power—*Ed.*

in the joint demonstrations of May 13. "If a couple of thousand kids can take over the university and at the same time keep the government at bay, why can't we do the same?" Thus, following May 13, and on the basis of a model which, at that point, came to them from the outside, the workers went on strike and took over the plants. The unifying and mobilizing element was not a platform of wage demands. These, in fact, came later as a justification of the strike, whose causes were definitely not lacking. What is interesting here is that wage demands came as the aftermath, when the plants had already been taken over.

INTERVIEWER: What you are saying, then, is that the causes of the May events had no immediate material foundation, no particularly explosive structural contradiction rooted in the present phase of French capitalism?

SARTRE: What had been commonly felt by all workers were the reactionary measures taken by the government concerning social security in the preceding autumn. These measures had hit every member of the working class, regardless of his position, by affecting everyone's wages. The unions had not been capable of opposing those measures, either because they had been caught by surprise or because they had not wanted to stick their necks out too far. If I remember correctly, there was a general strike for a day, and then things went back to normal. The unrest remained deep-seated and unexpressed and subsequently exploded during the May assemblies. Today another possible element of unification is brought into play by the invalidation of the wage increases won at that time, owing to the subsequent price increases and the devaluation of the currency. But it is not easy to foresee whether these common unifying elements of discontent will transform themselves into a common revolt. In May, however, there was such a revolt, and as far as I am concerned, the detonator was not the workers' awareness of exploitation as much as their awareness of their own strength and their own possibilities.

INTERVIEWER: The May revolt failed, however. It ended up as a victory for conservatism. Did it lack political guidance or the elements needed to carry out a revolution?

SARTRE: What was missing was the political guidance capable of giving to the May revolt that political and theoretical dimension without which the movement would have completely dissolved, as in fact did happen. What was missing was a party capable of fully absorbing the movement and its potentialities. It was missing, because an institutionalized structure, such as the Communist Party, could not adapt itself to something which caught it unprepared. How can such an institution find within its structure the necessary disposition to react, not with a "let us see what we can get out of it" nor with a "let us try to contain the movement so that it does not bypass us," but by saying, "This is how reality is, and this is how I must assume it to be, in order to give it a theoretical and practical interpretation which will allow it to grow and develop"? A Communist Party which is unable to do this becomes in effect what the French Communist Party has been for the last twenty-five years: an obstacle to any revolutionary struggle in France. It denies and suppresses anything that does not come from itself.

INTERVIEWER: In summary, though you criticize the Communist parties as they are, you also recognize the need for a moment of organization and unification of the movement.

SARTRE: Yes, this is the problem. We are witnessing a capitalist reaction which is both strong, complex, and fully able to bring about integration and repression. This necessitates a concomitant reorganization of the working class. The problem, though, is how to prevent it from degenerating into an "institution."

INTERVIEWER: Agreed, but it is interesting to note that the need for a political organization of the working class, demanded by the growing fragmentation of situations and of consciousness—as you previously described it—contradicts one of Marx's predictions— namely, that with the growth of capitalism, the proletariat immediately expresses itself as a revolutionary movement, without the need of any political mediation. The basis for this prediction was Marx's belief that a capitalist crisis was imminent and hence that alternative needs would develop within capitalist society, *e.g.,* an intensification of the contradiction between the forces and the relations of capitalist production. Later Lenin saw the socialization of property as a step which somehow would lead to socialist management, once the bourgeois political apparatus had been broken. As of today, we must admit the inadequacy of this thesis. First of all, the forces of production do not enter into a direct contradiction with the system. They are not neutral and objective, but the very product of the system. They have been adjusted to serve other priorities which they reflect. . . .

SARTRE: Yes, they are not necessarily bound to clash. They are the offspring of this type of development, as is shown, for example, by the priority given to space exploration in science. As far as the socialization of property is concerned, though I do not consider it correct to define the bureaucracy or the technocracy as a "class," it seems that it entails an extension of the possibilities of control and social integration.

INTERVIEWER: In other words, the transition from capitalism to socialism is not the same as the transition from feudal to bourgeois society. Capitalism developed within feudal society, so that when the latter fell, it was nothing but a shell containing a different structural reality, an already mature alternative within it. This cannot happen to the proletariat. Within capitalism it cannot express itself through alternative embryonic socialist organizations. . . .

SARTRE: Yes, it cannot express itself structurally either in terms of relations of production or of philosophical ideas. After the Renaissance, culture was no longer feudal, but bourgeois. Science was bourgeois. And even new social groups such as the *noblesse de robe* were bourgeois. This secular process accompanied and preceded the institutionalization of capitalist relations of production. Bourgeois management lasted for centuries and expressed itself as an alternative already present in the earlier society. For the proletariat, this does not even occur in the cultural domain. The proletariat does not have its own culture: It either borrows elements from bourgeois culture, or it expresses a total rejection of any culture—which is tantamount to admitting the nonexistence of its own culture. It is objected, however, that the working class has its own "hierarchy of values." Of course, by wanting the revolution, it wants something different from what it has. But I am skeptical of expressions such as "hierarchy of values," which are easily transformable into their opposite. The students' revolt is a typical expression of the difficulties faced by a counterculture. It is a refusal which, lacking its own elaboration, ends up by borrowing from the adversary, if even with opposite meaning, a series of ideologisms (conceptual simplification, overgeneralization, violence, etc.).

INTERVIEWER: Then, the anticapitalist revolution is simultaneously mature and immature. It produces the contradictions, but not the alternative. Upon what objective and material bases is it possible to reconstruct an alternative which would not fall back on pure evolutionism, without at the same time ending up in voluntarism or in pure revolutionary subjectivism?

SARTRE: Let me repeat: An alternative can be reconstructed more on the basis of alienation than on one of "needs." That is, upon the reconstruction of the person and of freedom. This is a need so omnipresent that even the most refined techniques of integration cannot avoid it. Rather, they try to satisfy it in a mystifying way. All "human engineering" is based on the notion that the owner must treat his employee as if the latter were his equal, for—and this is implicit—no man can renounce his right to equal treatment. And the worker that falls into the trap of "human relations" or paternalism is its victim precisely to the extent that he wants a real equality.

INTERVIEWER: Yes, but how can it be shown that these new needs are in fact new, that they are produced by advanced capitalism, that they are not mere leftovers of a "humanism" of precapitalist society? Perhaps the answer is to be sought in the very contradictions inherent in the development of capitalism, which require both the fragmentation of labor and a broader cultural formulation of the role of the fragmented laborer, the qualitative and quantitative extensions of education and a lack of social outlets, and an increase in demands and the impossibility of satisfying them. In other words, the permanent frustrations of that very fundamental productive force: man.

SARTRE: The growth of capital accelerates the process of proletarianization, not through absolute impoverishment, but through the constant degradation of new needs and roles. These are produced by capitalist development and not by crisis.

INTERVIEWER: Therefore, the moment of political organization of the working class implies not only an awareness of the contradictions and the unification of the struggle, but also the elaboration of an alternative. The "spontaneity" of May, on the contrary, assumed the solution of this problem. Neo-Marcusian or anarchist positions à la Cohn-Bendit aimed exclusively at the negation. But they could not even guarantee the continuity of the struggle, since in an advanced society the very rebelling groups must pose the problem of the "aftermath." The majority of men are alienated and oppressed. Yet they are provided with the means for subsistence. As a consequence, this leads them to seek a guarantee for further amelioration and an account of what will be substituted after the destruction (which explains why within a few weeks there was a shift from a position of struggle to one of fear of the consequences of the struggle). On the other hand, Touraine's or Mallet's theses assumed that the development of the forces of production and the subjective maturation of the masses made self-organization and self-management of society immediately possible. As we have seen, this is incorrect. Capitalist development precipitates the revolution by creating new needs, new forces, and new means of production. But these do reflect the capitalist mechanism, its priorities and structures, in such a way that a sudden breakdown of the system necessarily implies a decline in production. In other words, the immediate concerns of both the passive and the struggling masses, by themselves, do not seem to be able to express anything but the negation of their own condition. This is why the party is needed. It is needed not only as a generalizing moment of the struggle, but also as the agency from which the revolutionary project and the concept of a new society are derived or "invented."

SARTRE: Certainly, it is important to be aware of the difficulties inheret in the transition to socialism. Let us assume that the situation in France or Italy comes to the point of a power take-over. What do we know about a socialist economic reconstruction of a highly industrialized country, given the fact that such a country would probably be under fire from external boycotts, the immediate devaluation of the currency, and the freezing of exports? The USSR found itself in a similar situation after the revolution. Notwithstanding the terrible sacrifices and the enormous costs of the civil war and of the political and economic siege, the problems that it faced were less complex than those that would be faced by an advanced capitalist society today. From this viewpoint, we are all unprepared, especially the Communist parties. You mention the necessity of a transitional political perspective. Agreed. But which Communist Party has a fully elaborated theory of revolutionary change in advanced (yet not self-sufficient) capitalist societies?

INTERVIEWER: In advanced capitalist societies the problem of the transition to socialism has never been concretely raised by Communist parties after the 1920's.

SARTRE: Very true, especially after World War II and the Yalta

Agreements. Consequently, there has been no discussion of alternatives. This, however, is not unrelated to the new face of Communist parties. In Annie Kriegel's excellent book *Les Communistes Français,* the French Communist Party is severely criticized. Nevertheless, despite its politics and all the defects and errors listed by Kriegel, it is assumed that the FCP constitutes an alternative, or, better yet, the proletarian alternative, to French capitalist society. This is nonsense. In recognizing the need for the political organization of the working class, we must also recognize the total inadequacy of its "historical" institutions in relation to the tasks that we want to assign to them. A little while ago we were saying that without a unifying moment of struggle, a cultural mediation, and an alternative project it is not possible to go beyond the stage of mere revolt, which never succeeds politically. This, however, does not alter the fact that an institutionalized party is unable to function as a mediator between culture and struggles. The confused and unsystematic thought of the masses is *true* to the extent that it reflects experience. However, once this is translated into the ideological mechanism of the party, it becomes altogether different and presents a relationship totally different from culture. The party must be capable of continual struggle against its own institutionalization if it is to fit within the scheme which you propose. Without this premise, your whole argument fails. If the cultural import of Communist parties is almost nil, this is not because there is a lack of individually worthy intellectuals. Rather, it is the result of the parties' constitution which paralyzes their collective thinking. Action and thought are not separable from organization: One thinks in terms of the structures he finds himself in and acts according to the organization to which he belongs. This is why the official thought of Communist parties has become fossilized.

INTERVIEWER: Let us for the moment separate the theoretical hypotheses of the character of the revolutionary political organization of the working class from what it is in practice. Historically, Communist parties have followed in the path of the Third International and the political and ideological events of the Soviet Union and of the socialist camp. These are realities that have affected the growth of the working class and are an actual part of it. They have induced attitudes, ideologies, and power changes. Today, however, we face a working-class movement which, for the first time in Europe, tends to relate dialectically to the Communist parties without fully identifying with them. This movement is destined either to modify the parties or else to be rejected by them. It is unlikely that the movement can be simply absorbed, as is shown by the case of the students. Either way, we have the problem of a new concept of the "party." Returning to something you mentioned at the beginning, let me ask you this: Will this new party be condemned to gradual institutionalization and detachment from the very movement that has given rise to it? Is it actually possible to have an organization capable of continually overcoming its own limitations and the pitfalls of institutional sclerosis?

SARTRE: While I recognize the need for organization, I must confess that I cannot see how it is possible to resolve the problems brought about by established structures.

INTERVIEWER: From what you have said, the political party should guarantee the development of the struggling masses, rather than negate or minimize such a development. It should guarantee the development of a counterculture or an alternative culture. Also, it should be capable of producing syntheses in relation to the permanent dialectic within society. These seem to be specific tasks of the party, since their universality prevents them from being resolved by a group in fusion within the specific moment of the struggle.

SARTRE: Yes, they cannot be resolved without the party.

INTERVIEWER: Agreed. In order to escape this dilemma, we might advance a double hypothesis. First of all if the party is to avoid the logic of institutionalization, it must consider itself permanently at the service of the struggle, which has its own moment of power, and its own autonomous political levels. This implies going beyond the Leninist and Bolshevik model, which was subsequently adapted to popular fronts. According to this model, the struggle of the masses in and of itself never amounts to more than a struggle based on trade union demands. On the other hand, the "political use" of the struggle remains possible. This separation disappeared in the soviets or in the councils. The moment of power and its institutionalized embryo were already implicit in the means of the struggle— a struggle continuous with the hypothesis of a *social* revolution preceding a *political* revolution, where power was to be taken over by the soviets and not by the party. Second, we need to orient revolutionary theory differently. From Lenin on, revolutionary theory has been essentially concerned with how to take power, rather than with how to deal with society. Thus, it has failed both to supply an adequate analysis of the actual situation and to project what has to be attained by means of the revolution. This is one of the sources of the parties' inability to come in contact with the movement. They do not seem to be able to explicate the potentialities and needs of the movement. This is what happened to the students. It is easy to criticize them, but which party has answered the questions the students have asked about the function of education, its relationship to the rest of society, and the content of nonauthoritarian knowledge? Finally, we must keep in mind that a political organization of the working class, whether Marxist or not, is not just an a posteriori datum, but also the result of an interpretation of experience by means of an a priori methodology, from which the categories of capital, class, imperialism, etc., are derived. In other words, the theoretical-methodological Marxist moment which becomes dialectical through the experience of the struggle, carries, or should carry, the possibility of an alternative. If this relation between the party and the working class is kept open, can we guarantee a permanent counterinstitution and at the same time avoid the total fragmentation of the struggle?

SARTRE: I agree on one condition, *i.e.,* that this dialectic be depicted as a double power and that it not be wholly resolved within the political moment. And even then, many problems would remain unsolved. You speak of a theoretical-methodological element somehow given a priori and through which experience is to be interpreted. But does not "capital" remain a poor and abstract notion if the analysis of modern capitalism is not reconstructed through an investigation and through a constant challenging of the results of the investigation and of the struggle? True, thought is *one,* but its unity is dialectical. It is a living and developing reality. We must construct a relationship among men that guarantees not only freedom, but also the *revolutionary* freedom of thinking, a relationship that is able to grasp knowledge and to criticize it to the extent that it grasps it. This is how knowledge has always advanced—unlike the "Marxism" of the Communist parties. In order to contribute to culture and to truth, it is necessary that the party —the political organization of the working class—always leave open the possibility to be contradicted and created by its members and vice versa, rather than function as a superadministrator of a knowledge acquired once and for all. If we look outside official Communist circles, the debate concerning Marxism has never been as rich as it is today. Ever since the end of Stalinism, the problem of the diversity of socialism has come to the fore, and there have been many Marxist investigations which have openly clashed.

INTERVIEWER: It is, however, a clash concerning the exegesis of sacred texts. It is a debate between interpretations, rather than a rebirth of creativity and of creative interpretations of reality.

SARTRE: That is not exactly correct. Certainly, there has been a preliminary discussion of texts. But let us take Althusser as an example. His philosophy is not a matter of simple exegesis. He has a theory of concepts, of autonomous knowledge, and of the study of contradictions, starting from the dominating contradiction, the *surdétermination*. His investigations are original and cannot be challenged without a new elaboration. In order to oppose Althusser, I have been forced to reconsider the idea of "notion" and to draw from it a whole set of implications. The same can be said of the concept of structure introduced by Lévi-Strauss, which has been somewhat too easily adopted by certain Marxists. In other words, a genuine discussion always involves a new effort and new theoretical results. Wherever there are inquiries, there must also be a structure that guarantees the discussion. Without this, even the theoretical paradigm that the political organization proposes to the experience of the working class remains inconsequential. This is a permanent contradiction of the party, an actual limitation of all Communist parties. Similarly complex is the hypothesis of an "open" relationship between the party as a unifying political organization of the working class and the moment of self-government of the masses, soviets, or councils. We cannot forget that in postrevolutionary Russia, where this has been tried, the unifying organizations of the masses have rapidly disappeared and only the party has remained. It is a dialectically necessary process that in the USSR has led the party to take over the power that was meant to have been taken over and held by the soviets. Could it have been otherwise? This might not happen today. But during the years of the siege of the USSR by the capitalist countries—years of civil war and of terrible internal restrictions—it is easy to understand the sequence of events that eventually led to the elimination of the soviets. Thus, I saw fit to write that rather than a dictatorship *of* the proletariat, it should have been called a dictatorship *for* the proletariat. That is, the party had assumed the task of destroying the bourgeoisie for the proletariat, which was supposed to have done it directly, but which instead found itself taking orders of various kinds from an organism that both represented it and was above it. On the other hand, it was necessary for the survival of the USSR that the proletariat, as in every other country where there has been a revolution, be required to renounce what had been its more immediate objectives before the revolution, *i.e.,* wage increases and a reduction in working hours. What was asked of the proletariat was precisely the opposite. This was unavoidable. But would it not be difficult to pose these objectives from within a perspective of limited experience with local self-government? Finally, in terms of the present, it seems very difficult for an organization of soviets or councils to come into being in a situation dominated by a strong "historical" articulation of the working class, of the labor union, or of the party. In France, we have experienced the action committees. These have rapidly dissolved, not only because they have been outlawed or opposed, but because the labor unions have once again gained control of the movement.

INTERVIEWER: This last contradiction does not seem insurmountable. It is now being resolved in practice. Every labor struggle that deals not only with wage increases, but also with the rate of work, the hours, its organization and control, demonstrates that what is needed is some form of organization directed by the workers. For example, without the unitary base assembly, which is both autonomous and elevated to a high political level, this type of bargaining would be impossible. It is the level of unionist struggle that necessitates a rediscovery of the problem of the institutions directed by the working class. It is, then, a matter of experience, and not of an intellectualist invention. Certainly, these new forms clash with conservatism and bureaucratism. But they must also be aware of certain limitations of their own. In this respect, the Italian experience is interesting, insofar as within the party, or union, or movement, the alternative is not always, as you indicated, between rejection and instrumentalization. Rather, we are facing a social tension which expresses its own forms and which, while pressuring traditional working-class institutions, is unable to find an equilibrium in either of the two. In fact, although there are well-known limitations to the union, there are also limitations to the institution of direct democracy. The latter, by and large, functions perfectly well in the course of the struggle. But as it has happened in the Fiat factory during recent struggles, the workers ran the risk of unconsciously becoming instruments of separation, from department to department and from factory to factory, and, therefore, victims of the owners' logic. At this point, does the traditional union, with all of its limitations, constitute a defense against the fragility of the new institutions? In other words, today the movement appears richer and more complex than its political expression.

SARTRE: What is interesting in your scheme is, at any rate, the duality of power that it outlines, *i.e.,* an open and unabridgeable relation between the unifying moment of the political organization of the classes and the moments of self-government, councils, and heterogeneous groups. I stress this unabridgeable relation, since there will always be a permanent tension between the two moments. The party will always attempt to submit the movement to its own interpretive and developmental schemes, despite the fact that the party will consider itself "at the service" of the movement. The moments of self-government, on the other hand, will always attempt to project their living partiality on the contradictory whole of the social fiber. In this struggle, we might find the beginning or the guarantees of a twofold transformation, which can only lead— if we want it to be revolutionary—to the progressive dissolution of the political moment, to a society that strives toward unity, but still demands self-government, *i.e.,* to perform that social revolution which, with the state, abolishes also the other typically *political* moments. In other words, it is a dialectic which aims at leading us back to Marx's developmental scheme. Up to now, this has not happened. Perhaps the conditions for its existence are beginning to develop within advanced capitalist society. This, however, is a hypothesis requiring further thought.

Ernest Mandel

Ernest Mandel is editor in chief of the Belgian radical weekly *La Gauche* and is the author of the much-celebrated *Marxist Economic Theory* (1962). He is also the author of several important pamphlets, including *An Introduction to Marxist Economic Theory* (1968), *The Revolutionary Student Movement: Theory and Practice* (1969), *The Marxist Theory of the State* (1969), and *Revolutionary Strategy in the Imperialist Countries* (1970).

The following essay originally appeared in the *International Socialist Journal,* Year 2, Number 10, August, 1965.

The socialist strategy for Western Europe which Mandel constructs is based upon an analysis of "the objective conditions in which the masses could be mobilized and the situations of breakdown in which the balance of social forces with bourgeois society is upset." He argues that while the advanced capitalist economies have successfully avoided "catastrophic economic crises," they nevertheless are incapable of resolving "the basic contradictions of the capitalist mode of production." Furthermore, the very palliatives which corporate capitalism has introduced to avoid "catastrophic economic crises" create new contradictions which only exacerbate the already conflictual basis of the capitalist social system. Corresponding to these new contradictions and to the "new phase in the development of the productive forces" which advanced capitalism has engendered, there must be a "new roster of workers' objectives"—that is, one which is not purely defensive. Toward this end, Mandel outlines a strategy of anti-capitalist "structural reforms" whose aim is "to effect an integration between the immediate aims of the masses and the objectives of the struggle which objectively challenge the very existence of the capitalist system itself." Mandel concludes the essay by arguing for the "international coordination" of the workers' struggle. Far from destroying the possibility of revolution, Mandel believes that advanced capitalism "actually brings to fruition a series of circumstances which present revolution as an immediate and urgent necessity, demanded *by the facts.*" Although Mandel's argument was written in 1965 and for a European audience, its relevance to the anti-capitalist struggles now being waged both in Western Europe and in the United States is clear.

A SOCIALIST STRATEGY FOR WESTERN EUROPE

The debate over socialist strategy in western Europe must start from the prior assumption that, during the next decade, there will be neither a world nuclear war nor an economic crisis of comparable gravity with that of 1929–1933. It is not hard to see why we must limit our discussion by making this assumption: either one of the two alternatives would mean that the problem was completely transformed, in both its objective and subjective aspects. Nor need we waste much time on the reasons why it is plausible to make such an assumption. If the United States ruling class chose to unleash a world nuclear war in any *concrete* situation, except one in which it was directly threatened with extinction, it would simply be committing suicide. Even if the possibility cannot be entirely ruled out—and there is also the possibility of a war unleashed through error or insanity—it is not one on which we could (or need) build a strategy for the workers' movement.

As far as an economic crisis or catastrophe is concerned, it has been emphasized and re-emphasized that there are strong reasons why this can be avoided by neo-capitalism for a considerable time to come.[1] To go over the principal points very briefly: the size of the State budget and State intervention in the economy; the use of a whole arsenal of anti-crisis techniques; the use of "public investment" (particularly armaments) to compensate for any sagging in private investment, etc.

Certainly, the capitalist regime cannot transform threatening crises into mild recessions completely unscathed. There is a twofold price to pay for the conversion: first, a lasting tendency towards inflation

Reprinted by permission of the *International Socialist Journal*.

[1] Ernest Mandel, *L'Apogée du néo-capitalisme et ses lendemains* in *Les Temps Modernes*, August–September, 1964.

and a loss of purchasing power of leading currencies; second, an increasingly widespread surplus productive capacity (the other face of the coin of over-production). Without doubt, these two factors will make themselves strongly felt during the coming decade; already the United States payments deficit, and the ensuing dollar crisis, are giving the neo-capitalist success story a sharp jolt. But there is no reason to doubt that the system will be able to go on functioning, though rather bumpily, through several more monetary crises and anyway for a decade.

Finally, it should be said that, during the next decade, the colonial revolution will probably make further advances and we can also expect spectacular developments in the socialist countries; however, neither of these will *basically* alter the economic and social situation of the imperialist world (though of course they will have an undeniable influence, which there is no need to go into here).

It should also be remembered that those taking part in this discussion do not believe that social reforms of the type associated with the Swedish social-democratic government or the post-war Labour government in Britain can change the capitalist character of the economy or society in any way or serve as models for a socialist strategy whose purpose is the overthrow of capitalism.

Discussion must take place within this limited context; the various proposals on socialist strategy in western Europe cannot be evaluated outside this framework.

It does not follow that because there are no catastrophic economic crises there are no crises at all.

The first problem for marxists to face is the following: since we have established, as our initial hypothesis, that we cannot expect any catastrophic economic crisis comparable with 1929–1932 (or any near collapse of the bourgeois state, as occurred after defeat in war: Germany 1918–19, Italy 1943–45, etc.), does this imply that there will be no crisis at all to threaten the capitalist economy, society and State?

This is a crucial question, because only idealists—in the philosophical-sociological sense—can envisage the overthrow of capitalism without any kind of social, political or economic crisis. In such a case, the overthrow of capitalism would follow simply on a *prise de conscience*

by the great majority of the working population (or else a putsch!).
To accept a hypothesis of this kind would mean backsliding into
utopianism.

For a marxist, there is no doubt that we can only approach the
problems of the overthrow of capitalism and the conquest of power
by starting with the objective conditions in which the masses could be
mobilized and the situations of breakdown in which the balance of
social forces within bourgeois society is upset. These are what we call
"crisis situations". But these situations are not necessarily the same
as crises of catastrophic over-production, except for mechanistic de-
terminist economists, who are far from being marxists.

First of all, it should be emphasized that, though we consider that
neo-capitalism is perfectly capable of converting serious over-production crises into milder and briefer recessions, we do not think it capable of suppressing its repeated short-term fluctuations. The American
economy experienced regular recessions, in 1949, 1953, 1957–58,
1960–61. And I have tried to explain elsewhere the reasons for the
temporary shortening of the cycle, and the reasons which suggest that
there can be no *conclusive* shortening of it.[2]

The American economy is the typical economy of the neo-capitalist
system in the imperialist countries: it is the model which western Europe and Japan imitate with a lag of several years. It therefore seems
very likely that when these countries emerge from the special cycle of
the re-construction period, their economies will experience the same
kind of recessions, although this has not happened as yet (I am talking
of countries such as Great Britain, Belgium and, recently, Italy and
France).

These economic fluctuations will then themselves produce the mechanisms which *can* periodically disturb the balance of the capitalist societies and States; the difference between these milder recessions and
more serious crises mainly being that the socio-political consequences
are *much less automatic* (after the 1929–23 crisis there were serious
political and social repercussions in every capitalist country).

The explosive factors in present-day society are not restricted to
those coming from these short-term economic fluctuations. There are
also a number of unanswered structural problems: the problem of the
Mezzogiorno in Italy and the general problem of under-developed or

[2] *Ibid.*

declining regions; the problem of German unification; the problem of the downfall or extinction of the semi-fascist regimes of Spain and Portugal and the repercussions which would follow their revolutionary overthrow; attempts to establish "strong government" in other European countries; the constant possibility of monetary and financial crises, which on occasion can have very sharp effects (cf. the consequences of the banking crisis which has recently occurred in Uruguay, "the Switzerland of Latin America"); the constant possibility that any major social conflict will take a political form and provoke retaliation by the State (with the possible ensuing counter-retaliation of the working class movement and the working masses).

To put it in more general terms: we need not believe, simply because the neo-capitalist system has succeeded in avoiding catastrophic economic crises, that it is therefore capable of *solving all the economic and social problems* which face it. We do not believe that this system has, in the slightest way, resolved the basic contradictions of the capitalist mode of production. And we believe that, to these classical contradictions, it adds a whole series of new contradictions of its own.

In analyzing neo-capitalism, people often make the mistake of thinking that "solutions" which in fact create sharp new contradictions are evidence of a "conflict-less situation". I have already given one example,[3] which springs from one of neo-capitalism's apparently spectacular successes: long-term high employment. This "solution" inevitably leads to constant wage-rises, which finally end up by threatening to cut the rate of profit in a decisive way. Hence the necessity for the bourgeoisie of limiting or abolishing trade union independence in negotiating wages (incomes policies, etc.). Hence also the tendency to replace extensive by intensive investments, substituting depth for breadth, in order to economize on man-power (automation). All these developments tend to bring the crisis in the trade union movement to a head, rather than integrating it further into the State and eliminating conflict.

The problem of incomes policy gives rise to a larger problem which, in fact, has grown more serious under neo-capitalism than under classical capitalism: how can there be a constant and harmonious rise in the purchasing power of the wage-earners in a capitalist regime? To the extent that the capitalist system requires a multiplicity of de-

[3] *Ibid.*

cision centers, regarding both prices and investments,[4] it will be unable to avoid periodic fluctuations in real wages, out of step with the periodic fluctuations of the real cost of living. And, as the system becomes more and more a prey to international competition, there will also be periodic lags in the levels of real wages in different imperialist countries, which means that management will have to launch periodic attacks on "excessive wage rises". And as long as there is an independent working class movement (and, above all, an independent trade union movement) these periodic attacks by management will create at least objectively favourable conditions for the explosion of more far-reaching social struggle, which challenge the whole operation of the capitalist economy and might even lead to victorious workers' counter-attacks.

Similarly, if neo-capitalism cannot survive without periodic management attacks on "excessive" wage rises, it will not be able to avoid attacking the level of employment; it might even be said, under neo-capitalism, that recessions are more or less deliberately *provoked* by the bourgeoisie—principally as a result of deflationist squeezes—as well as occurring through the internal mechanisms of capitalism. Thus we have another example of objectively favourable conditions for an extensive struggle, particularly *at the turning-point when the recession sets in,* which has always been the most preferable time for working class struggles under classical capitalism.

Affluence does not mean that the workers feel there is nothing left to fight for.

If we accept that, although there will be no catastrophic crisis of the 1929–33 type, this does not mean that there will be no economic and social contradictions which could arouse far-reaching workers' struggles, then it follows that the vanguard forces within the workers' movement must put forward a whole series of objectives to galvanize the masses. The examples given above—struggle against rises in the cost of living, against various kinds of wage-freeze or "controlled growth of incomes", against recurrent waves of lay-offs—must be prominent features of the appropriate campaign.

[4] "Capital only exists and can only exist in the form of numerous separate capitals and, for this reason, its self-determination will be manifested as the mutual inter-action of these capitals." (Karl Marx: *Grundrisse der Kritik der Politischen Oekonomie,* p. 317, Dietz-Verlag, Berlin, 1953.

These are essentially *defensive* objectives. But neo-capitalism is bringing with it, nationally and internationally, a new phase in the development of the productive forces. There must be a new roster of workers' objectives, corresponding to the development of these forces and qualitatively and quantitatively different from those of the past.

Wages are the price of labour power; the price of labour power oscillates around its value. Now, Marx stresses that this value is not a stable physiological datum but a datum made up of variable historical and geographical factors. And he insists on the fact that new needs can and should be incorporated from time to time into the variable element of wages, which is evidence of the civilizing quality of trade union action.[5]

As the undeniable rise in the standard of living and real wages of the working class has reduced the proportion of purchasing power expended on basic nourishment and everyday clothing, the working class in the imperialist countries has developed a whole series of new needs which play an increasingly important role in its daily preoccupations: housing, transport, children's education, holidays, safety and, especially, protection against disease and unemployment. Corresponding to all these needs—whose satisfaction is under-developed or warped under capitalism—there are new forms of social consumption and socialization of the costs of satisfaction, which suggest a quite different model of distribution of the national income.

The more affluent he becomes, the more the worker runs up against new forms of alienation, supplementing the old. He is not alienated only as a producer; he is also alienated as a consumer. Any number of examples could be given of the way in which the so-called "successes" of neo-capitalism create new problems: the deterioration in quality of a whole series of mass consumption goods; the traumatic effects of increasingly intrusive advertising; the danger that new forms of leisure (such as TV!) will lead to class atomization. The working class movement can and must apply new solutions to these new problems—solutions which challenge the capitalist mode of production as such.

But, although workers are undergoing increased alienation as consumers, they are nonetheless alienated, first and foremost, as pro-

[5] Rosa Luxemburg, "The chief function of trade unions is that, by adding to the needs of the workers and raising them morally, it creates a cultural and social vital minimum in the stead of a physical vital minimum—in other words, it creates a definite level of cultural life for the workers." (*Einführung in die Nationalökonomie*, p. 275, E. Laubsche Verlagsbuchhandlung, Berlin, 1925).

ducers. During the neo-capitalist period, this alienation is given new dimensions arising from the very mechanisms which, for the time being, bring neo-capitalism its successes: the permanent technological revolution, the third industrial revolution, ever-spreading automation. The problems involved—control over speed-up and lay-offs; control over the organization of production; the effective role of the producer in the system—descend from the heady realms of philosophy to take their place, potentially at least, in the day-to-day trade union struggle. Everything connected with this group of problems is becoming increasingly important to the workers: the opportunity follows of raising the struggle for union demands onto a new level. If I may quote my own work: "In the same way that the daily experience of the nineteenth century worker taught him how the net product of each enterprise was divided between wages and profits, the daily experience of the worker in the neo-capitalist period teaches him how the national income is divided between the total of earned and the total of unearned income and how these mechanisms can only be mastered by the seizure of the means of production, the 'levers of power' of the whole of economic life." [6]

All the objectives I have listed above are *potentially revolutionary,* in the sense that they challenge the capitalist nature of the economy and the nature of the private ownership of the means of production themselves. And they are not merely ideological issues, but immediate aims of the masses. So, far from postponing the socialist revolution till the very distant future, neo-capitalism actually brings to fruition a series of circumstances which present revolution as an immediate and urgent necessity, demanded *by the facts,* without having to wait for the workers to understand the Theses on Feuerbach or the Third Volume of Capital first.

The Strategy of Structural Reforms

The main purpose of the strategy of structural reforms—invented by the left wing of the Belgian working class movement and now increasingly adopted by its counterparts throughout Europe—is to effect an integration between the immediate aims of the masses and the objectives of the struggle which objectively challenge the very existence of the capitalist system itself.

[6] *Traité d'Economie Marxiste,* II, p. 198.

It does not mean in the slightest that the workers' movement abandons wage claims, demands for shorter hours, the insistence on a sliding scale to combat the rising cost of living, etc.—all the traditional demands of the movement (or at least of its left wing). But it does mean that the movement does not *limit* itself to these immediate objectives or to a combination of struggle for these objectives together with vague propaganda for the "socialist revolution", the "socialization of the means of production", even "the dictatorship of the proletariat", which, while they are not part and parcel of the daily struggle, can exert no influence on the practical development of the class struggle.[7] It means that the working class movement, *in its day-by-day struggle*, combines the fight for immediate objectives which, rooted in the immediate interests of the masses, go on to challenge objectively the operation of the capitalist system.

There is no doubt that this is a daring strategy; it carries grave risks. The main risk is that we live in a period of development of the productive forces, in which the representatives of the most dynamic and aggressive sectors of capitalism themselves have an interest in various structural transformations of the economy. If the workers' movement is not vigilant, *it therefore risks lending its support to neo-capitalist strata,* who are engaged in a struggle against more conservative capitalist forces, whose interests are best served by the existing structures.

In other words the formula of "structural reforms" can be interpreted in two diametrically opposite ways: either it can mean *a reform of capitalism whose purpose is to ensure that the economy will function more satisfactorily* or it can mean "reforms" extorted by the working class struggle, completely incompatible with the normal operation of any kind of capitalist economy. These latter inaugurate a period in which there is a duality of power, whose conclusion must be either a defeat for the working class (in which case the "reforms" are

---

[7] We should not forget that the classic reformists of the beginning of the century did not in the slightest turn their backs on socialist propaganda. Reformism only abandons this propaganda in the final phase of its degeneration and then starts to jettison all references to socialist ideals or actually recants from them. So the real difference between socialist and reformist *action* cannot be seen in terms of whether there is socialist propaganda or not. The essential question is that of objectives for practical struggles: either these are limited to what can be achieved within a capitalist regime and digested by it or else they challenge the very existence of the regime, both by their goals and by their size.

destroyed) or a defeat for the bourgeoisie (in which case the "reforms" are consolidated by the conquest of power by the proletariat and the socialization of the means of production, democratically managed by the workers themselves).

In the first case, we are dealing with *"neo-capitalist structural reforms"*, the principal trap into which the socialist left in western Europe could fall; in the second case we are dealing with *"anti-capitalist structural reforms"*, which are the main way forward for a socialist strategy in Europe.

Since the term "structural reform" is naturally ambiguous, it is not good enough to try and distinguish an aggressive socialist strategy from a reformist social-democratic policy (essentially a support or even temporary consolidation of neo-capitalism) simply by applying different labels or even by making more comprehensive definitions. But, without claiming to have said everything there is to say, I would like to put forward five characteristics of a strategy of anti-capitalist structural reforms, which go together and which are indispensable if the neo-capitalist trap is to be avoided:

1. We must not try to capture "outlying positions" from capitalism as a first step, under the illusion that we will thereby lessen resistance and be able to advance "step by step" towards the heart of the capitalist fortress. Experience persistently teaches us that the nationalization of non-central sectors, or of raw material and energy producing sectors, if it is carried out apart from a general forward movement on all fronts, can be integrated without any trouble into the general scheme of rationalizing (and hence consolidating) the capitalist economy.

   Moreover, it is utterly impossible to operate an economy "at the same time" according to the criteria of collective interests and the criteria of the private interests of the big capitalists. There cannot be any consonance between these two criteria, when basic economic choices are at stake. Either the criterion of profit is uppermost, in which case the operation of the whole economy must necessarily be *subordinated* to the demands and profitability of the major monopolistic groups (which is perfectly compatible with the nationalization of specific sectors, socializing losses and providing state subsidies or hidden savings for the monopolies) or else things are taken to a different conclusion and private property must be abolished, if the whole economy is not to grind to a halt.

So the attack must be made, not on outlying sectors, *but on the key sectors,* the sectors which provide the bulk of the national income and the greatest volume and dynamic of investment, the "commanding heights" of the economy. Unless we try to seize these key sectors from capitalism, our policies will be not anti-capitalist but neo-capitalist, whatever our intentions may be.

2. We must raise the question of the hierarchic structure of the enterprise, of the power of decision over the organization of work, of workers' control over production (which can as easily spring from micro-economic problems, at enterprise level, as from such macro-economic problems as profit levels, price and credit policies, causes of inflation, etc.), the abolition of commercial and banking secrets and the opening of the books.

   This is the only way to avoid giving the strategy of structural reforms a technocratic character and giving it life in the factories, on the shopfloor and in offices, of tieing in closely to the mass of workers themselves. It is also the only way of making the duality of power a real threat to the survival of capitalism.

3. We must resolutely reject the institutionalization of workers' control and the institutionalization of anti-capitalist structural reforms in general. First and foremost, because otherwise we would be being utopian; it cannot be emphasized enough that no economy can function in practice according to two criteria, two sets of demands, two models of consumption, two opposed and contradictory powers in each enterprise. Secondly, because this is a trap, a very dangerous trap, which recalls the most vulgar reformist illusions: Léon Jouhaux imagined that he had already "started" to change the nature of capitalism the day he was named governor of the Bank of France! An army cannot be taken apart "battalion by battalion" any more than capitalism can be abolished "step by step". In practice, the institutionalization of workers' control in a context in which big capitalism would still control the main wealth and power points of the economy as a whole would quickly deprive it of any real substance and would turn it into a means of corrupting working class militants.

4. The programme of anti-capitalist structural reforms must be closely connected with a clear governmental formula, defining the replacement in power of one class by another (in Belgium, we use the formula: a workers' government based on the unions).[8] This is of the utmost importance, for it is essential to bring home to the mass of the workers that the question of structural reforms leads on to *the question of power* and that it is the struggle for power which will finally decide the issue of the battle. There is no need here to point out how illusions about putting through structural reforms "stage by stage" find their reflection in illusions about coalitions with the bourgeoisie which could put through this programme "bit by bit".

5. Propaganda for anti-capitalist structural reforms must be accompanied by an intense and systematic critique of capitalism as a whole, of its contradictions and its ludicrous methods of production, of its more and more idiotic and alienating model of consumption, of the monstrous social inequality which it continues to sustain—in short, by a systematic socialist education, which opposes the idea of socialist planning to the idea of capitalist "programming". This propaganda must also *play its part in demystifying,* in revealing the reality hidden behind phrases like "improving the workings of the economy" (read: the capitalist economy), "stabilizing the purchasing power of money", ensuring "a steady rate of growth", and so on and so forth.

The working masses are ready and waiting for a strategy of this kind.

The relatively high standard of living which the workers enjoy during the neo-capitalist period (until the long-term cycle marked by economic growth reaches its end and the financial crisis caused by incessant inflation brings about new explosions) is often said to make a strategy of anti-capitalist structural reforms, such as I have outlined, a utopian prospect. It is argued that, since it is no longer impelled to

---

[8] This is an alegbraic formula, unaffected by the form of organization adopted by christian workers (a key question, in both Belgium and Italy) or by the establishment of an independent christian workers' party, or by their entry *en bloc* into a socialist organization or by their alliance, with other working class parties.

action by hunger, misery and massive unemployment, the working mass is destined for "americanization", that is to say, de-politicization, the loss of its class consciousness under the influence of the mass media, which feed it ever more homogenous and co-ordinated propaganda, or, at the very least, for a persistent process of fragmentation, both at and away from work, as a result of automation.[9]

This is an important objection, which must be fully dealt with. I have shown above how neo-capitalism does not in fact put an end to the causes of workers' discontent and that it is still quite possible to launch powerful campaigns—perhaps even inevitable. But can these campaigns take on a revolutionary complexion, in the context of a welfare society? Or are they necessarily restricted to reformist objectives, as long as they take place in an atmosphere of more or less general prosperity? In other words, can "americanized" or "depoliticized" workers respond to anything else than reformism, even when they are fighting a wage-freeze, murderous speed-up or snowballing technological unemployment?

Before replying to this objection, we must first look at it more closely. If the objection is referring to the fact that, in the present economic atmosphere, there are going to be no repetitions of the 1918 German revolution or the 1941–45 Yugoslav revolution, then it is no more than a truism. We have already admitted this truism and included it in our prior hypothesis. And that brings us to the real point: are these particular kinds of revolution the only ones which can achieve the overthrow of capitalism? Are "catastrophic" conditions necessary? No. There is a different historic model which we can refer to: that of the general strike of June 1936 in France (and, to a lesser extent, the Belgian general strike of 1960–61, which came near to creating an analogous situation to that of 1936).

It is perfectly possible that, in the present general economic climate —that of "neo-capitalist affluence" or the "mass consumption society",

[9] There is obviously a great difference between the situation in the United States where, for well-known historical reasons, the proletariat has never attained political class consciousness—so that the class struggle is only a trade union struggle—and western Europe, where working class political apathy means that there has been a *loss* of class consciousness built up over half a century. It is quite likely that the American proletariat will end up by being politicized before the depoliticization of the European working class has become complete.

—the workers will become more and more radicalized as the result of a whole series of social, political, economic or even military crises (incomes policies, wage-freezes; anti-union measures, authoritarianism; recessions, sudden monetary crises; protest movements against imperialist aggression, imperialist military alliances, the use of tactical nuclear weapons in so-called wars, etc.) and that, once they are radicalized, they will launch more and more far-reaching campaigns, during the course of which they will begin to link their immediate demands with a programme of anti-capitalist structural reforms, until eventually the struggle concludes with a general strike which either overthrows the regime or creates a duality of powers.[10]

Naturally, all this pre-supposes a growing *prise de conscience* rather than a relapse into political apathy. But there is nothing unrealistic or utopian about this hypothesis. The experience of the last five years has shown how there is no automatic correlation between high wage rates (comparatively high on an international scale) and political apathy. In Italy, an unprecedented climb in wage rates has led to the strengthening of the Communist Party at the polls. In Belgium, the 1960–61 strike was called at a time when Belgian wage rates were among the highest in Europe, and its staunchest adherents were the best-paid sector of the Belgian working-class: the Liège iron and steel workers. And it could hardly be claimed that it was any fall in wages which led the working masses of Britain to elect the 1964 Labour government and oust the crestfallen tories.

Furthermore, the present situation of the western European workers' movement is extremely variegated; there are a multitude of nuances between its two extremes; on the one hand, there is the workers' movement in West Germany, the Netherlands or Switzerland, where autonomous class action and a comparatively high level of consciousness are only to be found among small, isolated groups (which does not necessarily mean that this will be the case for ever); on the other hand, there is Italy, Great Britain or Belgium, where, for all its weaknesses (and I am only too well aware of those in Belgium!), the workers' movement still displays a high level of autonomous class action, with a rich and diverse ideological life, a remarkable and widespread degree of combativity and genuine opportunities for making a real breakthrough.

[10] It would require a separate study to deal with the particular problems raised by the duality of powers.

Now, it is not possible to explain the differences between these two different sets of examples simply by referring to their different objective conditions. Average wage rates in Britain are still among the highest in western Europe; the same is true of Belgium (and since Belgian rates have relatively begun to fall back, the aggressive dynamism of the workers' movement has also fallen back with them, rather than surged forward); Italian wage rates have been rising faster than any others in Europe, for many years. It is quite untenable to explain the enormous differences in dynamism between the movements in Belgium and the Netherlands by referring to the objective conditions (and, in any case, Dutch wage rates have been comparatively low for two decades); the same is true of the differences between the French and Italian movements, over the last five years. It is quite clear that we are dealing with a whole complex of factors, among which that of "relative prosperity" cannot be shown to be particularly dominant.

It follows that *it is above all the subjective factor which plays the key role* in deciding whether or not the workers' movement makes use of the *opportunity* which neo-capitalism provides for an anti-capitalist strategic offensive. That is to say, in the last analysis everything depends on the action of the working class movement itself.

Here we can put our finger on the objective conditions which confront us today and those of, say, the thirties. During a period in which the worker is not irresistibly impelled against capitalism by hunger or misery, anti-capitalist action ceases to be the *automatic* result of his daily experience. But it can become so *through the mediation, the awakening of consciousness, which is the task of the workers' movement.* If the workers' movement is capable of fulfilling its task (not only little vanguard groups, but also those trade union and political forces which influence parts of the working class) it can throw a bridge, by action and education, between essentially defensive struggles (which are inevitable, though not "automatic") and struggles which can conclude objectively in the overthrow of the capitalist system. If on the contrary, it falls short, then undeniably there will be a process of gradual degradation and deterioration of class consciousness, of working class depoliticization, until the West German or Swiss model is arrived at, in which, as far as can be seen, the great majority of the working class no longer wants any part in far-reaching anti-capitalist struggles.

International co-ordination of the struggle.

There are two further problems which remain to be discussed: the problem of periodicity and the problem of the implications of European economic integration.

Any socialist strategy which is *based on mass action* (rather than electoral campaigns or guerrilla wars) must necessarily pay great attention to fluctuations in mass psychology, state of mind and relative capacity to respond to blows from the enemy and move on to the attack. Obviously, this capacity is not static. No individual—and *a fortiori* no group of individuals—can live over a long period, uninterruptedly, in a state of extreme tension. Theoretically and empirically, it has long since been shown that there are periodic fluctuations in the degree of mass action, no matter which country is being considered.

There is no need, in this context, to describe the delicate mechanism of inter-action between objective and subjective factors which explains this periodicity. Evidently, this is *related* to the economic cycle; but this relationship certainly does not mean that the peak point of mass action occurs when economic activity is in a trough. I have already pointed out that this peak point is much more likely to occur *at the time when the economic trend is reversed* (first waves of lay-offs or the favourable effect of full employment on the balance of class power).

The problem is complicated, however, because there is both a short-term and a long-term cycle of mass action (for example, in France the defeat of the workers' movement by the arrival in power of De Gaulle has led to conditions completely different from those prevalent in Italy). Various historical factors—the level of class consciousness attained in the past; the continuing influence of past forms of struggle —also have a considerable effect on the periodicity of struggles. The cycle can be slowed down or speeded up according to whether there is a greater or lesser degree of class unity. And there are many other important factors which might be listed.

It is of the utmost importance that *the internal logic of the periodicity of the workers' struggles* should be geared to the strategy outlined above. Obviously, a growing intensity of radicalization, enabling the struggle to be set more and more towards anti-capitalist objectives, must co-incide with a growing intensity of *mass* action in the cycle or else it will be doomed to failure, after which it may take as much as a decade or more to recover. It is also obvious that if we *let slip* the peak moments of mass struggle, without linking them to struggles for anti-capitalist reforms, we shall lose the chance of launching a decisive campaign for many years to come. In the present atmosphere, we cannot expect the proletariat, in western Europe at least, to launch a general strike every two years. A number of factors are of crucial importance: a correct analysis of the state of mind of the masses; the balance of power between the vanguard and the more retrograde and conservative forces within the workers' movement; the ability to produce the right slogans at the right moment, and so on and so forth. All these factors are crucial if a socialist strategy is to be applied with the least hope of success.

Concerning the European co-ordination of the struggle, I have already written at length elsewhere.[11] For as long as the working class in each of the six Common Market countries is able to exert pressure on the productive system of "its" country and "its" bourgeoisie, the best solution would be a country-by-country struggle, so that a victory in one would lead to favourable conditions for an international campaign against the movement towards the Common Market, NATO and other international organizations, sabotaging or destroying their effectiveness.

On the other hand, from the time that the interpenetration of capital reaches a certain point, there will be less and less possibility of an isolated victory in a single Common Market country and there will be a very strong likelihood that any isolated socialist experiment could be economically and financially strangulated. From this point on, the possibility of a socialist breakthrough must be an all or nothing affair, involving the whole Common Market. It must be admitted that this means a turn for the worse, at least in the short and middle term (in the long term, it has definite advantages). For whereas the first alternative requires a high degree of mass action and a successful outcome in only one country, the second requires a high degree of mass action in each country simultaneously, *co-inciding* with a successful simultaneous outcome! Obviously this is the harder to come by.

[11] Cf. my report to the seminar on *Intégration européenne et mouvement ouvrier,* organized by *Cahiers du Centre d'Etudes socialistes* in Paris.

André Gorz

The following essay originally appeared in the August/September, 1968, special issue of *Les Temps Modernes*. Part of Section 6 was omitted in the English translation of the original French essay published by *New Left Review*.

Against the background of the May, 1968, events in France, Gorz analyzes the viability of several different strategies for revolutionary change in the advanced capitalist countries. Most of the essay is devoted to a defense of the thesis that a new revolutionary party is needed and to a description of the nature and functions of such a party. "The important thing for the movement," Gorz concludes, "is to provide a framework within which all those who have now learned that revolution is possible" and that the Stalinist and post-Stalinist models are strategically obsolete "can be politically formed, can calculate their strength, and can exchange their experiences."

THE WAY FORWARD

Votes, as Marx and Engels used to say, give the right to govern, they do not give the power to do so. Conversely, to win votes, or to win by votes, the opposition must already have shown that it is capable of *taking* and *exercising* power in a substantially different manner from that which has prevailed hitherto.

This truth was resoundingly confirmed during the *abortive* May–June revolution. How could a Left, which had been unable to assert its power to govern when power was in its grasp, expect that votes would give it what it had been unable to take when nine million workers were on strike against the power of capitalism? From the moment that those political parties which historically claimed to represent the

Reprinted by permission of *New Left Review*.

working class showed themselves incapable of offering an outlet to the popular uprising and an alternative to the regime, it was only logical that they would be crushed by reaction and abandoned by a million of their voters.

It is now not so much a matter of seeking the reasons of this failure, or of denouncing those responsible, as of shedding light on certain fundamental aspects of the May–June crisis and of drawing the lessons for the future.

Because this revolutionary crisis was started by unorganized movements and reached its climax through the initiatives of the student and working-class base, there is now a strong temptation to pose the problem of how to overthrow the bourgeois State in anarcho-syndicalist terms: relying on mass spontaneity, seeing insurrection as the royal road to revolution, and repudiating not only the old bureaucratic apparatuses but also the preparatory work and political leadership of which the latter showed themselves incapable.

Attractive as it may seem in certain respects, a return to anarcho-syndicalism would, in fact, be an intellectual and political regression; worse still, it would be to misunderstand the nature of bourgeois power and the revolutionary process that is capable of bringing about its downfall and carrying the working class to power. The question of taking power was posed in May, and must continue to be posed; so too must the question of the instrument necessary for taking power, the new type of revolutionary party. But such questions cannot be posed and replied to simply in terms of a *gamble on the short-term repetition* of a spontaneous, insurrectionary general strike. That would be to return to revolutionary *attentisme;* to the theory of all or nothing according to which the revolution must be a quasi-instantaneous act or become bogged down in petty reformism, and until the great day there is nothing much to be done apart from agitation and propaganda.

It is this point that, once again, needs to be made today.

1. Maximalism

The May general strike was directed as much against the political and trade-union apparatuses of the working class as it was against the regime. The strike was neither foreseen, prepared, understood nor channeled by these apparatuses. It revealed the disjuncture between the

working class and its leaders; the latter were not aware of the depth
of working-class discontent, nor did they know its reasons; *a fortiori,*
they were incapable of translating these reasons into demands which
would at once raise the level of consciousness of the proletariat, take
account of the workers' refusal of their condition at the workplace and
in society, and orientate their combativity towards objectives which,
once attained, would transform the condition of the working class and
lastingly dislocate bourgeois power.

It was their inability to give the struggle a set of indissolubly linked
industrial and political objectives—which, once realized, would unleash a revolutionary process destined rapidly to transcend the initial
demands—that determined the ambiguous aspect of the general strike:
at once both trade-unionist and virtually insurrectionary. For the fact
that the strike's aims remained indeterminate meant that it appeared
as an undifferentiated, global rejection of the regime and of capitalist
society. Hence it became objectively maximalist: victory had to be
complete and immediate, or nothing would be won at all; between
total victory and total defeat there was no half-way stage; it was all
or nothing.

This objective maximalism gave an immediate, objective insurrectionary meaning to the strike, but it also contained the seed of its
own failure. For the insurrectionary general strike is closer to primitive
revolt than to revolutionary action *if it does not give way to a political
offensive* aimed at administering the coup de grâce to a weakened
enemy and at creating organs of workers' power and co-ordination,
with a *previously prepared* program and political openings. In the
absence of such preparation, the radicalism of the immediate global
refusal is merely the obverse of the indeterminate objectives, of the
lack of strategy. By remaining largely "instinctive," i.e. spontaneous
and un-thought out, the movement allows economic demands to express revolutionary aspirations and vice versa. This confusion should
surprise no one: maximalist or purely trade-unionist or both at the
same time, the movement remains at the level of immediate demands
because it lacks the mediations that would allow it to organize its
action in time and in space, with a conscious aim in view—that would
allow it to adopt a strategy.

The inadequacy of the traditional apparatuses thus condemned the
movement not to achieve any clear awareness of its potentialities, and
not to leave behind any political gains.

2. Spontaneity

Thus it is important not to take the May movement's elemental upsurge as a sign of originality and strength, when in fact this was the opposite face of its profound weakness. Nor, under the pretext that the movement revealed the revolutionary potential of the working class which had until then remained latent, must we throw overboard the work of political reflection on revolutionary strategy in the advanced capitalist countries which, though insufficient, has been undertaken in Europe during the past 20 years, simply to return to the theory of all or nothing, of "zero hour," of the system's sudden collapse.

This is all the more so because a similar potentially revolutionary crisis cannot be deliberately reproduced, with better chances of revolutionary victory the second time. On the contrary, the May movement was only possible because it took bourgeois power by surprise, and because, without either organization or revolutionary political leadership, its meaning from the start escaped even the masses who were its protagonists. The masses by surprise succeeded in rushing into the breach opened by the students; imitating the student's example, they exploited the retreat which the latter had forced the regime to make. Power at that moment seemed suddenly in their grasp. If a political force both able and determined to take power had existed, if such a force had spurred on the working class to create its own organs of control and local power, the working class would doubtless have followed. The first phase of a revolutionary process would have been won by surprise—but only the first phase. The trial of strength which would have followed would have taken place in circumstances extremely favorable to the working class. In control of the productive apparatus and of public services, it would in this first stage have been able to push a provisional government (a necessarily composite formation, since its leaders would not have been formed by a long revolutionary struggle) to take over the State apparatus; and by the strength of its own mobilization it would have deterred the partisans of armed repression. For all that, it is not certain that a trial of armed strength would have been avoided. For the revolutionary process to be carried through to its end, it would in fact have been necessary for the working class, led by a vanguard party which itself developed

324 THE WAY FORWARD

rapidly during the struggle, to have pushed beyond such programs as provisional governments are capable of conceiving, and to have imposed an acceleration and radicalization of social transformation. A second trial of strength, with the risk of civil war, would then have been engaged. Supposing it had been won, thanks to the combativity of the working class and to the important positions of power it had succeeded in winning in the country, this second trial would, like the first, have been the result—unforeseen at the start—of a revolutionary process whose logic and risks, though necessarily calculated and taken by the revolutionary leaders, *would not have been fully measured by the masses at the start.*

But they would have to be measured, and from the start, by a movement which proposed *deliberately* to repeat the May uprising. What is more, the inherent risks for such a movement have now increased; circumstances are less favorable. The bourgeoisie is on its guard, ready for a trial of armed strength, and the petite bourgeoisie is frightened. To suppose that the May uprising can be repeated is to suppose that the working class is subjectively prepared for civil war, both materially and politically.

This is not the case.[1] It is one thing to accept a trial of armed strength when this stems *from a movement which, though limited in its demands at the start, is radicalized by the effect of its success,* by the possibilities it discovers *en route,* by the victories it wins over bourgeois power: the trial of strength is then the last moment of a battle all of whose earlier stages have been victorious. The working class here is not mounting an assault on the fortress of bourgeois power; on the contrary it is defending the conquest it has won by "peaceful" means, and beating off the counter-attack from a position of strength. It is a different matter deliberately to accept from the start the risk of an insurrectionary confrontation with a State that is vigilant, intact and ready for battle. To accept such a risk is not and cannot be the task of the working masses, even when led by a resolute vanguard; it can only be the task of an active minority. And the latter's frontal struggle against the State only takes on the value and meaning of an example in the eyes of the masses in certain circumstances, notably when this struggle is based on a set of transitional aims which make explicit and politicize popular expectations.

---

[1] If, in fact, this can ever be the case in an advanced capitalist country, outside of an acute political and military crisis.

3. The "Guevarist" Strategy

We are touching here on the conditions of possibility for a "Guevarist" strategy, and on the limits of its validity. The immediate aim of armed insurrection by a minority is not to beat the forces of repression, not to conquer power, not to start a general insurrection—but progressively to create the conditions for a *political* radicalization of the masses. The first objective is to force the State openly to identify itself with violence and with the repressive forces on which its power rests. But this initial function—apparent precisely in the students' struggle which is *first and foremost* a refusal to accept an order experienced as authoritarian and repressive—has political effect only in so far as the corrupt and arbitrary character of the established authorities is latently evident, *before the insurrection,* to the working masses and to an important part of the petite bourgeoisie. In other words, in so far as the decomposition of the society (the corruption of the dominant class, the State's servility to oligarchic and foreign interests, its divorce from the nation's interests and identity) is evident, notably, in discredited institutions, in a crisis of State authority, in the practical impossibility for the dominant group or groups to base its power on any ideological hegemony: power then becomes synonymous with arbitrary, lying, cynical, brute domination. It is only in these conditions—conditions which existed in China and Cuba and presently exist in part of Latin America and the Caribbean—that armed insurrection, instead of being the *culmination* of a phase of political preparation (preparation that is impossible here by "peaceful" means) *itself takes the place of this preparation.*

Rebels of petit-bourgeois origin, the first groups of "Guevarist" insurgents aim to pose in dramatic fashion moral and national demands. But obviously they cannot remain at that level: to advance, they must find a social base for their revolt, win over the working class to revolutionary aims conceived outside it. The rebellion must differentiate its methods and objectives in accordance with the new aims; under threat of failure, it is thereby forced to learn the tasks of revolutionary struggle. Terrorism is thus not a *short-cut* which economizes on political work: it is the *point of departure* for such work, and creates the need and the conditions for it. The insurgents have to take on the role of vanguard political organization or be isolated and crushed.

The guerrilla has to become a school of political formation; create revolutionary cadres; work out in the field a transitional program adapted to the level of consciousness of the masses and constantly re-adapted as this level is raised by the struggle.

Thus, contrary to romantic and maximalist conceptions, "Guevarism" is fundamentally distinct from the theory of "all or nothing." It does not pose the seizing of power by the working classes as its immediate objective. It does not aim at a passage to socialism without any transitional stages. It does not claim that the revolution is an entity, complete as an idea before being made, and that transitional reforms and intermediate objectives are dangerous mystifications.[2] On the contrary, the program of the FLN is a democratic, not a socialist program; it does not claim to model South Vietnam in North Vietnam's image. The program of the 26 July movement, at the moment of its victory in Cuba, was neither socialist nor even explicitly anti-imperialist. In both cases (as also in China, in 1949) it was a question of transitional programs: i.e. of a set of fundamental reforms aimed at setting in motion a revolutionary process during which the self-education of the masses (and of their leaders) will lead to the superseding of the initial reforms and objectives.

In short, the unifying political perspective of a revolutionary movement cannot be the immediate construction of socialism and of communism, i.e. a post-revolutionary society. It can only be that of a revolutionary transformation of the present society by means of a range of intermediary objectives. By this must be understood not a succession of gradual and predetermined reforms, each posed as an end in itself, but the realization of a set of reforms linked to each other, corresponding to the aspirations of the masses. These must *irreversibly* shift the balance of power in favor of the working class, dislocate capitalist society and demand the transition to socialism as the only alternative to regression. Put another way, the function of intermediary objectives is to make evident the necessity for the transition to socialism, to prefigure it in certain concrete aspects, to set in motion the revolutionary process without necessarily taking socialism as its explicit short-term aim. Thus it is not of the masses that one should demand a prior socialist consciousness but of the vanguard. It is not at the programmatic level that socialism must be posed as the

[2] See Fidel Castro's speech of April 9, 1968.

aim, but through the inter-connection and the political dynamic of the programmatic objectives; through the method of struggle for these objectives which must in themselves constitute an apprenticeship and experience of workers' power; through the *conceptual* level of the program which, as a coherent articulation of intermediary objectives with the mass actions necessary to impose them, must be understood as the starting signal for a revolutionary process destined to go beyond all the initial objectives.

The socialist consciousness of the masses will only be created during this process, on condition of course that such a consciousness exists among the leaders, as a capacity to define the initial intermediary objectives which can take the movement to the point of non-return, and later those more advanced objectives which will supersede the initial ones: in other words as strategy.

4. The Failure of the PCF *

It would be illusory to believe that the next social crisis in France could start straightaway from the highest level reached during the course of the May–June crisis. It would be equally illusory to believe that it is necessary to start from a revolutionary general strike with, as its declared aim, the seizure of power by the working class. The abortive May revolution cannot take the place of political preparation or of formative experience. In this respect everything, or nearly everything, remains to be done.

This is why it would be foolish to reproach the PCF with not having launched the masses against the State last May, of not having inaugurated working-class power, socialism. To this kind of argument, the Party can answer, without embarrassment, that there is nothing to prove that the masses were ready for socialism. In fact, we know they were not, any more (or hardly more) than the PCF itself. It is more than probable that the Gaullist regime could have been overthrown; it is certain that by establishing centers of workers' power entire sections of the capitalist system could have been overthrown, and that the working class, properly led, could have prevented the provisional government from restoring the system. But that the capitalist system could have been swept aside in one fell

* French Communist Party—*Ed.*

swoop is an untenable thesis: for this, a revolutionary process far longer and more progressive than two to four weeks of potentially insurrectionary strike action would have been necessary.

More to the point is to reproach the PCF for its inability to set in motion the revolutionary process; for its inability to channel the combativity of the masses towards the creation of organs of popular and working-class power; for its inability to become the pole of political attraction of the workers' and popular committees which did arise spontaneously; for its inability to take advantage of the power actually won by the working class at the height of the struggle in order to undermine the basis and authority of the regime by the conquest of permanent positions of strength. For to have made no attempt, by creating nuclei of working-class power and organs of popular power, to capitalize on the state of mobilization of the working class; to have made no attempt to carry revolutionary consciousness to its apogee nor to fix it as a future point of reference by means of actions capable of serving as examples; to have repudiated as "contrary to the agreement" the demands for workers' power espoused by the CFDT* [3]; to have offered the movement as its sole conquest a rise in wages, which of all conquests is the one that capitalism reabsorbs most easily—unless (which was not the case) the working-class movement is prepared, politically and industrially, to prevent that reabsorption by exploiting the disequilibrium in the system provoked by the wage-increases; to have rejected any political and ideological union between the working class, the students and the

* French Democratic Confederation of Work, a left-wing Social Democratic trade union—*Ed.*

[3] Were these imprecise and ambiguous? No problem. It was merely necessary to point this out. They corresponded perfectly to the state of mind of the working-class base. They constitute the ideal type of dynamic conquest for whose defense and extension an appeal can be made to the initiative and imagination of the base. They represent the kind of gain which capitalism experiences the greatest difficulty in absorbing, and which is bound to sharpen class antagonism.

All this, naturally, on condition that workers' power is understood in the first place as a power exercised over the workplace and organization of work (at least partial technical self-management and mastery over the machine), and not as an administrative power accepting the limits and criteria of capitalist profitability. . . .

Workers' power could not at once be global, but it could concretize the global refusal of the system which it implies and unleash, by way of the demands which are inherent in its exercise, a process of struggle investing every aspect of the capitalist relations of production.

vanguards of the intellectual professions; to have gambled on an electoral victory which was ruled out from the moment that the regime was left intact, master of the field, and no perspective was offered for a future resurgence; all these demonstrate the highest degree of sheer bureaucratic stupidity of which a working-class and socialist party could possibly become guilty. . . .

It would be presumptuous to attempt to define here what might have been the intermediary objectives of a transitional program. It is not only their content that counts, but equally the method and climate of their creation through the direct participation of the base; the latter alone is capable of guaranteeing the democratic character of the program and, by multiplying its organs of popular power in the centers of production and habitation, of preparing and morally arming the masses against any attempt at restoration. Such a line, clearly, is not only incompatible with the present structure and methods of the PCF, but also with the belief . . . that the State is a *neutral instrument* "open to a revolution from above in the direction of socialism" [4]: in other words that the State of monopoly capitalism, provided that it is in the hands of a working-class party, can be utilized *just as it is* for the passage to socialism.[5] This belief, as Nicos Poulantzas notes, explains the constant oscillation of the PCF between a pseudo-maximalist position—what counts is to enter the control-room of the State; everything else will follow; the masses must mandate the communist deputies to do this, and meanwhile remain quiet—and a right-wing opportunist practice, which consists in paying for the right of entry into the control-room with compromises, alliances at the summit, and the demagogic defense of narrowly corporate interests.

5. Functions of the Revolutionary Party

The aim of these remarks is not so much to criticize gratuitously the leadership of the PCF as to pose the question of which type of revolutionary party and which strategy will permit a revolutionary process of transition to socialism once again to become possible in an advanced capitalist country. Indeed, the fact that the PCF is in-

[4] The formula was coined by Nicos Poulantzas, *Pouvoir politique et classes sociales,* Maspéro 1968, especially pp. 286–298.

[5] See Lucio Magri's article "State and Revolution Today," published in *Problemi del Socialismo* No. 22 for September 1967, and translated in *Les Temps Modernes* No. 266–7 for August/September 1968.

capable of assuming the functions of a revolutionary party by no means signifies that the problem of revolution must be envisaged henceforth, in the absence of any party capable of guiding it and bringing it to fruition, as the pure product of spontaneous movements. On the contrary, it must be re-remembered that the function of the party remains irreplaceable in at least four respects (which is not necessarily to say—we will come back to this—that the conditions for the creation of a revolutionary party are fully assembled):

a) *Function of theoretical analysis and elaboration.* The problem of a strategy for the struggle, and for the revolutionary transformation of society, cannot even be posed in the absence of a continually updated analysis of the evolution and contradictions of capitalist society at all its levels; of the conflicts of interest which fissure the ruling bloc; of the weak points which, if attacked, offer the possibility of breaking and discrediting the enemy front; of the respective positions of the forces and movements which are actually or potentially anti-capitalist within the productive process; of the position of the national bourgeoisie in the system of relations of the capitalist world; of the adaptation or inadaptation of the institutional structures, etc.

The fact that this function is not at present carried out by any party has a double consequence: the activity of the political apparatuses is limited essentially to day-to-day tactical maneuvers and demagogic improvisation, incapable of making any lasting impact on the stability of the system, within whose limits they by and large remain. Whence, inversely, the necessity for the revolutionary groups and movements to situate themselves outside the parties and pose the problem of the revolutionary transformation of society in terms of insurrectionary struggle. However, though insurrectionary struggle may detonate a revolutionary process in an already disintegrating society and State, in a politically and ideologically integrated society it can only succeed at best in revealing the limits of that integration, its possible points of rupture, and in throwing its political institutions into crisis. That is already a great deal, but it is only the beginning, the negative moment of the political work which has to be accomplished.

b) *Function of ideological synthesis* of sectional contradictions and demands, a synthesis which respects their specificity and their autonomy. This function can be identified with the ideological hegemony which the revolutionary party must win in order to be able to construct the "bloc" of anti-capitalist forces which will shatter the unity of the dominant bloc and wrest power from it. This "bloc" should not be taken to mean merely an "alliance" between the classes or strata exploited by the bourgeoisie. The weakness of the traditional type of alliance is that it is a juxtaposition of groups of sectional interests and grievances that are simply aggregated in their particularity, and translated into a catalogue of demands: from such an aggregate there can never spring a critique of existing society, nor the unifying perspective of transcending it through common struggle.

The absence of a revolutionary party is thus expressed by a multiplicity of demands and struggles for partial objectives, immanent to the system, with neither organic links between them nor unity of perspective. The potentially anti-capitalist forces engage in *parallel* and *successive* battles which, by virtue of a false conception of "the concrete," remain totally abstract. They lack the theoretical capacity to perceive, beyond the immediately apparent reasons for discontent, the determinant reasons—i.e. in the last resort the capitalist relations of production—and to oppose to neo-capitalist ideology (to its type of rationality and to its system of values) a higher conception of rationality, of civilization, of culture: a conception in the light of which sectional demands are at once critically illuminated in their relativity, integrated, and transcended at a higher level. . . .

In this respect too, the radicalism of the student movement is a positive contribution: the latter has from the start taken up a position outside the system, refusing the notion of objective impossibilities as *a priori* unacceptable and globally rejecting the system. However, by virtue of the fact that it is a sectional movement—and not the vanguard of a class—the student movement does not have the means to claim ideological and political hegemony for the construction of an anti-capitalist bloc. The student movement can only put itself forward as a theoretical and practical expression, at a specific level, of the contradiction between capitalist relations of production and productive forces. It can, at this specific level, be a suppurating wound in the side of the bourgeois political society and State, and, through the radicalism of its actions and positions, keep the latter in a state of permanent crisis—while at the same time bearing witness *vis-à-vis* the working-class movement to the possibility and necessity of a radicalization of the struggle at all levels.

Its contribution to the general crisis of the system can thus be decisive, and lasting, but on condition that it is integrated into the strategy of the class struggle as a specific and autonomous component of that struggle. It is because such integration is refused it that the student movement is permanently tempted to set itself up as a substitute for a revolutionary party and a working-class vanguard—naturally without being able to fill that role. Left to itself, the student movement can only transcend its sectional limits by an abstract appeal to the class-in-itself and to revolution-in-itself. The working-class movement, however, could only hold this against it on the condition that it match its critique of the student movement by an autocritique of its own corporate and economist deviations.[6] Only a revolutionary party, which integrated every dimension of the anti-capitalist struggle into a project of radical transformation of all levels of social life, could cause the student movement to transcend its limits, and could enable the working-class movement to harness the revolutionary potential of student struggles.

c) *Function of education and of political leadership.* A further function of the party is to incarnate the permanence of the struggle and its objectives even in periods when the tide of revolution is on the ebb. It prefigures the proletarian State, and reflects for the working class its capacity to be a ruling class. It incarnates the presence of socialism within capitalism, since it is a positive negation of the latter. It guarantees the survival of the movement and of revolutionary consciousness in trough periods in which the balance of forces precludes head-on battles. Yet, if it is to be able to carry out these functions, the party must aspire to being at once the memory and the prefiguration of struggles more advanced than those which are possible at a given moment. It must appear to every worker as the guarantee that all that can be done will be done, in all circumstances, to break the enemy front and emancipate the working class. Not that the party ought to direct every local or sectional struggle from the center. Its guiding function consists rather in situating any given struggle within the general framework of the class struggle; also in making explicit the way in which the immediate and local demands of the workers in reality transcend their specific situation, and the way in which these local demands mesh into and define the intermediary

[7] See Rossana Rossanda: *"L'anno degli studenti,"* De Donato 1968, of which a chapter was translated in *Les Temps Modernes* No. 266–7 for August/September 1968.

objectives of a transitional strategy. In this respect, far from setting itself up as the defender of a predetermined political line, to which social struggles should be subordinated at all costs, the party, through its total mobility, must appear capable not only of adopting, but also of *catalyzing* the demands thrown up by the base, in so far as they lead to a program of radical transformation of society and illustrate its necessity.

Let me underline the term *catalyze;* for the function of a program of structural transformations is not to reflect passively the kind of demands and level of consciousness of the workers at a given moment, but to stimulate demands by deepening the consciousness which the working class has of the intolerability of its condition, and by showing that very advanced demands can be satisfied and what the conditions are for their satisfaction. Pushing back the limits of the possible by revealing the possibility and the conditions of possibility of changes which seem out of reach (and which, indeed, cannot be lasting within the framework of the system) is one of the surest means of reinforcing working-class combativity.

The program *too* is such a means, particularly in so far as, through its coherence, it renders credible objectives to which the working class will fully commit itself only if the political instruments permitting their realization are defined. The objective of a 1,000 franc per month minimum salary in the car industry, for example, was not very credible, in May 1968, for many of the workers ("it will be taken away from us again by increased prices and a higher degree of exploitation"), although it was a demand thrown up from the base. But this objective, which in itself smacks of demagogy and is purely trade-unionist, takes on a revolutionary significance if it is defined by the ensemble of anti-capitalist structural reforms which are the condition of its effective realization.

What economic, social and industrial policy, what type of planning and distribution can permit large increases in low wages without any increase of unemployment, without inflation, without loss of efficiency in the economy as a whole? That is a typical question of economic policy in the transitional period: it brings into question the relations of production, the relations of exchange, the structure of the active population, the character of education, the choice of civilization, etc. —whence its educative value. It is a question to which the party's program must be capable of giving a reply. If it is incapable of providing such a reply and of translating it into objectives in the struggle; if it is not capable, armed with such a reply, of enacting an objective critique—on the political level and on that of mass action—of the measures by which the capitalist system seeks to reabsorb the increases in low wages which have been wrested from it; then in that case discouragement and skepticism tend to gain sway over the masses: everything that happens makes it seem as though they had demanded the impossible. In short, to break the equilibrium of the system, without being able to exploit and resolve its crisis to the advantage of the working class, means to allow one's victories to be transformed into defeats.

Similarly, momentarily to shake the power of the bourgeoisie without being able to wrest from it positions of power from which the struggle can be pursued and the power of the bourgeois State thrown into crisis means in the last resort to reinforce the bourgeoisie by allowing it to repair the breaches after its own fashion.

This brings us to the fourth function of the party.

d) *Function of seizing power and transforming the State.* A special study would be needed to show how the administrative and political centralization of power has weighed on political life in France, inciting popular movements to demand of the central power the solution to every and any problem, and inciting political parties to assume the role, more than anything else, of potential managers of a State held to be omnipotent. Centralization of the State in France leads to a statist distortion of political ideology and political life at all levels of society. Popular mobilizations are viewed in France either as protests demanding the intervention of central power in favor of the underprivileged categories (*"Pompidou, nos sous!"*), or, at best, as a mass support which should allow the opposition parties to express more forcibly their claim to manage the State.

This centralist, statist ideology is one of the principal obstacles to the birth and dissemination of a revolutionary ideology. It assigns a subordinate position to mass action, and stands in the way of any education or emancipation of the workers through self-determination of the methods and objectives of their struggle and through a democratic life at the base. The weakness of the French political parties, the relationship of patronage that exists between them and the electorate, the weight of their notables and their central bureaucracies, are to be explained to a considerable extent in this way—as too are the unchanging nature of the structures and Stalinist mentality of the PCF.

Yet even if they are more manifest there, the twin blights of centralization and bureaucratism are not peculiar to the French parties. Reinforcement of the central power, erosion of regional power and of autonomous local institutions are part and parcel of the domination of monopoly capital. It therefore follows that every party whose proposed vocation is to run the State apparatus and a modern capitalist society without changing them molds its structure on that of the State as it is. A revolutionary party, on the other hand, defines itself by its ability to make a critique at once theoretical and practical of the authoritarian centralizing character of the State—a character which expresses the domination of bourgeois monopoly. It defines itself by its ability to destroy the myth of the ineluctably authoritarian and centralizing nature of the "industrial State," whether capitalist or socialist. What would be involved in this act of destruction? Notably: to allow, in every area, the sovereignty and initiative of the base; to make the party, preeminently, the site of free debate and direct democracy; to encourage collective self-determination by the workers of the means and objectives of their struggle; to aim at the conquest of workers' power over the centers of production, not merely as an end in itself, but as the prefiguration of social self-management by the sovereign producers.

In short, the new revolutionary party should define itself by its ability both to seize and wield central power (an ability which, by definition, broad movements and trade unions lack), and to destroy at its very roots the authoritarian nature of that central power. And those roots, of course, lie in the social division of labor. If the struggle against the employers and against the bourgeois State does not involve the experience and the exercise of workers' sovereignty, then neither will the emancipation of the working class follow any hypothetical conquest of the State by its party. If wage demands are not also aimed at changing working-class *life*—not merely living conditions, but the quality and nature of the whole culture—and at smashing the old inter-craft divisions and hierarchical structures, then the political, ideological and cultural hegemony of the working class on which its final emancipation depends will not have been advanced an inch.

A working class which is not sovereign in production will not be sovereign in society. A working class which is not master of its local destiny, i.e. of the conditions and organization of production, will never be a ruling class with mastery over the organization of society. A working class which does not exercise power over its own workplaces, by its control of the means of production, will never exercise power in society, even though its representatives may be masters of the State. A working class which has not freed itself from the hierarchical division of labor in each firm will never free itself from the social division of labor, even though the private ownership of the means of production may have been abolished. The progress of the working-class struggle for the power of self-determination in the centers of production contains more revolutionary promise, even where the firms still remain in private hands, than nationalizations which leave intact the hierarchical structure of the actual company. A working class which is master of the means of production, and which itself determines the technical division of labor, will of necessity demand power in the society at large and the abolition of the social division of labor.

On all these points the contribution of the student movement is immensely positive. The practice of collective debate, of direct democracy, of decision-making in free assembly, of student self-management, of egalitarianism, of the positive negation of all authority, etc. all tie in with the libertarian tradition of the working class itself. It is not surprising that these features should serve as models for the latter, especially since the authoritarianism against which the students rebel indirectly reflects, on one particular level, the subordination of every area of social activity to the demands of monopoly capital.

The problem therefore: to construct a revolutionary party whose central organs, by their cohesion and capacity for political analysis, will prefigure the central power of the transitional period, without the party leadership claiming to control, direct or command the initiatives and movements that are born outside it, and that *are* the life-blood of the revolution. The hegemonic capacity of the party will be measured precisely by its capacity to enrich itself from movements born outside the party; to develop with them a common perspective while fully respecting their independence; and to become for them the center of attraction, the pole of doctrinal reference, the main political outlet.

To put it another way, this new type of revolutionary party can no longer follow the Leninist model. It is no longer confronted by a despotic and repressive State, but by a State which is essentially political and which bases the legitimacy of its repressive actions on its ability to mediate politically between contradictory interests that are continually reduced to forms of ideological expression which make this mediation possible. And it is no longer confronted by a homogeneous upsurge of the popular forces against repression, but by a number of upsurges, all relatively distinct in their anti-capitalist aspirations, all pursuing at differentiated and specific levels a sovereign self-determination by social individuals of the conditions, ends, and framework of their social activity. It is impossible to demand immediate unification —by a line imposed from above—of all the various movements (of manual, technical, scientific, artistic, cultural and other workers, etc.) as a pre-condition for the frontal conquest of the State. It is only possible to articulate their specific aspirations within the perspective of a common goal which contains them all and at the same time transcends them: the goal of a socialist society, itself pluralist and "articulated." This is the society which the revolutionary party must prefigure in its methods and action if it wishes to fulfill its proper function. It must *disintegrate* the power of the political State while presenting itself as the mediating and synthesizing instrument for the independent centers of power which are struggling to emerge on all the various levels of civil society.

I shall return shortly to the question of whether the birth of a new type of revolutionary party presupposes the creation of a new revolutionary party.

6. The Student Revolt

The foregoing reflections would have only circumstantial significance if the revolutionary radicalism of young people was a purely conjunctural phenomenon, destined to burn itself out; if the categories and gradualist solutions of the traditional left were to remain valid or become valid anew.

But the fact is that the radicalization of the under-25 generation is a world phenomenon; its themes are similar throughout the whole of the advanced capitalist world; it is this which indicates that the character of the movement is fundamental, and not merely circumstantial. To denounce it as adventurist and irresponsible is completely to miss the point. The real irresponsibility is to present an unavowedly reductionist explanation and say: "Basically these young people are revolting against their loss of class status; as children of bourgeois and petit-bourgeois parents, they are studying to enjoy the privileges of their class or to raise themselves in the social hierarchy. But the fact is that there are too many of them; there's no room for so many privileged people. So they will have to make do with the common lot."

This interpretation, particularly widespread in West Germany and Great Britain, calculates on the old ouvrierist hostility towards intellectuals and students, seen as a privileged and idle section of society. The French working-class movement makes itself an accomplice to this primitive hostility, when it refuses to take into consideration the material base of the student revolt in order to bind the students to the working class and propose to both a model of civilization and development which would suppress the barriers between intellectual and manual work; which would make the right to culture universal because it would cease to confer privileges, because manual work would have the same dignity as intellectual work, because—as in China and in Cuba —everyone would be obliged periodically to do both.

In fact, the European working-class movement has the undeserved good fortune that the students, the secondary-school children, the young workers do not formulate their problems within the framework of bourgeois society in corporate, quantitative terms (of jobs available, rates of increase, public credits, wage levels), but instead go right to the root of the problem. They radicalize to the left, demand the suppression of class barriers and elitist culture, and the onset of a universal (revolutionary) culture. They do not radicalize to the right through a demand for class privileges, through their rejection of proletarianization. The working-class movement, first by its indifference and then by its suspicion, insists that they *ought* to radicalize rightwards, and, if they do nothing of the sort, it is for accidental reasons in which no confidence should be placed.

In fact, if the student body radicalizes to the left, refuses elitism and cultural malthusianism at the same time as it refuses the technocratization of the university and bourgeois society, it is because there is no solution to the right: the students are trapped by the irrefutable logic of the cultural malthusianism of the bourgeoisie. If one accepts the capitalist criteria of efficiency and profit-earning capacity; if one accepts the bourgeois postulate that higher education—if it is not to be entirely wasted—must be the royal road to social and economic privilege; then it is certainly true that entry into higher education must be limited in the most draconian way: the university must be reserved for the future ruling elites, and the mass of young people sluiced off to schools producing experts on the cheap.

If, on the other hand, as the student movement demands, higher education should be open to all, then those who take it must renounce the least privilege in bourgeois society. They must renounce the capitalist criteria of efficiency and profit-earning capacity, the social division of labor, and all kinds of hierarchy. They must want culture for itself, independent of its utility. But at the same time they must desire a new kind of culture, a new type of society, a new scale of values. If the student vanguard, which formulates these demands theoretically, is followed by the general body, it is because the demands are not gratuitously extremist opinions, but a dialectical necessity which the general body experiences before expressing it in theoretical form.

For socialist and revolutionary theory, the question of culture as producer and product of the demand for a radical liberation appears in this light as the central question. Is it true that this question has remained unanswered in the socialist countries of Europe? That it was at the bottom of the present ferment in Czechoslovakia, and to a lesser degree in Poland and the Soviet Union? That it cannot be resolved by a mechanical transposition of Chinese and Cuban models? If this is the case, then the socialist forces must discover the guiding principles for an original model. After all, if parties aren't for that, they are for nothing.

7. The Way Forward

One of the great achievements of the May/June events is that for the first time in 35 years the question of revolution and of the passage to socialism has been posed in an advanced capitalist country in terms of needs and criteria that owe nothing to the schemas which, since the 7th Congress of the Comintern, have dominated the politics and ideology of the Communist parties. For the first time revolutionary forces (still embryonic) have sketched in mass action the prospect of an "affluent" socialism owing nothing to the Stalinist or post-Stalinist model which has been the more or less obligatory reference-point of the Marxist parties for the last 40 years.

Moreover, the question of the formation of a new revolutionary party capable of taking on the functions indicated above is now posed in France: one capable of defining a model of socialist democracy adapted to the demands—both cultural and for individual and collective liberation—of workers in an advanced country. Also, either in the short or the long term, the question of creating a new International —which would contain the independent revolutionary movements of the advanced capitalist countries and of the Third World—can only be avoided if what is left of the Third International ceases to be dominated by authoritarian and reformist tendencies, and declares itself open to all the varied revolutionary currents in the world. . . .

It matters little if the revolutionary groups in process of formation or development are not yet durable and coherent political entities, endowed with a hegemonic capacity. Every group devoted to action and theory—every group that gives itself the task of defining new forms of struggle; of defining the methods and objectives of dual power, particularly at the level of the big centers of production and the trusts; of defining the nature and sequence of middle-term objectives; of defining the economic and cultural policies of the transitional period—is at present the crucible from which the new party will emerge. The important thing for the moment is to provide a framework within which all those who have now learned that revolution is possible—and that it must arise from initiative at the base, from the installation of forms of direct popular control, from exemplary acts of rupture which immediately take one outside the logic of the system and which have an efficacy vastly superior to traditional modes of propaganda and centralized organization—can be politically formed, can calculate their strength, and can exchange their experiences.

The new party will be born from the growth and combination of these nuclei because the need is there. The need is there because in the absence of a synthesizing group—which facilitates national and international liaison; prefigures revolutionary power and symbolizes its possibility; guarantees the translation into political power and governing capacity of a working class that takes over the means of production—the chances of eliminating and defeating the bourgeois State are tiny, if indeed they exist at all. This does not mean that the new party will have to draw its strength from the power of its organization and its structures, but:

1. from the quality of its insertion into the centers of production and from its capacity to theorize the exercise of dual power, strategically,

particularly on the level of the trusts, and of key sectors and services;

2. from the presence at its head of men unimpeachable in the eyes of revolutionaries of all tendencies: men with the moral authority, the abilities and the political credibility to proclaim, when the hour arrives, the provisional government of the revolution; to convene a general assembly of the committees of popular power; and, prior to the construction of the revolutionary State, to devise holding measures (economic, monetary, administrative, military) which will provisionally ensure a minimum of central organization and a maximum of security against sabotage or a return in force of the enemy.

In the event of any recurrence of a generalized pre-insurrectionary situation, the prior existence of a provisional structure of this kind will be indispensable for victory. Spontaneous insurrectionary situations, in an advanced and complex economy, cannot be prolonged sufficiently to allow for the creation and organization of a revolutionary vanguard on a mass scale, and of a political force capable of channeling the movement towards the seizure of power. The destiny of a revolution is settled in a few days, once the revolutionary moment has arrived. If these days are not made use of to dislocate the bourgeois State, neutralize its repressive apparatus and install organs of popular power, the game will be lost—until the next occasion, which may well not arrive so soon. This is why a vanguard and a provisional political leadership, ready to make the most of any revolutionary situation, are indispensable.

Henceforward, we know that advanced capitalist society is vulnerable; that it is rent by contradictions which may explode into revolutionary crises; that the classic parties in their bankruptcy are not ideologically, politically or organizationally prepared to take advantage of these crises; that the essence of a revolutionary organization is to be ready for revolution, without advance notice. It is possible that the May uprising might recur, sooner or later, here or elsewhere, because the possibilities, under certain conditions, for its success have appeared so clearly that henceforward the power of the bourgeois State will have, as it were, an internal flaw.

But it is impossible, however, to rely solely on the return, *improbable in the short term*, of a spontaneous insurrection: just as they cannot be indefinitely prolonged, insurrectionary situations cannot be reproduced at will. The ability to make the most of a revolutionary situation when it arrives is only one of two eventualities for which a revolutionary organization has to prepare itself. The other eventuality is that of a long process, which must be utilized for political preparation in depth, and for actions of partial rupture, spaced out in time. This preparation and these actions include the constant repetition, by active minorities—of whom the SDS in West Germany has been the first to set the example—of insurrectionary acts of a symbolic and exemplary kind. These are the best means of propagating revolutionary ideas; of destroying fear and respect for "authority"; of revealing the limits, the insoluble contradictions, the blockages, the repressive nature and the absurdities of the existing social system; and of teaching contempt for that system. But these acts are not the insurrection itself; they will not get the better of the social system; they simply maintain areas of crisis within it which undermine its political credibility. They are one particular mode of preparatory political work; they presuppose the latter, win a wider receptivity for it, and need to be followed up by it.

Murray Bookchin

The following essay was originally published in *Anarchos,* Spring, 1969.

Bookchin's essay is an attempt to develop within an anarchistic and radical ecological frame of reference the concept of a post-scarcity society. The importance of spontaneity, of "revolution as self-activity," and of a liberatory technology for a reconstitution of the meaning of community and "for the very image of man in a liberated society" is discussed and defended. Bookchin's analysis of the concept of post-scarcity anarchy is one of the most insightful utopian statements of the anarcho-communist position.

POST-SCARCITY ANARCHY

Preconditions and Possibilities

All the successful social revolutions of the past have been particularistic revolutions of minority classes seeking to assert their specific interests over those of society as a whole. The great bourgeois revolutions of modern times offered an ideology of sweeping political reconstitution, but in reality they merely certified the social dominance of the bourgeoisie, giving formal political expression to the economic ascendancy of capital. The lofty notions of the "nation," of the "free citizen," of "equality before the law," concealed the mundane reality of the centralized state, the atomized, isolated man, the dominance of bourgeois interest. Despite their sweeping ideological claims, these particularistic revolutions replaced the rule of one class by another, one system of exploitation by another, one system of toil by another, one system of psychological repression by another.

What is unique about our era is that the particularistic revolution

Reprinted by permission of *Anarchos.*

has now been subsumed by the possibility of the generalized revolution: complete and totalistic. If it has achieved nothing else, bourgeois society at least revolutionized the means of production on a scale unprecedented in history. This technological revolution, culminating in cybernation, has created the objective, quantitative bases for a world without class rule, exploitation, toil and material want. The means now exist for the development of the rounded man, the total man, freed of guilt, the workings of authoritarian modes of training, and given over to Desire, to the sensuous apprehension of the marvelous. It is possible to conceive of future experience in terms of a coherent process: a process in which the bifurcation of thought and activity, mind and sensuousness, discipline and spontaneity, individuality and community, man and nature, town and country, education and life, work and play—all, are resolved, harmonized, and organically wedded in a qualitatively new realm of freedom. Just as the particularized revolution produced a particularized, bifurcated society, so the generalized revolution can produce an organically unified, many-sided community. The great wound opened by propertied society in the form of the "social question" can now be healed.

That freedom must be conceived in human terms, not in animal terms—in terms of life, not of survival—is clear enough. Men do not remove their ties of bondage and become fully human merely by divesting themselves of social domination, by obtaining freedom in its *abstract* form. They must also be free *concretely:* free from material want, from toil, from the burden of devoting the greater part of their time, indeed the greater part of their lives, to the struggle with necessity. To have seen these material preconditions for human freedom, to have emphasized that freedom presupposes free time and the material abundance for abolishing free time as a social privilege, is the great contribution of Karl Marx to modern revolutionary theory.

By the same token, the *preconditions* for freedom must not be mistaken for the *conditions* of freedom. The *possibility* of liberation does not constitute its *reality.* Along with its positive aspects, technological advance has a distinctly negative, socially regressive side. If it is true that technological progress enlarges the historical potentiality for freedom, it is also true that the bourgeois control of technology reinforces the established organization of society and everyday life. Technology and the resources of abundance furnish capitalism with the means of assimilating large sections of society to the established system of hierarchy and authority. They provide the system with the weaponry, the detecting devices, and the propaganda media for the threat as well as the reality of massive repression. By their centralistic nature, they reinforce the monopolistic, centralistic, bureaucratic tendencies in the political apparatus. In short, they furnish the state with historically unprecedented means for manipulating and mobilizing the entire environment of life, for perpetuating hierarchy, exploitation, and unfreedom.

It must be emphasized, however, that this manipulation and mobilization of the environment is extremely problematical and laden with crises. Far from leading to pacification (one can hardly speak, here, of harmonization), the attempt of bourgeois society to control and exploit its environment, natural as well as social, has devastating consequences. Volumes have been written on the pollution of the atmosphere and waterways, on the destruction of tree cover and soil, on toxic materials in foods and liquids. Even more threatening in their final results are pollution and destruction of a kind that involves the very ecology required for a complex organism like man. The changing ratio of carbon dioxide to other atmospheric gases, a product of the mindless combustion activities for domestic and industrial purposes, threatens the entire climatology of the planet. The concentration of radioactive wastes in living things is a menace to the health and genetic endowment of nearly all species. Worldwide contamination by pesticides that inhibit oxygen production in plankton or by near-toxic levels of lead from gasoline exhaust are examples of an enduring pollution that threatens the biological integrity of advanced life-forms, including man.

The human environment is being simplified to the danger-point. The inorganic, synthetic, and elemental are replacing the organic, the natural, and the complex. This is most clearly seen in the sweeping urban belts of America and Europe, where materials such as concrete, metals, glass—and smog—tend to completely replace every living feature of the environment. The same process of simplification occurs in the countryside, where the mass production of food transforms the traditional, variegated farmstead into an agricultural factory, based on monoculture, chemical controls, and insensate, large-scale mechanization, often in savage disregard of an area's natural ecology and the possibility of irreparable damage to the land.

But these changes are not limited to the biological realm alone. They are carried directly into every facet of daily life. In the great cities, swollen to the bursting point by masses of humans, only a mass concept of life can prevail. The need to employ, feed, educate, and transport millions of people reinforces the centralistic, totalitarian, and bureaucratic tendencies that inhere in modern industrial capitalism. The bureaucratic scale, reared on urban gigantism and the logistics of mass control, replaces the human scale. Life becomes as faceless, as homogenized as the manipulative apparatus itself. The wealth of social experience that marked earlier periods of history falls away and reveals man as an object, as a mass-manufactured commodity—the product of social factories euphemistically called the "family," the "school," the "home," the "church," and the "community."

Ecologically, bourgeois exploitation and manipulation are literally reversing organic evolution. By creating vast urban agglomerations of concrete, metal, and glass, by overriding and undermining the complex, often subtly organized ecosystems that constitute local differences in the natural world—in short, by replacing a highly complex, organic environment by a simplified, inorganic one, the prevailing society is disassembling the biotic pyramid that supported humanity for countless millennia. In the course of replacing the complex ecological relationships on which all advanced living things depend for more elementary relationships, the prevailing society is steadily restoring the biosphere to a stage which will be able to support only simpler forms of life. If this great reversal of the evolutionary process continues, it is by no means fanciful to suppose that the preconditions for higher forms of life will be irreparably destroyed and the earth will be incapable of supporting man himself.

Socially, bourgeois exploitation and manipulation have brought everyday life to the most excruciating point of vacuity and boredom. In converting society into a factory and market place, the very rationale of life is reduced to production for its own sake—and consumption for its own sake.* For all its different historical forms and combinations, capitalism has never transcended the commodity nexus

* It is worth noting, here, that the emergence of the "consumer society" provides us with remarkable evidence of the difference between the industrial capitalism of Marx's time and state capitalism today. When Marx spoke of capitalism as a system organized around "production for the sake of produc-

and the banalization of experience to the level of "business as usual." Hence everyday life becomes a business, marriage a partnership, children an investment. One budgets time and saves space. The reasons for the simplification of the natural world, of the city, indeed, of experience itself, cease to be a mystery if one bears in mind that the very essence of bourgeois society is the mediation of social relations by objects, the reduction of quality to quantity, the reduction of man himself to a commodity. It is from the commodity nexus, from the "free exchange" of objects of "equal value," that capitalism produced not only its great juridical fictions of the "free citizen" with "equality before the law," but also the bureaucratization of life, the statification of society, and the perversion of technology with the same inexorable force that "free competition" turns into monopoly. This commodity mode of society is beyond reform. For what is at stake is its very dialectic—the law of motion that inheres in its constitution as a social organism.

The Redemptive Dialectic

Is there a redemptive dialectic that can transform social development from its negative, destructive side into the positive conditions for an anarchic society, where men will attain full control over their daily lives? Or does the social dialectic come to an end with capitalism, its possibilities sealed off by the use of a highly advanced technology for repressive and co-optative purposes?

We must learn, here, from the limits of Marxism, a project which, in a period of material scarcity, understandably anchored the social dialectic and the contradictions of capitalism in the economic realm. Marx, it has been emphasized, examined the *preconditions* for liberation, not the *conditions* of liberation. The Marxian critique is rooted in the past, in the era of material want and relatively limited technological development. Even its humanistic theory of alienation turns primarily around the issue of work and man's alienation from the product of his labor. Today, however, capitalism is a parasite on the future, a vampire that survives on the technology and resources

---

tion," he regarded this as based on the economic immiseration of the proletariat. By contrast, "production for the sake of production" rests today on "consumption for the sake of consumption." Immiseration primarily takes on a spiritual rather than an economic form—a starvation of life.

of freedom. The industrial capitalism of Marx's time organized its commodity relations around a prevailing system of material scarcity; the state capitalism of our time organizes its commodity relations around a prevailing system of material abundance. A century ago, scarcity had to be endured; today, it has to be enforced—hence the importance of the state in the present era. It is not that modern capitalism has resolved its contradictions and annulled the social dialectic, but rather that the social dialectic and the contradictions of capitalism have been transferred from the economic realm to the hierarchical forms of propertied society, from the abstract "historic" domain to the concrete minutia of everyday experience, from the arena of survival to the arena of life.*

The dialectic of bureaucratic state capitalism originates in the contradiction between the repressive character of commodity society and the enormous potential for freedom opened by technological advance, between the exploitative organization of society and the natural world —a world that includes not only the natural environment, but also man's "nature"—his Eros-derived impulses. The contradiction between the exploitative organization of society and the natural environment is beyond co-optation: the atmosphere, the waterways, the soil, and the ecology required for human survival are not redeemable by reforms, concessions, or by modifications of strategic policy. There is no technology that can reproduce atmospheric oxygen in sufficient quantities to sustain life on this planet. There is no substitute for the hydrologic systems of the earth. There is no technique for removing massive environmental pollution by radioactive isotopes, pesticides, lead, and petroleum wastes. Nor is there the faintest evidence that bourgeois society will relent at any time in the foreseeable future in its disruption of vital ecological processes, in its exploitation of natural resources, in its use of the atmosphere and waterways as dumping areas for wastes, in its cancerous mode of urbanization and land abuse.

Even more immediate is the contradiction between the exploitative organization of society and man's Eros-derived impulses, a contradic-

---

* This is not to say that the economic contradictions of capitalism have disappeared, but, in principle at least, they are no longer beyond resolution by the system. They are not "inherent" or "inexorable" features of state capitalism, and they persist as a product of the unevenness of the development, of the "impurities" in the system, and of the social influences that linger on from earlier periods.

tion that manifests itself as the banalization and impoverishment of experience in a mass, bureaucratically manipulated, impersonal society. The Eros-derived impulses in man can be repressed, sublimated, but they can never be eliminated. They are renewed with every birth of a human being, with every generation of youth. It is not surprising that the young, today, more than any economic class or stratum, articulate the life-impulses in man's nature—the urgings of Desire, sensuousness, and the lure of the marvelous. Thus the biological matrix, from which propertied society emerged ages ago, reappears at a new level with the era that marks the end of property, only now this matrix is saturated with social phenomena. Short of manipulating humanity's germ plasm these life-impulses can be annulled only with the annihilation of man himself.

The contradictions within bureaucratic state capitalism permeate all the hierarchical forms developed and overdeveloped by bourgeois society. The hierarchical forms which nurtured propertied society for ages and promoted its development—the state, city, centralized economy, bureaucracy, patriarchal family, and market place—have reached their historic limits. They have exhausted their social functions as modes of stabilization. It is not a question of whether these hierarchical forms were ever "progressive" in the Marxian sense of the term. As Raoul Vaneigem has observed: "Perhaps it isn't enough to say that hierarchical power has preserved humanity for thousands of years as alcohol preserves a fetus, by arresting either growth or decay." For the present it is enough to say that these forms now constitute the target of all the revolutionary forces that are generated by modern capitalism and, whether one chooses to invoke the threat of nuclear catastrophe or ecological disaster, *they now threaten the very survival of humanity.*

With the development of hierarchical forms into a threat to the very existence of humanity, the social dialectic, far from being annulled, acquires a new dimension. It poses the "social question" in an entirely new way: if man had to acquire the conditions of survival in order to live (as Marx emphasized), now he must acquire the conditions of life in order to survive. By this inversion of the relationship between survival and life, revolution acquires a new sense of urgency. No longer are we faced with Marx's famous choice of socialism or barbarism; we are confronted with the more drastic alternatives of anarchy or annihilation. The problems of necessity and survival become congruent with the problems of freedom and life. They cease to require the theoretical mediation, "transitional" stages, and centralized organizations to bridge the gap between the existing and the possible. The possible, in fact, is all that can exist. Hence the problems of "transition," which occupied the Marxists for nearly a century, are eliminated not only by the advance of technology, but by the social dialectic itself. The problems of social reconstruction are reduced to practical tasks that can be solved spontaneously by self-liberatory acts of society.

Revolution, in fact, acquires not only a new sense of urgency, but a new sense of promise. In the hippy's tribalism, the Diggers' free food, in the dropout life-styles and free sexuality of millions of youth, in the spontaneous affinity groups of the anarchists, we already find those forms of affirmation that follow from acts of negation. With the inversion of the "social question" there is also an inversion of the social dialectic, a "yea" that emerges automatically and simultaneously with a "nay." The solutions take their point of departure from the problems. When the time has arrived in history that the state, city, bureaucracy, centralized economy, patriarchal family, and market place have reached their historic limits, what is posed is no longer a change in form but the absolute negation of *all* hierarchical forms *as such.* The absolute negation of the state is anarchy—a situation where men liberate not only "history," but all the immediate circumstances of their everyday lives. The absolute negation of the city is community—a situation where the social environment is decentralized into rounded, ecologically balanced communes. The absolute negation of bureaucracy is immediate as distinguished from mediated relations—a situation where representation is replaced by face-to-face relations in a general assembly of free individuals. The absolute negation of the centralized economy is regional biotechnology—a situation where the instruments of production are molded to the resources of the ecological biome. The absolute negation of the patriarchal family is free sexuality—a situation where all forms of sexual regulation are transcended by the spontaneous, untrammeled expression of eroticism among equals. The absolute negation of the market place is communism—a situation where collective abundance and cooperation transform labor into play and need into Desire.

Spontaneity and Utopia

It is not accidental that at a point in history, when hierarchical power and manipulation have reached their most threatening proportions, the very concepts of hierarchy, power, and manipulation are being brought into question. The challenge to these concepts comes from a rediscovery of the importance of spontaneity—a rediscovery nourished by ecology, by a heightened conception of self-development, and by a new understanding of the revolutionary process in society.

What ecology has shown is that in nature, balance is achieved by organic differentiation and complexity, not by homogeneity and simplification. In the case of pest control, for example, the more varied the flora and fauna of a biome, the more stable the population of a potential pest. The more environmental diversity is diminished, the greater will the population of a potential pest fluctuate, with the probability that it will get out of control. Left to itself, a biome tends spontaneously toward organic differentiation, greater variety of flora and fauna, and diversity in the number of prey and predators. This does not mean that interference by man must be avoided. The need for a productive agriculture—itself a form of interference in nature—must always remain in the foreground of an ecological approach to food cultivation and forest management. No less important is the fact that man can often produce changes in a biome that would vastly improve its ecological quality. But these efforts involve insight and understanding, not the exercise of brute power and manipulation. As Charles Elton, an outstanding English ecologist, puts it: "The world's future has to be managed, but this management would not be just like a game of chess—(but) more like steering a boat."

This concept of management, this new regard for the importance of spontaneity, has far-reaching implications for technology, community, indeed, for the very image of man in a liberated society. It challenges the capitalist ideal of agriculture as a factory operation, organized around immense, centrally controlled land-holdings, highly specialized forms of monoculture, the reduction of the terrain to a factory floor, the substitution of organic by chemical processes, the use of gang-labor, etc. If food cultivation is to be more like "steering a boat" than a contest between opponents, the agriculturist must become thoroughly familiar with the ecology of the land; he must acquire a new sensitivity to its needs and possibilities. This presupposes the reduction of agriculture to a human scale, the restoration of moderate-sized agricultural units, the diversification of the agricultural situation, in short, a decentralized, ecological system of food cultivation.

The same reasoning applies to industry in connection with pollution control. The development of giant factory complexes and the use of single- or dual-energy resources to the near exclusion of all other resources rank as major sources of atmospheric pollution. Only by developing smaller industrial units and diversifying energy sources by the extensive use of clean power (solar, wind, and water), will it be possible to significantly reduce industrial pollution. The means for this radical technological change are now at hand. Technologists have developed "miniturized" substitutes for large-scale industrial operations, small versatile machines, and sophisticated methods for converting solar, wind, and water energy into power usable in industry and the home. These substitutes are often more productive and less wasteful than the large-scale facilities that exist today.*

A "miniturized" technology, highly adaptable to regional production, has very little place in a centralized economy, based on a national division of labor and large-scale production. The small packets of energy which can be delivered by solar collectors, wind turbines, and small-stream dams, are nearly valueless for meeting the gargantuan demands of immense industrial complexes and megalopolitan cities. The extensive use of small-scale techniques and diversified forms of pollutant-free energy resources presupposes decentralized small or moderate-sized communities. The same conclusion applies to the use of the pollutant-free, nearly noiseless electric car (a vehicle that is excellent for local transportation, but of limited use for long journeys). It applies to the use of local resources, which are not large enough to meet the needs of giant industrial facilities, to microchemistry, and to many other related techniques and systems of technology.

* For a discussion of this "miniturized" technology, see "Towards a Liberatory Technology" in *Anarchy* 78 (August, 1967; London) or in two parts in *Anarchos* #2 and #3.

The implications of small-scale agriculture and industry for community are obvious: if man is to use the principles needed to manage an ecosystem, the basic unit of social life must itself become an ecosystem—an ecological community. It too must become diversified, balanced, and well-rounded. By no means is this concept of community motivated exclusively by the need for a lasting balance between man and the natural world; it is also anchored in the utopian ideal of the rounded man, the individual whose sensibilities, range of experience, and life-style are nourished by a wide range of stimuli, by a diversity of activities, and by a social scale that always remains within the comprehension of a single human being. Thus the means and conditions of survival become the means and conditions of life; need becomes Desire and Desire becomes need. The point is reached where the greatest social decomposition provides the source of the highest form of social integration, bringing the most pressing ecological necessities into a common focus with the highest utopian ideals.

We may pause, at this point, to form some vision of the new community:

We suppose the community has been established after careful study has been made of its natural ecology—its air and water resources, its climate, its geological formations, its raw materials, its soils, and its natural flora and fauna. The population of the community is consciously limited to the ecological carrying capacity of the region. Land management is guided entirely by ecological principles so that an equilibrium is maintained between the environment and its human inhabitants. Industrially rounded, the community forms a distinct unit within a natural matrix, socially and artistically in balance with the area it occupies.

Agriculture is highly mechanized, to be sure, but as mixed as possible with respect to crops, livestock, and timber. Floral and faunal variety is promoted as a means of controlling pest infestations and enhancing scenic beauty. Large-scale farming is permitted only where it does not conflict with the ecology of the region. Owing to the generally mixed character of food cultivation, agriculture is pursued by small farming units, each demarcated from the other by tree belts, shrubs, and where possible, by pastures and meadows. In rolling, hilly, or mountainous country, land with sharp gradients is covered by timber to prevent erosion and conserve water. The soil on each acre is studied carefully and committed only to those crops for which it is most suited.

Every effort is made to blend town and country without sacrificing the distinctive contribution that each has to offer to the human experience. The ecological region forms the living social, cultural, and biotic boundaries of the community or of the several communities that share its resources. Each community contains many vegetable and flower gardens, attractive arbors, park land, squares, even streams and ponds which support fish and aquatic birds. The countryside from which food and raw materials are acquired, constitutes not only the immediate environs of the community, accessible to all by foot, but also invades the community. Although town and country retain their identity and the uniqueness of each is prized and fostered, nature appears everywhere in the town, and the town seems to have caressed and left a gentle, human imprint on nature.

Social decisions are made in a general assembly, where all members of the community have an opportunity to acquire the full measure of anyone who addresses them. They are in a position to absorb his attitudes and demeanor, to explore his motives as well as his ideas in a direct personal encounter and through thorough debate, face-to-face discussion and close inquiry. The execution of public tasks is left to committees, formed of volunteers or selected by lot. Where specialized knowledge is required, the tasks are apportioned among technical groups, each member of which is subject to immediate recall. These committees and groups remain under constant public purview. Their work is limited exclusively to administrative tasks and they are answerable in every detail of their responsibilities to the assembly.

As a sense of regionalism grows in the community, every resource finds its place in a natural, stable balance, a truly organic unity of social, technological, and natural elements. Art assimilates technology in the deepest sense that art can exist: as social art, evoked by everyday human relationships. Small or moderate in size, the free community is able to rescale the tempo of life, the work patterns of its members, its buildings, architecture, systems of transportation, and communication, to completely human dimensions. Crafts regain their honored position as supplements to the factory; they become a form of domestic, day-to-day artistry. A high standard of excellence, based on a respect for the durability of goods and on the need to conserve raw materials, replaces the strictly quantitative, exploitative criteria of production that prevail today. The community becomes a beautifully molded arena of life, a vitalizing source of culture and a deeply personal, ever-nourishing source of human solidarity. From this point onward, the community ceases to be a *structural* concept and becomes a deeply human *process*—the process of communizing. It enters the still unexplored realm of the marvelous, a realm that no imagination of this era, however bold, can hope to encompass.

Spontaneity and Revolution

If it is true, as Guy Debord observes, that "Daily life is the measure of everything: of the fulfillment or rather the non-fulfillment of human relationships, of the use we make of our time," a question arises: who are "we" whose daily lives are to be fulfilled? Or put differently: how does the liberated Self emerge that is capable of turning time into life, space into community, and human relationships into the marvelous?

The liberation of the Self involves, above all, a social process. In a society that has shriveled the Self into a commodity, into an object manufactured for exchange, there can be no fulfilled Self. There can only be the beginnings of Selfhood, the *emergence* of a Self that seeks fulfillment, a Self that is defined by the obstacles it must overcome to achieve realization. In a society whose belly is distended to the bursting point with revolution, whose chronic state is an unending series of labor pains, whose real condition is a mounting emergency —only one thought and act is relevant: giving birth. Any environment, private or social, that does not make this fact the center of human experience is a sham and diminishes whatever Self remains to us after we have absorbed our daily poison of everyday life in bourgeois society.

It is plain that the goal of revolution, today, must be the liberation of daily life. Any revolution that fails to achieve this goal is counterrevolution. Above all, it is *we* who have to be liberated, *our* daily lives with all their moments, hours, and days, not universals like "history" and "society." *

---

* Despite its lip service to the dialectic, the traditional Left has yet to take old Hegel's "concrete universal" seriously, to see it not merely as a philosophical concept but as a social program. This has been done only in Marx's early writings, in the writings of the great utopians (Fourier and William Morris)— and, in our own time, by the drop-out youth.

The Self must always be *identifiable* in the revolution, not over-whelmed by it. The Self must always be *perceivable* in the revolution-ary process, not submerged by it. There is no word that is more sinister in the "revolutionary" vocabulary than "masses." Revolution-ary liberation must be Self-liberation that reaches social dimensions, not "mass liberation" or "class liberation" behind which lurks the rule of an elite, a hierarchy, and a state. If a revolution fails to pro-duce a new society by the Self-activity and Self-mobilization of revo-lutionaries, if it does not involve the forging of a Self in the revolution-ary process, the revolution will once again circumvent those whose lives are to be lived everyday and leave daily life unaffected. Out of the revolution must emerge a Self that takes full possession of daily life, not a daily life that once again takes full possession of the Self.

If for this reason alone, the revolutionary movement is profoundly concerned with life-style. It must try to *live* the revolution in all its totality, not only participate in it. It must be deeply concerned with the way the revolutionist lives, his relations with the surrounding environment, his degree of Self-emancipation. In seeking to change society, the revolutionist in turn cannot avoid those changes in him-self that involve the reconquest of his own being. Like the move-ment in which he participates, the revolutionist must try to reflect the conditions of the society he is trying to achieve—at least to the de-gree that this is possible today.

The treachery and failures of the past half century have made it axiomatic that there *can be no separation of the revolutionary process from the revolutionary goal*. A society whose fundamental aim is Self-administration in all facets of life can be achieved only by Self-activity. This implies a mode of administration that is always pos-sessed by the Self. If we define "power" as the power of man over man, power can be destroyed only by the very process in which man acquires power over his own life and in which he not only "discovers" himself but, more meaningfully, in which he formulates his Selfhood in all its social dimensions.

The point is that a libertarian society can be achieved only by a libertarian revolution. Freedom cannot be "delivered" to the indi-vidual as the "end-product" of a "revolution"; the assembly and community cannot be legislated or decreed into existence. A revolu-tionary group can seek, purposively and consciously, to promote the creation of these forms; but if assembly and community are not allowed to emerge organically, if their growth is not matured by the process of demassification, by Self-activity and by Self-realization, they will remain nothing but forms, like the soviets in post-revolutionary Russia. Assembly and community must arise within the revolutionary process; indeed, the revolutionary process must *be* the formation of assembly and community and, with these, the destruction of power, property, and exploitation.

Revolution as Self-activity is not unique to our time. It constitutes the paramount feature of all the great revolutions in modern history. It marked the *journées* of the *sans culottes* in 1792 and 1793, the famous "Five Days" of February, 1917, in Petrograd, the uprising of the Barcelona proletariat in 1936, the early days of the Hungarian Revolution in 1956, and the May–June events in Paris, 1968. Nearly every revolutionary uprising in the history of our time has been initiated spontaneously by the Self-activity of "masses," often in flat defiance of the hesitant programs advanced by the revolutionary organizations. Every one of these revolutions has been marked by extraordinary individuation, by a joyousness and solidarity that turned everyday life into a festival. This surreal dimension of the revolutionary process, with its explosion of deep-seated libidinal forces, grins irascibly through the pages of history like the face of a satyr on shimmering water. It is not without reason that the Bolshevik commissars smashed the wine bottles in the Winter Palace on the night of November 7, 1917.

The puritanism and work ethic of the traditional Left reflects one of the most critical problems in revolution today: the capacity of the bourgeois environment to infiltrate the revolutionary framework. The origins of this power lie in the commodity nature of man under capitalism, a quality that is almost automatically transferred to the organized group—and which the group, in turn, reinforces in its members. As the late Josef Weber emphasized, all organized groups "have the tendency to render themselves autonomous, i.e., to alienate themselves from their original aim and to become an end in themselves in the hands of those administering them." This phenomenon is as true of revolutionary organizations as it is of state and semi-state institutions, official parties, and trade unions.

The problem of alienation can never be completely resolved apart from the revolutionary process itself. It can be mitigated, partly by an acute awareness that the problem exists, partly by a voluntary but drastic remaking of the revolutionary and his group. This remaking can only begin when the revolutionary group recognizes that it is a catalyst in the revolutionary process, not a "vanguard." The revolutionary group must clearly see that its goal is not the "seizure of power," but the dissolution of power—indeed, that the entire problem of power, of control from below and control from above, can be solved only if there is no above or below.

Above all things, the revolutionary group must divest itself of the forms of power—statutes, hierarchies, property, prescribed opinions, fetishes, paraphernalia, official etiquette—in short, the subtlest as well as the most obvious of bureaucratic and bourgeois traits that reinforce authority and hierarchy, not only consciously, but unconsciously. It must remain open to public scrutiny not only in its formulated decisions, but in their very formulation. It must be coherent in the profound sense that its theory is its practice and its practice its theory. It must do away with all commodity relations in its day-to-day existence and constitute itself along the decentralized organizational principles of the very society it seeks to achieve: community, assembly, spontaneity. It must, in Josef Weber's superb words, be "marked always by simplicity and clarity, always thousands of unprepared people can enter and direct it, always it remains *transparent* to and controlled by all." Only then, when the revolutionary movement is congruent with the decentralized community it seeks to achieve, can it avoid becoming another elitist obstacle to the social development and dissolve into the revolution like surgical thread into a healing wound.

Prospect

The most important process going on in America today is the sweeping deinstitutionalization of the bourgeois social structure. A basic, far-reaching disrespect and a profound disloyalty is developing toward the values, the forms, the aspirations, and above all, the institutions of the established order. On a scale unprecedented in American history, millions of people are shedding their commitment to the society in which they live. They no longer believe in its claims. They no longer respect its symbols. They no longer accept its goals, and most significantly, they refuse almost intuitively to live by its institutional and social codes.

This growing refusal runs very deep. It extends from an opposition to war into a hatred of political manipulation in all its forms. Starting from a rejection of racial discrimination, it brings into question the very existence of hierarchical power as such. In its detestation of middle class values and life-styles, it rapidly evolves into a rejection of the commodity system; from an irritation with environmental pollution, it passes into a rejection of the American city and modern urbanism. In short, it tends to transcend every particularistic critique of the society and evolve into a generalized opposition to the bourgeois order on an ever-broadening scale.

In this respect, the period in which we live closely resembles the revolutionary Enlightenment that swept through France in the eighteenth century—a period that completely reworked French consciousness and prepared the conditions for the Great Revolution of 1789. In both cases, the old institutions are slowly pulverized by molecular action from below, long before they are toppled by mass revolutionary action. This molecular movement creates an atmosphere of general lawlessness: a growing personal, day-to-day disobedience, a tendency not to "go along" with the existing system, a seemingly "petty" but nevertheless critical attempt to circumvent restriction in every facet of daily life. The society, in effect, becomes disorderly, undisciplined, Dionysian—a condition that reveals itself most dramatically in an increasing rate of official crimes. A vast critique develops of the system—the actual Enlightenment itself, two centuries ago, and the sweeping critique that exists today—which seeps downward and accelerates the molecular movement at the base. Be it an angry gesture, a "riot" or a conscious change in life-style, an ever-increasing number of people—who have no more of a commitment to an organized revolutionary movement than they have to the society itself—begin to spontaneously engage in their own defiant propaganda of the deed.

In its concrete details, this disintegrating social process is nourished by many sources. It develops with all the unevenness, indeed all the contradictions, that mark every revolutionary trend. In eighteenth century France, radical ideology oscillated between a rigid scientism and a sloppy romanticism. New forms of dress were patterned on austere Roman republicans and colorful Italian shepherds. Notions of freedom were anchored in a precise, logical ideal of self-control and a vague, instinctive norm of spontaneity. Rousseau stood at odds with d'Holbach, Diderot at odds with Voltaire; yet, in retrospect, we can see that one not only transcended but also presupposed the other in a *cumulative* development toward revolution.

The same uneven, contradictory, and cumulative development exists today, and, in many cases, it follows a remarkably direct course. The beat movement created the most important breach in the solid, middle-class values of the 1950's, a breach that was widened enormously by the illegalities of pacifists, civil rights workers, and most recently, hippies. The merely reactive responses of rebellious American youth, moreover, have produced invaluable forms of libertarian and utopian affirmation: the right to make love without restriction, the goal of community, the disavowal of money and commodities, the belief in mutual aid, a new respect for spontaneity. Easy as it is for revolutionaries to criticize certain pitfalls within this orientation of personal and social values, the fact remains that it has played a preparatory role of decisive importance in forming the present atmosphere of indiscipline, spontaneity, radicalism, and freedom.

A second parallel between the revolutionary Enlightenment and our own period is the emergence of the crowd, the so-called "mob," as a major vehicle of social protest. The typical institutionalized forms of public dissatisfaction—in our own day: orderly elections, demonstrations, mass meetings—tend to give way to direct action by crowds. This shift from predictable, highly organized protests within the institutionalized framework of the existing society to sporadic, spontaneous, near-insurrectionary assaults from outside (and even against) socially acceptable forms reflects a profound change in popular psychology. The "rioter" and the "Provo" have begun to break, however partially and intuitively, with those deep-seated norms of behavior which traditionally weld the masses to the established order. They actively shed the internalized structure of authority, the long-cultivated body of conditioned reflexes, the pattern of submission sustained by guilt that tie them to the system even more effectively than any fear of police violence and juridical reprisal. Contrary to social psychologists, who see in these modes of direct action the submission of the individual to a terrifying collective entity called the "mob," the truth is that "riots" and crowd actions represent the first gropings

of the mass toward individuation. The mass tends to become de-
massified in the critical sense that it begins to assert itself against
the really massifying, automatic responses produced by the bourgeois family, the school, and the mass media. By the same token,
crowd actions involve the rediscovery of the streets and the effort to
liberate them. Ultimately, it is in the streets that power must be dissolved—for the streets, where daily life is endured, suffered, and
eroded, where power is confronted and fought, must be turned into
the domain where daily life is enjoyed, created, and nourished. The
rebellious crowd marked the beginning not only of a spontaneous
transmutation of private into social revolt, but a return from the abstractions of social revolt to the issues of everyday life.

Finally, another close parallel is the emergence of an immense and
evergrowing *déclasses,* a body of lumpenized individuals drawn from
every stratum of society. The chronically indebted and socially in-
secure upper and middle classes of our period compare loosely with
the chronically insolvent and flighty nobility of prerevolutionary
France. A vast flotsam of educated people emerges in both epochs,
living at loose ends without fixed careers and established social roots.
At the bottom of the structure we find a large number of chronic
poor: vagabonds, drifters, people with part-time jobs or no jobs at
all surviving on public aid and on the garbage thrown off by society,
a threatening, unruly *sans culottes*—the poor of the Parisian slums,
the blacks of the American ghettoes.

But here all the parallels end. The French Enlightenment belongs
to a period of revolutionary transition from feudalism to capitalism
—both, societies based on economic scarcity, class rule, exploitation,
social hierarchy, and state power. The day-to-day popular resistance
which marked the eighteenth century and culminated in open revolution was soon disciplined by the newly emerging industrial order as
well as by naked force. The vast mass of *déclasses* and *sans culottes*
were largely absorbed into the factory system and tamed by industrial
discipline. Formerly rootless intellectuals and footloose nobles found
secure places in the economic, political, social and cultural hierarchy
of the new bourgeois order. From a socially and culturally fluid condition, highly generalized in its structure and relations, society hardened again into rigid, particularized class and institutional forms—
the classical Victorian Era which appeared not only in England but,

to one degree or another, in all of western Europe and America. Critique was reconsolidated into apologia, revolt into reform, *déclassés* into clearly defined classes, "mobs" into political constituencies, "riots" into the well-behaved processionals we call "demonstrations," spontaneous direct action into electoral rituals.

Our own era, too, is a transitional one, but with a profound and qualitatively new difference. In the last of their great insurrections, the *sans culottes* of the French Revolution rose under the fiery cry: "Bread and the Constitution of '93!" The black *sans culottes* of the American ghettoes rise under the slogan: "Black is beautiful!" Between these two slogans lies a development of unprecedented importance. The *déclassés* of the eighteenth century were formed during a slow transition from an agricultural to an industrial era; they were created out of a pause in the historical transition from one regime of toil to another. The demand for bread could have been heard at any time in the evolution of propertied society. The new *déclassés* of the twentieth century are being created as a result of the bankruptcy of all social forms based on toil. They are the product of the end process of propertied society itself and the social problems of material survival. In the era when technological advances and cybernation have brought into question the exploitation of man by man, of toil, of material want in any form whatever, the cry—be it "Black is beautiful" or "Make love, not war"—marks the transformation of the traditional demand for survival into a historically new demand for life.* What underpins every social conflict in the United States, today, is the demand for the Self-realization of all human potentialities in a fully rounded, balanced, totalistic way of life. In short, the potentialities for revolution in America are now anchored in the potentialities of man himself.

What we are witnessing is the breakdown of a century and a half of embourgeoisement and a pulverization of all bourgeois institutions *at a point in history when the boldest concepts of utopia are realizable.*

---

* The above lines were written nearly a year ago. Since then, we have the example of the graffiti on the walls of Paris, painted during the May–June revolution: "Imagination to power," "I take my desires to be reality, because I believe in the reality of my desires," "Never work," "The more I make love, the more I want to make revolution," "Life without dead times," "The more you consume, the less you live," "Culture is the inversion of life," "One does not buy happiness, one steals it," "Society is a carnivorous flower." These are not graffiti; they are a program for Life and Desire.

And there is nothing that the present bourgeois order can substitute for the destruction of its traditional institutions but bureaucratic manipulation and state capitalism. This process is unfolding most dramatically in the United States. Within a period of little more than two decades, we have seen the collapse of the "American Dream," or what amounts to the same thing, the steady elimination in the United States of the myth that material abundance, based on commodity relations between men, can conceal the inherent poverty of bourgeois life. Whether this process will culminate in revolution or in annihilation will depend in great part on the ability of revolutionists to extend social consciousness and defend the spontaneity of the revolutionary development from authoritarian ideologies, both of the "left" and the right.

Addenda: The Affinity Group

What form of revolutionary organization is the most suitable to the social development described in the foregoing work?

A revolutionary organization that seeks to act catalytically on the development, that seeks to add its fund of consciousness without trying to manipulate the development, is best represented by the "affinity group"—a small group of revolutionary brothers and sisters who know each other intimately, who combine revolutionary life-style with consciousness, whose theory and practice are in concordance, who are not burdened by "leaders" and bureaucrats, who are autonomous, communal, directly democratic, and anarchic. The "seeding" of the social environment with these revolutionary groups, their cellular growth and proliferation, are vitally important today.

Much has already been written about this mode of organization in underground newspapers (see *The Rat,* Aug. 9–22, 1968 and Marvin Garson's articles in *San Francisco Express-Times* during July, 1968). A few points deserve emphasis here:

Affinity groups exist on a molecular level and have their own "Brownian movement." Whether they coalesce or separate (locally, regionally, or even nationally) depends entirely on living situations, not on bureaucratic fiat from a distant "center." Superbly resistant to infiltration by the state, they are not suited for conditions of repression. As intensely intimate groups, they offer serious barriers to police penetration. Even where there is penetration, the police infiltrator is localized and isolated in the scale of his activities by the single group and does not have access to a centralized apparatus—a position from which he can not only acquire vital information but determine policy for a nationwide movement.

Affinity groups are also ideally suited for revolutionary conditions, that is, for revolution seen as a spontaneous movement from below. In these conditions, nothing prevents the groups from collaborating closely on any scale required by the living situation, indeed, establishing wide contacts with each other and organizing common, self-disciplined activities. Yet these activities are rooted in the base of the revolution; their strong localism and autonomy provide them with the means for a sensitive appreciation of immediate possibilities in their area and, in the absence of a bureaucracy and an apparatus, they can preserve their revolutionary elan and spontaneity. Emerging and proliferating in the pores of society, they expand or contract, separate or coalesce, entirely according to the needs of the situation in which they exist. Intensely experimental and variegated in lifestyle and ideas, they act as a fermenting agent on each other, on every social situation that emerges, and range widely over all spheres of social and personal action. Each has its own resources to function completely on its own. Each seeks complete roundedness in experience, knowledge, and action—in itself trying to overcome the bifurcations that distort all individuals and groups in bourgeois society into one-sided organisms. Each continually enlarges its knowledge of the arena within its purview and stands ready to act in every change of situation. Each constitutes a nucleus of consciousness, experience, and action, serving to reinforce and advance the spontaneous revolutionary movement.

Ernesto "Che" Guevara

Ernesto "Che" Guevara was the revolutionary fighter and theoretician who played a key role in the Cuban revolution and who died in Bolivia at the age of thirty-nine trying to carry the revolution to that country. His writings on revolution can be found in his book *Guerrilla Warfare* (1961) and in John Gerassi's collection *Venceremos!* (1968).

The following essay was a letter to Carlos Quijana, editor-publisher of the Uruguayan weekly *Marcha,* written early in 1965 and then published in Cuba as *El socialismo y el hombre en Cuba* (Havana: Ediciones R). The official government translation is by Margarita Zimmerman.

Guevara's essay is a visionary statement of the new social possibilities opened up by the Cuban revolutionary experience. He devotes a great deal of attention to education ("Society as a whole must become a huge school") and to the need to build humanizing "revolutionary institutions" in Cuba. Throughout the essay, Guevara is sensitive to the many obstacles which stand in the way of developing libertarian socialism in Cuba. But his faith in the ability of the Cuban people to withstand hardship and to work together to create a new man and a new society is unstinting. The essay is a classic in the history of utopian socialist thought.

MAN AND SOCIALISM IN CUBA

DEAR COMRADE:

I am finishing these notes while traveling through Africa, moved by the desire to keep my promise, although after some delay. I should like to do so by dealing with the topic that appears in the title. I believe it might be of interest to Uruguayan readers.

It is common to hear how capitalist spokesmen use as an argument in the ideological struggle against socialism the assertion that such a social system, or the period of building socialism upon which we have embarked, is characterized by the extinction of the individual for the sake of the state. I will make no attempt to refute this assertion on a merely theoretical basis, but will instead establish the facts of the Cuban experience and add commentaries of a general nature. I shall first broadly sketch the history of our revolutionary struggle both before and after taking of power.

As we know, the exact date of the beginning of the revolutionary actions which were to culminate on January 1, 1959, was July 26, 1953. A group of men led by Fidel Castro attacked the Moncada military garrison in the province of Oriente, in the early hours of the morning of that day. The attack was a failure. The failure became a disaster and the survivors were imprisoned, only to begin the revolutionary struggle all over again, once they were amnestied.

During this process, which contained only the first seeds of socialism, man was a basic factor. Man—individualized, specific, named— was trusted and the triumph or failure of the task entrusted to him depended on his capacity for action.

Then came the stage of guerrilla warfare. It was carried out in two different environments: the people, an as yet unawakened mass that had to be mobilized, and its vanguard, the guerrilla, the thrusting engine of mobilization, the generator of revolutionary awareness and militant enthusiasm. This vanguard was the catalyst which created the subjective condition necessary for victory. The individual was also the basic factor in the guerrilla, in the framework of the gradual proletarianization of our thinking, in the revolution taking place in our habits and in our minds. Each and every one of the Sierra Maestra fighters who achieved a high rank in the revolutionary forces has to his credit a list of noteworthy deeds. It was on the basis of such deeds that they earned their rank.

It was the first heroic period in which men strove to earn posts of greater responsibility, of greater danger, with the fulfillment of their duty as the only satisfaction. In our revolutionary educational work we often return to this instructive topic. The man of the future could be glimpsed in the attitude of our fighters.

At other times of our history there have been repetitions of this utter devotion to the revolutionary cause. During the October Crisis and at the time of the hurricane Flora, we witnessed deeds of exceptional valor and self-sacrifice carried out by an entire people. One of our fundamental tasks from the ideological standpoint is to find the way to perpetuate such heroic attitudes in everyday life.

The revolutionary government was established in 1959 with the participation of several members of the "sell-out" bourgeoisie. The presence of the rebel army constituted the guarantee of power as the fundamental factor of strength.

Serious contradictions arose which were solved in the first instance in February 1959, when Fidel Castro assumed the leadership of the government in the post of Prime Minister. This process culminated in July of the same year with the resignation of President Urrutia in the face of mass pressure.

With clearly defined features, there now appeared in the history of the Cuban Revolution a personage which will systematically repeat itself: the masses.

This multifacetic being is not, as it is claimed, the sum total of elements of the same category (and moreover, reduced to the same category by the system imposed upon them) and which acts as a tame herd. It is true that the mass follows its leaders, especially Fidel Castro, without hesitation, but the degree to which he has earned such confidence is due precisely to the consummate interpretation of the people's desires and aspirations, and to the sincere struggle to keep the promises made.

The mass participated in the agrarian reform and in the difficult undertaking of the management of the state enterprises; it underwent the heroic experience of Playa Girón; it was tempered in the struggle against the groups of bandits armed by the CIA; during the October Crisis it lived one of the most important definitions of modern times, and today it continues the work to build socialism.

Looking at things from a superficial standpoint, it might seem that those who speak of the submission of the individual to the state are right; with incomparable enthusiasm and discipline, the mass carries out the tasks set by the government whatever their nature: economic, cultural, defense, sports, etc. The initiative generally comes from Fidel or the high command of the revolution: It is explained to the people, who make it their own. At times local experiences are taken up by the party and the government and are thereby generalized, following the same procedure.

However, the state at times makes mistakes. When this occurs, the collective enthusiasm diminishes palpably as a result of a quantitative diminishing that takes place in each of the elements that make up the collective, and work becomes paralyzed until it finally shrinks to insignificant proportions; this is the time to rectify.

This was what happened in March 1962 in the presence of the sectarian policy imposed on the party by Anibal Escalante.

This mechanism is obviously not sufficient to ensure a sequence of sensible measures; what is missing is a more structured relationship with the mass. We must improve this connection in the years to come, but for now, in the case of the initiatives arising on the top levels of government, we are using the almost intuitive method of keeping our ears open to the general reactions in the face of the problems that are posed.

Fidel is a past master at this; his particular mode of integration with the people can only be appreciated by seeing him in action. In the big public meetings one can observe something like the dialogue of two tuning forks whose vibrations summon forth new vibrations each in the other. Fidel and the mass begin to vibrate in a dialogue of growing intensity which reaches its culminating point in an abrupt ending crowned by our victorious battle cry.

What is hard to understand for anyone who has not lived the revolutionary experience is that close dialectical unity which exists between the individual and the mass, in which both are interrelated, and the mass, as a whole composed of individuals, is in turn interrelated with the leader.

Under capitalism certain phenomena of this nature can be observed with the appearance on the scene of politicians capable of mobilizing the public, but if it is not an authentic social movement, in which case it is not completely accurate to speak of capitalism, the movement will have the same life span as its promoter or until the rigors of capitalist society put an end to popular illusions. Under capitalism man is guided by a cold ordinance which is usually beyond his comprehension. The alienated human individual is bound to society as a whole by an invisible umbilical cord: the law of value. It acts upon all facets of his life, shaping his road and his destiny.

The laws of capitalism, invisible and blind for most people, act upon the individual without his awareness. He sees only the broadness of horizon that appears infinite. Capitalist propaganda presents it in just this way, and attempts to use the Rockefeller case (true or not) as a lesson in the prospects for success. The misery that must be accumulated for such an example to arise and the sum total of baseness contributing to the formation of a fortune of such magnitude do not appear in the picture, and the popular forces are not always able to make these concepts clear. (It would be fitting at this point to study how the workers of the imperialist countries gradually lose their international class spirit under the influence of a certain complicity in the exploitation of the dependent countries and how this fact at the same time wears away the militant spirit of the masses within their own national context, but this topic is outside the framework of the present note.)

In any case we can see the obstacle course which may apparently be overcome by an individual with the necessary qualities to arrive at the finish line. The reward is glimpsed in the distance and the road is solitary. Furthermore, it is a race of wolves: He who arrives does so only at the expense of the failure of others.

I shall now attempt to define the individual, the actor in this strange and moving drama that is the building of socialism, in his twofold existence as a unique being and a member of the community.

I believe that the simplest approach is to recognize his unmade quality: he is an unfinished product. The flaws of the past are translated into the present in the individual consciousness and constant efforts must be made to eradicate them. The process is twofold: On the one hand society acts upon the individual by means of direct and indirect education, while on the other hand the individual undergoes a conscious phase of self-education.

The new society in process of formation has to compete very hard with the past. This makes itself felt not only in the individual consciousness, weighed down by the residues of an education and an upbringing systematically oriented toward the isolation of the individual, but also by the very nature of this transition period, with the persistence of commodity relations. The commodity is the economic cell of capitalist society: As long as it exists, its effects will make themselves felt in the organization of production and therefore in man's consciousness.

Marx's scheme conceived of the transition period as the result of the explosive transformation of the capitalist system torn apart by its inner contradictions: Subsequent reality has shown how some countries, the weak limbs, detach themselves from the imperialist tree, a phenomenon foreseen by Lenin. In those countries capitalism has developed sufficiently to make its effects felt upon the people in one way or another, but it is not its own inner contradictions that explode the system after exhausting all of its possibilities. The struggle for liberation against an external oppressor, the misery which has its origin in foreign causes, such as war, whose consequences make the privileged classes fall upon the exploited, the liberation movements aimed at overthrowing neocolonial regimes, are the customary factors in this process. Conscious action does the rest.

In these countries there still has not been achieved a complete education for the work of society, and wealth is far from being within the reach of the masses through the simple process of appropriation. Underdevelopment and the customary flight of capital to "civilized" countries make impossible a rapid change without sacrifices. There still remains a long stretch to be covered in the building of the economic base, and the temptation to follow the beaten paths of material interest as the lever of speedy development is very great.

There is a danger of not seeing the forest because of the trees. Pursuing the chimera of achieving socialism with the aid of the blunted weapons left to us by capitalism (the commodity as the economic cell, profitability and individual material interest as levers, etc.), it is possible to come to a blind alley. And the arrival there comes about after covering a long distance where there are many crossroads and where it is difficult to realize just when the wrong turn was taken. Meanwhile, the adapted economic base has undermined the development of consciousness. To build communism, a new man must be created simultaneously with the material base.

That is why it is so important to choose correctly the instrument of mass mobilization. That instrument must be fundamentally of a moral character, without forgetting the correct use of material incentives, especially those of a social nature.

As I already said, in moments of extreme danger it is easy to activate moral incentives: To maintain their effectiveness, it is necessary to develop a consciousness in which values acquire new categories. Society as a whole must become a huge school.

The broad characteristics of the phenomenon are similar to the process of formation of capitalist consciousness in the system's first stage. Capitalism resorts to force, but it also educates people in the system. Direct propaganda is carried out by those who are entrusted with the task of explaining the inevitability of a class regime, whether it be of divine origin or due to the imposition of nature as a mechanical entity. This placates the masses, who see themselves oppressed by an evil against which it is not possible to struggle.

This is followed by hope, which differentiates capitalism from the previous caste regimes that offered no way out. For some the caste formula continues in force: The obedient are rewarded by the *post mortem* arrival in other wonderful worlds where the good are requited, and the old tradition is continued. For others, innovation: The division in classes is a matter of fate, but individuals can leave the class to which they belong through work, initiative, etc. This process, and that of self-education for success, must be deeply hypocritical: It is the interested demonstration that a lie is true.

In our case, direct education acquires much greater importance. Explanations are convenient because they are genuine; subterfuges are not needed. It is carried out through the State's educational apparatus in the form of general, technical, and ideological culture, by means of bodies such as the Ministry of Education and the party's information apparatus. Education takes among the masses, and the new attitude that is praised tends to become habit; the mass gradually takes it over and exerts pressure on those who have still not become educated. This is the indirect way of educating the masses, as powerful as the other, structured, one.

But the process is a conscious one: The individual receives the impact of the new social power and perceives that he is not completely adequate to it. Under the influence of the pressure implied in indirect education, he tries to adjust to a situation that he feels to be just and whose lack of development has kept him from doing so thus far. He is educating himself.

We can see the new man who begins to emerge in this period of the building of socialism. His image is as yet unfinished. In fact it will never be finished, since the process advances parallel to the development of new economic forms. Discounting those whose lack of education makes them tend toward the solitary road, toward the satisfaction of their ambitions, there are others who, even within this new picture of over-all advances, tend to march in isolation from the accompanying mass. What is important is that people become more aware every day of the need to incorporate themselves into society and of their own importance as motors of that society.

They no longer march in complete solitude along lost roads toward far-off longings. They follow their vanguard, composed of the party, of the most advanced workers, of the advanced men who move along bound to the masses and in close communion with them. The vanguards have their eyes on the future and its recompenses, but the latter are not envisioned as something individual; the reward is the new society, where human beings will have different characteristics: the society of communist man.

The road is long and full of difficulties. At times the route strays off course, and it is necessary to retreat; at times, a too rapid pace separates us from the masses, and on occasions the pace is slow, and we feel upon our necks the breath of those who follow upon our heels. Our ambition as revolutionaries makes us try to move forward as far as possible, opening up the way before us, but we know that we must be reinforced by the mass, while the mass will be able to advance more rapidly if we encourage it by our example.

In spite of the importance given to moral incentives, the existence of two principal groups (excluding, of course, the minority fraction of those who do not participate for one reason or another in the building of socialism) is an indication of the relative lack of development of social consciousness. The vanguard group is ideologically more advanced than the mass; the latter is acquainted with the new values, but insufficiently. While in the former a qualitative change takes place which permits them to make sacrifices as a function of their vanguard character, the latter see only by halves and must be subjected to incentives and pressures of some intensity; it is the dictatorship of the proletariat being exercised not only upon the defeated class but also individually upon the victorious class.

To achieve total success, all of this involves the necessity of a series of mechanisms, the revolutionary institutions. The concept of institutionalization fits in with the images of the multitudes marching toward the future as that of a harmonic unit of canals, steps, well-oiled apparatuses that make the march possible, that permit the natural selection of those who are destined to march in the vanguard and who dispense rewards and punishments to those who fulfill their duty or act against the society under construction.

The institutionality of the Revolution has still not been achieved. We are seeking something new that will allow a perfect identification between the government and the community as a whole, adapted to the special conditions of the building of socialism and avoiding to the utmost the commonplaces of bourgeois democracy transplanted to the society in formation (such as legislative houses, for example). Some experiments have been carried out with the aim of gradually creating the institutionalization of the Revolution, but without too much hurry. We have been greatly restrained by the fear that any formal aspect might make us lose sight of the ultimate and most important revolutionary aspiration: to see man freed from alienation.

Notwithstanding the lack of institutions, which must be overcome gradually, the masses now make history as a conscious aggregate of individuals who struggle for the same cause. In spite of the apparent standardization of man in socialism, he is more complete; his possibilities for expressing himself and making himself heard in the social apparatus are infinitely greater, in spite of the lack of a perfect mechanism to do so.

It is still necessary to accentuate his conscious, individual and collective, participation in all the mechanisms of direction and production and associate it with the idea of the need for technical and ideological education, so that the individual will realize that these processes are closely interdependent and their advances are parallel. He will thus achieve total awareness of his social being, which is equivalent to his full realization as a human being, having broken the chains of alienation.

This will be translated concretely into the reappropriation of his nature through freed work and the expression of his own human condition in culture and art.

In order for it to develop in culture, work must acquire a new condition; man as commodity ceases to exist, and a system is established that grants a quota for the fulfillment of social duty. The means of production belong to society, and the machine is only the front line where duty is performed. Man begins to free his thought from the bothersome fact that presupposed the need to satisfy his animal needs by working. He begins to see himself portrayed in his work and to understand its human magnitude through the created object, through the work carried out. This no longer involves leaving a part of his being in the form of labor power sold, which no longer belongs to him; rather it signifies an emanation from himself, a contribution to the life of society in which he is reflected, the fulfillment of his social duty.

We are doing everything possible to give work this new category of social duty and to join it to the development of technology, on the one hand, which will provide the conditions for greater freedom, and to voluntary work on the other, based on the Marxist concept that man truly achieves his full human condition when he produces without being compelled by the physical necessity of selling himself as a commodity.

It is clear that work still has coercive aspects, even when it is voluntary: Man has still not transformed all the coercion surrounding him into conditioned reflexes of a social nature, and in many cases he still produces under the pressure of the environment (Fidel calls this moral compulsion). He is still to achieve complete spiritual recreation in the presence of his own work, without the direct pressure of the social environment but bound to it by new habits. That will be communism.

The change in consciousness does not come about automatically, just as it does not come about automatically in the economy. The variations are slow and not rhythmic; there are periods of acceleration, others are measured and some even involve a retreat.

We must also consider, as we have pointed out previously, that we are not before a pure transition period such as that envisioned by Marx in the "Critique of the Gotha Program," but rather a new phase not foreseen by him: the first period in the transition to communism or in the building of socialism.

Elements of capitalism are present within this process, which takes place in the midst of violent class struggle. These elements obscure the complete understanding of the essence of the process.

If to this be added the scholasticism that has held back the development of Marxist philosophy and impeded the systematic treatment of the period, whose political economy has still not been developed, we must agree that we are still in diapers. We must study all the primordial features of the period before elaborating a more far-reaching economic and political theory.

The resulting theory will necessarily give preeminence to the two pillars of socialist construction: the formation of the new human being and the development of technology. We still have a great deal to accomplish in both aspects, but the delay is less justifiable as far as the conception of technology as the basis is concerned: Here, it is not a matter of advancing blindly, but rather of following for a sizable stretch the road opened up by the most advanced countries of the world. This is why Fidel harps so insistently on the necessity of the technological and scientific formation of all of our people and especially of the vanguard.

In the field of ideas that lead to nonproductive activities, it is easier to see the division between material and spiritual needs. For a long time man has been trying to free himself from alienation through culture and art. He dies daily in the eight and more hours during which he performs as a commodity to resuscitate in his spiritual creation. But this remedy itself bears the germs of the same disease: He is a solitary being who seeks communion with nature. He defends his environment-oppressed individuality and reacts to esthetic ideas as a unique being whose aspiration is to remain immaculate.

It is only an attempt at flight. The law of value is no longer a mere reflection of production relations; the monopoly capitalists have surrounded it with a complicated scaffolding which makes of it a docile servant, even when the methods used are purely empirical. The artist must be educated in the kind of art imposed by the superstructure. The rebels are overcome by the apparatus, and only exceptional talents are able to create their own work. The others become shame-faced wage-workers, or they are crushed.

Artistic experimentation is invented and is taken as the definition of freedom, but this "experimentation" has limits which are imperceptible until they are clashed with, that is, when the real problems of man and his alienated condition are dealt with. Senseless anguish or vulgar pastimes are comfortable safety valves for human uneasiness; the idea of making art a weapon of denunciation and accusation is combatted.

If the rules of the game are respected, all honors are obtained—the honors that might be granted to a pirouette-creating monkey. The condition is not attempting to escape from the invisible cage.

When the Revolution took power, the exodus of the totally domesticated took place; the others, revolutionaries or not, saw a new road. Artistic experimentation took on new force. However, the routes were more or less traced, and the concept of flight was the hidden meaning behind the word freedom. This attitude, a reflection in consciousness of bourgeois idealism, was frequently maintained in the revolutionaries themselves.

In countries that have gone through a similar process, endeavors were made to combat these tendencies with an exaggerated dogmatism. General culture became something like a taboo, and a formally exact representation of nature was proclaimed as the height of cultural aspiration. This later became a mechanical representation of social reality created by wishful thinking: the ideal society, almost without conflict or contradictions, that man was seeking to create.

Socialism is young and makes mistakes. We revolutionaries often lack the knowledge and the intellectual audacity to face the task of the development of the new human being by methods different from the conventional ones, and the conventional methods suffer from the influence of the society that created them (once again the topic of the relation between form and content appears). Disorientation is great and the problems of material construction absorb us. There are no artists of great authority who also have great revolutionary authority.

The men of the party must take this task upon themselves and seek the achievement of the principal aim: to educate the people.

What is then sought is simplification, what everyone understands, that is, what the functionaries understand. True artistic experimentation is obliterated and the problem of general culture is reduced to the assimilation of the socialist present and the dead (and therefore not dangerous) past. Socialist realism is thus born on the foundation of the art of the last century.

But the realistic art of the nineteenth century is also class art, perhaps more purely capitalist than the decadent art of the twentieth century, where the anguish of alienated man shows through. In culture, capitalism has given all that it had to give and all that remains of it is the foretaste of a bad-smelling corpse; in art, its present decadence. But why endeavor to seek in the frozen forms of socialist realism the only valid recipe? "Freedom" cannot be set against socialist realism because the former does not yet exist: It will not come into being until the complete development of the new society. But let us not attempt to condemn all post-midnineteenth-century art forms from the pontifical throne of realism-at-all-costs. That would mean committing the Proudhonian error of the return to the past, and straitjacketing the artistic expression of the man who is born and being formed today.

An ideological and cultural mechanism must be developed which will permit experimentation and clear out the weeds that shoot up so easily in the fertilized soil of state subsidization.

The error of mechanical realism has not appeared (in Cuba), but rather the contrary. This is so because of the lack of understanding of the need to create a new human being who will represent neither nineteenth-century ideas nor those of our decadent and morbid century. It is the twenty-first-century man whom we must create, although this is still a subjective and unsystematic aspiration. This is precisely one of the basic points of our studies and work; to the extent that we make concrete achievements on a theoretical base or vice versa, that we come to broad theoretical conclusions on the basis of our concrete studies, we will have made a valuable contribution to Marxism-Leninism, to the cause of mankind.

The reaction against nineteenth-century man has brought a recurrence of twentieth-century decadence. It is not a very serious error, but we must overcome it so as not to leave the doors open to revisionism.

The large multitudes of people are developing themselves, the new ideas are acquiring an adequate impetus within society, the material possibilities of the integral development of each and every one of its members make the task ever more fruitful. The present is one of struggle; the future is ours.

To sum up, the fault of many of our intellectuals and artists is to be found in their "original sin": They are not authentically revolutionary. We can attempt to graft elm trees so they bear pears, but at the same time we must plant pear trees. The new generations will arrive free of "original sin." The likelihood that exceptional artists will arise will be that much greater because of the enlargement of the cultural field and the possibilities for expression. Our job is to keep the present generation, maladjusted by its conflicts, from becoming perverted and perverting the new generations. We do not want to create salaried workers docile to official thinking or "fellows" who live under the wing of the budget, exercising freedom in quotation marks. Revolutionaries will come to sing the song of the new man with the authentic voice of the people. It is a process that requires time.

In our society the youth and the party play a big role. The former is particularly important because it is the malleable clay with which the new man, without any of the previous defects, can be formed.

Youth receives treatment in consonance with our aspirations. Education is increasingly integral, and we do not neglect the incorporation of the students into work from the very beginning. Our scholarship students do physical work during vacation or together with their studies. In some cases work is a prize, while in others it is an educational tool; it is never a punishment. A new generation is being born.

The party is a vanguard organization. The best workers are proposed by their comrades for membership. The party is a minority, but the quality of its cadres gives it great authority. Our aspiration is that the party become a mass one, but only when the masses reach the level of development of the vanguard, that is, when they are educated for communism. Our work is aimed at providing that education. The party is the living example; its cadres must be full professors of assiduity and sacrifice; with their acts they must lead the masses to the end of the revolutionary task, which means years of struggle against the difficulties of construction, the class enemies, the defects of the past, imperialism.

I should now like to explain the role played by the personality, the man as the individual who leads the masses that make history. This is our experience, and not a recipe.

Fidel gave impulse to the Revolution in its first years, he has always given it leadership and set the tone, but there is a good group of revolutionaries developing in the same direction as Fidel and a large mass that follows its leaders because it has faith in them. It has faith in them because these leaders have known how to interpret the longings of the masses.

It is not a question of how many kilograms of meat are eaten or how many times a year someone may go on holiday to the seashore or how many pretty imported things can be bought with present wages. It is rather that the individual feels greater fulfillment, that he has greater inner wealth and many more responsibilities. In our country the individual knows that the glorious period in which it has fallen to him to live is one of sacrifice; he is familiar with sacrifice.

The first came to know it in the Sierra Maestra and wherever there was fighting; later we have known it in all Cuba. Cuba is the vanguard of America and must make sacrifices because it occupies the advance position, because it points out to the Latin American masses the road to full freedom.

Within the country, the leaders have to fulfill their vanguard role; and it must be said with complete sincerity that in a true revolution, to which you give yourself completely without any thought for material retribution, the task of the vanguard revolutionary is both magnificent and anguishing.

Let me say, with the risk of appearing ridiculous, that the true revolutionary is guided by strong feelings of love. It is impossible to think of an authentic revolutionary without this quality. This is perhaps one of the great dramas of a leader; he must combine an impassioned spirit with a cold mind and make painful decisions without flinching. Our vanguard revolutionaries must idealize their love for the people, for the most hallowed causes, and make it one and indivisible. They cannot descend, with small doses of daily affection, to the terrain where ordinary men put their love into practice.

The leaders of the Revolution have children who do not learn to call their father with their first faltering words; they have wives who must be part of the general sacrifice of their lives to carry the Revolution to its destination; their friends are strictly limited to their comrades in revolution. There is no life outside the Revolution.

In these conditions the revolutionary leaders must have a large dose of humanity, a large dose of a sense of justice and truth, to avoid falling into dogmatic extremes, into cold scholasticism, into isolation from the masses. They must struggle every day so that their love of living humanity is transformed into concrete deeds, into acts that will serve as an example, as a mobilizing factor.

The revolutionary, ideological motor of the Revolution within his party, is consumed by this uninterrupted activity that ends only with death, unless construction be achieved on a worldwide scale. If his revolutionary eagerness becomes dulled when the most urgent tasks are carried on a local scale, and if he forgets about proletarian internationalism, the revolution that he leads ceases to be a driving force and it sinks into a comfortable drowsiness which is taken advantage of by imperialism, our irreconcilable enemy, to gain ground. Proletarian internationalism is a duty, but it is also a revolutionary need. This is how we educate our people.

It is evident that there are dangers in the present circumstances. Not only that of dogmatism, not only that of the freezing up of relations with the masses in the midst of the great task; there also exists the danger of weaknesses in which it is possible to incur. If a man thinks that in order to devote his entire life to the Revolution, he cannot be distracted by the worry that one of his children lacks a certain article, that the children's shoes are in poor condition, that his family lacks some necessary item; with this reasoning, the seeds of future corruption are allowed to filter through.

In our case we have maintained that our children must have, or lack, what the children of the ordinary citizen have or lack; our family must understand this and struggle for it. The Revolution is made by man, but man must forge his revolutionary spirit from day to day.

Thus we go forward. Fidel is at the head of the immense column— we are neither ashamed nor afraid to say so—followed by the best party cadres, and right after them, so close that their great strength is felt, come the people as a whole, a solid bulk of individualities moving toward a common aim; individuals who have achieved the awareness of what must be done; men who struggle to leave the domain of necessity and enter that of freedom.

That immense multitude is ordering itself; its order responds to an awareness of the need for order; it is no longer a dispersed force, divisible in thousands of fractions shot into space like the fragments of a grenade, trying by any and all means, in a fierce struggle with their equals, to achieve a position that would give them support in the face of an uncertain future.

We know that we have sacrifices ahead of us and that we must pay a price for the heroic fact of constituting a vanguard as a nation. We, the leaders, know that we must pay a price for having the right to say that we are at the head of the people that is at the head of America.

Each and every one of us punctually pays his share of sacrifice, aware of being rewarded by the satisfaction of fulfilling our duty, aware of advancing with everyone toward the new human being who is to be glimpsed on the horizon.

Allow me to attempt to come to some conclusions:

We socialists are more free because we are more fulfilled: We are more fulfilled because we are more free.

The skeleton of our complete freedom is formed, but it lacks the protein substance and the draperies. We will create them.

Our freedom and its daily sustenance are the color of blood and swollen with sacrifice.

Our sacrifice is a conscious one: It is in payment for the freedom we are building.

The road is long and in part unknown; we are aware of our limitations. We will make the twenty-first-century man; we ourselves.

We will be tempered in daily actions, creating a new human being with a new technology.

The personality plays the role of mobilization and leadership in so far as it incarnates the highest virtues and aspirations of the people and does not become detoured.

The road is opened up by the vanguard group, the best among the good, the party.

The basic raw material of our work is the youth: In it we place our hopes and we are preparing it to take the banner from our hands.

If this faltering letter has made some things clear, it will have fulfilled my purpose in sending it.

Accept our ritual greetings, as a handshake or an "Ave María Purísima."

Patria o muerte